本书为：

浙江省2013年度高等教育教学改革项目成果（编号：jg2013209）
浙江大学宁波理工学院P^3实践教学体系建设成果
浙江大学宁波理工学院校园文化建设成果

用声音叙事：义乌，我来了

浙江大学宁波理工学院2013—2014年度“用声音叙事”活动调研报告

2013年度“用声音叙事”活动指导委员会

主　　任：费英勤
副 主 任：杨建刚 陈小兰 黄光杰
主任委员（按姓氏拼音为序）：
陈　斌 陈立明 谌晓煜 庞继贤 杨祥龙 周树红
策　　划：蔡　亮

编委及指导教师（按姓氏拼音为序）

蔡　亮　蔡　蕾　李　炜　刘　杰　南二丽　欧　琛
吴丹苹　徐志敏　俞　峰　喻旭燕　张静燕
Michael C. Milam [美国]

浙江省2013年度高等教育教学改革项目成果

用声音叙事：义乌，我来了

Beyond the Voices:
Yiwu, Here I Am

主　　编◎蔡　亮
副 主 编◎吴丹苹 欧　琛 李　炜
英文校对◎Michael C. Milam [美国]

ZHEJIANG UNIVERSITY PRESS
浙江大学出版社

架起沟通的桥梁 聆听世界的声音

董凤鸣

经过改革开放三十多年的发展，义乌已经成为全球最大的小商品贸易集散中心，商品辐射到全球219个国家和地区，初步形成了“购全球、全球购”的市场格局。近些年，每年到义乌的外国客商逾50万人次，来自100多个国家和地区的13000多名外商常驻义乌进行国际采购。在义乌的大街小巷，各种肤色的外国人随处可见，义乌也因此有了“小联合国”的美誉！

浙江大学宁波理工学院发起和组织的“用声音叙事”大型文化传播语言实践活动，是校地互动与合作的一个有益探索。该活动自2008年开展以来，通过调研—创作—研讨—服务的模式聚焦在华外籍人士，深入外籍人士的工作和生活，服务城市发展，并先后整理和出版了《用声音叙事：筑梦宁波》、《用声音叙事：我的企业在宁波》、《用声音叙事：我要学汉语》等一系列实践成果，有力地推动了中外文化交流与传播，在社会各界引起了极大的反响。义乌作为全国国际化程度最高的城市之一，同样十分需要“用声音叙事”这类文化载体，来丰富城市的涉外文化内涵。

在浙江大学宁波理工学院和义乌市外事与侨务办公室等相关单位的共同推动下，从2011年至2013年，“用声音叙事”活动连续三年走访义乌。项目组的师生们以“国际贸易综合改革试点背景下的义乌和义乌外籍人士”为题开展调研实践活动。他们走上街头、深入市场、植根企业，站在学者和学子的角度，聆听在义乌的外籍客商的心声。师生们以对话的形式和朴实无华的语言，记录了外籍客商在义乌工作和生活的一个个精彩片段，这些片段有的真实地再现了外籍客商在义乌的奋斗和成长历程；有的则与大家分享了创业的艰辛和成功的喜悦。比如，在对外商的采访中，来自巴西的时装设计师朱莉安娜·阿桑卡小姐与大家分享了她在义乌的快乐生活。她说，她喜欢义乌这样的小城市，上班不用坐地铁，家与办公室很近，很方便，去有生意往来的公司也很方便，尽管很忙，但她很享受这样的生活。来自巴基斯坦的伊兹哈克先生说，他来义乌已经9年了，专门做条形码生意，产品虽不起眼，但市场需求巨大，生意十分红火。用他的话说："Enter Futian Market, and I am embracing the world."（走进福田，拥抱世界。）瑞典商人 Tumaag 在 13 年前就已来到义乌，经营外贸公司。他感觉义乌人热情、好客、真诚，义乌市场国际化程度高，商机无限，他已完全融入义乌的生活。他说，中国梦就是他的梦。像以上这些生动的例子在书中还有许多。很多外国朋友已经把自己的生活和理想紧紧地与义乌联结在一起，把义乌当作自己实现梦想的地方。

《用声音叙事：义乌，我来了》一书共七个部分，分别是：创业义乌、商赢义乌、情定义乌、筑梦义乌、共建义乌、乌伤城里扶桑人以及品读义乌。在聚焦外籍人士圆梦义乌的同时，"用声音叙事"活动的师生们也在以一种全新的视角解读义乌，用清新、质朴的语言，描绘出了一个新丝绸之路的起点，一个放飞梦想的创业天堂，将义乌梦与中国梦有机地结合在一起。

2011 年 3 月，随着义乌开展国际贸易综合改革试点的获批，义乌的发展已经上升为国家战略。如今改革的目标已经明确，但是改革的征程任重道远。在推进国际贸易综合改革的道路上，我们需要勇气，需要担当，需要智慧，更需要凝心聚力，团结奋进。浙江大学宁波理工学院"用声音叙事：义乌，我来了"大型采访实践活动，正好从一个侧面为我们搭建了一个深入了解外籍客商心声的平台。更难能可贵的是，青年学子也发出了未来参与建设义乌的声音，义乌也真诚地欢迎各方有志之士将义乌视作成就梦想的舞台。

我们相信，《用声音叙事：义乌，我来了》的出版，对于展示义乌的独特商业文化、促进跨域文化交流将会产生积极的影响；对于我们优化涉外服务、提升义乌国际化层次、加快推动国际贸易综合改革也有很好的参考价值。

最后，衷心祝愿浙江大学宁波理工学院开展的"用声音叙事"大型文化传播语言实践活动越办越好！

是为序。

（董凤鸣　中共义乌市委常委、义乌市人民政府副市长）

序　二

教育提升学生价值

——教学案例“用声音叙事”的启示

金伟良

“教育提升学生价值”的办学理念是浙江大学宁波理工学院基于高等教育的现实关注和未来指向而提出的创新办学模式，其内涵在于：教育要在服务和引领社会经济文化发展方面扮演重要角色，设计和组织具有“服务社区”性质的教育与学术活动可以促进学生解决现实问题和适应未来社会等能力的提高；因此，提升学生价值的教育活动就是要将教育的社会服务功能和高校的人才培养目标有效地结合在一起，为学生创造一种具有在场感和成就感的学习环境。

在场感就是将学生的学术成长、思想成长放置于一种有现场感的教学环境之中，教育活动所创造的现场感与学生对客观世界的认知过程紧密关联，与学生的现实生活紧密关联。学习过程中个体的经历具有不可替代性，学生体验教学实践、参与社会服务，这种参与是真实的、主动的和自觉的；个体对学习的思考和行动具有统一性，教育活动的在场，是学生身、心融入学习活动之中，既是“我思故我在”，也是“我行故我在”，用一种简单的方式来诠释，那就是：“我来了，我做过，我收获”。我们提倡的教育活动就是为学生创造真实的体验机会，激发学生对自我学习的责任意识，让每个细微的收获和挫折都可以成为未来前行的动力。

学校是激发学生成就感的物理空间和情感空间，有成就感的教育就是让学生体味到学习的快乐和收获。课堂上回答问题后的赞许是成就，竞赛中赢得奖杯时的喜悦是成就，自己作品印成铅字是成就，团队项目被社会采纳同样是成就；成就不可以被简单地量化为利益的加加减减，成就是自我价值实现时由衷的快乐，解决一个现实的问题，放下一段感情的困扰，突破一个事业的瓶颈，都可能是成就感产生的源泉。要提升学生价值，教育活动就要把学生的能力发展放在首位，把创造快乐的学习体验放在首位，用有意义的教学实践发掘学生的现实潜能，成就学生的未来可能。

经过全校师生数年的辛苦耕耘,“教育提升学生价值”这一办学理念的生命力在实践中不断得到验证和充实。“用声音叙事”就是一个提升学生价值的典型教学案例,活动立足专业学习,参与城市建设,不重复,不说教,创造了一个有在场感和成就感的教学环境。伴随活动的开展,一批批学生成长起来,我们欣慰地看到了活动不断取得突破,《用声音叙事:义乌,我来了》的出版就是活动开展六年来的新成绩,本次活动走出宁波调研义乌外籍人士圆梦中国的故事,活动师生以一种“我来了”的气势参与到教学活动中,前后三载,学生融入学习活动之中,感受学习活动带来的乐趣,稚嫩的文笔中流露出一种对自我成长、对城市建设、对民族文化和对国家成就的自豪感,这就是教育成就人生价值的最好体现。

(金伟良 浙江大学教授、博导,浙江大学宁波理工学院院长)

序　三

教育是谁的？

费英勤

谈到当代大学生的教育问题，无论是专业能力的培养还是人文精神的提升，一些人总会从各种现象的罗列中发现一大堆问题，继而习惯性地把责任一股脑地推到大学生身上，这种简单的思维忽视了一个最基本的事实：教育从来不是受教育者单方面的事情，对于“教育是谁的”这个问题，卸责的回答固然可以轻松且冠冕堂皇，但是套用时下的一句流行语：教师去哪儿啦？学校去哪儿啦？家长去哪儿啦？社会又去哪儿啦？

教育是教育生态系统内部所有成员的事情，任何个体的成长，都是系统环境内众多组织、机构、成员通力协作的结果，任何一个环节的缺失都无法成就成功的教育。大学生无论作为个体还是群体都处在一个天然的教育共同体内，这个共同体涵盖了学校、家庭、社区、社会组织等诸多因素，理想的教育形态是所有教育生态系统内的成员都将自己视为利益相关方，且真诚关心大学生的成长，充分调动一切社会资源，形成促进大学生健康成长的合力。学校作为教育生态系统的核心，应该深入研究教育的内容、载体和过程等问题，积极引导大学生健康成长。

评价教育活动是否成功的一个重要标准是教育生态系统内各个成员的参与程度。从这个角度讲，浙江大学宁波理工学院“用声音叙事”活动是一个充满生命力的教学实践活动、思想教育活动、文化交流活动。自 2008 年以来，活动就是教学实践、社会实践和校园文化建设的统一，在校园内有教学、科研、学工、外事等相关部门对活动给予的积极支持和帮助，在社会上有公共服务部门、外籍人士、学生家长等多方的热情加入。以 2011—2013 年义乌外籍人士调研为例，义乌市委宣传部、义乌市政府外侨办，学校义乌校友会、学生家长和兄弟院校等都积极参与。活动创造了多方参与的对话环境，在这样的对话中，教师没有缺位，学校没有缺位，社会没有缺位。

《用声音叙事：义乌，我来了》是浙江大学宁波理工学院“用声音叙事”活动的第四本书。在该书即将出版之际，我们再次审视“用声音叙事”活动的发展历程，从文化到商务，从英语到汉语，从宁波到义乌，活动主题和空间不断地扩大，教育一直以一种多方合作的姿态出现在我们面前，并且为大学生创造出无数解决实际问题的机会，这些对大学生的专业能力培养和人文精神的提高都弥足珍贵，活动也很自然地回答了“教育是谁的”这个问题，教育从来都是一个社会问题，只要各方的关心不缺席，教育就会带给大家一个惊喜！

（费英勤 浙江大学研究员，浙江大学宁波理工学院党委书记）

目　录 CONTENTS

第一章 创业义乌：义乌，我来了

1

兄弟齐心，义乌打拼　Abdul Mejid　/ 3
　脚踏实地，闯出一片天地　钱　晨　/ 14
留学中国，创业义乌　Zhuo Han　/ 16
　义乌，创业者的乐园　沈丹妮　/ 24
商海义乌，择机而行　Adriano Santos　/ 26
　义乌：特别的爱给特别的你　朱小曈　/ 36
货比三家，义乌最佳　Kamal　/ 38
　商品之都，传奇之城　林萌萌　/ 49
心系义乌，乐享生活　Juliana　/ 51
　印象义乌："娜"样精彩　邵丽霞　/ 61

第二章 商赢义乌：拥义乌者，拥天下

63

走进福田，拥有世界　Ishaq　/ 65
　多元文化城市的独特之旅　岑　烨　/ 77
中国梦，我的梦　Tumaag　/ 79
　活在当下　赵雅婷　/ 90
义乌，理想的采购中心　Saman　/ 92
　小城市，大舞台　潘晶晶　/ 102
义乌，建在市场上的城市　Teign　/ 104
　中国名片——义乌；义乌名片——福田　陈　圆　/ 114
我心已定　Orlov　/ 116
　言出必行　尚梦丹　/ 126

127
第三章
情定义乌：
义乌有爱，心有了家

我和义乌的不解之缘 Bady / 129
商业之都——璀璨的东方明珠 郑 媛 / 142
我的梦，在中国 Ahmet Turan / 144
人以群分，物以类聚 王菁璟 / 156
义乌，我的梦工厂 Nigel Cropp / 158
义乌印象 李新新 / 171
随心，随性 Ghansham / 173
让生活绽放光彩 楼一博 / 186
义乌，与你共同成长 Bouda / 188
义乌，因你而精彩 黎 苗 / 199

201
第四章
筑梦义乌：
义乌梦，文化情

事业之梦，诚信铸就 Harry / 203
成功路上，事在人为 姚 星 / 216
成长，壮大，成功——扎根义乌 Mamadou Sall / 218
梦想之城，希望之都 谢之悠 / 229
义乌，繁都的华丽转身 Rida / 231
情系东方，梦圆中国 朱江珊 / 241
义乌，我的第二故乡 Subhi / 243
小城市，大世界 罗一圆 / 253
义乌情，中国梦 Manson / 255
奇妙宝地义乌 黄 爽 / 266

269
第五章
共建义乌：
义乌有我更精彩

多彩义乌，应有尽有 Zack / 271
商海义乌，文化为舟 赵艳艳 / 280
自由竞争：为商业而生 Swidan / 282
小城大市，“城”“市”并肩 罗 倩 / 295
经商之道，“诚”“信”二字 Mohammed / 297
稳中求进，诚信为本 刘 璐 / 308
趣意盎然在义乌 Stephen / 309
义乌，不可貌相 陈佳露 / 319

第六章 乌伤城里扶桑人：日籍人士在义乌

321
义乌之缘　古賀崇嗣　/ 323
　樱花般盛开的中国梦　侯　朋　/ 338
义乌情结　佐藤日春　/ 340
　义乌之旅　刘　李　肖　琳　/ 347
能者多劳　木田清隆　/ 348
　精通三国语言的采购　章李可　郑立冬　/ 355
中国式奇迹　杉本哲夫　/ 357
　小商品海洋，购物者天堂　陈林杰　杨侠剑　/ 363

第七章 品读义乌

365
义乌初印象　楼星烨　/ 367
义乌说“义”　沈　洁　马莉莉　张斯惠　/ 371

后记　用心讲故事的人　郑　媛　/ 386

Table of Contents

Chapter One
Business in Yiwu: My Ideal Choice
1

Our Main Battlefield Abdul Mejid / 3
Working in a Down-to-earth Way Qian Chen / 11
Study in China, Trade in Yiwu Zhuo Han / 16
Yiwu, a Paradise for Business People Shen Danni / 22
Learn to Choose, Learn to Live Adriano Santos / 26
I Love You Especially, Yiwu Zhu Xiaotong / 34
My First Choice Kamal / 38
Yiwu: A Legendary City Lin Mengmeng / 46
I'm Happy in Yiwu Juliana / 51
Yiwu: A Wonderful City Shao Lixia / 59

Chapter Two
Fortune in Yiwu: Business Brings You the World
63

Enter Futian Market, and Embrace the World Ishaq / 65
Unique Experience in the Multi-cultural City Cen Ye / 74
China Dream, My Dream Tumaag / 79
Live for Now Zhao Yating / 87
Yiwu, an Ideal Sourcing Center Saman / 92
A Small City on a Large Stage Pan Jingjing / 100
Yiwu, a City Established on a Market Teign / 104
Chinese Business Card: Yiwu; Yiwu's Business Card: Futian Chen Yuan / 112
I Just Decided Orlov / 116
So Said, So Done Shang Mengdan / 124

Chapter Three
Love in Yiwu: Love Brings Me back Home
127

My Indissoluble Bond with Yiwu Bady / 129
Capital of Commerce: a Vivid Oriental Pearl Zheng Yuan / 139
Dreams in China Ahmet Turan / 144
Good People Meet Good People Wang Jingjing / 154
My Yiwu Dream Works Nigel Cropp / 158
Impression of Yiwu Li Xinxin / 168
Live Life to the Fullest Ghansham / 173
Make Every Day Count Lou Yibo / 183
To Be with You, Yiwu Bouda / 188
Yiwu, Wonderful Because of You Li Miao / 197

Chapter Four
Dream in Yiwu: Cultural Bond that Links You and Me
201

Honesty Is the Best Policy Harry / 203
On Our Way to Success Yao Xing / 213
Grow, Thrive and Achieve in Yiwu Mamadou Sall / 218
The City of Dream and Hope Xie Zhiyou / 227
Yiwu, the Conversion of a City Rida / 231
Rida and His Family in Yiwu Zhu Jiangshan / 239
Yiwu: My Second Home Subhi / 243
Small City, Big World Luo Yiyuan / 251
Fall in Love with Yiwu Manson / 255
Wonderland: Yiwu Huang Shuang / 263

Chapter Five
Construction of Yiwu: It'll Be Better with Me
269

We Have Whatever You Want Zack / 271
Cultural Construction of Business City Yiwu Zhao Yanyan / 278
Equality—Born for Business Swidan / 282
Small City but Big Market: City or Market? Luo Qian / 292
Honesty and Trust Are Our Need Mohammed / 297
Honesty and Trust Contribute to Stable Development Liu Lu / 306
The Wonderland of Yiwu Stephen / 309
Yiwu: More than the Appearance Chen Jialu / 316

Chapter Six
義烏城の日本人
321

義烏の縁　古賀崇嗣 / 323
桜の夢　侯　朋 / 335
義烏へのコンプレックス　佐藤日春 / 340
義烏への 旅行　劉李　肖琳 / 345
僕は仕事がたくさんできる　木田清隆 / 348
三ヶ国語ができる仕入れ係　章李可　鄭立冬 / 353
中国式の奇跡　杉本哲夫 / 357
雑貨の海洋、買い物の天国　陳林杰 楊侠剣 / 361

Chapter Seven
Tales of Yiwu
365

The First Impression of Yiwu　Lou Xingye / 367
The Interpretation of "Yi" in Yiwu　Shen Jie　Ma Lili　Zhang Sihui / 371

Postscript　Sincere Story-teller Wins Hearts　Zheng Yuan / 386

第一章

Business in Yiwu: My Ideal Choice

创业义乌：义乌，我来了

导言

义乌，一座以国际商贸而闻名于世的城市，每年都吸引着大量外商前来经商创业，谋求发展。长久以来，义乌小商品为人所津津乐道，在国内外享有盛誉，加之义乌市政府坚持开放包容的政策，营造良好的国际贸易环境，并着力构建便捷、完善的国际贸易服务体系和公共服务体系，这一切使得义乌这座本就具有悠久商业历史和发达商业文明的城市发展成了如今的“小商品海洋、购物者天堂”。义务人吃苦耐劳、踏实肯干、热情好客的精神也由此彰显。

本章中提及的五位外商千里迢迢来到义乌这块风水宝地，他们有的依托于义乌商品的种类繁多与价廉物美的优势而将此地选为进货首选地，有的则被义乌广阔的经商天地和良好的创业环境所吸引，慕名而来，开创自己的事业：或开餐馆，或办公司，或买卖商品，或提供资讯。义乌，是这些怀揣梦想、渴望成功的外商实现抱负、一展宏图的乐园。他们，因义乌而成功；义乌，也因他们而在国际商贸的舞台上绽放了光彩。

通过他们的叙述，可以看到义乌的成功绝非偶然。义乌如今的繁荣与发展正是热情友好的义乌人敢于争先、不断创新，脚踏实地、吃苦耐劳所造就的。他们的这些品德感染着、影响着来此创业的外商，而外商在义乌的奋斗与成功也不断推动着义乌向前发展，持续展现蓬勃向上、欣欣向荣的局面。

Abdul Mejid

Abdul Mejid: Our Main Battlefield

兄弟齐心，义乌打拼

Abdul Mejid is from Pakistan. Ten years ago, his elder brother started a business of hair accessories in Yiwu. Three years ago, Abdul followed his brother to Yiwu, and worked together with him. They mainly purchased hair accessories in Yiwu, and brought them back to Pakistan for sale. Today, the brothers manage their business well in Yiwu, and their goods are well received in Pakistan. As for the future, Abdul hopes that he can keep his business steady and run it smoothly.

阿卜杜勒·迈吉德来自巴基斯坦。十年前，他的哥哥来到义乌创业，专营头饰用品。三年前，他追随哥哥的脚步而来，与哥哥并肩打拼，从义乌采购头饰带到巴基斯坦国内销售。如今，兄弟俩已经在义乌站稳了脚跟，他们的头饰经营在巴基斯坦国内也已经闯出了一片小天地。对于未来，阿卜杜勒希望能够稳扎稳打，让现有的生意长盛不衰。

Our Main Battlefield

By Abdul Mejid

Transcript of the Interview:

【BTV①】Mr. Abdul Mejid, thank you for agreeing to our interview. We are from Ningbo Institute of Technology, Zhejiang University, and we are doing a research program in Yiwu.

【Abdul】That's okay. Please feel free to ask what you want to know, I'd like to share all I know with you.

【BTV】OK, first of all, could you please briefly introduce yourself?

【Abdul】No problem. My name is Abdul Mejid. You can call me Abdul, and I'm 35 years old. I am a businessman from a small city in Pakistan. And I'm dealing in hair accessories.

【BTV】How long have you been in Yiwu?

【Abdul】Three years.

【BTV】Do you like the food in Yiwu, and do you often eat local food?

【Abdul】No. I am not quite accustomed to Chinese food. There are a lot of Muslim food restaurants in Yiwu, and I often eat there. It makes me feel as if I were home.

【BTV】What do you think of people in Yiwu?

【Abdul】They are very cooperative and friendly.

【BTV】What do you think of Yiwu?

【Abdul】You can live in Yiwu and work here. It is a business city.

【BTV】Did you know anything about Yiwu before you came here? How did you know it?

【Abdul】It's all because of my family. My elder brother came here about ten years ago. He told me a lot about Yiwu. And he also took me here.

【BTV】Is your brother the first one in your family to come to Yiwu?

【Abdul】Yes.

【BTV】Apart from Yiwu, have you and your brother been to some other

① BTV 为"Beyond the Voices"缩写。

cities?

【Abdul】We have been to Guangzhou for business, and we have also traveled to many other cities in China for sightseeing.

【BTV】It seems that you've been to a lot of places in China, why do you choose Yiwu as your business base? How does it attract you?

【Abdul】My business is a family business. My other three brothers and uncles are all involved in it. Our business was started in Pakistan first. My brother started it in 1984. In 2002, my brother knew about Yiwu from a friend on the Internet. His friend strongly recommended that he should come to Yiwu, saying that he would love this city as long as he came here in person. So he came, and ran business. And we have been doing it until now.

【BTV】Could you tell us how you run your business?

【Abdul】We buy things in Yiwu and bring them back to Pakistan to sell them to local people. We have shops in Pakistan to sell the products. 70% of the goods we buy here are the goods that are popular among local people. We would buy one thousand or two thousand pieces, and bring them back to Pakistan to sell. The rest are samples. We just buy a small quantity, and bring them to Pakistan to see whether they are sold well or not. If they are sold well, we will buy more, and if not, we will choose other items. This time I come to Yiwu is to choose the sample.

【BTV】Why are you interested in hair accessories?

【Abdul】Because my brothers did this business first, and in Yiwu there are many products of this kind, and they are very good. And selling hair accessories can bring us great profit.

【BTV】As you mentioned just now, you have your business in Guangzhou and Yiwu. Could you tell us the similarities and differences that you think they have?

【Abdul】The similarity is that these two cities are trading cities; many overseas businesspersons would choose these two cities to do business. For the difference, I think Yiwu has almost all the products that I need, but Guangzhou has just a few. We are dealing in hair accessories; and Yiwu is our most suitable choice. So a small proportion of my family's business is in Guangzhou, about 5%, and the rest are in Yiwu. Yiwu is our main battlefield.

【BTV】Do the hair accessories you find in Yiwu meet your standards?

【Abdul】Yes, they are quite good. I always go to the Futian Market.

【BTV】Are there any similar markets in your country?

【Abdul】We have a market in Lahore. The market is very small, not like the one in Yiwu. And it provides me so many business opportunities. I like it.

【BTV】Do you have any local partners here?

【Abdul】Yes, I have.

【BTV】Can you use a word to describe your Chinese partners?

【Abdul】Hard-working. Very hard-working. With their great help, my business is running quite smoothly. I chose the right place.

【BTV】Do you have any local employees? And how do you think of them?

【Abdul】Yes, I used to have one. She was a very good person. She now is not working for me, and she once did as a secretary. She grouped the people and put things in great order.

【BTV】What do you think of the investment environment in Yiwu?

【Abdul】I think the investment here is good. There are many good chances.

【BTV】Have you encountered any difficulties such as communication?

【Abdul】I think it's not really a problem for me because I can say a little Chinese, and I have no problem in English to communicate with people.

【BTV】We know that Yiwu is a very successful business city. What do you think contributes to its success?

【Abdul】Well, first, it has abundant resources; second, Yiwu government's policy is facilitating us to do business; and third, the people here are really very hard-working, and working with them is quite good.

【BTV】You have business in China and Pakistan. Do you think the business style of these two countries is different?

【Abdul】Yes, they are different countries, and their cultural backgrounds are also different, but if you know something about the culture or something else in your business target city, it would help you so much. I can speak Chinese, and I'm also very interested in Chinese culture. So as a result, my business here is quite well, I think.

【BTV】Yes, you are right. I think you have caught the key point in doing business in a foreign country. Then how did you learn Chinese? Did you learn it by yourself?

【Abdul】I bought some books and video tapes from bookstores and also practiced speaking Chinese at any time if possible. Just like the way of learning English, but these two languages are quite different. Learning Chinese is much more difficult than English.

【BTV】The China Dream is frequently mentioned nowadays; do you have a Pakistani Dream? What is your company's blueprint?

【Abdul】I just want to run my small company well, that's okay.

【BTV】Don't you want your company to grow bigger and bigger?

【Abdul】Not yet. The bigger the company becomes, the more problems it would have. Many people developed their business fast, and then they met lots of problems. They became very worried. I don't want to have very big business, because big business has big problems.

【BTV】So your dream is to keep your business steady and run your business smoothly?

【Abdul】To some extent, it's right.

【BTV】It doesn't matter whether your dream is small or big. It's crucial that you have one in your mind, and you are working very hard to achieve it.

【Abdul】Yes, you are right.

【BTV】I sincerely hope that your dream comes true. Thank you very much for your participating in our interview. Thank you for your cooperation. Thank you!

【Abdul】You are welcome!

Group Members: Qian Chen, Cen Ye, Chen Jialu, Zhu Jiangshan

叙事记录

【BTV】阿卜杜勒·迈吉德先生，感谢您接受我们的采访。我们是浙江大学宁波理工学院的学生，来义乌做一项调研。

【Abdul】不客气。你们想了解什么就尽管问好了。我知无不言，言无不尽。

【BTV】首先，您能否简单地介绍一下自己？

【Abdul】没问题。我叫阿卜杜勒·迈吉德。你们叫我阿卜杜勒就行了。我今年 35 岁，来自巴基斯坦的一座小城。我是一名商人，专营头饰用品。

【BTV】您来义乌有几年了？

【Abdul】有三年了。

【BTV】您喜欢吃义乌当地的食品吗？经常吃吗？

【Abdul】没有。我还不太习惯吃中餐。义乌有很多穆斯林餐馆，我常去那儿吃。那儿让我有种在家的感觉。

【BTV】您觉得义乌人怎么样？

【Abdul】他们待人友善，乐于助人。

【BTV】那义乌这个城市呢？

【Abdul】适合生活，便于工作，商贸气氛浓厚。

【BTV】您来义乌之前对这儿有所了解吗？又是如何获取相关信息的？

【Abdul】主要是受我家人的影响。我哥哥十年前就来这儿了。他和我说了很多有关义乌的事。也是他带我来这儿的。

【BTV】您哥哥是您家人中最早来义乌的吗？

【Abdul】是的。

【BTV】除了义乌，你们兄弟俩还去过中国其他城市吗？

【Abdul】我们去过广州经商，也去过许多别的城市旅游观光。

【BTV】你们兄弟俩去过挺多地方的，为何最终扎根义乌开展业务？义乌魅力何在？

【Abdul】我们家人都是从事这方面贸易的，除了我们兄弟俩，还有其他三兄弟和几位叔叔参与其中。我们家的生意开始于巴基斯坦国内，由我哥哥于1984年创立。2002年的时候，我哥哥的一位网友和他说起了义乌。那位网友强烈建议我哥哥来义乌看看，他说只要我哥哥来到义乌就会爱上这个城市。我哥哥就来了，生意也做起来了，至今还一直经营着。

【BTV】可以说说你们是怎么经营的吗？

【Abdul】我们在义乌进货，然后运到巴基斯坦国内销售。我们在巴基斯坦国内开了几家商店专营这些货品。我们所进货品的70%都是当地热销产品。我们会采购一千甚至两千件运回巴基斯坦国内销售。其余30%的货品都是试销品，我们小批量地采购一些带回国内，看看是否有销路。如果畅销的话，我们就再多进些货；如果市场反应不佳，我们就转而采购其他商品。我这次来义乌，就是来采购样品的。

【BTV】为何专营头饰？

【Abdul】因为我们兄弟就是做这个起家的；而且义乌这类商品量多质优。经营头饰让我们获利颇丰。

【BTV】您之前提到，您在广州和义乌都有生意，那么在您看来，这两个城市有何异同？

【Abdul】相同之处就是，这两个城市都是商贸之城，外商大多乐意到这个两城市去经商；有所不同的是，在义乌，我可以找到我所需的绝大多数货品，可在广州我要的货品就比较少了。我们家是做发饰生意的，义乌是我们的最佳选择。正因为如此，我们只有大概5%的生意在广州，其余都在义乌。义乌是我们生意的主战场。

【BTV】那义乌市场上的这些发饰用品都符合你们的进货标准吗？

【Abdul】是的，都挺好的。我经常去福田市场采购。

【BTV】你们国家有类似的这种大型市场吗？

【Abdul】拉合尔有一个市场，不过规模很小，比不上义乌的福田市场。我喜欢福田市场，因为这儿机会多。

【BTV】您在这儿有本地的合作伙伴吗？

【Abdul】有的。

【BTV】可以用一个词来形容一下您的中国合作伙伴吗？

【Abdul】勤奋。真的很勤奋。正因为有了他们的帮助，我的生意才能做得顺风顺水。我来对了地方。

【BTV】您在这儿雇有中国员工吗？觉得他们工作如何？

【Abdul】是的，我曾有过一个。她为人很不错。她曾做过我的秘书，不过现在已经不在这儿做了。之前她在的时候，组织人员、安排事务都井然有序。

【BTV】您觉得义乌的投资环境如何？

【Abdul】我觉得这儿的投资环境还不错，机会很多。

【BTV】您在这儿有没有遇到过什么困难？语言交流有问题吗？

【Abdul】我想这不是什么问题，因为我会说一点点汉语，而且与人用英文交流也没什么大问题。

【BTV】义乌是个商贸之城，运作得很成功，您认为义乌为何会如此成功呢？

【Abdul】嗯，首先，这里有丰富的物资；其次，义乌市人民政府出台了一些利于我们外商从商的政策；再次，义乌人吃苦耐劳，和他们一起工作很愉快。

【BTV】您不仅在中国经商，也在巴基斯坦经商。您觉得两国的经商之道有所不同吗？

【Abdul】不一样。中巴两国国情不同，文化背景也不同。但是，如果你打算去一个地方经商，能事先了解那儿的文化及其他方面的情况，就会受益匪浅。我会说汉语，也对中国文化很感兴趣，因此我在义乌的生意就做得不错。

【BTV】嗯，有道理。我想您已经找到了在异国经商的窍门。那么您是如何学习汉语的呢？是自学的吗？

【Abdul】我在书店买了很多有关汉语学习的书籍和碟片，而且只要一有机会，我就会练习说汉语。这和学英语有些类似。但英语与汉语不太一样，学汉语要比学英语难得多。

【BTV】现在我们都在谈论“中国梦”，您有“巴基斯坦梦”吗？贵公司又有何蓝图呢？

【Abdul】我只想把我的小公司经营好就好了。

【BTV】您不想把公司发展壮大吗？

【Abdul】目前暂无此意。公司越壮大，问题也就会越多。很多人的生意拓展得飞快，麻烦也就接踵而至。他们因此烦心不已。我不想把生意做得很大，要是做大了，麻烦也就多了。

【BTV】那您的梦想就是保持现有生意平稳顺利地运行，对吗？

【Abdul】嗯，差不多。

【BTV】梦想无关乎大小，只要心中有梦想，并为之奋斗，这才是关键。

【Abdul】你说得对。

【BTV】真心祝愿您梦想成真。感谢您接受我们的采访，感谢您的配合！谢谢！

【Abdul】不客气！

团队成员：钱晨，岑烨，陈佳露，朱江珊

Working in a Down-to-earth Way

By Qian Chen Supervised by Ou Chen & Cai Liang

When people mention Yiwu, they always talk about its small commodities. As for me, apart from the small commodities, I know that its development, to some extent, originated from a kind of deal called "Ji Mao Huan Tang" (Bartering chicken feathers for candy). More than 30 years ago, in a time when supplies of materials were insufficient, many vendors journeyed north and south and traveled to exchange inexpensive goods such as candy or coarse paper with residents for chicken feathers in order to gain a little profit. This deal originated in Yiwu. It fully revealed that Yiwu people were economical, courageous, innovative, strong-willed and hard-working. It also inspired Yiwu people to gradually develop Yiwu into an international center of small commodities.

This summer, Ningbo Institute of Technology, organized an activity entitled "Beyond the Voices: Yiwu, Here I Am" to conduct a research on the business environment of Yiwu and how expatriates live and work in Yiwu. I volunteered to be a participant, and seized the chance to get to know Yiwu in person. Then what I knew about Yiwu would not just be confined to the information I got from books or the Internet.

On arriving in Yiwu, I was amazed to see the grand Yiwu Market. Inside the market, I saw countless stores, various commodities, and bustling business people. Though many stores were not big in size, they were of international style. The Chinese signs in the stores were always accompanied by their English version. The owners of the stores could also speak a little English. The convenience in communication in addition to abundant supplies of materials attracted more and more overseas business people to come to Yiwu to start their business. What I saw fully convinced me that Yiwu was truly a paradise for shopping and doing business.

During the interview, I exchanged ideas with some expatriates on Yiwu's business environment and their working experiences. Their praise for Yiwu's business environment and their attitude on working in a down-to-earth way impressed me greatly. One of the most representative interviewees was Abdul Mejid.

Abdul was from Pakistan. He accepted my interview amicably and answered my questions enthusiastically. From our conversation, I got to know that he was not a sophisticated man. His faith in being a plain and honest person in business as well as in life left a deep impression on me. He told me that his brother came to do business in Yiwu ten years ago. Three years ago, he came to Yiwu to work with his brother, dealing hair accessories. They searched Futian Market for what they wanted, purchased the goods, and then took them back to Pakistan for sale. Since they did not buy and sell goods within one country, they had to travel between China and Pakistan. When I asked him whether he felt tired of it, he said with a smile, "I love my business." His words revealed that he was an optimistic and steady man. He was the kind of man who would love whatever job he took up, and devoted himself to the work that he loved.

While Abdul was talking about his working experience, I truly understood that he was hard-working. Although selling hair accessories was not a big deal, he treated his business carefully. From the purchasing in Yiwu to the selling in Pakistan, he did almost everything in person. In order to achieve better development in China, he studied Chinese himself and paid much attention to Chinese culture. What Abdul has achieved today was a reward for his hard work. There is a Chinese saying, "A huge tree that fills one's arm grows from a tiny seedling; a nine-story tower rises from a heap of earth; a thousand li journey starts with the first step." I was moved by Abdul's perseverance and his conscientiousness, and his story told me that one could obtain one's success if one could work in a down-to-earth way.

When I asked why Abdul and his brother chose to start their business in Yiwu, he told me that Yiwu was suitable for doing business. He not only appreciated abundant resources and a sound business environment in Yiwu, but also enjoyed the favorable policies issued by Yiwu civil government for facilitating expatriates in doing business. He felt that his business activity as well as his lawful rights and interests could be protected. Moreover, he said that people in Yiwu were very hard-working and friendly, which made it a pleasant experience to work with them. Abdul said that he and his brother had already chosen Yiwu as their main battlefield and ideal location for developing their business.

When the interview was about to end, we talked about his future plans. He said that he did not have an aggressive plan for his business. What he wanted most at present was to keep his business steady and run it smoothly. He said that he did not have a big dream because he thought that a contented mind was a perpetual feast. He told me that it did not matter whether one's dream was big or not. What really mattered was that one should keep a dream in mind and work hard to achieve it.

For Abdul and his brother, Yiwu is a business paradise. Working in a down-to-earth way, they have cultivated a business environment of their own hand in hand.

脚踏实地，闯出一片天地

文：钱　晨　指导老师：欧　琛　蔡　亮

说起义乌，“义乌小商品”总是出自人们之口的第一个词。而我对于它的了解还来源于“鸡毛换糖”。“鸡毛换糖”是指在早在数十年前，在那个物资匮缺的年代，小商小贩走南闯北走街串巷，以糖、草纸等低廉物品，换取居民家中的鸡毛等废品以获取微利。最早的鸡毛换糖就形成于义乌。它是毫厘争取、积少成多、勇于开拓的创新精神和百折不挠、善于变通、刻苦务实的实干精神的完美体现，也是义乌逐渐发展成为国际小商品贸易中心的精神内核。

今年暑假，为了深入了解义乌创业环境以及外商的工作和生活状态，学校组织了“用声音叙事：义乌，我来了”暑期社会实践活动。我有幸成为该活动的一员，有了一次能亲身实地了解义乌的机会。由此，我对义乌的认知也不仅仅停留在书本或是网络带给我的信息。

初到义乌，我立刻惊叹于义乌小商品市场的宏大规模。那里商铺林立、商品繁多、客商汇聚。走进一家家门面不算大的店铺，凡有文字标识之处便可见英文标注，店主们不仅中文说得溜，简单英文也能来上几句，颇有一种国际范儿。这样好的“语言环境”，加上丰富的物资供应，让越来越多的国外客商选择来到义乌，开创事业。我的这番所见也印证了对义乌原有的印象——“购物者的天堂，创业者的乐园”。

在采访的过程中，我和不少外商就义乌的商贸环境和他们的创业经历进行了交流。他们对义乌创业环境的认同以及他们脚踏实地、事必躬亲的创业态度都给我留下了深刻的印象，其中最具代表性的就是阿卜杜勒·迈吉德。

阿卜杜勒来自巴基斯坦。他非常友好地接受了我的采访，并十分热情地回答了我的问题。通过和他的交谈，我发现他为人实在。说老实话，做老实事，本本分分做生意，这是他给我最深刻印象。他告诉我，十年前他的哥哥就来到义乌创业了。三年前，他跟着哥哥一块儿来到义乌闯荡，专营头饰用品。他们从义乌进货，在福田市场寻觅他们眼中的“珍宝”，然后再带回巴基斯坦，在他们所开的专营店里销售。由于进货地和销售地分处两个国家，他们时常需要在中巴两国往返。当我问及这样的奔波是否让他倍感疲惫时，他只是轻轻一笑，淡淡地说道：“因为我喜欢这一行当。”就这一句“我喜欢”，让我感受到了他的乐观与踏实。“爱一行干一行、干一行爱一行”的真谛也在他身上得到了很好的诠释。

在了解阿卜杜勒创业经历的过程中，我真真切切地感受到了他的刻苦和实干。虽然经营头饰用品并不是什么大生意，阿卜杜勒还是仔仔细细地对待经营的每一环节。从义乌市场的选购、货物的付运到巴基斯坦国内的销售，每一环节他都亲力亲为，一丝不苟。为了能够更好地在中国发展，他还自学汉语并关注中国文化。阿卜杜勒今日的业绩是他脚踏实地付诸努力的收获。“合抱之木，生于毫末；九层之台，起于累土；千里之行，始于足下。”他的坚持、他的踏实，让我感动，也让我领悟到一个道理：凡事只有一步一个脚印，踏踏实实走好每一步，才能有所成就。

当我问及他和他的哥哥为何将创业地选在义乌时，他告诉我义乌物资丰富，经商氛围浓厚，非常适合开展贸易。此外，义乌市人民政府也出台了不少有利于外商从商的政策，让他们的经商活动及合法权益有了制度的保障。再者，义乌人吃苦耐劳、踏实肯干、待人友好，和他们一起工作很愉快。阿卜杜勒说义乌是他们弟兄俩经商的主战场，也是他们创业的理想场所。

临近采访结束，我们谈及了他今后的事业规划。他说他不求自己的事业突飞猛进，只要能保持现有生意的平稳运行就好。他说他的梦想并不高远，他懂得知足，因为知足才能常乐。梦想无关乎大小，心中有梦想，并为之努力奋斗，这才是关键。

义乌是阿卜杜勒和哥哥打拼的乐园，他们兄弟齐心、脚踏实地，闯出了一片属于他们的天地。

Zhuo Han

Zhuo Han: Study in China, Trade in Yiwu

留学中国,创业义乌

Zhuo Han comes from Uzbekistan. He is a boy of good manners and great passion. He was an overseas student at Zhejiang University, and he can speak Chinese fluently. Influenced by his brother, Zhuo Han came to Yiwu after graduation. Now, he is running a restaurant in Yiwu, and he is intending to open a clothing store. Zhuo Han likes Yiwu very much, especially its commercial atmosphere. He plans to settle down in Yiwu for a long time, and he is full of confidence about the future development of his business.

卓翰来自乌兹别克斯坦,为人热情而有礼貌。他曾在浙江大学留学,能说一口流利的中文。毕业后,受他哥哥的影响,卓翰来到了义乌。目前,他在义乌经营着一家餐厅,并且还打算开一家服装店。卓翰很喜欢义乌,尤其是义乌的商业氛围。他打算长期在义乌营生,并对自己事业的未来发展充满了信心。

Study in China, Trade in Yiwu

By Zhuo Han

Transcript of the Interview:

【BTV】Nice to meet you, Zhuo Han. Would you please briefly introduce yourself?

【Zhuo Han】I come from Uzbekistan. I was an overseas student of Zhejiang University. I like making friends in peacetime.

【BTV】An overseas student of Zhejiang University? What is your major?

【Zhuo Han】My major is Chinese.

【BTV】You may have many choices for study, why do you finally choose to study in China?

【Zhuo Han】I think it is convenient to do business here. I come here for my future work. In my country, most of the goods are from China. The goods there are two or three times more expensive than they are here, so I think that I will have a better career in China.

【BTV】Did you have much contact with Chinese people when you were at Zhejiang University? How was your campus life?

【Zhuo Han】Most of the people around me are foreigners. We went to school five days a week. Every day we had four hours of classes. We also had reading and listening classes. Now I can roughly understand Chinese.

【BTV】Your Chinese is good. Did you learn Chinese after you came here or had you studied it before?

【Zhuo Han】I started to learn Chinese one year before I came to China and continued studying it for half a year after I got to China. There is a Confucius Institute in my country, and I learned Chinese there.

【BTV】Really? What do you think about Confucius? Do you know him?

【Zhuo Han】I know he is a culture giant of China. I don't know much about him, but I am willing to learn more about him if I have a chance.

【BTV】So how do you know Yiwu? Why did you come to Yiwu to do business?

【Zhuo Han】Because my brother was doing business in Yiwu, and he once brought me to Yiwu, and I got to know Yiwu then. It is very suitable for business.

【BTV】How long have you been in Yiwu?

【Zhuo Han】Not very long. It's only been about two or three months because I just graduated from school.

【BTV】Which aspects attract you most in Yiwu?

【Zhuo Han】It is very convenient to do business here, and I can learn many good ways of doing business. And there are many kinds of goods here.

【BTV】When you are doing business, what do you pay more attention to, quality or price?

【Zhuo Han】First I will think about the quality of the products. If the quality is good, then I will consider the price.

【BTV】Do you work here? What is your job?

【Zhuo Han】I have a restaurant near the market, offering Uzbekistan and some other western food.

【BTV】How is the business of your restaurant?

【Zhuo Han】I just opened the restaurant, and the business is not so bad.

【BTV】During your stay in Yiwu, have you made any new friends?

【Zhuo Han】Yes, I have made some new friends. They are all very friendly and enthusiastic. We get along with each other well.

【BTV】If you introduce Yiwu to your friends, what will you say?

【Zhuo Han】I will tell them Yiwu is a place which is suitable for business. Of course, other aspects of Yiwu are also very good.

【BTV】It seems that you like Yiwu, so what is Yiwu like in your eyes?

【Zhuo Han】I will use one word to describe Yiwu: business.

【BTV】Who do you hire in your restaurant, Chinese or foreigners? And what are your standards for employment?

【Zhuo Han】The staff in my restaurant are foreigners. I don't have specific standards. I think being hard working and careful are very important.

【BTV】Do you have any problems in the process of running a restaurant?

【Zhuo Han】Yes, we have some, but not big problems. I haven't met big problems so far.

【BTV】Does the government have any special provisions for your opening a restaurant here?

【Zhuo Han】Yes. We must do the things according to the law. The requirements for us from the government are strict. Our time here is also restricted. I came to China to study, so I just had a student visa. It will expire in a month, so I have to go back to my country and come back here next month.

【BTV】Apart from opening the restaurant here, do you want to open other shops?

【Zhuo Han】Yes, I want to open a clothing store.

【BTV】Did the economic crisis affect your business?

【Zhuo Han】No big influence. My business in the restaurant is still good.

【BTV】Do you have some suggestions for the local government? Some suggestions that can help you open a restaurant better?

【Zhuo Han】I haven't considered that yet. I think my work in Yiwu is good. My life at Zhejiang University was also nice. The college specifically opened a restaurant for us, and the food there was authentic. I lived there very happily.

【BTV】Thank you very much for accepting our interview. Hope your restaurant will be better and better, and we wish you success in business.

Group Members: Luo Yiyuan, Shen Danni, Yang Xiajian

叙事记录

【BTV】很高兴见到你，卓翰。能简单地做个自我介绍吗？

【Zhuo Han】我来自乌兹别克斯坦，是浙江大学的留学生。我平时比较喜欢结交朋友。

【BTV】浙大留学生？什么专业呢？

【Zhuo Han】中文。

【BTV】你有多种求学的选择，为什么最后决定来中国留学？

【Zhuo Han】我觉得来中国做生意比较方便，我来这儿是为我将来的工作打算的。在乌兹别克斯坦，很多商品都来自中国。那些商品比这儿的同类商品要贵上两三倍，所以我觉得来中国会有更好的发展。

【BTV】在浙大时你和中国人接触得多吗？你大学的生活怎么样呢？

【Zhuo Han】我身边的人多数都是外国人。我们一周上五天课，每天上四个学时，有阅读课也有听力课。我现在大致能听懂中文。

【BTV】你中文说得挺好的。你的中文是来这里之后学的还是之前就学过了？

【Zhuo Han】来中国前我学了一年的中文，来中国后又学了半年。我们国家设有孔子学院，我是在那里学的中文。

【BTV】是吗？那你知道孔子吗？对他了解多少呢？

【Zhuo Han】我知道他是中国的文化巨匠。我对他了解不深，若有机会，我还想多了解些。

【BTV】你是怎么知道义乌的呢？为什么选择来义乌做生意？

【Zhuo Han】因为我哥哥是在义乌做生意的，他之前曾带我来过义乌，我对义乌就有了一定的了解。这里是一个非常适合做生意的地方。

【BTV】你在义乌生活有多久了？

【Zhuo Han】没多久，也就两三个月，因为我刚从学校毕业。

【BTV】你觉得义乌有哪些方面吸引了你？

【Zhuo Han】在这儿做生意很方便，也可以学到不少精妙的经营之道，而且这儿的商品种类繁多。

【BTV】做生意时，你更看重什么？是质量还是价格？

【Zhuo Han】我会先看看商品的质量，如果质量好，再考虑价格。

【BTV】你现在在义乌工作吗？从事什么工作呢？

【Zhuo Han】我在这个市场边开了一家餐厅，主供乌兹别克斯坦风味的菜肴以及其他一些西餐。

【BTV】那餐厅的生意如何呢？

【Zhuo Han】餐厅开张不久，生意还算过得去。

【BTV】你在义乌的这段时间里有没有结交新朋友？

【Zhuo Han】有，我交了几个新朋友。他们都很友好，也很热情。我们相处得挺好的。

【BTV】如果你向朋友介绍义乌，会怎么说呢？

【Zhuo Han】我会跟他们说义乌是一个很适合做生意的地方，当然义乌的其他方面也很好。

【BTV】你好像很喜欢义乌，能说说你眼中的义乌吗？

【Zhuo Han】我会用一个词来表示：生意。

【BTV】你餐厅招录的是中国人还是外籍人士？有什么招人的标准吗？

【Zhuo Han】我餐厅的员工都是外国人。我没有特定的招聘标准。我觉得做起事来要既勤快又认真，这点很重要。

【BTV】那你在开餐厅的过程中有没有遇到困难？

【Zhuo Han】有是有，但都是小事，迄今为止还没遇到过大问题。

【BTV】你在这儿开餐厅，政府有没有相关的特别规定？

【Zhuo Han】有的。我们必须依法行事。政府对我们的要求还是比较严格的。对于我们在此驻留的时长也有限制。我之前是来中国学习的，所以办的是学生签证，还有一个月就要到期了，所以我要先回国，下个月再来义乌。

【BTV】除了在这儿开餐厅，你还想过开其他的店吗？

【Zhuo Han】有想过。我想开一家服装店。

【BTV】之前的经济危机有没有影响到你的生意？

【Zhuo Han】没有大的影响，我餐厅的生意还可以。

【BTV】那你对当地政府有何谏言？怎样能帮助你更好地经营餐厅？

【Zhuo Han】这个我倒还没想过。我觉得在义乌工作挺好的。我以前在浙江大学的生活也不错，那儿有专门为我们开设的餐厅，所供菜肴口味纯正。我在那儿过得很开心。

【BTV】非常感谢你接受我们的采访，期盼你的餐厅越办越红火，也预祝你事业有成。

团队成员：罗一圆，沈丹妮，杨侠剑

Yiwu, a Paradise for Business People

By Shen Danni Supervised by Ou Chen & Cai Liang

Yiwu, a city located in the hinterland of Zhejiang Province, has become world-famous because of the Yiwu Market. Various goods and their competitive prices attract customers from all parts of the world to do business in Yiwu. Many of them are overseas customers. In order to get a comprehensive view of Yiwu's business environment and expatriates' life in Yiwu, Ningbo Institute of Technology, Zhejiang University, carried out a research project entitled "Beyond the Voices: Yiwu, Here I Am", and I was lucky enough to be one of the participants.

Before I went to Yiwu, my knowledge about Yiwu was just based on hearsay. I had never paid much attention to her. In order that I could complete my task better, I surfed on the Internet to get some information about Yiwu. It was not until then that I was deeply attracted by the descriptions such as "home to the biggest wholesale market of daily consumer goods in the world", "an important international center of small commodities, information and exhibitions", "where the new Silk Road begins", and "an important bridgehead for foreign products to access China", and I became really interested in the coming visit to Yiwu.

After I got to Yiwu, what I saw of the International Trade City in Yiwu fulfilled my expectations. I was deeply impressed by the grand and vast market. No wonder Yiwu was called "an ocean of small commodities and a paradise for shoppers". The shops in the market were orderly, and the goods were dazzling. While we were doing surveys in the market, voices of bargaining from the international and local customers filled my ears. Some of the expatriates could speak Chinese quite fluently. I visited several shops and interviewed their owners. They all told me that the market in Yiwu was really open and well organized.

When I was searching for my interviewee, I saw Zhuo Han, the Uzbekistan guy with a big smile on his face. Zhuo Han told me proudly that he used to be an overseas student of Zhejiang University. That was why he became excited when he saw my working card saying that I was from Ningbo Institute of Technology, Zhejiang University. His words and his friendliness erased my nervous tension, and I started to talk with him.

Zhuo Han said that he got to know something about Yiwu before he came here to start his business. While he was studying as an overseas student, he learned that Yiwu was a suitable place for business. Then, under his brother's advice, he made up his mind to start his own business in Yiwu.

Since Zhuo Han had been studying in China for some time, he got to know Chinese culture a little bit. As for the culinary culture, he found that the style of Chinese cooking was quite different from that of western cooking, and it was also different from the style of Uzbek cooking. He also noticed that many overseas business people in Yiwu not only wanted to try traditional Chinese food and western food, but also wanted to try food of other cultures. Then, he got an idea and decided to open a restaurant serving western and Uzbek food. Although his restaurant had just been set up, it was always full of customers, and some of them were regular diners. The brisk business showed that he was right in opening a restaurant like this. Zhuo Han told me that he also wanted to open a clothing store and that he thought Yiwu was very suitable for business and investment.

While talking with Zhuo Han, I learned how he started his business in Yiwu and how he worked and lived in Yiwu. During the interview, Zhuo Han expressed his love for Yiwu through his words. He loved Yiwu because he really appreciated the grand market and convenient business environment there, because his business was successful in Yiwu, and because he was fully satisfied with his life in Yiwu. He said he had quite a number of Chinese and international friends in Yiwu, whose passion and friendliness strengthened his resolution to stay in Yiwu.

After the interview, I was really excited. As a local resident in Zhejiang, I felt proud of hearing praise for Yiwu from an expatriate. I also learned a great deal from Zhuo Han's studying and working experiences. His story was worth learning. In addition to his strong desire for learning foreign culture, his creativity and endeavor was inspiring for us students who were about to graduate and step into the society. It was important to have a sound environment for one's developing career, but one's strong will was the key to success. Zhuo Han told me that he was just one of many ambitious and hard-wording young people who came to Yiwu to start their own businesses. For them, Yiwu was a paradise because it offered them a favorable environment for their development. They, through hard work, could realize their business dream, and their success in turn propelled the further development of Yiwu. I thought that this might be one of the reasons why Yiwu could always retain her attractiveness and vigor.

Yiwu, you are a real paradise for business people!

义乌，创业者的乐园

文：沈丹妮　指导老师：欧　琛　蔡　亮

义乌，一个地处浙江腹地的城市，因其拥有义乌国际小商品市场而闻名于世。琳琅满目的商品和极具竞争力的价格吸引着四海客商前来创业经商。这些人中有很大一部分是来自海外的客商。为了更好地了解义乌的创投环境和外商在义乌的生活及工作，今年暑假浙江大学宁波理工学院组织了“用声音叙事：义乌，我来了”社会实践活动，我有幸成为其中的一名参与者。

在去义乌之前，我对义乌的认识仅仅停留在“道听途说”的阶段，自己并没有真正去关注过她。为了能够更好地完成暑期的调研活动，我又上网恶补了有关义乌的信息。“全球最大的日用消费品批发市场所在地”、“重要的国际小商品贸易中心、信息中心和展示中心”、“新丝绸之路的起点”、“外国商品进入中国的重要‘桥头堡’”，这些描述牢牢地吸引了我的眼球，也让我对将要开始的义乌之行充满了期待。

来到义乌之后，展现在我眼前的义乌国际小商品市场就印证了我之前对义乌的期待。市场的宏伟和广阔给我留下了深刻的印象，难怪义乌被称为“小商品海洋，购物者天堂”。市场的店铺规格整齐划一，店铺里的商品让我们眼花缭乱。我们在市场里做问卷调查时，外国客商和店家讨价还价的声音不绝于耳。有些外商甚至能用非常流利的中文跟店主商议价格。我走访了几家店铺，也采访了一些店主。从店家口中得知，这里的市场自由开放，商店经营秩序井然。

在调研的过程中我遇到了卓翰，那个带着微笑的乌兹别克斯坦大男孩。卓翰很自豪地告诉我他是浙江大学的留学生。也正是因为如此，他在看到我们的工作牌上印有“浙江大学宁波理工学院”的文字时就显得很兴奋，而他的这番介绍也让我倍感亲切。加之他的友好态度，更是让我之前紧张的心情得以平复，开始和他侃侃而谈。

卓翰说他来义乌发展之前就对义乌有所了解，早在他留学时，就对义乌广阔的经商天地和良好的经商环境有所耳闻。随后他在哥哥的建议下决定来义乌创业，决心闯出一番属于自己的事业。

因为有过在中国学习的经历，卓翰对中国的文化已经有些熟悉。在饮食文化方面，他发现中餐和西餐以及他本国的餐饮风格不一，而义乌的外商云集，他们在体验中餐的过程中也对西餐念念不忘，对其他风味的餐饮也跃跃欲试。于是，一个想法在他脑海里产生了，他决定开一家餐厅，里面主营乌兹别克斯坦风味的食品和西餐。虽然他的餐厅刚开不久，但常常顾客盈门，而且已经有了一些固定的客户群。这红火的生意也印证了他最初的创业决定是明智的。他告诉我，除了开一家餐厅，他还想有一家服装店。他觉得义乌是创业和投资的宝地。

在与卓翰对话时，我了解到了他在义乌创业的过程以及他在义乌工作和生活的经历。在访谈中，卓翰言语间透露着对义乌的喜爱。这种喜爱源自于他对义乌广阔的市场和便捷的经营环境的赞许，源自于他创业成功的喜悦，也源自于他对义乌生活的满足。他说他在当地已经结交了一些外国朋友和中国朋友，也正是这些朋友的热情和友好更加坚定了他留在义乌的决心。

采访结束后，我的内心也起了不小的波澜。不仅仅是因为我作为浙江人听到了外籍人士对义乌的赞扬而倍感骄傲，还因为我对卓翰求学和创业的经历有所感悟。卓翰有许多闪光点值得我学习。除了他对异国文化的求知欲望，他的创新精神、奋斗精神也是我们这些即将毕业并踏入社会的大学生所应该具备的。对于个人的发展，良好的环境固然重要，但个人的坚强意志是决定成功的关键。卓翰告诉我们，在义乌还有许多像他一样雄心勃勃、踏实肯干的青年，他们都选择来到义乌这个创业乐园。义乌为他们的发展提供了良好的环境。这样的环境孕育出了一批批志在创业的商业人士，而这些商业人士的成功也推动着义乌不断朝前发展。我想，这也正是义乌多年来能够魅力不减，发展不滞的因素之一吧。

义乌，一个创业者的乐园！

Adriano Santos

Adriano Santos: Learn to Choose, Learn to Live

商海义乌,择机而行

Adriano Santos is from Brazil. He loves Chinese very much and has given himself a Chinese name—A Deli. Influenced by his brother, Adriano came to Yiwu three years ago and started his own business, running a company which provides services for those foreigners who come to Yiwu to do business. Though he has not been in Yiwu for a long time, he has come to know how things work in China and has learned to make choices. He thinks that Yiwu is full of opportunities, and that he is right in starting a business in Yiwu.

阿德利亚诺·桑托斯来自巴西。热爱中文的他给自己取了个名字,阿德利。三年前,受到哥哥的影响,阿德利亚诺来到了义乌,开办了一家服务公司,为来义乌做生意的外国人提供各种资讯服务。虽然他在义乌做生意的时间不算长,但他已经在打拼中悟出了在中国的经商之道,学会了取舍。在他看来,义乌遍地是商机,来义乌发展是他人生中的一个正确选择。

Learn to Choose, Learn to Live

By Adriano Santos

Transcript of the Interview:

【BTV】Hello, my name is Zhu Xiaotong. I'm a student from Ningbo Institute of Technology, Zhejiang University. My team is conducting a research on the expatriates in Yiwu. May I ask you several questions?

【Adriano】Okay, with pleasure.

【BTV】First, can you make a brief self-introduction?

【Adriano】Okay, my name is Adriano Santos. I'm from Brazil. I've been here for three years.

【BTV】When did you first get to know Yiwu? How did you know about it?

【Adriano】Before I came here, I heard about Yiwu from my brother. He already had a company here. After I came here, especially after I started my own business, I came to know Yiwu more. Many foreign businessmen like to buy goods from Yiwu and then export them to their own country. They make quite a lot of money in this way.

【BTV】Well, which aspect of Yiwu attracts you most?

【Adriano】Convenience. I think everything is easy to do. Everything is convenient. And everything you need is quite easy to find here.

【BTV】How about the communication?

【Adriano】I think no problem. Since I have learned Chinese, I think it's okay because I can speak Chinese.

【BTV】Did you learn it by yourself?

【Adriano】Yes, I learned it by myself. I've been in America for eight years, and I learned English. When I was in Mexico, I learned Spanish. Now, I'm in China, I can speak Chinese.

【BTV】You are so great. Can you give us some suggestions? Because you know we major in English.

【Adriano】I think environment is the most important thing. And you should practice, practice and practice.

【BTV】It's a useful suggestion. Maybe you can talk about your life in Yiwu during these three years.

【Adriano】The life here at the beginning was difficult because each different country has different culture. And the way to express friendship is the hardest thing. In our country, friendship is like touching, hugging, and it's happy to touch, to hug, but in China, we see somebody, we say "Hello", nobody hugs, nobody touches.

【BTV】Maybe the way we show friendship is different. You said that was in the beginning, and then?

【Adriano】Then we got used to it and had many foreign friends.

【BTV】Have you ever experienced any culture shock in Yiwu? Tell us some interesting stories if you have any.

【Adriano】Totally. About one time, we went to Haixin School. It's an English school. We went together for Saturday trip. We went to a lake. Near the lake, there were many people barbecuing. It was a place for barbecue. Also there were some people fishing. The lake was so nice that I couldn't help swimming in it. When people saw me swimming in the lake, they were shocked and shouted because they thought it was very dangerous. They tried their best to persuade me not to do so, and I didn't continue swimming, but actually I didn't think it was dangerous.

【BTV】So how did you feel about it? Over-protection?

【Adriano】Yeah, I felt it was. But I had to give up because it was totally a mess.

【BTV】Okay, that's a very interesting story. And how do you spend your leisure time in Yiwu?

【Adriano】Like this, chatting, and making friends and swimming. I like making friends and doing some sports.

【BTV】Then do you often take part in some local activities?

【Adriano】I sometimes participate in some local social activities. Sometimes, the local government organizes some affairs for foreigners like us. They invite me to take part in them.

【BTV】Oh, that's interesting. How about the food in Yiwu?

【Adriano】Food is okay. It's no problem to eat Chinese food for me. But we sometimes cook at home.

【BTV】Oh, you cook? Can you cook Chinese food?

【Adriano】No, I don't know how to cook Chinese food. Mostly I cook foreign food.

【BTV】Many restaurants in Yiwu serve western food and Muslim food, and they cater to the needs of foreign businessmen. And what do you think of the investment environment in Yiwu?

【Adriano】I think it's good. You will make a lot of money if you take a chance to make a business. And the chance of doing business here is good.

【BTV】Then what do you think should be improved?

【Adriano】Maybe the traffic. Both the driver and the pedestrian should be polite and obey the traffic rules.

【BTV】Yeah, it should be improved. And I know your company does not produce goods. Instead, it offers services. Can you tell me more about your company?

【Adriano】Okay. Many foreign people come to China to buy goods, but they do not exactly understand how things work in China. It's easy for Chinese people to understand, but for foreigners, it's not easy. So our company is just like a bridge between the Chinese and the foreigners.

【BTV】As we know, there are many companies like yours in Yiwu. So what's your opinion about this business?

【Adriano】I think for me it's okay because there are still a lot of customers, and there is still a big market. Many people need somebody's help. I don't need to worry about how to find customers.

【BTV】You are quite confident. And what's the blueprint for your company?

【Adriano】Well, maybe not so much my blueprint as my wishes. What I want in the future is to have less work to do.

【BTV】Less work? Why? In my view, more work means more money.

【Adriano】No, absolutely not. You know, there are many types of customers. For some customers, you have to do a lot of work, but you make little money; while for some other customers, you don't have to do much work, but you can make a lot of money. That is what I want. I don't want to be so busy. I want to live a more easy-going life. So, now I choose customers. If some customers come to me for help, and I think it's comfortable, then I will do, but if not, I will refuse.

【BTV】When did you start to choose your customers?

【Adriano】Well, when I had my own company at the beginning, I wanted to earn more money, so I always provided services to people who came to me for help, but later, I found some people ask for many more services than they paid me. I was very busy, very tired. After that, I learned to choose customers. I didn't regret to refuse some customers because it was worth to do that. I can meet other comfortable customers. Learn to choose, learn to live, that is life.

【BTV】Well, do you have any difficulties in running your business?

【Adriano】The staff. I don't need too many staff. I need capable staff.

【BTV】Are your staff Chinese or foreigners?

【Adriano】Chinese people who can speak a little English. At the beginning, I choose to hire staff who speak a little English, so I can also learn Chinese.

【BTV】Do you communicate with them in Chinese?

【Adriano】Yes, I communicate with them in Chinese. I've learned a lot of Chinese from them.

【BTV】Are you busy all year long?

【Adriano】No, May and August are the busiest months. Do you know Canton Fair? It is held twice a year, and it has three phases. The first phase is for big machines, and the second is for home decorations, and the third is for sports, clothes and something else. It's a very big market.

【BTV】What did you do at the Canton Fair? Translation?

【Adriano】No, most of them can speak English. What I did is to choose customers, and then I can do business in Yiwu.

【BTV】Oh, that's really a good idea. So, thank you very much for accepting my interview. I've really learned a lot from you.

Group Members: Zhu Xiaotong, Zhao Yating, Huang Shuang

叙事记录

【BTV】您好,我叫朱小曈。我是浙江大学宁波理工学院的一名学生。我的团队正在做一个关于义乌外商的调查。我可以问您一些问题吗?

【Adriano】可以,我很乐意回答。

【BTV】首先,您能否简单介绍一下您自己?

【Adriano】好的,我的名字叫 Adriano Santos(阿德利亚诺·桑托斯),来自巴西。我来义乌已有三年了。

【BTV】您初识义乌源于何时?又是如何知晓?

【Adriano】来义乌之前,我哥哥和我说了一些义乌的情况。他早已在义乌开了公司。我来到义乌之后,尤其是开始自己的营生之后,就更进一步认识了义乌。很多外国客商喜欢来此进货并出口到他们自己的国家。借此，他们获利颇丰。

【BTV】那么，义乌最吸引您的是什么？

【Adriano】便捷。我觉得在这儿办事很简单，很便捷，想要什么也能轻松找到。

【BTV】那语言交流呢？

【Adriano】不成问题。我学过中文，能说汉语，所以语言交流尚可。

【BTV】您中文是自学的吗？

【Adriano】是的，我是自学的。我在美国待了8年，学会了英语。在墨西哥时又学会了西班牙语。如今，在中国了，我就学会说中文了。

【BTV】真厉害。您能给我们这些学英语的人一些建议吗？

【Adriano】我认为环境是最重要的因素，而且你需要不断地练习、练习、再练习。

【BTV】受教了。那么您能谈谈在义乌的三年生活吗？

【Adriano】初来乍到时，有些不习惯，因为不同的国家有着不同的文化。比如友谊的表现方式就是最大的难题。在我们国家，朋友间可以拥抱，可以有肢体的接触，人们也乐于以此传达友情；但在中国，当我们遇见别人时，我们就说声“你好”，打个招呼，不拥抱也没有肢体接触。

【BTV】也许我们表达友谊的方式不一样吧。您刚刚说的是开始阶段，那后来呢？

【Adriano】后来我们慢慢也就习惯了，还结交了各国朋友。

【BTV】那您是否经历过“文化冲突”？如果有的话，可否和我们说说趣事？

【Adriano】当然。有一次，我们去海信英语学校。周六我们一起去湖边度假。湖边有很多人在烧烤，因为那是一个可供烧烤的地方。湖边也有人在钓鱼。湖很美，美得我情不自禁地下水游起泳来。人们看到我在游泳，又惊又叫，因为他们认为这样太危险了。他们极力劝说我不要游泳，我也就作罢了，但事实上我没觉得这么做有什么危险。

【BTV】那您当时有何感受？被过度保护了？

【Adriano】是的，我感觉是这样的。但当时局面有点乱，我也就不坚持了。

【BTV】故事挺有趣。那么，您在义乌闲暇之余都做些什么呢？

【Adriano】像这样聊天，交友，还有游泳。我喜欢结交朋友，也爱好运动。

【BTV】那您经常参加义乌当地的活动吗？

【Adriano】我有时会参加本地的一些社会活动。有时当地政府会为我们这些外国人组织些活动。他们会邀请我参加。

【BTV】挺有意思的。那义乌的食物怎样？

【Adriano】挺好的。对我来说，吃中国菜没问题。但有时，我会在家做菜。

【BTV】是吗？那您会做中国菜吗？

【Adriano】我不会做中国菜。我常做外国菜。

【BTV】义乌有不少餐馆供应西餐和穆斯林风味的菜，应该可以满足许多外商在吃方面的需求。那么您认为义乌的投资环境怎么样？

【Adriano】我觉得挺好的。如果你能抓住商机做生意，你就能赚大钱。这里商机颇好。

【BTV】那您认为有什么需要改进的地方吗？

【Adriano】应该是交通吧。司机和行人都应该文明出行，遵守交通规则。

【BTV】嗯，这方面确实需要改进。据我所知，贵公司并不生产商品，而是提供服务，可否具体介绍下？

【Adriano】好的。许多外商来华采购，但他们并不了解中国的经商之道。中国商人早已熟知的商道，对外国商人而言，想要弄懂绝非易事。我们公司就像是一座联通中外商人的桥梁。

【BTV】据我了解，义乌有不少公司和贵公司类似，对此您有何看法？

【Adriano】我觉得没什么，因为需要服务的客户依然很多，这方面的市场依然很大。很多人需要帮助。所以我无须担心客户源。

【BTV】您挺有信心的。那么，贵公司有何发展蓝图？

【Adriano】嗯，与其说是蓝图，不如说是我的愿望。我希望将来要做的工作会少些。

【BTV】工作少一些？为什么？在我看来，多干就能多赚钱。

【Adriano】并非如此。要知道，客户类型多种多样。有些客户，要求你干的活儿挺多，但付给你的报酬却很少；而有些客户，要求你干的活儿不多，但给你的报酬却挺丰厚的。我想要的客户正如后者。我不想太过忙碌。我想轻轻松松生活。所以，现在我接客户时会有所选择。若有客户上门，我觉得适合做生意的就做，不适合的就婉言谢绝。

【BTV】您从何时起开始选择客户做生意？

【Adriano】嗯……公司成立之初，我想多赚钱，所以我对需要我提供服务的客商几乎是来者不拒。但后来，我发现有些客户要得多，给得少。我很忙、很累。在那之后，我就开始尝试着选择客户来做生意。我不后悔拒绝一些客户，因为这么做是值得的。我可以为其他优质客户服务。学会选择，学会生存，这就是生活。

【BTV】那您开公司有没有遇到什么困难呢？

【Adriano】招工问题。我所需员工的数量不多，但能力要强。

【BTV】贵公司的员工是中国人还是外国人？

【Adriano】会说点英语的中国人。自公司创办起，我就录用能说些英语的中国人，这样，我也可以学习汉语。

【BTV】那您和他们说汉语吗？

【Adriano】是的，说汉语。通过和他们交流，我已学到了不少汉语。

【BTV】您整年都忙吗？

【Adriano】也不是，五月和八月最忙。你知道广交会吗？广交会每年举行两次，分三期。第一期是大型机械及设备，第二期是家居装饰，第三期是运动产品和服饰及其他。广交会规模很大。

【BTV】广交会上您做些什么？当翻译？

【Adriano】不是，很多人都会说英语。我去那里物色客户，之后就可以在义乌拓展业务了。

【BTV】哦，这主意真不错。非常感谢您接受我的采访，我获益良多。

团队成员：朱小曈，赵雅婷，黄爽

I Love You Especially, Yiwu

By Zhu Xiaotong　Supervised by Ou Chen & Cai Liang

When I was a child, I heard my parents talking about Yiwu. What they mainly mentioned was the wholesale market. From what they said, I got to know that the goods there were low in price but good in quality. At that time, I just got a vague view of Yiwu, thinking that it might be a good place for shopping. It was not until I took part in the research project entitled "Beyond the Voices: Yiwu, Here I Am" organized by the Ningbo Institute of Technology, Zhejiang University that I got to know Yiwu more. After I completed my interview with some expatriates in the wholesale market, Adriano Santos in particular, I sensed the unique beauty of Yiwu. As a result, my special love for Yiwu welled up in my heart.

Friendly and Passionate People in Yiwu

Adriano Santos was the first expatriate whom I interviewed in Yiwu. Three years ago, he came to Yiwu from Brazil and set up a company offering advisory services. He warmly accepted to do my interview and was really eager in communicating with me. During the interview, he listened to my questions patiently and offered replies in detail with a smile on his face. His friendliness and passion erased my nervousness and timidity, drowning me in unexpected warmth just like a spring breeze kissing my face. Besides Adriano Santos, almost all the people whom I interviewed or contacted in Yiwu, expatriates and local people, were kind and enthusiastic. I think that the kindness and enthusiasm that they expressed might be one of the reasons why many businessmen choose to settle down in Yiwu to start their businesses.

Abundant Opportunities in Yiwu

During the interview, Adriano Santos told me that the abundant opportunities in Yiwu attracted him here. He said that while he was wondering what he should choose as his business, he noticed that many difficulties occurred in the processes of business deals because of language barriers and cultural differences. Some expatriates were in urgent need of finding someone to help them facilitate cross-cultural communication. They wanted to adapt to the local environment quickly so that they could run their businesses in Yiwu better. Adriano seized this chance. Since he could speak quite a few languages, he set up a company to offer advisory services to international business people to help them find an effective access to the Yiwu market. Though having been faced with fierce competition by many similar companies, Adriano was still confident about his future career. For him, Yiwu was full of opportunities. As long as one could observe and think carefully, he would find a way to succeed in business.

From what Adriano told me, I came to understand why Yiwu kept thriving. It had been offering chances to those business people who were in pursuit of their dreams. They came to Yiwu, got to know Yiwu, and then started their businesses. They seized the chances to sow the seeds of their dreams and then waited to reap success. Yiwu provided the business people with a good environment to fulfill their dreams, and their success in turn propelled the development of Yiwu.

Adriano's Business Strategy

My interview with Adriano not only allowed me to understand the favourable business conditions in Yiwu, but also made me realize the importance of making choices. Before the interview, I always thought that the busier your business became, the more customers you had, then the more profit you could reap. However, Adriano told me that it was not always true. When he first started his business, he regarded each customer as god and served every customer with his heart and soul. He was really exhausted at that time, but his income was not much. Later, he changed his business strategy and began to choose comfortable customers to serve. Although the customers that he had became fewer, his work was more relaxing, and his income began to increase. Adriano said, "Learn to choose, learn to live, that is life." He learned what this really meant after he came to Yiwu, and after the interview, I took it as an attitude for my life.

After I spent several days in Yiwu interviewing expatriates, I obtained a more comprehensive view of Yiwu. It is not like Beijing, the capital of China, nor is it like Shanghai, the most prosperous city in China, nor is it like Guilin or Hangzhou which are famous for fabulous scenery. Yiwu is unique as a business city. Its uniqueness owes a great deal to its friendly and passionate people and is exemplified by its vigorous development. Its uniqueness can provoke ideas and arouse people's affection.

Yiwu, I love you especially.

义乌:特别的爱给特别的你

文:朱小曈　指导教师:欧　琛　蔡　亮

我记得小时候就在大人们的交谈中听到过义乌这个名字。他们提得最多的就是小商品市场,我也由此知道了那里有很多物美价廉的商品。那时对义乌的印象是泛泛的,朦朦胧胧地感觉那里应该是购物的好去处。直到我参加了学校组织的"用声音叙事:义乌,我来了"暑期实践活动,实地采访了义乌小商品市场里的客商,我对这座城市的印象才逐渐丰满起来。尤其是对阿德利亚诺·桑托斯的采访,让我切实感受到了义乌这座商贸之城的独特魅力,我不由得对她产生了一种特别的喜爱之情。

一、义乌之人,热情友好

阿德利亚诺·桑托斯是接受我采访的第一位外籍客商。三年前,他从巴西来到义乌,开办了一家提供资讯服务的公司。对于我的采访要求,阿德利亚诺·桑托斯热情地予以配合。在采访过程中,他微笑以对,积极与我交谈,耐心地倾听我提出的各类问题,并详细地进行了回答。他的友好与热情消除了我采访前的紧张与胆怯,让我感受到春风拂面般的温暖。不仅仅是阿德利亚诺·桑托斯,我所采访过、接触过的其他外商以及义乌本地居民大都是和善有礼、热忱相待的。我想,他们所展现的这种热情友好的正能量也正是往来客商驻足义乌的缘由之一吧。

二、义乌之地,商机遍布

采访中,阿德利亚诺·桑托斯告诉我,他之所以来义乌发展是看中了义乌的遍地商机。他告诉我创业之初,他了解到义乌有不少外国客商因为中外文化有异、语言不通而在经商时遭遇困难,急需有人帮助他们跨越中外文化差异的藩篱,尽早"入乡随俗"以便更好地开拓业务。他敏锐地捕捉到了这一商机,凭借自己通晓多国语言的优势,开办了提供资讯服务的公司,旨在帮助外国客商有效地融入义乌市场。如今,即使面对多家同类型公司的竞争,阿德利亚诺·桑托斯依然对未来的发展充满信心。因为在他看来,义乌是个充满商机的城市,只要肯留心、善思考,就会抓住适合自己发展的商机,开辟创业的新天地。

阿德利亚诺的一席话让我看到了义乌的蓬勃之源。她为有梦想、敢追求的四海客商提供了充足的机会。这些客商来到义乌、认识义乌、了解义乌之后,便可在这片充满机遇的沃土上,看准时机,播撒梦想的种子,等候收获成功。是义乌良好的创业环境促成了这些客商的创业之梦,而这些客商的成功又进一步促进了义乌的发展。

三、经商之道，取舍有度

与阿德利亚诺的交谈不仅让我感受到了义乌经商的“地利”和“人和”，还让我领悟了取舍之道。在采访前，我总以为做生意应该是越忙越好，顾客是越多越好，这样才能赚大钱。但阿德利亚诺告诉我，事实并非如此。创业之初，他秉承着“来者便是客”的理念，对上门的每一位客户都不加以区分地对待，结果他疲于工作，盈利却很少。后来他改变了策略，开始选择服务的对象，只接待优质客户。虽然客户较之前少了些，但工作轻松了，盈利也增加了。学会选择，学会取舍，学会生存是他来义乌创业后的一种领悟，也是我这次采访所学到的一种人生态度。

通过数日的采访，我对义乌有了更为全面的了解。她不像北京，有首都的光辉笼罩着；不像上海，有繁华的景象映衬着；不像桂林，有柔情的山水呵护着；也不像杭州，有美丽的西湖滋润着。义乌这座商贸之城有其独特的气质。这种气质源自于热情友善的义乌人，造就了蓬勃向上的义乌城，也激发着人们的感悟与爱她之情。

义乌，我将特别的爱给予特别的你！

Kamal

Kamal: My First Choice

货比三家,义乌最佳

Kamal is from Jordan. He is a young businessman dealing in products such as faucets and water pipes. He devotes himself to his business and shops around to maximize profit. At present, Yiwu is his first choice for buying products in China because the competitive prices and wide variety of goods in Yiwu have left a deep impression on him.

卡马尔来自约旦,主要经营水暖管件。他是一个潜心于事业的年轻商人,为了追求利润的最大化,他经常往返于各地,货比三家。如今,他将义乌作为在中国进货的首选地,因为义乌商品的种类繁多与价廉物美给他留下了非常深刻的印象。

My First Choice

By Kamal

Transcript of the Interview:

【BTV】Shall we begin now?

【Kamal】Yes. I am ready.

【BTV】So where are you from?

【Kamal】I am from Jordan. It is a small country in the Mideast, and it is very very beautiful.

【BTV】How often do you come to China? And what do you think of China?

【Kamal】I come to China five or six times a year to buy some products. Most of my products come from Yiwu. So it is my first choice if I want to buy some products in China. China is a beautiful country, and I love Chinese food, especially sea foods. I went to Ningbo last month, and I can still remember the excellent taste of the sea foods. Besides, China does business with many countries in the world, so China is a big market for businessmen in other countries. We can not only send merchandises to China, but also find supplies in China.

【BTV】I am glad that China has left a good impression on you. Except China, have you ever been to other countries? What for?

【Kamal】I have been to many countries, such as Turkey, Italy, United Arab Emirates, Egypt, Syria, and Libya, etc. Generally, I went there for business. I think if you do a business, you have to pay all your attention to it, or you will make some mistakes. I do not want to regret. I will try my best to avoid mistakes. Besides, I need many goods, so I have to visit many countries and make comparison of products in different countries. I have to think about the quality, the price and so on, choose what to buy, and decide which one will bring me more profit.

【BTV】It seems that you spend much of your time doing your business instead of something relaxing. What do you do when you are free or feel stressed? I mean in China.

【Kamal】In China, I just concentrate on my business. I do not think of other things. We are businessmen; we are not visitors. We have to think about many things.

【BTV】Okay. You have been to many other places. Compared with them, what's special about Yiwu?

【Kamal】To be honest, it is a good market. Many people say that Yiwu is a small city but a big market. Yiwu became very famous many years ago. So I came here. Besides, compared with other places, the price of products in Yiwu is lower. This is the most important character. As for the weather, it is hot in Yiwu. But I think it is okay because it is also very hot in my country. And the transportation is a little crowded. People in Yiwu are very friendly. I think most of the Chinese people that I have met are all very friendly and talkative. I like Chinese people, especially people in Yiwu.

【BTV】Can you recall something interesting or unforgettable during your first visit to Yiwu?

【Kamal】I cannot remember clearly. But there are really many differences in cultures. You know, in my country, females cannot wear short pants or shorts or tee shirts like you do. We do not drink beer or eat pork. Once, one of my friends, who didn't know the taboo, invited me to have meal and treated me with roast suckling pig. I refused because of my religion. I have a big family. I am the youngest one. I have five sisters and five brothers. But in China, maybe many families just have one or two children.

【BTV】Yes, there are some cultural differences. Then how about friends? Do you have Chinese friends here?

【Kamal】No, because every time I come here, I just stay for several days. You know, business is business. I do not think it is a good idea to make friends with my business partners. If my business partners and I become friends, then I have to take their feelings into consideration, and this will make it more difficult for me to deal with some issues. And, I am always busy in working, so I have no time to make some friends. But I really have some friends in Ningbo. They will take me to eat some delicious food in Ningbo. But we are just friends, no business.

【BTV】Now that you have mentioned business, would you mind telling me something about your business?

【Kamal】Of course not. You can ask anything you want to know.

【BTV】That is very kind of you. Well, what are you selling now?

【Kamal】I am selling things such as taps and water pipes. They are often used in toilets, bathrooms or kitchens.

【BTV】So you buy some products here and transport these goods back to your country and sell them?

【Kamal】Yes, yes, like this. I go to frontier market to get my goods. Sometimes I go to Taizhou. I also went to Ningbo last month. It is a very beautiful and modern city. Many countries build their factories in China because of the lower price of labor. Big cities have many factories, but markets are rare. So one city cannot meet my needs because one city cannot offer all kinds of products I want. I have to go to various factories in different cities to get my products.

【BTV】Is this the difficulty that you confront currently? Do you have any ways to deal with the problem?

【Kamal】Yes, this is a big problem. It is difficult to solve. What I can do is to make a little more profits from other aspects, such as the decrease of transportation fee or cheaper goods.

【BTV】We all know that the price of products in Yiwu is lower than that of other places in China. Is this one of the reasons that made you choose Yiwu?

【Kamal】Yes. Buying things in lower price is likely to bring more profits for me. So it is also a way to remit the problem mentioned above.

【Emily】Any other reasons?

【Kamal】Yes. Many people here can speak some English. You know, if people can say some English, there will be fewer difficulties in our communication. And we can find almost everything in Yiwu. And I will tell you something else. Three years ago, I came to Yiwu to get my products. The price was very low. But now, the price is higher and higher. Then I go to some other new markets, not in China.

【BTV】Not in China? Then where are the new markets? Why do you choose those countries?

【Kamal】Turkey and Italy. Because of the increase of the cost of living, the price of products in Yiwu is also increasing. It is much more difficult for me to find satisfactory products in Yiwu.

【BTV】Is there any similar market in your country?

【Kamal】Unlike China, my country just has some small factories. China has people and technology.

【BTV】What do you think of the market in Yiwu? Is it satisfactory?

【Kamal】It is difficult to say. You know the price of things is higher and higher. But RMB is devaluing. So it is more and more difficult to do business.

【BTV】Are there any problems that trouble you or your company?

【Kamal】For example, if I want to get visa to China, I have to pay 300 dollars. But if I want to go to Turkey or Italy, I just need my passport because our government and government in Turkey and Italy have cooperation.

【BTV】Do you have any suggestions for the policy of Yiwu?

【Kamal】Maybe more communication and cooperation between our governments will be better. It will be more convenient for us.

【BTV】What is the blueprint for your business?

【Kamal】I hope that my business can be better and better. I do not need to go here and there. It is tiring and also expensive.

【BTV】Finally, we are English major students. Maybe we will deal with foreign trade after graduation. Do you have any suggestions for us?

【Kamal】No matter what you will do in the future, now, just try your best to study and live a good life. Because you know, the females in my country are in low position. You have good environment and chance and you have to hold them. This is important.

【BTV】Thank you for your sincere suggestions. And thank you for your cooperation. Best wishes to you.

Group Members: Lin Mengmeng, Zheng Yuan, Luo Qian

叙事记录

【BTV】访谈可以开始了吗?

【Kamal】是的,我准备好了。

【BTV】请问您来自哪里?

【Kamal】我来自约旦,一个中东的小国家,那里风景优美。

【BTV】您时常来中国吗? 多久来一次? 对中国印象如何?

【Kamal】我来中国进货,大概一年会来五六次。我进的货大多数来自义乌。可以说,义乌是我在中国进货的首选地。中国是个美丽的国家。我特别喜欢中国的食物,尤其是海鲜。上个月我去了宁波,宁波海鲜的美味让我久久难以忘怀。此外,中国和很多国家都有贸易往来,所以,对于外商而言,中国是个大市场。我们这些外商不仅可以售货也可以进货。

【BTV】我很高兴听到这些赞美之词。除了中国，您去过别的国家吗？为什么去呢？

【Kamal】我去过很多国家，像土耳其、意大利、阿联酋、埃及、叙利亚、利比亚，等等。我去这些国家多数是工作之故。我觉得一旦开始经商就要全身心投入，否则就会出错。我不想留有遗憾。我会竭尽全力避免犯错。此外，我要进货，就要去不同的国家，货比三家，关注产品的质量和价格等，选我所需、择优下单。

【BTV】看来您把很多时间都投入到工作中了，而不是去休闲娱乐。那么就您在中国的生活而言，您在闲暇之余或是压力重重之时都做些什么呢？

【Kamal】在中国，我一心扑在工作上，不作他想。我们是商人，不是游客，必须考虑周全。

【BTV】嗯。您游历丰富，和您去过的其他地方相比，义乌有何独特之处？

【Kamal】说实话，义乌是个好市场。很多人都说义乌是小城市大市场。多年以前，义乌就已经名扬海内外了。我也是慕名而来。和其他地方相比，义乌商品的价格更为低廉，这一点最为关键。都说义乌天气热，我倒觉得还好，因为约旦也很热。义乌的交通有些拥堵。义乌人非常友好。我觉得所接触过的中国人大都热情友好、能说会道。我很喜欢中国人，尤其是义乌人。

【BTV】您还记得初到义乌时所经历过的一些趣事、难忘的事吗？

【Kamal】我记不太清了。但的确有一些文化上的差异让我印象深刻。在约旦，女性不能像你们这样穿短袖短裤。我们不喝啤酒，不吃猪肉。有一次，一位朋友邀我吃饭，由于不知我们的禁忌，他请我吃烤乳猪。我只能拒绝，因为这关乎我的信仰。我出生在一个大家庭，排行老幺，上面有五个姐姐和五个哥哥。但在中国，很多家庭只有一个或两个孩子。

【BTV】嗯，两国在文化上确有不同。那交朋友方面呢？您在义乌有中国朋友吗？

【Kamal】没有。我每次来义乌只待几天。在商言商，我觉得和生意伙伴做朋友不是明智之举。如果我和他们成了朋友，凡事就要顾及他们的情面，这样做起事来就比较麻烦。再说，我总是很忙，所以也没空结交朋友。但我在宁波倒有几个朋友。每次我去那儿，他们总会带我去吃美食。但我们仅是朋友而已，并没有生意上的来往。

【BTV】既然您提到了做生意，那么您介意和我说说您生意上的事情吗？

【Kamal】没事，你想知道什么尽管问就是了。

【BTV】谢谢您。请问您现在销售什么产品？

【Kamal】我卖水龙头和水管之类的东西。这些东西适用于卫生间、浴室和厨房。

【BTV】您在这里进货然后运到自己的国家进行销售，是这样吗？

【Kamal】是这样的。我到前沿市场去进货。有时我也会去台州。上个月我还去了宁波。宁波很美很现代化。许多外资进入中国投资建厂，因为这儿劳动力便宜。大城市里不乏工厂，但形成的市场寥寥。所以，仅在一个城市进货满足不了我的需求，我必须往来多个城市，走访多家工厂，来获取我所需的产品。

【BTV】这就是您现在所面临的困境吗？那您有何脱困的良方？

【Kamal】是的，这是个大问题，而且很难解决。我只能削减其他方面的成本，尽量做到利润最大化，比如降低运费成本或者进货成本。

【BTV】义乌商品的价格较之中国其他地区的商品价格相对要低，这是您来义乌的原因之一吗？

【Kamal】是的，如果进货价格低就可以让我赚取更多的利润。这也是我之前提到的脱困方法之一。

【BTV】还有其他原因吗？

【Kamal】嗯，有的。这儿很多人都能说些英文，这样有助于顺畅交流。义乌的商品应有尽有，想要什么几乎都可以找到。嗯，我也有点别的要说。三年前我来义乌进货时，这儿的商品很便宜，但现在价格越来越高了。那么我就要转向海外其他新市场了。

【BTV】海外？哪里的新市场？为何做此选择？

【Kamal】土耳其和意大利。生活费用的上升使得义乌商品的价格也在不断提升。现在要在义乌找到价廉物美的商品是越来越难了。

【BTV】贵国有此类市场吗？

【Kamal】约旦只有一些小工厂，不像中国，既有技术也有人力资源。

【BTV】您觉得义乌的市场怎样？您满意吗？

【Kamal】怎么说呢。物价在涨，人民币在贬值，生意越来越难做了。

【BTV】您和贵公司是否碰到过什么困难？

【Kamal】举个例子来说，我办赴华签证，就要交 300 美金。但我若是去土耳其或意大利，只需出示护照就行了，因为约旦政府跟土耳其政府以及意大利政府都有合作。

【BTV】那您有何提议？

【Kamal】我希望我们两国政府能有更多的交流合作，这样我们做生意就方便多了。

【BTV】您对未来有何展望？

【Kamal】我希望我的生意能够越做越红火，自己也不用各地奔波，这样太累太费钱。

【BTV】我们是英语专业的学生，毕业后可能会从事与外贸有关的工作，您对我们有何建议？

【Kamal】不论你们以后从事什么工作，现如今，你们应该努力学习，好好生活。要知道，妇女在约旦地位不高。你们有这么好的环境，这么多的机会，就应该紧紧抓住不放手。这一点非常重要。

【BTV】谢谢您的建议，感谢您的配合。祝您一切顺利。

团队成员：林萌萌，郑媛，罗倩

Yiwu: A Legendary City

By Lin Mengmeng　Supervised by Ou Chen & Cai Liang

When people talk about small commodities, the first word that comes to my mind is "Yiwu". The world-famous Yiwu Market is the landmark of the city. In 1982, the Yiwu municipal government took the lead in setting up the first generation market. Within the following 30 years, the market has been developed and optimized to be one of the most well-known markets of small commodities in the world, which is really a miracle in the business universe. How could Yiwu demonstrate such a marvelous development? How could Yiwu possess such a huge market of small commodities and attract such a large number of overseas business people? With these questions in mind, I participated in a research project entitled "Beyond the Voices: Yiwu, Here I Am" which was organized by Ningbo Institute of Technology, Zhejiang University.

In the middle of July, I went to Yiwu with my teammates. When I entered the Yiwu Market, what I saw was quite different from the image that I had in my mind. I used to think that the market would be as old and noisy as some other markets, but actually it was well-planned, neat and tidy. Although it was swarming with business people, everything there seemed orderly. I was greatly motivated to carry out the research project in such a comfortable environment.

One of the foreigners who accepted my interview was Kamal, a young businessman from Jordan. He could speak English fluently, and our conversation went smoothly. He told me that many people in Yiwu could speak a little English, which was conducive to international communication and business. What he said reminded me of what I saw on the first night I came to Yiwu. The city was brilliantly illuminated and a hubbub of voices bubbled up. The streets were lined with stands which offered a rich supply of different commodities. Most of the customers were foreigners. Though they came from various countries, they could still communicate with the owners of the stands because they could talk to each other in English. I believed that the pervasive use of English which facilitated interpersonal communication might be one of the reasons why foreign business people chose Yiwu to run their businesses.

During the interview, Kamal told me his way of managing business. He said that he had been to many places to make a comparison of products that he needed. Finally, he regarded Yiwu as his first choice for buying goods in China. He said that the market in Yiwu was huge, and he could meet business people from all over the world. The goods in the Yiwu Market were an excellent variety, and he could find almost everything that he wanted. Moreover, the goods were low in price but good in quality, which made it possible for him to gain more profit. What Kamal said accorded with what I saw. Before I came to Yiwu, I thought that small commodities were things just like pendants or stationery. However, after I visited the Yiwu Market, I realized that the variety of goods there was beyond my anticipation. What was even more amazing was that almost all the foreign business people whom I contacted during my research thought highly of the competitive prices and good quality of commodities in Yiwu. I then understood that it was the advantages that Yiwu commodities enjoyed in variety, price and quality that attracted a large number of business people to come to Yiwu from abroad.

At the end of the interview, Kamal told me that he had been to many cities in China, but he found that only Yiwu had such a large and internationalized market of small commodities. What he said made me think about the legend Yiwu had created. How could Yiwu stand out among many cities in China to become a world-famous capital of small commodities? I received the answer after the research project. In my opinion, the success of Yiwu owed greatly to the innovation of the Yiwu people. If they had not taken the lead to set up the first generation market thirty years ago, there would not have been such a world-famous market of small commodities. Moreover, after the market had been built, it was relocated five times and expanded ten times, changing from a "street market" to a "world supermarket". Hence, the success of Yiwu Market also owed a great deal to the Yiwu people's desire to advance with the times and their constant pursuit of the "Yiwu Dream". Because they kept pace with the times, seized the chance for development, and kept progressing to strive for the best, they made Yiwu boom and flourish.

The trip to Yiwu was really beneficial to me. I had the opportunity to know Yiwu better and was enlightened by its legendary development. The Yiwu Market was obscure when it was first built, but now it outshines others in the world of small commodities industries. However, the Yiwu people did not stop. Instead, they continued to pursue a higher goal and spare no efforts to keep their legend. The development of Yiwu taught me that nothing could be accomplished overnight. To be successful, one should not only have the courage to be a pioneer, but also to be innovative and stick to the faith of "Good is better, but better best". Only in this way could a person progress and develop.

商品之都，传奇之城

文：林萌萌　指导老师：欧　琛　蔡　亮

说起小商品，我脑海中浮现出的与之关联的第一个词就是“义乌”。闻名于世的义乌国际小商品市场就是这座城市的标志。自1982年义乌市政府“敢为天下先”地创办了第一代市场起，义乌人用了30多年的时间演绎了“无中生有、有中生奇、无奇不有”的发展奇迹，义乌小商品也由此享誉海内外。那么，为什么这么一座县级城市可以展现如此巨大的发展？为什么义乌会有规模如此之大的小商品市场以及源源不断的外国客户群？带着这些疑问，我参加了今年暑假学校组织的主题为“用声音叙事：义乌，我来了”的暑期社会实践活动。

七月中旬，我随着实践小分队来到了义乌。走进义乌国际小商品市场，我眼前呈现的并不是想象中的那种老旧嘈杂的交易市场的景象，这里规划合理，整洁明亮，虽然客商云集，但秩序井然。能在这样一个舒适的环境中进行实践活动，我动力倍增。

接受我采访的外籍客商中有一人名叫卡马尔，是一个来自约旦的年轻商人。卡马尔能说一口流利的英语，这使得我们之间的交流进行得颇为顺利。他告诉我，在义乌很多人都能说些英文，这样有助于顺畅交流，也有助于贸易的有效开展。他的话也让我想起了刚到义乌那晚我的所见所闻。夜色下的义乌灯火通明，人声鼎沸，街道两旁摆满了地摊，商品琳琅满目。光顾这些摊位的顾客大多是外籍人士。虽然他们来自世界各地，但这并未影响他们和摊主们的交流，因为他们都可以用国际通用语——英语进行交谈。我想这种语言上的“国际化”，这种语言交流上的便利，应该是许多外籍商人选择义乌开展贸易活动的原因之一吧。

在采访中，当我和卡马尔谈到他的生意经时，他告诉我他经商去过很多地方，但货比三家之后，他把义乌定为他在中国进货的首选地，因为这里的市场庞大，他可以接触到世界各地的客商；这里的商品种类繁多，他几乎可以找到他想要的所有商品；这里的商品价廉物美，从义乌进货他更有利可图。卡马尔所说的也与我在义乌的所见相符。来义乌之前，在我的印象中所谓的小商品就是一些小挂件或者是文具之类的小东西，但当我真正来到小商品市场后，映入我眼帘的是各种各样我所能想到或是想不到的物品，其品种的繁多远超我的想象。更令我惊喜的是，我在调研过程中所接触到的外籍客商均对义乌商品的价廉物美津津乐道。我由此顿悟，正是义乌小商品在品种、质量及价格上的优势吸引了众多四海客商不远万里而来，汇集于义乌。

在采访将要结束时，卡马尔说他去过中国的很多城市，但只有义乌拥有这么大规模的国际化的小商品市场。他的一席话触动了我对义乌所缔造出的传奇的思考。中国有这么多城市，为什么义乌会从中脱颖而出，成为举世闻名的小商品之都呢？通过此次义乌之行，我有所感悟。我想义乌今天的成功，首先要归功于义乌人的创新精神，若是没有他们30多年前敢于开创先河建立第一代市场，也很难有今天的这个世界级的小商品市场。此外，从创建市场之初到现在的30多年间，义乌小商品市场五易其址、十次扩建，实现了从“马路市场”到“世界超市”的跨越。因此，义乌小商品市场今天的成功，也应该归功于义乌人的“与时俱进”以及他们对“义乌梦”的不断追寻。正是因为他们紧跟时代发展的步伐，把握时代发展的脉搏，不断进取，争创一流，义乌才有了如今蓬勃发展、欣欣向荣的局面。

此次义乌之行让我受益匪浅，不仅仅是因为我借此对义乌有了更深刻的认识，更是因为义乌小商品贸易的发展传奇给了我许多启迪。义乌小商品市场从初创时的名不见经传到如今在国内外小商品业的一枝独秀，义乌人一直没有停下进取的脚步。他们在不断追求更高的目标，努力续写着新的传奇。义乌的发展轨迹告诉我没有什么事情是可以一蹴而就的。凡事要想获得成功，除了要具备“敢为天下先”的勇气，还要秉承创新创优的理念，坚守“没有最好、只有更好”的信念，如此才能不断进步、持续发展。

Juliana

Juliana: I'm Happy in Yiwu

心系义乌,乐享生活

Juliana Assuncao is a fashion designer from Brazil. Having been invited by one of her Chinese friends, she came to Yiwu five months ago and works for an international trade company. She is ardent, hardworking, optimistic and kind-hearted. Though she has not been in Yiwu for long, she has already adapted herself to life in Yiwu and is leading a happy life.

朱莉安娜·阿桑卡来自巴西,是一名时装设计师。5个月前,她受一个中国朋友的邀请来到了义乌,就职于一家国际贸易公司。她是个热心而又勤奋的人,乐观开朗,诚恳善良。虽然来义乌的时间并不长,但她已经完全适应了义乌的生活,并乐在其中。

I'm Happy in Yiwu

By Juliana

Transcript of the Interview:

【BTV】Hello, Nana, we are from Ningbo Institute of Technology, Zhejiang University. Thank you for agreeing to our interview. Can we start now?

【Juliana】Okay.

【BTV】Can you introduce yourself first?

【Juliana】Okay. My name is Juliana Assuncao. I am from Brazil. I am 26 years old. I'm a fashion designer, and I have a Chinese friend. He offered me a job here in China, and I started it last December. At that time, I really felt excited because I thought it would be a good experience for my life.

【BTV】After you came to China, apart from Yiwu, did you go to other Chinese cities?

【Juliana】Yeah, I have already been to other cities. Shenzhen, Hangzhou, Hong Kong and Shanghai.

【BTV】Anything different between Yiwu and those cities? What advantages does Yiwu have?

【Juliana】I like living in Yiwu rather than in big cities. In big cities like Shanghai, you need to use subway. I don't like to use it for work. I like Yiwu more because of this. My home is near my office, my office is near the supermarket, near my friends, near other companies I need to go, and near Futian Market. I like this kind of life. I don't like big cities.

【BTV】Did you hear anything about Yiwu before you came?

【Juliana】No. I didn't know Yiwu until my boss told me about it.

【BTV】How long have you been in Yiwu?

【Juliana】Five months.

【BTV】And what do you often do in your spare time? Will you join in some activities?

【Juliana】Yeah! Yeah! I really like Yiwu. I start to do exercise in a gym center. I also have a place to dance. It's a normal enjoyment in my country. Sometimes my friends and I go to some places and dance together. And I also like shopping and buying clothes. I don't buy many, but I like buying clothes. And I go to market to buy food and other kinds of things for my home needs.

【BTV】Do you still miss your family in Brazil?

【Juliana】Yeah, but I can call them and chat in video with them.

【BTV】Maybe you can invite them to visit China and see you.

【Juliana】Maybe. My mother really wants to come to China. She likes traveling. But from Brazil to China, it is really a long distance. But some day, maybe she can come.

【BTV】You are so warm-hearted. I guess you have made many new friends here.

【Juliana】Yeah, yeah, sure. I have Chinese friends, American friends and French friends. China is my new home. Office guys are my new family members. I'm trying to make friends. I'm far away from my family and my friends. If I stay here and just cry because of loneliness, I will never feel happy. I choose to come to China. I choose to come to Yiwu. It's my choice, so I need to live here and get used to the life here.

【BTV】Can you use one word to describe Yiwu?

【Juliana】Hm, I have a lot of words to describe Yiwu. Hm, and now, I think is happiness. Yeah, I think so. I am happy in Yiwu, and many people here are happy.

【BTV】That's very nice. How about Chinese culture?

【Juliana】I already like Chinese culture before I come here, and I know a few things about Chinese culture. I respect it. The culture of my country is different from that of China. I think I can learn a lot from Chinese culture.

【BTV】Chinese culture is splendid. China has a long history. I am glad that you like it. Hm, have you adapted yourself to the life in Yiwu? Did you encounter any difficulties when you first came here and started your work?

【Juliana】I have already adapted to my life here. My life in Brazil is not very different from my life here.

【BTV】Do you have much work to do here? It seems that you are quite busy.

【Juliana】I really work hard. The time difference between Brazil and China is eleven hours. It's the night here, but it's the day in Brazil. So when I finish my work in China now, I should go back home and begin my work for a Brazilian company on the Internet. So I have two jobs for a day. For most of my time, I am working.

【BTV】Oh, you must be very tired.

【Juliana】Yeah, and sometimes I only have five hours to sleep. But on Sunday, there is no work for me. I can take a rest on Sunday.

【BTV】You have been in Yiwu for five months. Do you think it's a good place to do business?

【Juliana】Yes. Futian Market is the biggest market in the world, and there are a lot of companies and factories around. It's good for business.

【BTV】What kind of international business do you do?

【Juliana】We sell nothing. We help Brazilian customers to buy stuff in China and send it in containers to Brazil. We import or export the products our customers need by big ships.

【BTV】And can the goods in Yiwu satisfy the market in your country?

【Juliana】Almost. I think a lot of companies can find the stuff they need in Futian Market. Just for specific materials, you need go to Shenzhen, or Ningbo.

【BTV】When you first came here, how did you communicate with people?

【Juliana】By body language. But now, I know a few Chinese words. I start to communicate with Chinese in Chinese language. I can write an E-mail to my Chinese friends and use QQ to communicate with them in some Chinese words. I also have friends who know English, and I can communicate with them in English. Sometimes I can find other Brazilian people, and I can communicate with them.

【BTV】Language is really important in communication.

【Juliana】Yes. When you arrive in a new country, if you can communicate with local people, you will feel better.

【BTV】But learning a foreign language is not an easy task.

【Juliana】Yeah, but you need to believe that you can. You should try your best. Never close yourself.

【BTV】What you said is really right. You are so confident, easy going and positive.

【Juliana】Yeah. I try to do my best. I know sometimes I don't want to smile, but I would smile. If you keep a straight face, nobody will like you. Every time, I try to do my best. It's not just for me, but for every one who stays near me. I tell myself that I should be myself. Sometimes I will go to an orphanage in Yiwu, and help the children who lost their father and mother. I know every child there needs help and happiness. They need our help. I smile to them. I believe smiling can open a lot of persons' hearts.

【BTV】If they feel happy with you, they will like being around you.

【Juliana】Yeah. You know if you feel bad every time and don't smile every time, just say bad words and don't like your life, nobody will like you. You won't have happiness in your life. You need to choose other ways. You can choose your life.

【BTV】We will graduate from school in two or three years. Can you give us some suggestions?

【Juliana】Maybe you can learn from what Yiwu does. I think Yiwu chooses the best way because Yiwu is always studying. Yiwu is trying. It tries the best way. Studying is the best for the young people. If you study, you can improve your life. If you don't have money, you need to study to find a good job in the future. If you have money, you need to study, too. You need to know the way for using your money. Otherwise, you will lose your money. If you study, work well, have a good friend and have a good relationship with everybody, everything will be easy for you. Never stay alone, never. You should have a good person around you.

【BTV】Thank you so much for agreeing to our interview.

【Juliana】I feel happy when you talk with me. When someone needs my help, I'm always happy to offer help.

Group Members: Shao Lixia, Wang Jingjing, Zheng Lidong

叙事记录

【BTV】你好，娜娜，我们是浙江大学宁波理工学院的学生。感谢你接受我们的采访。我们现在可以开始了吗？

【Juliana】可以。

【BTV】你能先自我介绍一下吗？

【Juliana】好的。我的名字是朱莉安娜·阿桑卡。我来自巴西，今年 26 岁了。我是一名时装设计师。我的一个中国朋友邀我来华工作，于是去年 12 月份我就开始在这儿工作了。那时，我真的很兴奋，因为我觉得来华工作会成为我人生中一段精彩的经历。

【BTV】来华之后，除了义乌，你去过中国的其他城市吗？

【Juliana】去过。我去过其他城市，比如深圳、杭州、香港，还有上海。

【BTV】那么义乌和那些城市有什么不同吗？义乌有何优势？

【Juliana】与大都市相比，我更喜欢在义乌生活。像上海这样的大都市，出行要坐地铁。我不喜欢乘坐地铁上班。正因为如此，我更喜欢义乌。我的家就在我办公室附近，我的办公室又紧邻超市，靠近我朋友那儿，离与我有生意往来的公司也不远，还紧挨着福田市场。我喜欢这样的生活，不喜欢大都市的生活。

【BTV】你来义乌之前对义乌有所了解吗？

【Juliana】没有。我老板和我说起义乌，我才知道。

【BTV】你来义乌有多久了？

【Juliana】5 个月了。

【BTV】那你空余时间常做些什么？会参加一些活动吗？

【Juliana】嗯，会的！我真的很喜欢义乌。我已开始在体育中心锻炼，也找到一个可以跳舞的地方。跳舞在我们国家是很常见的娱乐方式。有时候，我会和我朋友一起去跳舞。我也喜欢购物，买衣服。衣服买得不多，但我喜欢买。我也会去市场买吃的和家用品。

【BTV】你思念在巴西的家人吗？

【Juliana】是的，不过我可以和他们打电话或者视频聊天。

【BTV】或许你可以邀请他们来中国玩，来看看你。

【Juliana】也许吧。我妈妈真的很想来中国。她喜欢旅游，但巴西到中国的距离真的太远了。不过，或许有一天她会来。

【BTV】你是个热心肠的人。我想你在这儿已经交了很多新朋友吧。

【Juliana】嗯，是的，的确如此。我有中国朋友、美国朋友、法国朋友。中国是我的新家，办公室同事是我的新家人。我尝试着多交些朋友。我的家人和之前的朋友都远在巴西。如果我因为在这儿感觉孤单而独自落泪，我永远不会开心。我选择来到中国，来到义乌，这是我的选择，我就必须在这儿生活下去，适应这儿的生活。

【BTV】嗯。你可以用一个词来形容义乌吗？

【Juliana】嗯。有很多词可以用来形容义乌。嗯，现在的话，我想说的是快乐。是的，我是这么认为的。我在这儿很开心，很多来这儿的人也都很开心。

【BTV】真好。那你觉得中国文化怎么样？

【Juliana】我来这儿之前就喜欢中国文化，对中国文化也有所了解。我尊重中国文化。它和巴西的文化有所不同，我可以从中学到很多东西。

【BTV】中国历史悠久，文化灿烂。听到你说喜欢中国文化，我倍感骄傲。嗯，你已经适应这儿生活了吗？你初来义乌工作时有没有遇到什么困难呢？

【Juliana】我已经适应了这儿的生活。跟我在巴西的生活相比，我在这儿的生活并没有多少不同。

【BTV】你在这儿有很多工作要做吗？你好像挺忙碌的。

【Juliana】我确实很努力地工作着。巴西和中国之间的时差是11个小时。现在这里是晚上，但在巴西就是白天。倘若在中国我完成了一天的工作，回家之后，就要通过互联网开始为在巴西的公司工作。我一天要完成两份工作，所以一天中大部分时间都是在工作。

【BTV】那你一定很累吧？

【Juliana】是的，有时我只睡5个小时。但星期天我没什么工作要做，可以休息一下。

【BTV】你来义乌已经有5个月了，你认为义乌是块做生意的风水宝地吗？

【Juliana】是的。福田市场是世界第一大市场，而且其周边工厂和公司密集分布。这对于做生意很有利。

【BTV】你在这儿做什么生意呢？

【Juliana】我们公司不经销商品，只是帮助巴西客商在中国购货，然后用集装箱把货物运到巴西。我们通过海运发送客商所需的进出口货物。

【BTV】义乌的货品可以满足你们国内市场的需求吗？

【Juliana】差不多。我觉得很多公司都可以在福田市场找到他们所需的货品。只有一些特定的货品，可能还需去深圳或宁波进货。

【BTV】初来义乌时，你如何与人交流？

【Juliana】用肢体语言。但现在，我已学会了一些中文词语。我开始和中国人用中文交流。我会用简单的中文给我的中国朋友写电子邮件，也会用简单的中文和他们在QQ上聊天。此外，我有一些朋友懂英语，我就和他们用英语交流。有时候我遇到巴西人，也会和他们交流。

【BTV】语言在交流中至关重要。

【Juliana】是的。到了一个新的国度，如果你能和当地人交流，就会感觉更加舒服。

【BTV】但是外语学习并非易事。

【Juliana】嗯，但你要相信自己的能力，竭尽全力，决不能把自己封闭起来。

【BTV】你说得很对。你真是充满自信，易于相处，还很乐观向上。

【Juliana】是的。凡事我总是竭尽所能。有时我虽不开心，但还是微笑以对。如果你总板着脸，没人会喜欢你。我之所以尽力而为，不仅仅是为了我自己，还为了我身边的每一个人。我告诉我自己，要活出自我风采。有时候，我会去义乌的一家孤儿院，帮助那些没有爸爸和妈妈的孩子。我知道那里的每一个孩子都需要帮助、渴望快乐。他们需要我们的帮助，我会笑着面对他们。我相信微笑可以打开人的心扉。

【BTV】如果他们感到和你在一起很开心，他们就会很乐意和你在一起。

【Juliana】是的。如果你每次都郁郁寡欢、冷面以对、满腹牢骚、厌倦生活，那么没人会喜欢你。你一辈子都不会快乐。你应该做些改变，重新布局你的人生。

【BTV】我们几个再过两三年就要毕业了。你能给我们一些建议吗？

【Juliana】或许义乌这个城市能给你们一些启迪。义乌在发展中不断学习提高，这一点非常好。义乌为求最佳，不断尝试。对于年轻人而言，学习是最佳途径。你们通过学习就能改善生活。若你们家境贫寒，就要好好学习，这样将来就能找到一份好工作。当然，若你们家境殷实，也应该好好学习，知晓如何合理理财，否则就会荡尽家财。好好学习、勤奋工作、诚心交友、与人为善，你的人生之路就会是坦途。不要过形单影只的生活，人的一生需要有好人相伴、贵人相助。

【BTV】非常感谢你接受我们的采访。

【Juliana】你们和我交流，我很高兴。有人需要我帮忙的时候，我总是乐于相助。

团队成员：邵丽霞，王菁璟，郑利冬

Yiwu: A Wonderful City

By Shao Lixia　Supervised by Ou Chen & Cai Liang

When I was a little child, I heard of Yiwu City. Nowadays, people talk about it quite often, and I have begun to pay more attention to it. From what I found on the Internet and in the newspapers, I got to know Yiwu a little bit. It was home to the biggest wholesale market of consumer goods in the world, and it also took the lead in other aspects. Until 2011, compared with other specialized markets in China, the total trade volume of the Yiwu Market had been the highest for 21 consecutive years. Also, the Yiwu Municipal People's Court became the first local court that could handle foreign-related business disputes. In 2011, the competitiveness of Yiwu ranked first among all the county-level cities in Zhejiang Province. All these facts revealed the uniqueness of Yiwu and fully demonstrated its potential for development. The achievements of Yiwu became world-famous and attracted business people from home and abroad. They came to Yiwu to learn from Yiwu, to study in Yiwu, to start business in Yiwu, or to settle down in Yiwu. Their arrival added vigor to the city. I really admired Yiwu for its success and aspired to visit it in person. Hence, when I learned that my school planned to carry out a research project entitled "Beyond the Voices: Yiwu, Here I Am", I volunteered to be a participant without hesitation.

When I walked into this legendary city, I saw row upon row of stores, a stream of cars and people, varied restaurants serving Chinese or Western food, and ubiquitous signs in different languages. In the world-famous Futian Market, I met Juliana Assuncao, a beautiful young lady from Brazil. Although she was busy communicating with a store owner at that time, she told me how to contact her after I expressed my intention to interview her. She was really amiable and told me to call her "Nana". Then things went on as I had expected. I arranged a meeting with her and interviewed her successfully.

During the interview, Nana, with a charming smile on her face, answered all my questions patiently and passionately. Nana told me that she was from Brazil and was 26 years old this year. She said that she came to Yiwu at the invitation of one of her Chinese friends. She told me that she came to Yiwu from Brazil 5 months ago to manage an international trade company named Bvista with that friend.

When Nana first arrived in Yiwu, she was often homesick and upset. However, she knew that it was no use being melancholy, so she tried various ways to get rid of her homesickness. Sometimes, she would call her family members or contact them through a video chat, and sometimes, she would go out with her new friends in Yiwu, dining and chatting. Now, she had already adapted herself to the life in Yiwu and no longer felt lonely. In her spare time, she would go shopping, dine in restaurants, chat with friends, and enjoy dancing. Sometimes, she would also go to an orphanage in Yiwu to see the orphans there and share her happiness with them. Nana said that she enjoyed her life in Yiwu very much. Although Yiwu was not big, Nana thought it was a good place for living because it had satisfactory facilities and convenient transportation. She also added that the local residents in Yiwu were very friendly. They often took the initiative in greeting her, which filled her heart with warmth.

When we talked about the business conditions in Yiwu, Nana praised Yiwu again. She said that Yiwu was a good place to do business. The favorable policies, the prosperous market, and the gathering of business people were favorable objective and subjective factors for Yiwu's success. Nana believed that Yiwu had a promising future.

When our interview was about to end, Nana gave me some suggestions, taking Yiwu's development as an illustration. She said that Yiwu kept learning and changing in its course of development. The idea of striving to be better contributed to its success, which was also enlightening for young people. In her opinion, studying was the most important thing for young people. For those who were poor, unceasing study could help them escape poverty, whereas for those who were rich, unceasing study could propel them to advance.

The interview gave me a chance to get to know Nana, a Brazilian lady who lives happily in Yiwu. During the interview, what she said really revealed her praise for Yiwu as well as her fondness for Yiwu, and I could truly sense that her life in Yiwu was rich, bright and wonderful.

On my way back home, what Nana said echoed in my ears, and the whole interview recurred in my mind. Through this research project, I got a chance to know Yiwu directly, and from Nana's words, I got to know Yiwu better.

Just as Nana had described, Yiwu is a wonderful city!

印象义乌:“娜”样精彩

文:邵丽霞　指导老师:欧　琛　蔡　亮

我小时候就听说过义乌,近年来,这个名字又频繁被人提及,让我不由得对她多了几分关注。借助网络和报纸的信息来源,我对义乌有了些许了解。她拥有全球最大的日用消费品批发市场,拥有多项第一:义乌市场总成交额至2011年已连续21年居全国各大专业市场榜首;义乌法院成为全国第一所可管辖涉外民商事案件的基层法院;2011年,义乌的综合竞争力名列浙江省县级市首位……这些第一彰显了义乌的独特,也充分说明了她的发展潜力。义乌的成就闻名于世,吸引着海内外客商纷至沓来。他们或观摩、或学习、或创业、或安居。他们的到来又给这座商贸之城增添了活力。义乌的成就让我心生敬佩,也激发了我想一睹风采的欲望。于是,当学校组织“用声音叙事:义乌,我来了”的暑期社会实践活动时,我毫不犹豫地报了名。

当我踏入义乌这座充满传奇色彩的城市时,映入我眼帘的是鳞次栉比的商铺,川流不息的车流和人流,风格各异的中西餐馆以及随处可见的各国文字标识。在闻名于世的福田市场里我遇见了朱莉安娜·阿桑卡,那位年轻美丽的巴西姑娘。虽然那时她正忙于和一家商铺的老板交流,但当我向她表达了采访意向后,她还是抽空给了我她的联系方式,并很平和地让我叫她娜娜。之后,正如我所愿,约谈、会面、采访,一切都开展得很顺利。

采访时,娜娜的脸上始终绽放着迷人的微笑,她用流利的英文耐心而又热情地回答我的提问。娜娜告诉我,她来自巴西,现年26岁。5个月前,她受一个中国朋友之邀,自巴西来到中国,来到义乌,开始与这个朋友一起经营一个叫宾威斯特(Bvista)的外贸公司。

初来义乌时,娜娜时常想家,难免有情绪低落的时候,但她深知郁郁寡欢于事无补,于是,她想了各种办法排解乡愁。她有时会与家人打电话或者视频聊天,有时也会和在义乌新交的一些朋友吃饭聊天。如今,她已完全适应了在义乌的生活,也不再感到孤单。闲暇之余,娜娜会逛街、购物、吃饭、聊天、跳舞。有时她还会去义乌的一所孤儿院看望那些失去双亲的孩子,将自己的乐观开朗的正能量传递给他们。娜娜说她现在很享受在义乌的生活。义乌虽然城市不大,但设施齐全,通行便利,是个宜居之处。她还补充说义乌当地人待人友善,经常会主动和她打招呼,这让她倍感亲切。

当我们谈及义乌的商贸环境时,娜娜又是一番称赞。她说义乌是个做生意的风水宝地,政策的眷顾、市场的繁荣以及客商的汇聚,使得义乌拥有了“天时、地利、人和”。义乌未来的发展令人期待。

临近采访结束时，娜娜以义乌的发展为例给了我一些建议。她说义乌在发展中不断求学求变，这种“没有最好、只有更好”的理念造就了义乌传奇，这对于我们年轻人也是一种启迪。她说年轻人最重要的就是学习。不断的求学可使贫者脱困，亦可使富者进取。

短短的一次采访让我认识了娜娜，这位乐享生活的巴西姑娘。在与我交谈的过程中，娜娜言语间透着对义乌的赞许与喜爱。我也真切地感受到她在义乌的生活是充实的、阳光的、精彩的。

回程的路上，我耳边依然回响着娜娜的一言一语，眼前浮现着采访的点点滴滴。通过这次实践活动，我对义乌有了更为直观的感受；通过与娜娜的交流，我对义乌有了更进一步的了解。

印象义乌，“娜”样精彩。

第二章

Fortune in Yiwu: Business Brings You the World

商赢义乌：拥义乌者，拥天下

导言

经过30多年改革开放的历程，义乌从一个名不见经传的贫穷小县发展到2013年成为综合实力全国百强县市第11位、发展质量第2位的经济强市。这种脱胎换骨式的巨变得益于义乌人坚持不懈的努力。他们一直努力发展小商品市场，通过市场化推动工业化、城市化、城乡一体化，走出了一条经济社会快速发展的成功道路。义乌，不仅为世界倾听中国前进的脚步声锁定了准确生动的音准，而且也为外国人走进中国、了解中国市场、分享中国改革的成果，提供了精彩纷呈的舞台。借助她，每一位心存善念与梦想，希望凭借自身实力在中国市场竞争中独占鳌头的"老外"，都有了创造奇迹的机会。

此章节中，"用声音叙事"实践小分队与5位在义乌创业的外国商人的访谈，充分展示了义乌的核心竞争力，让人领略到她作为"小商品海洋，购物者天堂"的独特魅力。无论是Tumaag、Orlov和Ishaq的"中国梦"、创富热情，还是Saman、Teign对义乌市场和城市的独到见解，都表现出了他们对这一广阔市场的深刻认同。同时，也让人感受到他们对于这片创业热土的浓情厚谊。

2011年，国务院批复同意在义乌市开展国际贸易综合改革试点，以此为起点，义乌市场开始了国际化的新征程！相信义乌能在为全国提供成功经验和创新样本的同时，为更多的外商接受、融入和改变这座城市创造无穷的机遇。

拥义乌者，拥天下。

Ishaq

Ishaq: Enter Futian Market, and Embrace the World

走进福田,拥有世界

Ishaq is from Palestine and now lives in Yiwu. Nine years ago, he came to China and chose Yiwu as his dream land. He runs a printing company here and three shops in Palestine, dealing in blankets, towels and underwear. He is seeding his dream here and is about to establish a new shop in Futian Market. With a deep insight into the potential of the Yiwu market, he gradually attempts to develop and enlarge his business in Yiwu.

伊兹哈克来自巴勒斯坦,现居义乌。9年前,他来到中国并将义乌选作他的圆梦之地。他在义乌经营着一家印刷公司,在巴勒斯坦还拥有3家店铺,分别销售毛毯、毛巾和内衣。他将梦想的种子撒播在义乌的大地上,打算在福田市场新开一家商铺。伊兹哈克深谙义乌市场的发展潜力,正逐渐尝试着发展并壮大他在义乌的事业。

Enter Futian Market, and Embrace the World

By Ishaq

Transcript of the Interview:

【BTV】Ishaq, thank you for agreeing to the interview. We are from Ningbo Institute of Technology, Zhejiang University. The purpose of this project is to explore how foreign businessmen develop their business in Yiwu and to learn what difficulties that they have during this development. As a component of our service-learning course, this project will serve as a bridge between overseas-funded enterprises and the local government.

【Ishaq】Just go ahead. I'm very happy to have you here to talk with me about the business I have established. So just ask what you want to know, and I'll share my stories and experiences with you as long as you like them.

【BTV】Okay, first can you give me a brief introduction to yourself, such as your name, how many years you have had your business here and anything else?

【Ishaq】Er... My name is Ishaq, a normal Arabian name, and I have settled here for almost nine years, from 2004 to now.

【BTV】What aspects of Yiwu attract you most, or in other words, why did you just choose Yiwu, a small city, rather than Hangzhou, Shanghai, or Beijing, as a starting point for your business?

【Ishaq】When I first heard of Yiwu, it was such a small city, but at that time, I was sure it would become an international city one day. Now, Yiwu has Futian, where thousands of customers gather and do their business each year. What's more, numerous cartons of commodities here in each booth in Futian market can be found very conveniently and quickly.

【BTV】So what does your company deal in?

【Ishaq】We produce codes and labels printed on the cartons about the quantity and features for the commodities in Futian Market. We are not selling certain items.

【BTV】That's a great idea. In this case, you don't have to establish a factory here.

【Ishaq】We don't need a factory, as you see. I have my office in my apartment, and I have two interpreters who work for me, and a few staff to help me handle some trivial affairs. But if I have a factory in Ningbo, I will produce cartons for the markets there. I think that's another business opportunity.

【BTV】I know that most of the foreigners in this district are from Arabian countries, so you have to print in many languages?

【Ishaq】Yes. When you walk in the Futian Market, you will feel you are entering Arabian countries. We use Arabian, English, Israel, and so forth.

【BTV】So how can the customers know your company and contact you?

【Ishaq】I advertise my company on the website and some trading booths in Futian Market. Every day, a lot of customers will hang out and purchase things they want in the market. The shop owners will help to inform them of my location. It is quite easy for the customers to find my office.

【BTV】After referring to your business background, I'd like to know if you are fond of Yiwu cuisine and are you accustomed to the Chinese cultural life here?

【Ishaq】I love Yiwu. I love my customers, too. As for the food, I can make meals at home on my own. During my free time, I will cook for my staff. They once praised my cooking skills. Believe it or not, I can use chopsticks quite well, even better than some Chinese. Forks and knives seem to get away from my life. And I bought my car seven years ago in Yiwu. I will hang out at night to have a cup of coffee with my friends or business partners in the open-air seats of the coffee shops although the traffic is fairly terrible here.

【BTV】Great! Have you gotten acquainted with new friends here, like the local people?

【Ishaq】Of course, because of my poor Chinese, I only make few Chinese friends, including you. Most of my business partners and friends are from Arabian countries for there are no language barriers between us.

【BTV】So are you and your business partners feeling culture shock here?

【Ishaq】Seldom, it is a multicultural city. I ask many people, among whom my Arabian friends say that they are just living in an Arabian city in Yiwu. Egyptians regard Yiwu as Egypt. Jordan people also take Yiwu as Jordan.

【BTV】Can you give some adjectives to describe the characteristics of Yiwu people?

【Ishaq】Sorry, I seldom get along with the Chinese people except for the business. So it's hard for me to describe the people who I am not familiar with.

【BTV】It is known to all that the Chinese way of doing business differs very much from the foreigners' way. Can you share your experiences from this perspective?

【Ishaq】Wow... Chinese people focus on my mood in doing the business because they care which time they shall come and how they carry on the conversations, with few attentions paid to the dealing itself. Sometimes they confused me. After a long talk, we might just shoot the breeze, rather than hit the point of the business.

【BTV】Are there any similar markets in your own country like Yiwu?

【Ishaq】No, commodities in my country are quite scattered, not densely-gathered like in the Futian Market. It's handy to purchase what you want within this market. You know, efficiency and timing are the most important part in my business. I also have three shops in my own country, but the market is not so well-stocked like Yiwu. Thus, I have to drive far away to buy blankets, towels and underwear to supply to our customers and fill the goods shelves in my shops.

【BTV】Terrific! You have so many shops, but you have settled down in China. How do you manage the daily business in your own country, via the Internet?

【Ishaq】That's not a problem. I have four daughters and one son. Two girls had already graduated from college, so they are running the shops as managers in Palestine for me. They will tell me the business achievements each month, and we can deal with some financial problems through the Internet. Technology helps us to overcome these problems.

【BTV】You have so many children, so no doubt you are doing big business around the world.

【Ishaq】Oh, that really costs me a large sum of money, but my God will help me.

【BTV】When you hire employees, what do you mainly pay attention to? And do you agree that the labor resources are advantageous in China?

【Ishaq】People come to my office for the job-hunting. I prefer people who are patient to the customers and honest about the business with me. Moreover, their English and Arabian should be quite good for the convenience of my company. The labor cost here is as low as my own country, but compared with the cost in European countries, it's much lower.

【BTV】You have been here for nine years, so you must have experienced the financial crisis in those years?

【Ishaq】The fuel! The house price! They are rising rapidly each year. You see, I have to drive to different cities in China to buy machines for the business, and I rent the apartment as the role of office temporarily. Before I came to Yiwu, the gasoline was about 5 RMB per liter. But now, it's between 7—8 RMB. So is my office, from 17,000 to 28,000 per year. And some customers stopped doing business during those years. As a result, I faced a tremendous challenge. Countries all over the world are troubled by the financial crisis.

【BTV】On this ground, do you have your own insights about China within the fierce international environment?

【Ishaq】Developed countries are still eating other countries' resources. China is short of the fuel according to its large population. Most fuel resources are in Arabian counties, and China is always advocating peaceful international cooperation.

【BTV】In the long run, will you focus on your own shops in Palestine or will you broaden your business range in Yiwu?

【Ishaq】I think I will open up my new business here because the shops are quite stable-operated in Palestine. I am about to establish shops in Futian Market this year.

【BTV】Crowds of foreign businessmen came here. Do you think it's due to certain government policies that encourage the foreign trading here?

【Ishaq】Personally, I just find it easy to do business in Yiwu. To import and export is also not a big problem, thanks to the loose tariff policy. I do feel the business environment is really comfortable and encouraging new opportunities here.

【BTV】Does Futian Market contribute to other industries in Yiwu?

【Ishaq】There are side industries booming thanks to the market, like restaurants, hotels, coffee shops and other entertaining places to meet the different needs of different foreigners. Many foreign businessmen just live near the market. They walk to the market or take a taxi for less than five minutes. It is an easy city!

【BTV】Do you seed your dream here, your Yiwu Dream?

【Ishaq】Yeah. I once had been to Ningbo, your hometown. If you do business like Yiwu people do in Ningbo, you will definitely lose money. But here, I feel the impulse of the business potential. Although Ningbo is a harbor city, with numerous modern factories and industrial zones, the market is the core of the trading process. I see China is inside Futian Market. Once you enter the market, you are seeing the world. That's the reason for your asking why so many foreigners come to Yiwu. Futian refreshes the vigor in Yiwu. I am also realizing my dream here. If I were given another chance to set my business in Shanghai, Beijing, or Hangzhou, I will not hesitate to choose Yiwu again for my dream.

【BTV】So today, I'm very happy that you have taken the interview. Your insights and suggestions are quite meaningful for our project. Our book will come out next year, and I will send you a copy for your kind cooperation. This is the end of our conversation. Thank you very much again.

【Ishaq】You are welcome. I will come to see you next time I go to Ningbo on my business trip.

Group Members: Cen Ye, Qian Chen, Zhu Jiangshan, Chen Jialu

叙事记录

【BTV】伊兹哈克，感谢你接受我们的采访。我们是来自浙江大学宁波理工学院的学生，本次采访的目的是探究外商如何在义乌开启事业之门，了解外商在创业过程中所遇到的困难。这是我们服务学习课程的一部分，它将为义乌的外企和当地政府搭建一座沟通的桥梁。

【Ishaq】那我们就开始吧。我很开心能够在这里和你们聊聊我所创立的事业。你们想知道什么就尽管问好了，只要你们愿意听，我就和你们说说我的创业故事和生意经。

【BTV】好的。首先，请简单介绍一下你自己，比如姓名、来义乌经商的时长，等等。

【Ishaq】我叫伊兹哈克，一个很普通的阿拉伯人的名字，从 2004 年来到义乌算起，至今在这儿已有 9 年了。

【BTV】义乌有什么闪光点最吸引你，换句话说，你为什么会选择义乌这个小城市，而非杭州、上海、北京这样的大都市来作为你事业的起点？

【Ishaq】当我第一次听说义乌的时候，它还是一座非常小的城市，但那时我已经确信它总有一天会变成一个国际化的城市。现在义乌有了福田市场（义乌国际商贸城），每年都有成千上万的客商来此经商。市场内的每一个摊位都备有种类繁多的货物，你想要买什么，都可以便捷快速地找到。

【BTV】那请问你们公司经营什么产品呢？

【Ishaq】我们为福田市场里的商品生产印在包装纸箱上的条形码和商标，用来注明货物数量和特征。我们不卖特定的货物。

【BTV】这真是一个好的商业渠道，这样的话你们就不需要在这造一个工厂了。

【Ishaq】正如你所说的，我们不需要工厂。我把自己的公寓作为办公室，雇了两个翻译，还有一些为我处理琐事的员工。以后若有机会在宁波建厂，我就可以为宁波的商品市场生产纸箱，这或许是另一个商机。

【BTV】我知道福田市场这片区的外商大多来自阿拉伯国家，那你们就要印多种文字了？

【Ishaq】确实如此，当你走在福田市场，你仿佛就走进了阿拉伯国家。因此我们承接阿拉伯语、英语、以色列语等多种文字的印刷项目。

【BTV】那么你的客户是怎么知晓你的公司并且联系你呢？

【Ishaq】我在各大网站和福田市场的一些摊位上都做了宣传。每天都有许多顾客在市场里转悠和采购。一旦交易成功，许多铺位的老板就会向他们提及我的所在。他们很容易就能找到我的办公室。

【BTV】我们刚刚聊了聊你的生意，现在我想知道你是否喜欢义乌菜，是否已经习惯了这儿的中国式文化生活呢？

【Ishaq】我爱义乌，跟客户们也很合得来。至于中国菜，我经常在家里自己做着吃。在闲暇之余，我也会为员工们掌厨做一桌菜。他们经常褒奖我的厨艺，也许你不信，我可以很熟练地用筷子吃饭，甚至比一些中国人用得好。刀叉似乎已经从我的生活中消失了。七年前，我就在义乌买了一辆车。虽然义乌的交通不怎么样，但是晚上我还是会经常和朋友以及生意上的伙伴去咖啡馆的露天座位喝咖啡。

【BTV】听起来很不错！那么你在这里结交了一些新朋友吗，比如义乌当地人？

【Ishaq】当然！不过我中文水平不太好，中国朋友不是很多，但其中包括你。所以我大多数朋友都是阿拉伯国家的，毕竟我们之间没有语言障碍。

【BTV】那么你和你的朋友在这里有没有感受到不同文化背景带给你们的冲击呢？

【Ishaq】那倒不会，这是一个文化多元化的城市。我问过许多朋友，阿拉伯朋友说他们住在义乌和住在阿拉伯没什么区别。埃及的朋友感觉这里就是埃及，约旦的朋友说这里就是约旦。

【BTV】你可以用一些形容词来描述义乌本地人吗？

【Ishaq】不好意思，因为语言关系，除了贸易往来外，我和中国人接触比较少，因此让我来描述不熟悉的人太难了。

【BTV】大家都知道中国人做生意的方式和外国人的方式大相径庭，你可否和我们分享下你在这方面的见解呢？

【Ishaq】中国人喜欢关注我在做生意时候的情绪，因为他们在意什么时候他们过来和我谈生意、怎么把这笔生意谈成。他们很少会十分关注交易本身。有时候，他们让我很困惑，比如我们谈了很久，但都是闲聊，根本没谈生意。

【BTV】那在你们国内有没有像义乌一样的市场呢？

【Ishaq】没有，我们国家货物都相当分散，不像福田市场这样高度集中，想买什么就能买到什么。效率和时机是经商至关重要的两点。在我自己的国家，我有3家店铺，但不像义乌一样货源齐全。因此我常常需要开车到很远的地方购买毛毯、毛巾和内衣来供应客户，并给货架补货。

【BTV】你拥有如此多家店铺，真是棒极了！但你长期住在中国，怎么处理店铺的一些日常商业事务呢，通过互联网么？

【Ishaq】那倒不是问题。我有五个小孩——四个女儿和一个儿子。两个女儿已经大学毕业了，她们任经理一职帮忙在巴勒斯坦经营店铺。她们会通过互联网向我报告业绩和经济状况，科技让一切问题都不再是问题了。

【BTV】你有这么多孩子，怪不得生意做这么大。

【Ishaq】抚养他们确实是很大的经济负担，不过我坚信神会帮助我。

【BTV】你在招聘员工时，会主要关注他们什么方面？你认为在中国劳动力资源是一个巨大优势吗？

【Ishaq】许多人来我的办公室求职，我最看中他们对客户的耐心和对我报告业绩的诚实度。此外，他们要精通英语和阿拉伯语，以便工作需要。这里的劳动力报酬和我家乡差不多，不过和欧洲国家相比，简直低多了。

【BTV】你来中国9年了，那么你肯定在这里经历过那几年的经济危机吧？

【Ishaq】燃油啊，房价啊，每年都涨得太快了！你看，我得开车去中国不同的城市购买特定的印刷机器，还有我租的这个临时办公室。来义乌之前，油费只需要每升5元，但是现在，已经涨到每升7～8元了。我的办公室也是如此，从每年1.7万租金涨到了现在的2.8万。这些年，有些客户不再经商，而我也经历了前所未有的大挑战。世界各地的其他国家也在经受金融危机的考验。

【BTV】那你觉得中国在当前如此严峻的国际形势下该怎么发展？

【Ishaq】发达国家依旧吞噬着其他相对弱小国家的资源。中国是一个人口大国，能源相对来说十分短缺，而且大部分的能源在阿拉伯国家，所以中国一直提倡和平的国际化合作。

【BTV】从长远的角度来看，你会着重发展在巴勒斯坦的事业还是开拓你在义乌的事业呢？

【Ishaq】我想我会扎根于此，因为在巴勒斯坦的商铺已经运营稳定了，今年我打算在福田市场也开一个新的店铺。

【BTV】如此多的外商蜂拥而至，你觉得是得益于政府所采取的鼓励对外贸易的政策吗？

【Ishaq】我个人觉得在义乌做生意十分容易。得益于宽松的关税政策，进口出口都不是什么大问题。我确实感受到这里舒适的商业环境，和各种新的商机。

【BTV】福田市场带动了义乌其他产业的发展吗?

【Ishaq】依托福田市场,饭店、酒店、咖啡厅、娱乐场所这样的服务业蓬勃发展,以满足不同外国人的不同需求。许多外国人就住在市场边上,他们可以走着去采货,就算坐出租车,也不过五分钟的路程。这真是一个便捷的城市!

【BTV】你在这里有梦想吗,你的义乌梦是什么?

【Ishaq】有,我曾经去过你的家乡宁波,如果你像义乌人一样在宁波做生意,肯定会亏本。但是在这,我感受到了商业潜力的脉搏。虽然宁波是一个港口城市,拥有众多的工厂和工业区,但是市场才是贸易的核心。我觉得福田市场浓缩了整个中国,一旦你踏进这个市场,你可以感受到全世界。这其实也可以回答你刚才的问题:为什么如此多的外国人会来义乌。福田市场让义乌变得更有活力。同时,我也在这里实现我自己的梦想,如果上天再给我一次选择的机会,我还是会对上海、北京抑或是杭州说"不!",我会再一次毫不犹豫地选择义乌来作为我的圆梦地。

【BTV】那么今天,很荣幸你能接受我们的采访。你的见解和建议对我们的项目很有意义。我们的书将会在明年出版,为了感谢你慷慨的合作,届时我会寄一本给你。在采访的最后,再次感谢你抽出时间配合我们完成本次采访。

【Ishaq】不用谢,下一次我出差去宁波一定会去看你的。

团队成员:岑烨,钱晨,朱江珊,陈佳露

Unique Experience in the Multi-cultural City

By Cen Ye Supervised by Yu Xuyan & Cai Liang

Yiwu, located in the middle of Zhejiang Province, has become a household name over the years; it is also the mecca for all the businessmen and young people who yearn to get the hang of the international market system to broaden their horizons.

Several years ago, I heard of this small city, but at that time people only offered a general comment that the quality of the goods in the market was quite inferior. What is worse, the price could not satisfy the customers' need as well. But now, Yiwu has already been making a fine reputation all over the world, with the quality of the commodities being improved and the market system being perfected.

While walking in the streets of this small city, I always wonder if I were on vacation abroad, for there are so many foreigners walking by. As a result of so many foreigners, the housing prices have been rising at a rapid rate. For the residential areas, the price here has surpassed that of Guangzhou, let alone the business areas. Undoubtedly it is a miracle that Yiwu can top history's greatest trade city, Guangzhou, in terms of housing prices. With this fact, we can understand the potential of this new star in the trading world. The fast-paced life style forces the traffic to deteriorate so that pedestrians have to be really careful when crossing the street. However, thanks to the westernized life style, people are accustomed to hanging out to have a cup of coffee with friends or colleagues, and a hectic day ends with a sound sleep.

One Year Is Not Enough for Visiting All the Booths in the Market

"If there were no market, Yiwu would not have become such a trade city today" is the most frequent point that almost every foreign businessman will refer to when talking about their enterprises here.

During the decade after China joined the WTO, the marketing scale in Yiwu has grown about ten times, covering 4,700,000 square meters and dealing in 1,700,000 kinds of commodities. It has been estimated that if a person stays at a booth for three minutes, and he works eight hours each day, he would have to spend more than one year to finish visiting all the booths.

To soothe the everyday routine, the business people live near the Futian Market, most of whom even rent their business offices in the buildings near the market. One is Ishaq, a Palestine businessman who came to Yiwu nine years ago, and hired five employees to help him purchase commodities, which become best-sellers in his own country. He said that 70% of the ornaments in Arabian countries are from China.

Yiwu is like a magnet, appealing to many businessmen from all over the world to seek fortunes in this small city. Some foreigners just take a fancy to the manufacturing capacity in Yiwu. Ishaq said, "Many of my business partners are my fellows in my hometown. From the visa to the business license, I teach them step by step. As for me, I'll spend three quarters of my time each year in China, and my son is studying international trade in Palestine. I can foresee the bright future here, so I will suggest him to come along to do business here when he graduates."

A Tiny "United Nations" in a Small City

From the perspective of local folks, Yiwu is a city that flourishes along with the market. Mutual understanding and tolerance play an essential part in accommodating people from different backgrounds, races and customs. Foreign businessmen describe the city as a well-separated district. The Arabian people live in the areas just near the market while people from different countries occupy the different parts of this small city.

Various food stands can be seen beside the residential areas. Because most of the foreign businessmen are from the Middle East, the so-called Middle East food street is still the most densely-crowded social area. Mutton kebabs and Arabian dim sum full of sugar are so aromatic that travelers are always tempted to indulge in this street. If you want to eat other gourmet food, you can go to the other districts to taste the authentic food in different areas. But most importantly, you can enjoy this without going abroad.

440,000 Foreign Businessmen Are Pursuing Their Yiwu Dream

As is known to all, the American Dream influenced a generation. With the rising international status, China now has its China Dream, so many foreign businessmen flood into the burgeoning market to realize their Yiwu Dream.

Different from the American Dream which focuses on individual success, we have our dream on the basis of the nation's prosperity. Only when the nation or the collectivity is on the track to success, can we feel a sense of belonging and achievement. And then we can seed our dream in this land; undoubtedly we will harvest a fruitful success.

Yiwu is a place worth visiting and reading and writing about again and again. We should be proud of its force in boosting the Chinese economy.

多元文化城市的独特之旅

文：岑　烨　指导教师：喻旭燕　蔡　亮

位于浙江中部的义乌这几年来家喻户晓，几乎是所有商人和有志成为商人的年轻人熟悉国际市场系统，并扩大国际视野的必经之地。

几年前就听闻义乌小商品市场，当时人们的评价是商品质量不够好，而且价格也难以满足大众消费者的需求。但现在，随着商品质量的不断提升和市场系统的不断完善，义乌誉满全球。

走在这个小城市的街道上，我总在想自己是否在国外旅游，因为不经意间就会有许多的外国人映入我的眼帘。正因为如此，这里的房价才一直处于迅猛上升的趋势。就居民区而言，这里的房价已经超过了广州，更不用说商业区域了。在房价方面，义乌能够超越著名的贸易城市广州，无疑是个奇迹。由此，我们可以预见到这颗贸易市场新星的崛起。快节奏的生活方式使得这里的交通日益拥堵，行人在穿马路的时候需要格外小心。然而，得益于西化的生活方式，人们似乎已经习惯在晚上约上几个好友，抑或是生意上的伙伴出来喝一杯咖啡，安然结束一天的匆忙生活，换来一夜好眠。

遍览所有摊位，一年太匆匆

“如果没有市场，义乌就不会发展成为今日的贸易之都”，几乎所有外商在说到自己在义乌的生意时都会作此感慨。

在中国“入世”的十年间，义乌的市场规模也随之扩大10倍之多。目前经营总面积达到470万平方米，市场里销售着单品170万种。据测算，如果在每个摊位前停留3分钟，按一个人一天工作8小时来计算，逛完全部的商铺要花一年多的时间。

为了日常行程的便捷，许多商人就住在福田市场的周边，他们中大多数人甚至就把办公区安置在临近市场的商务楼内。伊兹哈克9年前就来到义乌，目前已经雇用了5名员工帮助他日常采购。他说，义乌的商品在他自己的国家十分畅销，在阿拉伯国家有70%的饰品都是中国货。

义乌就像一块吸铁石，吸引世界各地的商人来此寻求财富。一些外商说，他们看中义乌的小商品制造能力。“我的很多商业伙伴都是我的同乡，从办签证到申请营业执照都是我手把手教的。”伊兹哈克说，“现在我每年有四分之三的时间留在中国，我的儿子在巴勒斯坦，也在读国际贸易，义乌让我预见到了一个光明的未来，我会建议他毕业之后来这里和我一起做事业。”

小城市里的“联合国”

在当地人眼中，义乌就是一个随着市场而繁荣的城市。这么多来自不同社会背景、种族、文化习俗的人们能够在这里一起生活，相互理解和宽容起到了不可或缺的作用。他们会打趣地把义乌描述成“片区型”城市。例如阿拉伯人住在靠近市场的这片区域，而来自其他国家的人分布在这个城市不同的角落。

与住宅区相辅相成的是一条条的美食街，由于外商里中东人居多，因此那条“中东美食街”仍旧是外商最密集的社交场所。烤羊肉串和蘸满糖的阿拉伯点心散发着诱人的香味，让游客不禁驻足于此，流连忘返。若你想品尝其他国家正宗的特色美食，你大可去不同的区域一饱口福。最重要的是，一切的一切，你不必出国便可享受到。

44 万外商共圆“义乌梦”

众所周知，当年的“美国梦”影响了一代人；随着国际地位的日益上升，如今中国也有了“中国梦”。如此多的外商蜂拥而至，在这个迅猛发展的新兴市场共圆“义乌梦”。

“美国梦”更注重于个人的成功。与之不同的是，我们的梦想建立在祖国繁荣的基础之上。只有当祖国或者是集体走上成功的轨道，我们才能体会到强烈的归属感和成就感。随后，我们就会在这片神州大地上播种我们的梦想。无疑，我们将收获累累硕果。

义乌值得你我再访、再读、再写。义乌有力地推动了中国经济的发展，我们应当为此自豪！

Tumaag

Tumaag: China Dream, My Dream

中国梦,我的梦

Tumaag comes from Sweden. He came to Yiwu thirteen years ago. He is running a trading company. His company provides services for people who come to Yiwu. Maybe they are looking for products or new models from Yiwu market that offers the cheapest prices from local factories. Maybe they need to take pictures of samples, or send the samples to clients to develop new business. Living in such a world full of of desires, he still believes that we should live for now.

Tumaag是瑞典人,13年前来到义乌。他自己开了一家贸易公司,为来到义乌的人提供服务。他们当中,有些是来市场里寻找商品和新模型,因为这里的市场能从当地工厂拿到最优惠的价格;有些需要给货品拍照或者是向顾客发送样品,从而发展新的业务。在这个充满欲望的世界里,他仍然相信我们应该活在当下。

China Dream, My Dream

By Tumaag

Transcript of the Interview:

【BTV】It is nice of you to agree to our interview.

【BTV】Could you give us a brief self-introduction?

【Tumaag】Of course. I'm Tumaag. I come from Sweden. And I have been here for more than ten years. Then I started my own business. I think my office is growing into a bigger one.

【BTV】Great! You are the one we are looking for.

【Tumaag】Okay. It's my pleasure.

【BTV】What about your life in Yiwu? What kind of food do you eat here?

【Tumaag】All kinds of food. I like Chinese food. It's very delicious, such as "suan cai yu", you know?

【BTV】Yeah, spicy fish with pickled vegetable. We all know it is very spicy, but a lot of people love the dish. It tastes good. And have you made any new friends here?

【Tumaag】I have some business friends. They are Chinese. Many people want to talk with me. But I would like to stay alone. I am quiet, and I don't have a lot of friends. Just for business.

【BTV】I see. What do you think about the local residents in Yiwu?

【Tumaag】Anyway they are hospitable. They seem to be ready to help people at anytime. It is really helpful when we first came here.

【BTV】Really? Then are there any stories about the local people?

【Tumaag】I think Chinese people are all very kind, not just the people in Yiwu. You know, when I first came here, I had some problems in finding the place I want to go. I asked the passers-by, but surprisingly they were willing to show me the way. Go this way, turn left and something like that. Even sometimes they will take me to the place. It is fantastic.

【BTV】So you feel at home, don't you? Then is it the same in your country?

【Tumaag】Aha, I come from Europe. But it is actually different in my country. The people in my hometown are very busy. They may not have the time to show the way to others. So Chinese are very hospitable even they don't have enough time.

【BTV】Do you still remember some examples of cultural shock you have confronted? Would you share them with us?

【Tumaag】Yeah. Let me think. For example, when Chinese are eating or talking on the phone. They sometimes talk too loud that I think it is a little noisy. Maybe they are just talking something that is really interesting. You know. I have lived here for a long time, but I think it could be a kind of cultural shock for me.

【BTV】Oh, I understand. Do you participate in some activities in your spare time?

【Tumaag】Yes. I do exercise after I finish my work. You know, as a businessman, I may be too much filled with so many business affairs. We need to relax ourselves to refresh our brain. Maybe just taking a walk is enough.

【BTV】OK. Are you satisfied with the life style here?

【Tumaag】Yeah. I am happy here totally.

【BTV】Then let's talk about your own company. What kind of business are you doing?

【Tumaag】Trading company. In a way, we offer some help for different businessmen. We will provide service for people who come to Yiwu. Maybe they look for products or new models from Yiwu market that offers the cheapest price from the local factory; maybe they take the pictures or express the sample to clients to develop a new business.

【BTV】I see. Do you have a brand for your office?

【Tumaag】A brand? No. My company is just like a shipping company. I have a large number of customers all over the world. So they order the goods, and we send to them. We don't have any brand.

【BTV】Okay. Then why do you choose Yiwu as your working place?

【Tumaag】First, Yiwu is an international market. There are a lot of foreigners here. It is like a cultural melting-pot. Yiwu makes it possible to do business with all kinds of people from different countries.

【BTV】It is convenient, right? Then what else?

【Tumaag】Besides there are many goods here. Indeed there are many choices. You can have many opportunities to choose the goods you like and the company you want to run.

【BTV】What about the people?

【Tumaag】People here are very hard-working and warm-hearted. It does great help. I like to work with people here.

【BTV】Are your staff Chinese? How do you communicate with them?

【Tumaag】They are Chinese actually. But they can speak Russian. I communicate with them in Russian.

【BTV】Wow! That's cool. I am wondering why you do business with foreigners by speaking Russian?

【Tumaag】Yeah. You know. Most of my customers are Russian and Ukrainian. They speak Russian. So there is no problem in language.

【BTV】Then what are the standards for hiring in your company?

【Tumaag】If they can speak Russian, I will hire them. Seriously, I mean that the more kinds of languages they can speak, the more chances they will have in a foreign company. And they should be smart anyway.

【BTV】Okay. Thank you for your suggestions for college students. What are the differences between Yiwu and your country in doing business?

【Tumaag】In my country, they order something. For example, we will make an appointment at 8:00. Then we will be on time. But it is a little different here. People may not be punctual sometimes.

【BTV】Yeah. That can be annoying. But I think it is reasonable. Because people here are busy in doing business. So they may be late. What's your suggestion for doing business in Yiwu?

【Tumaag】I think they would better make the goods they want more clearly. Another one is the time. Apart from this, we should communicate with each other more. Both the foreigners here and the local people should make some efforts together to expand the business.

【BTV】Thank you. We will value your advice. I believe the situation will improve.

【Tumaag】Yes. I hope so. Actually, I have seen the changes in Yiwu these years.

【BTV】Can you give us some examples?

【Tumaag】When I came here at first, I walked to the Futian Market, just few people could speak English, so we had difficulty in communicating. Obviously, the problem has been easily changed. People here can do business in simple English. It is a great change I have seen. There are also some changes in traffic and buildings. The cars are getting more and more. There is a heavy traffic in Yiwu. And there are a lot of the cloud-kissing buildings now with the rapid development. I think China must be proud of Yiwu.

【BTV】Yeah, we take pride in Yiwu. Have you ever heard about the reform and opening-up policy in China?

【Tumaag】Yes. I know that. You know, with the policy, China has been more open now. In my country, if I do business, I must write down how much I pay, how much I buy and how much I have commercialized. So doing business is much easier in China.

【BTV】Is there anything interesting in China that you want to share with us?

【Tumaag】Yeah. I like Chinese culture. The men may not be at home and may go out to play with friends. But the women are great. They will be at home to do some housework. I mean the life style in China is great, just fifty-fifty. I like it very much.

【BTV】Okay. And do you like the way we live?

【Tumaag】Yeah. Because in my country, if one person goes out, maybe the whole home will be left empty, and there is no one to care about the house and the family. I appreciate the Chinese culture sometimes.

【BTV】Then have you heard of the China Dream?

【Tumaag】No. Sorry.

【BTV】That's okay. What about your dream here or your dream about the office?

【Tumaag】My dream? To be honest, I don't have any dream. Also, I never think about the plans of my company here. You know, we cannot know what is going to happen tomorrow or in next few years. And the situation in the world is not easy. I just live for now. I don't want to take any plans, and I am happy at this moment. That's what I wish. It is my idea.

【BTV】Great. In my view, your opinion is not the same as others. You are sparing your efforts to live a happy life, not just make more money. Although you don't have future plans, I appreciate your belief about life style.

【Tumaag】Thank you.

【BTV】Thank you very much for your great support to our project. It is really nice to have such a meaningful talk with you.

Group Members: Zhu Xiaotong, Huang Shuang, Zhao Yating

叙事记录

【BTV】你愿意接受我们的采访，我们很高兴。

【BTV】可以做一个简短的自我介绍吗？

【Tumaag】当然，我叫 Tumaag，瑞典人。我来义乌已经有十多年了。来到义乌之后，就开始做生意。我觉得我的生意会越做越大的。

【BTV】太棒了，你就是我们要找的人。

【Tumaag】好的，这是我的荣幸。

【BTV】你在义乌的生活怎么样？喜欢吃什么菜呢？

【Tumaag】各种食物我都会吃，我很喜欢美味的中国菜，比如说酸菜鱼，你知道吗？

【BTV】是的！酸菜鱼，我们都知道。很辣的一道菜，但是，很多人都特别钟爱这道菜。味道真的不错。那么，在义乌，你结交了一些新朋友吗？

【Tumaag】我有一些商业伙伴，他们都是中国人。许多人都想过来和我聊聊天，但我比较喜欢一个人待着。我是一个比较喜欢安静的人，所以朋友不多，只是一些生意场上的朋友。

【BTV】我懂了，那么，你觉得义乌本地人怎么样？

【Tumaag】义乌人很热情。他们助人为乐，我刚来这里的时候，他们真的是帮了我很多很多。

【BTV】是吗？有没有这样的事例可以跟我们分享呢？

【Tumaag】嗯。我认为不仅仅是义乌人，中国人都很友好。你知道，我刚来这里的时候，找不到想要去的地方，就问过路人，但是很意外的是，他们都非常愿意告诉我具体的路线，走这条路，左拐，类似的一些指示。甚至有些时候，他们还会直接把我带到那个地方，真的是太好了！

【BTV】所以，你感到宾至如归？那在你的家乡那儿也一样吗？

【Tumaag】啊哈，我来自欧洲，但是，这点和中国真的不太一样。我家乡的人都很忙，他们可能没时间去给其他人带路吧。所以，中国人真的十分热情，即使他们很忙，没有足够的时间，也会这么做。

【BTV】那有没有遇到过文化冲突呢，可以和我们分享吗？

【Tumaag】好的，让我想想。比如说，中国人在吃饭或者打电话的时候，有时讲话讲得太响，我会觉得有点吵。可能他们在谈一些比较有意思的事情。虽然我在这里住得比较久了，但对我来说这还是一种文化冲突。

【BTV】哦，我知道了。你在工作之余有没有参加一些活动？

【Tumaag】是的。完成工作后，我会去锻炼身体。你知道，作为一个商人，我可能太忙于商业事务。我们需要放松自己，理清思绪。也许，散个步就足够了。

【BTV】那你对这里的生活方式满意吗？

【Tumaag】是的，总的来说，我在这里很开心。

【BTV】那我们现在就谈谈你的公司吧？你是做哪一行的？

【Tumaag】贸易公司。从某种程度来说，我们为不同的商业人士提供一些帮助。我们会为来到义乌的人提供服务。他们当中，有些是来市场里寻找商品或新的款式，因为这里的市场能从当地工厂拿到最优惠的价格；有些需要给货品拍照或者是向顾客发送样品，从而发展新的业务。

【BTV】我明白了。那你的公司有没有什么商标品牌？

【Tumaag】商标品牌？没有，我们公司就像是一个船运公司。我的客户来自全球各地，他们下订单给我们，我们就发货给他们，不需要任何品牌。

【BTV】好吧。那你为什么会选择义乌作为你事业的开始呢？

【Tumaag】首先，义乌是一个国际市场。这里有很多外国人，就像一个文化大熔炉。在义乌，来自不同国家的人们都有机会实现自己的商业理想。

【BTV】所以这十分方便，是吧？还有其他理由吗？

【Tumaag】除此之外，这里有许多的物品，实际上是有很多的选择吧，你可以有很多机会去选择你想要的东西，并且经营自己的公司。

【BTV】这里的人怎样？

【Tumaag】这里的人们都十分努力工作，乐于助人。这确实大有裨益，我喜欢和这里的人一起工作。

【BTV】你的员工是中国人吗？你是如何和他们沟通的呢？

【Tumaag】确实，他们是中国人，但是他们都会说俄语，所以我们用俄语交流。

【BTV】哇！好酷啊，我很好奇为什么你们和外国人做生意时说俄语。

【Tumaag】嗯，我的大部分顾客来自俄罗斯和乌克兰，他们说俄语，所以我们就没有语言问题了。

【BTV】原来如此，那你雇用员工的标准是什么呢？

【Tumaag】如果他们会说俄语，我当然愿意雇用他们。严格来讲，我的意思是说，在一个外企公司，一个员工会说的语言种类越多那被雇佣的可能性会越高吧。不过，不管怎么说，他们也要有商业头脑。

【BTV】好的，谢谢你对大学生的建议。我们还想知道在做生意方面，义乌和你的家乡那边有什么不同？

【Tumaag】在我的家乡那边，顾客下订单，如果约了 8 点见面，我们就会比较准时。不过，这里有点不同，有时候人们不太准时。

【BTV】是的，我知道这有点让人不高兴，但我觉得是可以理解的，毕竟人们都忙着做生意，所以可能会迟到。那对于如何在义乌经营贸易，你有没有好的建议呢？

【Tumaag】我觉得他们应该明确自己想要的物品，另外就是时间问题吧。除此之外，我们应该多交流交流，不论是当地人还是外国人都应该一起努力去扩大贸易。

【BTV】谢谢你，我们会重视你的意见，并且相信这种状况会改变的。

【Tumaag】是的，我也希望。事实上，这些年，我看到义乌变化很大。

【BTV】能给我们举些例子吗？

【Tumaag】我第一次去福田市场，只有极少数人会讲英语，所以我们沟通有问题。显然，现在问题已经轻松地解决了，人们可以通过简单的英语交流做生意了。这是个大变化吧。交通和建筑方面也有一些变化。汽车越来越多，交通负载量也很大。随着义乌的快速发展，许多大楼高耸入云。我觉得中国一定为义乌感到骄傲吧。

【BTV】是的，我们为义乌而自豪。你有没有听过中国的一项政策：改革开放？

【Tumaag】是的，我知道这个。因为这个“改革开放”政策，中国变得更加开放了。在我们国家，如果要做生意，必须上报付了多少，买了多少，交易了多少。所以在中国做生意更加方便。

【BTV】你有没有其他有关中国的趣闻轶事可以和我们分享？

【Tumaag】是的，我喜欢中国文化。一个家庭里，男人可能出去玩了，但是中国女人很不错，她们会在家里做一些家务。我的意思是说中国的家庭生活方式很好，很平衡。我很喜欢！

【BTV】那么，你喜欢我们的生活方式么？

【Tumaag】喜欢，因为在我们国家，如果一个人出门了，那么全家都会出去。没人会照顾家里了，所以有时候我很欣赏中国文化。

【BTV】那你有没有听说过中国梦？

【Tumaag】没有，不好意思。

【BTV】没事，那么你有自己的梦想或者说有关公司的梦想吗？

【Tumaag】我的梦想？说实话，我没有什么梦想。另外，也没有什么有关公司的计划。你知道的，我们没法预知明天或者接下去的几年会发生什么，而且现如今的世界局势不是很明朗。我不想有计划，这一刻我高兴满足就够了。活在当下，这就是我的想法。

【BTV】很好！在我看来，你的观点和其他人不太一样，你想过一种快乐的生活，而不仅仅是赚钱。尽管你没有计划，我很欣赏你的生活方式！

【Tumaag】谢谢！

【BTV】谢谢你对我们实践活动的支持，很高兴和你进行了如此有意义的对话！

团队成员：朱小曈，黄爽，赵雅婷

Live for Now

By Zhao Yating Supervised by Yu Xuyan & Cai Liang

The Melting Pot of Cultures

Wandering in the streets in Yiwu, we meet foreigners with different skin colors in diverse groups of three and four, or just alone. They walk in the streets anxiously or freely. While walking into the bright and spacious International Trade City equipped with first-class facilities and walking around so many shops, you can see a lot of foreigners with deep socket eyes, high nose and full beard. With the help of translator, they talk about the goods and make bargains with shopkeepers. The influx of foreigners gives an exotic atmosphere to the local culture. The North Chouzhou Street near the International Trade City is regarded as a place with much exotic flavor. There are many restaurants, cafés and big hotels with signs in English, Korean and Arabic on this street. In the evening, the air, filled with the aroma of coffee, roast mutton and apple hookah, comes to you. A number of foreign businessmen from Africa and the Middle East come here and stay together to relax after they finish a day's work. When we walk into a restaurant, the rhythm of the background music is Middle East style. The television hanging on the wall is broadcasting Arabic news. Waiters wearing robes are shuttling back and forth among the guests. All these make us feel like we are living in a foreign country.

Because of the gathering of foreigners, there appears a foreign street and a "United Nation". Having experienced much in Yiwu for years, many foreigners can speak Chinese and even the local dialect now. Some of them, with their families, have been living here for more than ten years. Therefore, they have integrated themselves into this city deeply. Foreigners with different skin colors, foods of all kinds and the fusion and conflict of cultures made us believe that we had come to the melting pot—Yiwu.

A Good Place to Make Money

Word has it that Yiwu is a city where all the local residents are businessmen. Everyone there has a strong wish to earn more money. There is an additional book in Yiwu's primary schools, which is entitled "The Urban and Rural Business in Yiwu". What is more surprising is that every person is sure that he will make a lot of money there. In this way, the local people and the foreigners come to Yiwu to pursue and achieve their dreams of making money. During the interview, they answered us with smiles, explaining that they came here for money when they were asked why they choose Yiwu. Compared with other countries, the business here is much more free and open. Yiwu is called the "Canton Fair Opened All Year Round". Before 2008, buyers all over the world went to Yiwu crazily. Every customer ordered a large quantity of goods. It was very common that one kind of goods could sell in the hundreds to the thousands, and each order was worth hundreds of thousands of RMB. So it was easy to do business at that time. Even with a thin profit margin, it was very common to earn hundreds of thousands of RMB. Some did even bigger, and their annual income reached tens of millions of RMB.

With the development of electronic commerce in recent years, domestic consumption has made many young men's dreams come true through online business. Most of the goods sold online come from Yiwu market which serves as a supplier of goods. Although many goods are not made locally, they are sold out from Yiwu market. What makes it a place to make money is that the prices of all goods now are fair, and the markets there are not only open but also large. In addition, foreigners are learning Chinese eagerly while Chinese are trying hard to learn all kinds of foreign languages nowadays. Therefore, Yiwu comes to be the best place to do business. There is an old saying that tolerance is great. In order to make the business environment more comfortable, local government has taken a series of actions, such as symposia for businessmen. In this way, the government can understand what foreigners think and need, solve problems about their children going to school and extend the time of the visa. It is not only the 320,000 kinds of goods that attract foreign businessmen but the tolerance that the local government and people express as well. This gives the city passion and energy. As for Tumaag, a Swede who has been living here for more than ten years, the local residents are very hospitable. He was greatly helped both in life and business when he first came to Yiwu. Tumaag said that he has fallen in love with Chinese culture after he came although some cultural shocks exist. Tumaag chose Yiwu for his business dream. So he came alone more than a decade ago to start his own dream. Tumaag is running a trading company which mostly ships goods to customers. He said this company is just like a ship on the sea, "We will set out whenever it is needed." With a decade's development, the company has become bigger even though their customers are mainly from Russia and Ukraine. Personally, he now feels satisfied. I believe that his dream has come true, and we wish that all men and women like him can realize their own dreams in Yiwu.

Now Is Good

In Yiwu, stories are easy to find about foreigners who come to make a fortune and often do. These gold diggers come to Yiwu from all over the world because of their dreams. China has her own dream of renaissance. Every country has a dream. So does everyone. We came to know some foreigners' dreams during those days. The economic development of China has made great progress through the WTO, and Yiwu has been the most outstanding place in business. Thus all those cute foreigners earn more than they wanted with much satisfaction. Now they consider Yiwu as their hometown.

Some people want to make more money. Some are trying to enlarge their business. Some just like to live a comfortable life. However, there are still some people who think they should be happy at this moment. They don't care how much they earn or spend. Tumaag said, "I don't have any dreams now. I have realized my dream here. I just want to live for now." Just like when we first met Tumaag, he sat there with ease playing the phone and smoking in the restaurant alone. He looked like a kid who doesn't have to worry and lives for now. Actually, I appreciate the idea highly. Seizing each moment in our lives allows us to prolong its value and make it more meaningful.

It is a short but wonderful journey to carry on this project in Yiwu. Now standing in the international market of trading, Yiwu is sure to go further and do better. We believe firmly that she will be more prosperous when we pass by next time.

活在当下

文：赵雅婷　指导老师：喻旭燕　蔡　亮

文化熔炉

徜徉在义乌的街头，肤色迥异、着装不一的外国人，或三五成群，或独自一人，或急或徐地行走在大街上。走进宽敞明亮、设施一流的国际商贸城，穿梭于琳琅满目的商品之间，一抬头便可以看到深眼窝、高鼻梁、满脸络腮胡的外国人，在翻译的帮助下，与店主讨价还价。老外们的涌入，给义乌本土文化注入了异国情调。义乌最有洋味儿的地段，是距国际商贸城不远的稠州北路。在这条路上，分布着标有英文、韩文、阿拉伯文的餐厅、咖啡馆和大酒店。傍晚时分，空气里弥漫着咖啡、烤羊肉和苹果水烟混合的味道，许多来自非洲和中东地区的外商忙完了一天的工作便聚集到这里放松。进入一家餐厅，背景音乐是中东风格的节奏，挂在高处的电视机播放着阿拉伯电视新闻，身着长袍的服务员在客人中间穿梭忙碌着，让人感觉仿佛置身于异国他乡。

由于老外的集聚，义乌这座城市也出现了"异国风情一条街"、"联合国社区"。经过多年的经商磨炼和生活积累，很多外国人已经会讲汉语，甚至会讲义乌当地的方言，有的已经携家带口在义乌生活了十来年，他们已经深深融入义乌这座城市。各种肤色的外国人，各类风格的食物和各种文化的交融与冲突使我们相信我们真正地来到了这个文化大熔炉——义乌。

淘金之地

人称义乌是一个"全民皆商"的城市，每一个人都在想着赚钱，义乌小学课本中专门加了一本《义乌的城乡贸易》。更让人感慨的是，每一个人都认为自己可以在这个城市赚到钱。本地的、外地的，还有外国的，都在义乌追寻着他们自己的淘金梦。在采访过程中，问及来义乌的原因，他们总会笑着说是为钱而来。相比其他国家而言，义乌的商品贸易显得更为自由和开放。义乌市场被誉为"天天开门的广交会"。在 2008 年以前，各国的采购商都在义乌大量采购商品，每个客户的需求量都非常大，单款产品几百件到上千件都很平常，每个订单也都是货值几十万，所以当时的生意好做。即使利润率不高，每年下来挣个几十万的比比皆是，甚至有人做得更大，年收入达到了上千万之多。

最近这几年，随着电子商务的崛起，国内消费也成就了许多有梦想的年轻人在互联网上的创业，义乌又成了他们坚实的货源地，网上商城的很大一部分产品都来自义乌市场。很多虽然不是义乌制造，却也是通过义乌市场销售出去的。义乌商品物美价廉，市场开放广阔，使义乌成长成为如今的金源地，再加上现在外商如饥似渴地学习中文，而中国人也在努力地学习各种外语，因此义乌成了做生意的最佳城市。整个商城不仅弥漫着浓浓的商业气息，也流露着酽酽的异国情调。古人云：有容乃大。为了给外商营造良好的综合环境，市政府采取了一系列的措施，如召开外商座谈会，倾听他们的呼声，解决他们的孩子入学问题，延长签证时间……不仅仅是那32万种如海洋般的小商品吸引着外商，还有义乌市政府及人民的那种兼收并蓄的博大胸怀，使义乌这座城市散发着激情与活力。对于在义乌生活了十多年的瑞典人Tumaag来说，义乌的当地人十分热情。他第一次来义乌，在生活和生意上都受到了当地人的帮助。Tumaag说，虽然有着文化的冲突，但感受着义乌当地的风土人情十余年之久，他已经爱上了中国的文化。十多年前，Tumaag只身一人来到这里，开始了自己的淘金之路。他在这里开了一家贸易公司，主要就是向下了订单的顾客发送货物。他说自己的公司就是一艘在海上航行的船，“只要有需要，我们就出发。”现如今，经过十余载发展，虽然主要顾客是来自俄罗斯和乌克兰，但公司已经不断地壮大。Tumaag觉得很满足。我相信他的淘金之梦已经稳稳地在义乌实现了，祝福所有像他一样的淘金人能在义乌圆梦。

当下即好

在义乌，老外“穿着裤衩而来，西装革履而去”的淘金故事屡见不鲜。这些来自世界各地的“淘金客”，因为梦想而来到义乌。中国有自己的复兴之梦。每个国家也都有各自的梦想，每个人也是如此。在义乌的这些天，我们了解到了一些外国人的梦想。入世后，中国经济长足发展；而义乌，在商贸方面的贡献尤其显著。因而在义乌，这些可爱的“老外”们如鱼得水，赚足了腰包。如今，他们把义乌当故乡。一些人想赚更多钱，一些人努力拓展他们的贸易，一些人只想过舒适的生活。但是，也仍然有些人觉得此时此刻开心便可。他们不介意赚了或花了多少。Tumaag说：“现在，我没有什么梦想。我已经实现了梦想，现在只想活在当下。”就像我们初次遇见Tumaag一样，他一个人悠闲地坐在餐馆里抽着烟玩着手机，仿佛孩子一般，无忧无虑地活在当下。事实上，我很欣赏这种想法。抓住生命中的每一刻，会让我们延长其价值并且使它更有意义。

能在义乌开展这项调研就是一段短暂而美好的旅程。如今，置身于国际贸易大市场，义乌一定会走得更远更好！我们坚定地认为当我们下次再途经义乌时，她会变得更加繁荣！

Saman

Saman: Yiwu, an Ideal Sourcing Center

义乌，理想的采购中心

Saman Tofip is from the northern part of Iran. He has been in China for six years and has a great impression of China. He is a friendly person with a great sense of humor. Now, he is a successful businessman with his own company. Yet, he is still ambitious with lots of dreams to be realized.

萨曼来自伊朗北部，在中国已有6年之久，对中国的印象相当好。他既友善又幽默。如今，拥有一家属于自己的公司，已经成为一名成功的商人，但是雄心壮志的他仍怀有远大的理想。

Yiwu, an Ideal Sourcing Center

By Saman

Transcript of the Interview:

【BTV】Good afternoon. I'm Monica. May I have your name?

【Saman】I'm Saman.

【BTV】Okay. Let me introduce myself first. I'm a college student from Ningbo Institute of Technology, Zhejiang University. We're doing a project about foreign people's life and work in Yiwu. I am going to ask you some related questions. Thank you for your time of the interview! First, would you mind introducing yourself?

【Saman】You know my name. And I'm from Iran. I have three brothers and two sisters. I came to Yiwu with my friends in 2007. Then I set up my own company here.

【BTV】Where's your family?

【Saman】My family all stay in Iran. I came here alone.

【BTV】Wow, how often do you go back to see your family?

【Saman】Once a year. Only at Chinese Lunar New Year, I go back to my hometown and see my family.

【BTV】Oh, you must miss your family very much. Would they come here to see you?

【Saman】Yes. Of course, I miss my family very much. But I'm doing my business, not having fun. I have a lot of things to do every day. And I have many meetings with my customers. My families rarely have the opportunity to see me. They have their own things to do. We just can reunite once a year.

【BTV】Venturing far from your family to a foreign country is not an easy thing. What makes you do this? Why did you choose Yiwu?

【Saman】In order to offer a better life for my family. I came here to work harder. Yiwu is the ideal sourcing center with its variety and reasonable prices.

【BTV】I think your business must be successful. I see your schedule is very busy.

【Saman】Yeah. I have to associate with my customers. Every day I have lots of business affairs.

【BTV】I wonder what your business is? I mean, what do you mainly engage in?

【Saman】I do many business here. But the business is about auto tyres and spare parts of tyre. And I have one department dealing with tyres and spare parts of tyre. There are many others I also engage in. For example, house decoration, and baby clothes. I have already opened my stores about these in the Futian Market.

【BTV】Great. Your company is big. You are a successful businessman. I think it will still develop better.

【Saman】Thank you. I hope so.

【BTV】And have you ever been to other countries apart from China?

【Saman】Many countries, like Malaysia, Netherlands, Thailand, Dubai and so on.

【BTV】By the way, I heard that there are a great number of Chinese people in Dubai, aren't there?

【Saman】Yes. Many Chinese people do business there about five or six years ago. And people who are from Thailand and Netherlands also go there. But nowadays Dubai's business is not good. Recently more and more people come to China and India.

【BTV】Why did this happen?

【Saman】The reason that why less and less people go to Dubai is complicated.

【BTV】Are there any other difficulties or challenges in your business?

【Saman】The difficulties? Yeah, of course, the biggest problem is visa. It's very difficult for me. Visa is very important to every foreigner. If you don't have your visa, it will be a big trouble for you to go abroad. Every foreigner here must handle it first. As a foreign businessman, every six months, three months or even two months you have to renew your visa.

【BTV】This sounds somewhat inconvenient. What about other countries? Are they the same as in China?

【Saman】No. It's completely different from China. In other countries, it's easy to get a visa for a long time.

【BTV】What is the difference in other countries? How can it be more convenient than China?

【Saman】You can ask the people in your country who had been to other countries. For example, when Chinese people go to Europe, the valid time of their visa depends. Policy there is more flexible and convenient.

【BTV】What is the standard of visa in western countries?

【Saman】It depends on the purpose of your tour. If you come here for business and you may stay here for a certain period of time, and you are ensured the safety. Then you'll get a visa for a long time as you expected.

【BTV】Oh, it sounds like that western visa is more convenient than the Chinese visa. And have you ever got trouble with the visa in China?

【Saman】Yes, I have. Once I went abroad with my customers. They told me that my visa was no longer valid. I should go to get a visa again. But I was in a hurry at that time. And I almost lost a big customer.

【BTV】I'm sorry to hear that. Maybe the Chinese government should take actions to improve the current policy. Then, getting a visa would be more convenient and you need not to worry about it.

【Saman】I hope I would still be in China when it happens.

【BTV】You have been here for many years, what do you think of Yiwu and the people of Yiwu?

【Saman】Yiwu is a pretty city. Yiwu has the biggest market all over the world. It's a good place to develop business. There are all kinds of commodities. What's more, the commodity here is cheap. In a word, Yiwu has many advantages to start one's career here. And Yiwu people are industrious and capable, with a spirit of innovation.

【BTV】In addition to Yiwu, have you been to other places in China?

【Saman】I've been to some of the other places in China. Every month, I have to travel to Shanghai and Shandong. Overall, the Chinese people are very friendly. I was there to eat and shop, and I can feel their respect. It makes me feel very comfortable. In comparison, the need to improve traffic in Yiwu is urgent. You can see cars everywhere during the rush hours.

【BTV】Yiwu is not perfect. There are many areas that need to be improved. Why did you come here and start your career here?

【Saman】As you know, Yiwu has a big market, which is famous all over the world. People in most places of China, even from other countries in the world come here to purchase the things. Yiwu can provide me a better market.

【BTV】Are there any good policies that the government provides for your benefit?

【Saman】I can load my goods directly. It's easy to deliver things, even big goods, like woods. I no longer need to load somewhere, but just deliver it to my destination directly. It not only saves my money, but also shortens my time. It works more efficiently.

【BTV】What else do you expect the government to provide? I think you may say visa, right?

【Saman】Yeah. You are smart. I believe if visa problem is solved, I can go out more conveniently. Like what I said just now. Visa to me is a very big problem.

【BTV】Through these years, what's your greatest achievement? Would you like to share your business experience with us?

【Saman】Since I came here, I have set up my own company. And I manage it successfully. From 2007 to 2009, the business was good. There were a lot of customers every month. But from 2010, the business is a little low because there are more and more companies. When I came here, only one fifth people of my hometown come here too. But now most people of my hometown come here. And they set up their companies too. The customers are divided to every company. So business is not as good as before.

【BTV】I think it's a challenge for you. But I believe that you can overcome it.

【Saman】Thank you! I hope so!

【BTV】My interview is over. Thank you again for your cooperation. Hope to see you again.

【Saman】I hope so. Bye-bye.

Group Members: Pan Jingjing, Wang Yujia, Li Miao

叙事记录

【BTV】下午好。我是 Monica。怎么称呼你?

【Saman】我叫 Saman。

【BTV】好的。下面我先自我介绍一下。我是一名来自浙江大学宁波理工学院的大学生。我们现在正在做一项调研,旨在了解外国人在义乌的生活和工作。所以接下来的采访中我将会问你一些相关问题,非常感谢你能抽时间接受我们的采访!请你先自我介绍一下好吗?

【Saman】好的。名字你已经知道啦。我来自伊朗,有三个兄弟,两个姐妹。

2007年，我跟朋友一起来到中国，来到义乌，在这里开了一家自己的公司。

【BTV】你的家人在哪里呢？

【Saman】我的家人全都在伊朗。我是自己一个人来到这边的。

【BTV】你多久回去一次看望你的家人？

【Saman】一年一次。只有在中国农历新年的时候，我才回到家乡和家人见上一面。

【BTV】那你一定很想念你的家人吧！他们会来这边看你吗？

【Saman】是的，那是当然，我非常想念我的家人。但是我来这边是来做生意而不是来玩的。我每天有大量的事情要做。要与客户谈判，还有许多会议。而我的家人很少有机会来看我，因为他们都有自己的事要做。所以我们一年只能团聚一次。

【BTV】远离亲人在异国他乡创业是件很不容易的事，你这样做的动力是什么呢？为什么选择义乌？

【Saman】为了让家人过得更好，我来到这里，更努力地工作。义乌小商品市场品种多样，价格合理，是理想的采购中心。

【BTV】你的事业一定很成功，我看到你的日程安排得满满的。

【Saman】嗯。我要跟客户联系谈生意。每天都有很多公司的事要处理。

【BTV】你从事什么业务？我是说你的公司主要经营什么？

【Saman】我的业务很广，主要是汽车轮胎和轮胎骨、配件之类。我有一个部门就是负责汽车轮胎和零部件的。还有其他许多方面公司也有涉及，例如：房屋装修、婴儿服装。而且我现在已经在福田市场开了一些这样的店。

【BTV】很不错！你的公司真的挺大的。你是一个很成功的商人，我认为一定会发展得越来越好的。

【Saman】谢谢。借你吉言。我也希望能越来越好。

【BTV】除了中国，你去过其他国家吗？

【Saman】许多国家，比如马来西亚、荷兰、泰国、迪拜，等等。

【BTV】说到迪拜，我听说很多中国人在那边，是吗？

【Saman】是的。在五六年前是有许多中国人在迪拜做生意。而且很多来自泰国、荷兰的人都会去那里。但是现在迪拜的生意不如从前了，并不是那么繁荣。最近，越来越多人选择印度和中国去发展他们的事业。

【BTV】这是为什么？

【Saman】越来越少的人去迪拜做生意，原因比较复杂。

【BTV】你在事业上还有什么其他困难或挑战吗？

【Saman】困难吗？有的，当然有，最大的困难是签证。这对我来说是最大的麻烦。签证对每一个外国人来说都是很重要的。如果你没有签证，出国就很麻烦。

每个外国人必须先把这个处理好。作为一个外国商人，每六个月、三个月、甚至两个月就不得不重新签证一次。

【BTV】这听起来有些不方便。办签证在其他国家是怎样的呢？也和中国一样吗？

【Saman】不，和在中国完全不同。相对来说，在其他国家获得长期签证更容易。

【BTV】那么其他国家有哪些不同呢？为什么说比中国方便？

【Saman】你可以去问问去过外国的中国人。举个例子，中国人去欧洲，签证的有效期是视情况而定的，政策更灵活，更方便。

【BTV】西方国家的签证标准是什么呢？

【Saman】这视你出行的目的而定。如果你出差，需要待上一段时间，而且确保安全，你就可以跟他们沟通让签证的可用时间变得长一点。

【BTV】听起来西方的签证是比中国方便多了。那你在中国是否遇到过签证麻烦？

【Saman】嗯，遇到过一次。有次，我和客户一起出国。在海关的时候，他们说我的签证不能用了，应该去重新办理。但是那次我很赶时间，还因此差点失去了一个大客户。

【BTV】我很抱歉听到这些。可能中国政府应当采取行动调整当前政策。到那时候签证会变得方便，你也不需要担心这个啦。

【Saman】希望那时我还在中国。

【BTV】你在这里也有好几年了，你觉得义乌和义乌人怎样呢？

【Saman】义乌是个很漂亮的城市。它是世界上最大的小商品市场，是发展商业的好地方。商品种类齐全，价格便宜。总的来说，义乌具备开拓市场的优势。而且义乌人勤劳能干，具有创新精神。

【BTV】除了义乌，你去过中国其他地方吗？

【Saman】我也去过中国的其他地方，每月我都要去上海、山东出差。总的来说，中国人是很友善的。我在那边吃饭、购物，都能感受到他们对我的尊重。这让我感觉很舒服。相比较而言，义乌的交通状况需要改善，你可以看到高峰时段到处是车。

【BTV】义乌并不完美，还有不少地方需要改善，你为什么仍然选择义乌开始创业？

【Saman】你也知道，义乌有很大的市场，这一点世界闻名。很多地方，甚至其他国家的人都到这里来采购。义乌可以提供给我一个很好的市场。

【BTV】这里的政府是否提供了好的政策让你受益？

【Saman】我可以直接运货。运输货物很容易，甚至包括一些大的货物，如木材之类，不用再像以前那样需要找个中转站卸货，而是直接送到目的地。这样不仅节省了钱，而且缩短了运输时间。工作更加高效了！

【BTV】你觉得政府还可以提供哪些政策？你是不是想说签证？

【Saman】哈哈，你真是太聪明了。如果签证解决了，出去就更方便了。就像我之前说的，签证于我而言是一个大问题。

【BTV】经过这些年的奋斗，你获得了哪些成就，可以和我们分享一下吗？

【Saman】自从来到这里，我创立了一家属于自己的公司，也经营得相当成功。从2007年到2009年，生意相当好，每个月客户都很多。但是2010年之后，生意有些淡了，因为这里的公司越来越多。我刚来的时候，我们那边只有五分之一人口来到这边做生意，而现在我家乡大部分人都过来这边开公司。那么顾客就无疑被很多公司平分了，所以公司的利润相比以前有所下降。

【BTV】这是对你的一个挑战。我相信你可以做好的。

【Saman】谢谢！我也希望自己可以！

【BTV】我的采访结束了。再次感谢你的配合。希望有机会再见！

【Saman】后会有期。拜拜！

团队成员：潘晶晶，王宇佳，黎苗

A Small City on a Large Stage

By Pan Jingjing　Supervised by Yu Xuyan & Cai Liang

Once arrived in Yiwu, I was deeply shocked at its pace of integration into an international metropolis. When you look around, high-rise buildings stand everywhere. Anyone who has visited Yiwu will certainly marvel at the bustling streets and the landscape: Is this just a small county-level city? You must wonder how they created today's miracle.

People all say that the Chinese nation is a magical nation, and indeed Yiwu can be called a real myth and miracle since China's reform and opening-up nearly thirty years ago.

Yiwu is a small city with a long history and rich cultural heritage. It has nurtured many attractions and talents. As the country's largest commodity market, the whole city is filled with a deep entrepreneurial atmosphere. "An ocean of small commodities and a paradise for shoppers" has become synonymous with Yiwu, well known throughout China and abroad. In the world's largest small commodity wholesale market, the daily trading volume becomes the "Yiwu index", known as the "wind vane" and "barometer" of the global commodity trade industry. As the world's largest commodity distribution center, Yiwu small commodity exports continue to grow. What is hidden behind the booming business? Obviously, it's the culture behind the economy and the spirit of Yiwu. The promising achievements facilitate Yiwu's rapid economic development, contributing to the rise of the Yiwu market. Yiwu people, who dare to do the things that no one did before, step out of Zhejiang, step out of China, and go to the world.

The miracle comes not only from Yiwu people's tireless pursuit but also from the support and encouragement that the local government provides for the entrepreneurs. Over the years, the Yiwu municipal government has issued many policies that encourage exports and expand the international market, such as support for export enterprises to register overseas trademarks, encouragement to export enterprises to establish overseas branches, increased credit support and so on. There is a complete set of local services in Yiwu. It is rare in the country that the Yiwu municipal government subsidies a large proportion of enterprises. This allows Yiwu to fully demonstrate the charm of "a small city on a large stage".

During the interview with Saman, I learned many interesting things. First, I found that Yiwu is a city that never sleeps. Many cars are still running on the street late at night. Early in the morning, when most people are still immersed in sweet dreams, a group of people drag themselves out of bed, overcome their sluggishness, and wash up as fast as they can. These are the hard-working and ambitious people of Yiwu.

Another finding was that in Yiwu Arab and Muslim restaurants are present everywhere. I began to realize that, in addition to the cities of Gansu, Qinghai, Xinjiang, and Ningxia Hui Autonomous Region, this is also a place where Muslim restaurants flourish. Arabs dressed in national attire can be seen everywhere on the streets. They are like Wenzhou people, where there is business, there they are. Of course, people of different colors and clothes come to do business here, so most Chinese people in the markets can speak some simple English with strong local accents for bargaining.

The most crowded night market can attract many young people. Commodities in the night market are dazzling, affordable and, diverse. Young girls are easily attracted by pendants and bracelets. At the night market, we met an enthusiastic foreign friend who agreed to be interviewed in no time and took the initiative to communicate with us. He is a businessman from Iraq, but just recently came to Yiwu due to business. This was an unforgettable night.

Sometimes we fall in love with a city with not so many reasons. A stranger's smile, a little support, a surge of enthusiasm will also suffice. Although we only stayed a few days in Yiwu, I have a special feeling for the city. I believe that under the guidance of the local government, Yiwu will radiate new vitality. Honesty, generosity and credibility will make businessmen from all over the world feel at home in this land. With the integration of the expatriates, the Yiwu people have become the people of the new era. Yiwu is writing a new commercial chapter with innovation, integrity, and entrepreneurship.

Yiwu is a small city on a large stage.

小城市,大舞台

文:潘晶晶　指导教师:喻旭燕　蔡　亮

初到义乌,我深深地惊诧于义乌融入国际化大都市的脚步。放眼望去,幢幢高楼耸立。只要去过义乌的人,一定会为其街道上车水马龙的景观而感到惊叹:这只是一个县级小城吗?你一定会想他们是如何创造今天的奇迹的。

世人都说:中华民族是一个神奇的民族,而义乌确实可以被称为是当代中国改革开放30多年以来真正的神话和奇迹。

义乌是一座具有悠久历史和深厚文化底蕴的小城市。这里孕育了不少人才,留下了不少名胜古迹。义乌作为全国最大的小商品市场,整座城市充满了浓浓的创业气息。“小商品海洋,购物者天堂”成了义乌的代名词,享誉中外。在这个世界最大的小商品批发市场里,每日交易量汇聚成“义乌指数”,被称作全球小商品贸易的“风向标”和“晴雨表”。作为全球最大的小商品集散地,义乌小商品出口量不断增大。而这发达的商业背后隐藏着的是什么呢?显然,是经济背后的文化,是“勤耕苦学,刚正勇为”的义乌精神。义乌人的奋发有为成就了义乌经济的飞速发展,促成了义乌市场的崛起。敢为天下先的义乌人走出了浙江,走出了中国,走向了世界。

奇迹的创造不仅源于义务人孜孜不倦的追求,也源于政府对创业者的支持和鼓励。多年来,义乌市政府颁布了很多关于鼓励出口和拓展国际市场的政策,如:支持出口企业到境外注册商标,鼓励出口企业到境外设立分支机构,加大信贷支持力度等等。义乌当地有完善配套的服务体系。大量企业在义乌享有政府津贴,这在其他地方很少见。如此,才让义乌充分展现了“小城市大舞台”的魅力。

而采访期间也有不少有趣的事。首先我发现义乌是一个“不眠城”。深夜,大街上依然是车来车往。清晨,当大多数人还沉浸于甜美的梦乡时,就已经有那么一群人拖着疲惫的身躯,咬牙战胜清晨的困意,以最快的速度起床洗漱。这就是勤劳有斗志的义乌人。

另外,义乌有很多阿拉伯和穆斯林餐厅。我这才意识到,不仅仅是在甘肃、青海、新疆和宁夏回族自治区的城市里穆斯林餐馆鳞次栉比,义乌也是如此。大街上随处可见身穿民族服装的阿拉伯人,我不得不感叹他们和温州人一样,有买卖的地方就有他们的身影。当然了,在义乌也随处可见各种肤色各种打扮的外国人。因此,小商品市场里的中国人大都会说一点简单又带有地方口音的英文,用来讨价还价。

人来人往的夜市最吸引年轻人。夜市上小商品琳琅满目,物美价廉,款式多样，让人爱不释手。年轻女孩子很容易被吸引买些挂坠、手链之类的饰品。在那里，我们碰到了一个热情的老外，很爽快地答应了我们的采访，主动与我们交流。他是来自伊拉克的商人，而最近刚好因商出差到义乌。这是一个令人难忘的夜晚。

有时候爱上一座城不需要太多理由，一个陌生人的微笑，一点微薄的支持，一股跳动的热情便也足矣。尽管在义乌只有短短几天，可是对这座城市已有种特殊的情感。我相信义乌在政策的指引下将焕发新的活力。诚信、包容、信誉让四方商客在这一方热土倍感宾至如归，外来商客融入义乌，成了新时代义乌人。富而思进的新时代义乌人，在创新发展、诚信经营中，正勤劳快乐地书写着新的商业篇章。

义乌，小城市，大舞台。

Teign

Teign: Yiwu, a City Established on a Market

义乌,建在市场上的城市

Teign comes from Malaysia. He is on the staff of a company in Shanghai and also the boss of a shop in Malaysia. This enthusiastic young man was once an exchange student in Shanghai Jiao Tong University. He studied Chinese during his stay and is good at listening, speaking, reading and writing. He has been in China for seven years. To collect commodities for his shop, he comes to Yiwu every July.

代振来自马来西亚,既是上海某公司的职员,也在马来西亚经营着自己的生意。热情大方的他曾是上海交通大学的交换生,在一年的交换生生涯中,代振苦学中文,现在听说读写都没有问题。他在中国已经7年了,每年7月都为他的店来义乌采购商品。

Yiwu, a City Established on a Market

By Teign

Transcript of the Interview:

【BTV】Hi, Teign.

【Teign】Hi!

【BTV】We are the team of "Beyond the Voices". We are from Ningbo Institute of Technology, Zhejiang University. We are doing a research aimed at acquiring a basic understanding of the living and working demands of foreign expatriates in Yiwu.

【Teign】OK, I will tell you the things I know. But I have to say maybe I don't know much about your questions.

【BTV】Thank you! Since you know the purpose of our project, let's just start our interview. Could you tell us where you're from?

【Teign】Malaysia.

【BTV】Malaysia is a beautiful country. How many years have you been here in Yiwu?

【Teign】Seven years, I mean I have been in China for seven years, but I come here in Yiwu every year in July for collecting the products.

【BTV】Do you live in China with your family?

【Teign】No, my family is in Malaysia. I came to China for study.

【BTV】You came to China for study? Where did you study?

【Teign】Shanghai Jiao Tong University. I was an exchange student.

【BTV】Since you were an exchange student in Jiao Tong University, why did you choose the occupation of a businessman?

【Teign】I do business just for part-time. This is part-time. I'm not doing this full-time. I have a shop in Malaysia, so I buy some products and someone send them to my country. My parents help me to manage my shop in Malaysia.

【BTV】Oh, I see. You are a part-time boss. So, what's your main occupation?

【Teign】Haha... Yes, I am a part-time boss and my main occupation right now is marketing management. I'm a trading specialist in Shanghai. I work and live in Shanghai now.

【BTV】Since you are working and living in Shanghai now, how much do you know about Yiwu?

【Teign】About Yiwu... I know Futian, Chouzhou Beilu, and... another is Binwang Market. Also I've been to the Night Market, Huangyuan Market and the riverside.

【BTV】Wow, you know the Night Market?

【Teign】Yeah, I know the Night Market. It's very crowded there, and I've heard that many people in Yiwu said that the quality of things there are not good, but I think it is okay. Some products are okay and some are not good. Even I heard that some foreign people like me like to buy things and, place an order there.

【BTV】I agree with you. I've heard that, too. I can see that you know almost all the markets in Yiwu. Do you know the changes in the markets in Yiwu?

【Teign】Not much. Although I've lived in China for seven years, I come to Yiwu only once a year. I know the Binwang Market and Futian. When I came to Yiwu the first time, there were many shops in Binwang Market and... maybe only one district in Futian Market. Now, the Futian Market is bigger, and Binwang Market does not exist. Well, changes of the market in Yiwu are quite good, very convenient.

【BTV】Yes, these are convenient. You seem to know the changes in Yiwu very well. So, what do you think is convenient in Yiwu?

【Teign】Of course the market in Yiwu is convenient. We can find anything here, and all products are cheap. That's why I came to Yiwu. And it's not as crowded as Shanghai. And... the hotels are cheap, so it may reduce my cost here. Like Hai Yang. It's not really expensive, it's okay. That I can say.

【BTV】Can I understand this as the living environment or condition in Yiwu is good?

【Teign】Yes, that's what I mean.

【BTV】Thank you! Then how about the food in Yiwu? Can you make any comment?

【Teign】Okay, food? For me it is convenient, because there are lots of Indian restaurants here. I like Indian food. There are many Indian restaurants near the Night Market. Haha... that's why I know the Night Market. I went there for eating the first time. So, it's good and it's all right now I think.

【BTV】Thank you! I understand the food environment is good and convenient. And do you like the people here?

【Teign】Yeah! I mean all over China. I like China. I like Chinese people. So, I like the people around here. People in Yiwu are different from that in Shanghai. People here are quite busy. They are all businessmen. They are friendly. The business partners treat me well. Yes, they are good. And... people here are very hard-working. People in Shanghai like shopping. I think people here like working. That's what I know.

【BTV】So, do you have local friends here?

【Teign】Eh... not exactly. People like doing business here. They are quite busy. As I come here not very often, only once a year, the people I know here are all business partners. We do business and talk about business. But I have Chinese friends in Shanghai. Some are my classmates and some are my colleagues. We play football together when we do not work in the company.

【BTV】Okay, then. Although you do not come here often, what do you think of the security in Yiwu?

【Teign】I think it's secure, but some Chinese people don't think so. You don't live in Yiwu, right?

【BTV】I live in Yiwu.

【Teign】Okay, so how do you think of the security in Yiwu? Do you feel it is safe in Yiwu?

【BTV】Yes, I feel it is good. It's safe here.

【Teign】It's good, yes, because Chinese people do not like violent people.

【BTV】Compared with your country...

【Teign】It's much safer, of course. I mean all the countries I've been to: England, some other countries in Europe, India. I think China is safer.

【BTV】Wow, you've been to many countries. So, do you know some similar markets in other countries or cities like Yiwu?

【Teign】In other countries... Well, I've been to, some countries in Europe, India and so on. They are probably some places I've been to, but only in Yiwu, I come for business. They do have markets in other countries, but the market in Yiwu is bigger. The Futian Market is the biggest. Of course, if I want to buy products, I come to Yiwu. I can find everything here.

【BTV】Okay. Can you use one word or one sentence to describe Yiwu?

【Teign】One word to describe Yiwu? It's very hot. Not only the weather but also the people. Well, business like. I think it is really profitable. You can make really good deals here. Because as for us, since I came here two years ago, I was buying products here and selling to my country. You can get products really cheap and you can sell for really high prices. For example, earrings, you can buy them for 2 RMB or 3 RMB, then you sell them for like 30 RMB. Do you know that? It's a big profit. That's the main reason I came here. Then, I want to use the word "market" to describe. There are different markets here. I think the whole city is a city established upon market. We can see markets all around the city. That's what I say and that's one thing I really like here.

【BTV】Thank you! I think you have given us your deep understanding of this city. Finally, can you give your best wishes or some advice to this city, Yiwu?

【Teign】Well, I like people and the markets in Yiwu. I wish Yiwu a promising future with more markets. I think Yiwu has done very well. Thank you!

【BTV】Thank you very much for your cooperation. You've provided us much useful information for our book. I wish you better business, a better life in China!

【Teign】Thank you!

Group Members: Chen Yuan, Si Wenjun, Zhao Yanyan

叙事记录

【BTV】你好,代振!

【Teign】你们好!

【BTV】我们是来自浙江大学宁波理工学院的“用声音叙事”团队。我们正在做一个调研,旨在了解在义乌的外籍人士的生活和工作环境。

【Teign】好的,我会告诉你们我所知道的,不过不得不告诉你们我可能知道得不多。

【BTV】谢谢!既然你已经知道了我们这个活动的目的,就让我们开始吧。可以告诉我们你来自哪里吗?

【Teign】我来自马来西亚。

【BTV】马来西亚是一个很美丽的国家吧。你来义乌有多少年了呢?

【Teign】7 年。我的意思是我来中国已经 7 年了,不过我每年 7 月会来义乌采购商品。

【BTV】你们一家都住在中国吗?

【Teign】不是的，我的家人都在马来西亚，我之前来中国是来上学的。

【BTV】你来中国上学？在哪儿呢？

【Teign】上海交通大学，我是交换生。

【BTV】既然你曾经是上海交通大学的交换生，为什么选择了商人这个职业呢？

【Teign】我经商只是业余的，并不是全职。我在马来西亚有一家商店，所以我来这儿采购商品然后让人送到我的国家。我的父母在那儿帮我管理。

【BTV】哦，我了解了，你是一个业余老板。那你的主要职业是什么呢？

【Teign】哈哈，是的，我是个业余老板。现在我的主要职业是营销管理，我是上海外贸公司的一名贸易专员。现在我在上海工作生活。

【BTV】既然你现在在上海工作和生活，那你对义乌了解多少呢？

【Teign】关于义乌……我知道福田市场、稠州北路，然后是宾王市场。我还去过夜市、篁园市场、江滨。

【BTV】哇，你还知道夜市？

【Teign】是啊，我知道夜市。那里人很多很拥挤，我还听很多人说那里的商品质量不好，不过我觉得还行。那里有些商品很不错，有些质量有待提高。我还听说过有像我这样来义乌采购的外国人在那里买东西下订单呢。

【BTV】嗯，是的，我也听说过。听你的回答似乎你已经知道义乌全部的市场了。那你知道这些市场这些年来的变化吗？

【Teign】知道得不多吧。虽然我在中国已经 7 年了，不过我一年只来义乌一次。好吧，我知道宾王市场和福田市场。第一次来义乌时，宾王市场里还有很多的商铺在营业，福田市场好像也才只有一个区，而现在，宾王市场已经不营业了，福田市场则变得更大了。义乌市场的变化还是很不错的，很方便。

【BTV】是的，是很方便。你似乎对义乌这些年的变化还挺了解。那么，你觉得义乌有哪些方面是便利的呢？

【Teign】毫无疑问，义乌的市场是便利的。我们可以在那儿买到任何东西，而且全部商品的价格都很便宜。正因如此，我来义乌采购。义乌也不像上海那样拥挤。而且……这里的酒店很便宜，这为我节省开支，比如“海洋酒店”，那里就不是很贵，还可以。这些是我知道的。

【BTV】我可以把这些理解为义乌的居住环境和居住条件还不错吗？

【Teign】是的，我就是这个意思。

【BTV】谢谢！那义乌的饮食怎么样呢？你如何评价？

【Teign】好的，饮食？对我来说挺方便的，因为这边有很多印度餐厅。我喜欢吃印度风味的美食。夜市边上有很多印度餐厅，哈哈，这就是为什么我会知道夜市了，第一次去那边就是去吃饭的。所以我觉得还不错，挺好的。

【BTV】谢谢！我把它理解为义乌的饮食环境还不错，挺便利的。那你喜欢这里的人吗？

【Teign】喜欢啊！我的意思是全中国的人们，我喜欢中国，所以我也喜欢这儿的人们。义乌与上海不同。这儿的人都很忙，他们都是生意人，但都很友好，我的生意伙伴都对我很好。是的，他们很好。而且大家都很勤劳，不像上海人，他们爱逛街，这儿的人们爱工作，这些是我知道的。

【BTV】那你有当地的朋友吗？

【Teign】这个……不是很确切。这儿的人都喜欢做生意，他们都很忙。我也不是经常来，一年只来一次，所以我在这儿认识的都是生意上的伙伴，我们只一起做生意，谈论生意。不过我在上海有中国朋友，有的是同学，有的是同事。我们会在工作之余一起踢足球。

【BTV】很好啊！虽然你不是经常来义乌，你觉得这边的治安怎么样呢？

【Teign】我觉得很好！但有些中国人不这么认为。你们不住在义乌对吗？

【BTV】我住在义乌。

【Teign】好吧，那你认为义乌的治安如何呢？你觉得义乌安全吗？

【BTV】是的，我觉得很好，我觉得义乌治安很好。

【Teign】是的，很好，因为中国人都不喜欢暴力。

【BTV】比起你的国家……

【Teign】中国安全多了，这是肯定的。我的意思是在我去过的一些国家里，比如欧洲的一些国家、印度等，我觉得中国安全多了。

【BTV】哇，你去过很多国家。那你知道有哪些国家或城市有像义乌这样的市场吗？

【Teign】在别的国家……我去过欧洲的一些国家、印度等。去过的这些地方可能也会有市场，不过只有来义乌是来做生意的。别的国家的确也有市场，不过义乌的市场更大，福田市场是最大的。毫无疑问，需要采购商品的时候我肯定会来义乌，我能在这儿买到任何东西。

【BTV】好的，那你能用一个词或一句话来描述义乌这座城市吗？

【Teign】用一个词描述义乌？"热"，不仅仅是天气很热，义乌的人们也很热情。在这做生意，利润可观，我们都做得很顺利。自从两年前来这儿，我就在这儿采购，再把商品卖到我的国家。我们可以用绝对低的价格买到产品，再以很高的价格卖掉。以耳环为例吧，你可以用 2 至 3 元买到再以 30 元卖掉，你知道吗？这是很大的利润。这是我来这里很主要的原因。然后呢，我想用"市场"这个词来描述义乌。这里有各式各样的市场，我觉得这就是一座建在市场上的城市，市场遍地，这是我非常喜欢这里的一个原因。

【BTV】谢谢你为我们阐述了你对义乌这座城市很深入的理解。最后，你可以给义乌这座城市献上你最美好的祝愿或提出一些建议吗？

【Teign】好的，我喜欢义乌的人民和义乌的市场。我希望义乌有更辉煌的发展，扩建更多市场。我觉得义乌已经做得很好了，谢谢！

【BTV】感谢你的合作，你的合作为我们的书稿提供了很多有用的信息，希望你的生意越来越好，在中国的生活越来越好！

【Teign】谢谢！

团队成员：陈圆，斯文骏，赵艳艳

小组成员在讨论实践方案

Chinese Business Card: Yiwu; Yiwu's Business Card: Futian

By Chen Yuan Supervised by Yu Xuyan & Cai Liang

Yiwu is my hometown. I took part in the project "Beyond the Voices", with profound love for my city. I took it as an opportunity to know it better from the view of expatriates in Yiwu. Unexpectedly, I came to make many foreign friends and understood more about my hometown from their perspectives during this survey.

If someone asks why such a small city can attract so many foreign businessmen, the answer must be the market, without any question. The first market in Yiwu was called Yiwu Small Commodity City, and then it was Yiwu Binwang Market. Now, the Small Commodity City has transformed into Yiwu International Trade City. It is the market that brings all kinds of commercial opportunities to this city. What interests me is that "Futian" has become an alternate name to Yiwu. More foreign businessmen prefer to call the market "Futian" rather than the "International Trade City". Statistics show that the market now covers over 4.7 million square meters, and has 7,000 shops, including 16 basic categories, 4,202 kinds and over 170 million articles. There are five districts which sell different kinds of products. In order to promote the exchange between different countries, there are international halls to sell all featured commodities from all countries. What is more, if you visit every shop for three minutes, it will take you one and a half years to visit all the shops given eight hours a day. Can't such a large market attract large amounts of foreign businessmen?

I interviewed a foreign businessman from Malaysia during the survey. His Chinese name is Dai Zhen. He expressed his love for this city with full enthusiasm. Although he didn't come to Yiwu frequently, he knows a lot about the market. He knows that the market has moved many times before finally settling in "Futian". Actually, the Yiwu commodity market has become the international center for the daily circulation, exhibition and information for consumable goods through changing sites five times and extending the area nine times. Now, the commodities from the Yiwu market have radiated to all countries and areas of the world. When chatting, I recognized that a small city is going global in Dai Zhen's eyes. We also recognized that Yiwu market has evolved from "buying and selling across China" to "buying and selling across the globe". Now, either in the Yiwu market or on the exotic street, different countries blend characters; either in the classroom of public school or at cultural sites, or where people travel and entertain, foreigners who have different skin colors and different languages can be seen everywhere. It is apparent that Yiwu has become an immigrant city.

Teign has said that Yiwu is a city established upon a market. When we asked him to use one word or one sentence to describe Yiwu, he used "hot" first, and then "market". In his point of view, the weather here is hot and the people here enthusiastic and friendly. Furthermore, he considered Yiwu as a city established on a market. Wherever he goes, there is a market. He can buy whatever he wants in this city. Certainly, Yiwu has been regarded as the biggest small commodity wholesale market in the world by the United Nations, the World Bank and other international authorities. This legendary city has been approved as a comprehensive reform spot for international trade, and its development has opened a new chapter in international trade.

Through the interview, I have formed a new image of Yiwu from the perspective of expatriates working or living here. I firmly believe that the publication of *Beyond the Voices: Yiwu, Here I Am* will be a great boost for Yiwu's reputation.

In Yiwu, for 365 days a year, all kinds of businesses are booming, just like economic blood continuously circulating, making the town's business much stronger and dynamic. I feel so proud of being a native of Yiwu. Yiwu is just like a share of auspicious stock, and I believe that it will maintain its trajectory and lead development in the future with a global perspective!

义乌国际商贸城二区市场

中国名片——义乌;义乌名片——福田

文:陈 圆 指导老师:喻旭燕 蔡 亮

义乌是我的家乡,怀着对家乡的爱,我参加了这次暑期活动——“用声音叙事:义乌,我来了”,旨在了解外国人眼中的义乌。这次的活动,让我结交了很多外国朋友,让我从他们眼中更好地了解了自己的家乡。

要问为什么义乌这座不起眼的小城能吸引这么多外商?毋庸置疑,答案一定是市场。从最早的义乌小商品城,到后来的义乌宾王市场,再到现在的义乌国际商贸城,就是它们为这座小城市带来了各种商机。有意思的是,虽然如今的市场已更名为义乌国际商贸城,但更多的外商愿意称它为“福田市场”,在他们眼中,“福田”已成为义乌的代名词。在市场的宣传册中可得知,现在“福田”市场的经营总面积达470余万平方米,商位7000个,经营16大类4202个种类1亿7千多万种单品。市场一共有五个区,每个区经营种类不同。为增进与各个国家的交流,市场还专门设有国际馆,专卖来自各个国家的特色商品。有人曾做过一个有趣的计算,那就是如果你在每个商位前逗留3分钟,按每天8小时计算,需要一年半才能逛完。如此大的一个市场能不引来各国的外商吗?

活动期间,我采访的是一名来自马来西亚的外籍商人,他的中文名叫代振,采访中他热情地向我讲述了他对义乌这座城市的热爱之情。虽然他并不常来,但他对义乌市场的了解并不少。他知道义乌市场经历了一次次的搬迁,最终在福田落户。的确,通过了解义乌市场的历史可以知道,通过五易其址、九次扩建,它才成为国际性日用消费品流通中心、展示中心和信息中心。如今,市场商品已辐射到世界各个国家和地区。闲聊中,我还从代振眼中看到了一个国际化水平显著提升的城市正跨步走向全世界。采访之余,我们还专门走访了义乌市场历史的讲解员,我们了解到,义乌市场正从“买全国货、卖全国货”向“买全球货、卖全球货”转变。如今,无论是在万商云集的义乌市场,还是在闪烁着各国文字的异国风情街;无论是在市民学校的课堂里,还是在义乌人相邀出游、同堂而乐的文化场所,处处都可以看到操着不同语言,有着各种肤色的外国人。看得出义乌已成为一座名副其实的“移民城市”。

代振说这就是一座建在市场上的城市,让他用一个词或一句话来描述义乌,他用的第一个词是“热”或者“热情”——这里天气炎热,这里的人们十分热情友好;第二个词便是“市场”,他觉得这整座城市就像建在市场上一样,走到哪儿都是市场,走到哪儿他都能找到自己想要的东西。不错,义乌是全球最大的小商品集散中心,是被联合国、世界银行等国际权威机构确定的世界上最大的小商品批发市场。这座传奇城市在2011年获批国际贸易综合改革试点，开启了新篇章。

在此次采访过程中，我从外籍人士眼中领略了一个崭新的义乌形象。我相信，《用声音叙事：义乌，我来了》的成功出版一定会成为义乌宣传的助推器，吸引来自更多国家的外商。

义乌，这里一年365天，汹涌的商潮周而复始，为经济发展注入新鲜血液，使商城义乌脉动有力，活力流传。作为一名义乌人，我很骄傲。义乌就是一支潜力股，相信她会一如既往，以全球化的视野，蓬勃发展！

Orlov

Orlov: I Just Decided

我心已定

Orlov Volodymyr, from Ukraine, is a typical businessman. He has been in China for twelve years and in Yiwu for eight years. He set up a company near the Yiwu International Trade City (more popularly known as the Futian Market), which sells products from the market to Ukraine. Although it is a small company, he is confident to run it successfully. My first impression of this European gentleman is that he is friendly, hardworking and full of vigor and enthusiasm. In addition, he can speak Chinese very well.

奥罗芙·弗拉迪米尔,来自乌克兰,是一位典型的商人。他来中国已经 12 年,其中在义乌就生活了 8 年之久。他在义乌国际商贸城(福田市场)的附近成立了一家自己的外贸公司,将该市场的产品销售到乌克兰。规模虽然不大,但是他有信心做成功。第一次见到他,我就觉得这位来自欧洲的绅士十分友好、勤奋,浑身散发着活力和热情。此外,他还能说一口流利的中文。

I Just Decided

By Orlov

Transcript of the Interview:

【BTV】Hello, Orlov Volodymyr. We are from the Ningbo Institute of Technology, Zhejiang University. Thank you for granting our interview. Would you please talk a little bit about yourself first?

【Orlov】My name is Orlov Volodymyr, and I am from Ukraine. I've been in Yiwu for nearly eight years.

【BTV】What is your first impression of Yiwu?

【Orlov】I came to Yiwu eleven or twelve years ago. I thought it was a small city. You know, it had not set up the Futian Market, yet. I was eager to know such a small city, so I just decided to start my business in Yiwu.

【BTV】Why?

【Orlov】Though Yiwu is a small city, it can create miracles.

【BTV】Would you please use one word to describe Yiwu?

【Orlov】I don't know. I just know I am used to living here.

【BTV】What do you think of the weather in Yiwu?

【Orlov】It's okay. I can accept it.

【BTV】Which aspect of Yiwu attracts you most?

【Orlov】Oh, you see, it is convenient to drive in Yiwu. And it's not crowded in the street.

【BTV】Have you got used to the Chinese food now?

【Orlov】At the beginning, I couldn't eat any Chinese food, and I didn't find places to eat. Because Chinese food is too peppery. However, I can eat anything now, and there are all kinds of food in Yiwu.

【BTV】Can you cook Chinese food?

【Orlov】I can't. But I enjoy eating it. Haha...

【BTV】Did you bring your family here?

【Orlov】Of course! We also traveled to other cities. But now I am living here by myself.

【BTV】Is language a problem for your life or work here in Yiwu?

【Orlov】Yes, it was difficult to speak and write. Though it is not very good now, it's a little better than before. Also, I think Chinese is a beautiful language.

【BTV】You speak Chinese so fluently. I want to know how you learned Chinese.

【Orlov】I just learned Chinese when I communicated with the local businessmen. In fact, I don't speak it very well.

【BTV】How wonderfully you speak! Well, do you know the Yiwu spirit?

【Orlov】I'm sorry. I just know people in Yiwu are very hard-working.

【BTV】You mentioned one aspect of the Yiwu spirit. It includes industriousness, braveness, honesty and inclusiveness.

【Orlov】So that explains it.

【BTV】Did you set up your own company?

【Orlov】Yes.

【BTV】What kind of business do you do?

【Orlov】I do foreign trade.

【BTV】Really? What kind of products does your company sell?

【Orlov】We sell all the things found in Yiwu International Trade City.

【BTV】Wow! All?

【Orlov】Yeah, all.

【BTV】So great. Well, where do your products mainly go?

【Orlov】Of course we sell to Ukraine.

【BTV】How did you start to know Yiwu?

【Orlov】I came to China with my boss twelve years ago, and I came to Yiwu.

【BTV】How many staff members are there in your company now?

【Orlov】About seven or eight people.

【BTV】Are they local people or Ukrainian?

【Orlov】All Chinese people.

【BTV】Is your company close to the Yiwu International Trade City?

【Orlov】Yes, it is just in the International Trade Building.

【BTV】And could you tell me what was your reason for starting a business in Yiwu?

【Orlov】Because there is such a big market that other cities don't have. The Yiwu International Trade City has a huge potential to develop. Only in Yiwu, people can buy more goods or buy less goods.

【BTV】I agree with you. Well, have there been any changes in Yiwu during these eight years?

【Orlov】I think before it there was a small city which was just like a farm village. Now, it is an international global city.

【BTV】How about the changes of the Yiwu International Trade City during these years?

【Orlov】Of course, it has changed. The air-conditioner used to take a long time to come on when it was too hot or too cold before. Now, it comes on immediately. For us, if customers feel uncomfortable, they may not want to do business. Don't you think so?

【BTV】As the saying goes, "The customer is God." And did you have some unforgettable experiences during these eight years? For example, did you have bad experiences when you carried out business with the local businessmen?

【Orlov】It's hard to say good or bad. But sometimes they don't know what I say.

【BTV】What do you mean?

【Orlov】I just say simple words, but they think different meanings.

【BTV】For example?

【Orlov】For example, I tell a manufacturer to make the same item every time. You see, it's easy, and I needn't explain. The first product is a sample, and it takes a long time to make the sample. The manufacturer says that he can do it. However, after several times, they still make a completely different product.

【BTV】Yiwu is known as "an ocean of small commodities and a paradise for shoppers", what have you achieved here?

【Orlov】Because Chinese people are smart in doing business, I figured that I would gradually become smart when I do business with them and other foreigners, and my company will develop better. So I just decided to live here. Haha...

【BTV】Are there other difficulties when doing business with the local businessmen?

【Orlov】The time of delivery. Sometimes, we agree on a delivery time, but they are late.

【BTV】They are unpunctual, right?

【Orlov】Yeah, it's a small problem to them, but it's a big one to us.

【BTV】So, what do you think is the most important quality when you do business with people?

【Orlov】Do what you say. The behavior and language should be consistent.

【BTV】You know, there are many foreigners in Yiwu, and they have contributed greatly to the local economy. Would you introduce your friends to Yiwu to start their businesses?

【Orlov】Of course. I have done this.

【BTV】Okay. How much do you know about the policies of the local government? Which aspects do you think should be improved to help foreign businessmen in Yiwu?

【Orlov】I know few policies. But I think the prices are a problem. They were cheap, and we could bargain several years ago. Now, they become much higher, and we can't bargain any more.

【BTV】Are you worried about prices?

【Orlov】Yeah. The manufactures make products with higher profits than before.

【BTV】If you were the executive of Yiwu City, which aspect of Yiwu should be improved most?

【Orlov】There is a problem in Yiwu. It's difficult to get visas.

【BTV】Is it inconvenient?

【Orlov】Yes, it's very inconvenient. We have to renew our visas every one or two months. You know, there are many foreign friends. No matter how short or long we stay, we have to renew the visa often.

【BTV】Is it the same to renew a visa whether you stay a long time or a short time? Do you want to prolong the time for visas?

【Orlov】Yes, yes! As a matter of fact, the government could decide the length of visas on the basis of the reason for coming to Yiwu. Sometimes, I want a three-month visa, but the government gives me a one-month visa.

【BTV】Will you stay in Yiwu to develop your company for a long time?

【Orlov】It's hard to say. Maybe I will stay in Yiwu for ten years.

【BTV】Thank you very much for agreeing to our interview. I wish you a nice stay in Yiwu, and your suggestions are very meaningful for improving the city's image. Thanks.

【Orlov】You are welcome.

Group Members: Liu Li, Shang Mengdan, Liu Lu

叙事记录

【BTV】你好，奥罗芙·弗拉迪米尔，我们是来自浙江大学宁波理工学院的学生，感谢你能接受我们的采访。首先，能简单地介绍一下你自己吗？

【Orlov】我的名字叫奥罗芙·弗拉迪米尔。我来自乌克兰，在义乌已经8年了。

【BTV】请问你对义乌的第一印象怎么样？

【Orlov】我十一二年前来义乌，觉得义乌是个小地方。当时还没有开发福田市场呢。当然，也就是这么一座小城市吸引了我，才让我决定留在这里。

【BTV】为什么这么说呢？

【Orlov】因为义乌虽小，但是它能够创造奇迹。

【BTV】如果用一个词形容义乌，你觉得是什么样的词？

【Orlov】不知道，我只知道我习惯了在义乌的生活。

【BTV】那太好了！你觉得这里的气候怎么样？

【Orlov】挺好的。我还比较适应这里的天气。

【BTV】你觉得义乌在哪方面最吸引你？

【Orlov】义乌的交通很方便，不会堵车。

【BTV】那你现在习惯吃中国菜吗？

【Orlov】刚开始我都吃不惯，而且不知道去哪吃，因为到处都是辣的东西。不过，现在我什么都能吃！而且，在义乌，什么吃的都有。

【BTV】那你会做中国菜吗？

【Orlov】不会做。但是我很享受吃中国菜！哈哈。

【BTV】那你以前带家人来这里玩过吗？

【Orlov】当然有！我们还去过其他城市旅游。不过我现在是一个人在这里。

【BTV】你觉得不熟悉中文对你来义乌发展是一种障碍吗？

【Orlov】开始的时候说不来，也写不来。虽然现在我的中文也不是很好，但是比以前好点。并且，我认为它是很美的语言。

【BTV】你中文说得很流利，我想知道你是通过什么方式学习中文的？

【Orlov】就是自己在做生意的时候和当地人多交流。其实我中文说得不是很好。

【BTV】哈哈。你已经说得很棒了！那么，请问你知道义乌精神吗？

【Orlov】对不起，我不太清楚。我只知道义乌人都很勤奋。

【BTV】你说对了其中一点。义乌精神包括"勤耕好学，刚正勇为，诚信包容"。

【Orlov】哦，原来如此。

【BTV】那你现在是自己开公司吗？

【Orlov】对。

【BTV】做什么样的生意呢？

【Orlov】做外贸。

【BTV】是吗？那你的公司一般销售什么种类的产品呢？

【Orlov】所有义乌国际商贸城的东西。

【BTV】哇，所有的？

【Orlov】是的。

【BTV】太棒了。那贵公司的产品主要销售到哪里？

【Orlov】当然是销售到乌克兰那边了。

【BTV】请问，你是通过什么方式知道义乌的呢？

【Orlov】我12年前和老板来中国工作，然后就来到了义乌。

【BTV】你的公司现在有多少名员工？

【Orlov】大概七八个人。

【BTV】他们都是当地人还是乌克兰人？

【Orlov】都是中国人。

【BTV】那你的公司离义乌国际商贸城近吗？

【Orlov】很近的，就在国贸大厦。

【BTV】那我想知道是什么原因让你来义乌投资做生意呢？

【Orlov】因为其他城市没有像义乌一样有一个这么大的市场。义乌国际商贸城发展潜力巨大。只有在义乌，人们买货可多可少。

【BTV】我很赞同你的看法。那么，你来义乌8年，觉得这8年中义乌有没有什么改变呢？

【Orlov】义乌啊，我感觉以前的义乌真的是一个农庄一样的小地方，现在它正成为一个走向全球的国际城市。

【BTV】那义乌国际商贸城有没有什么变化呢？

【Orlov】市场当然也有改变。以前天气太热或太冷，空调启动都要很长时间，而现在，一会儿就开启了。这都是为了照顾客人，如果客人觉得不舒服的话，我们可能生意也比较难谈成功。是吧？

【BTV】俗话说顾客就是上帝。那你在义乌8年有没有发生过什么让你难忘的事情呢？比如在和当地人做生意的过程中，有没有发生过不愉快的经历呢？

【Orlov】没有什么不好的。就是有时候义乌人不太领会我的意思。

【BTV】为什么这么说呢？

【Orlov】就是我简单明了地说一件事，他们理解得却完全不一样。

【BTV】比如？

【Orlov】比如，每次我对生产商说制造一模一样的东西，很简单的，不用解释。第一个产品就是样品，样品做出来要花很长时间。商家说可以做一模一样的，但是往往做很多次还是不一样。

【BTV】义乌被誉为“小商品海洋，购物者天堂”。你觉得你在此做生意有什么收获呢？

【Orlov】因为中国人做生意很精明。我在和中国人还有许多来这里的外国人做生意的同时，能够让自己逐渐变聪明，这样公司也会发展得越来越好。所以我才决定留在这里。哈哈。

【BTV】那你觉得和当地人做生意还有没有什么困难的地方呢？

【Orlov】还有就是送货时间的问题。有时候，我们定好了交货时间，可他们总是晚交货。

【BTV】不守时，对吗？

【Orlov】对。虽然对于他们是很小的问题，但是对于我们却是很大的问题。

【BTV】那你觉得人和人做生意的时候，最重要的品质是什么？

【Orlov】说到做到。要言行一致。

【BTV】你知道义乌有很多外国人，他们对当地的经济做出了巨大的贡献。那么，你会介绍你的朋友来义乌发展他们的生意吗？

【Orlov】当然。我已经在这么做了。

【BTV】好的。那你对当地政府的政策了解多少？你认为有没有什么方面需要加强，从而更好地服务在义乌的外籍人士？

【Orlov】我知道的政策不是很多，但是我觉得价格是一个问题。以前价格很便宜，还可以很厉害地还价。但是，现在价格越来越贵，都不让还价了。

【BTV】现在要为价格担忧，是吗？

【Orlov】是的，现在生产商的利润变高了。

【BTV】假如你是义乌市市长，你觉得哪方面是最应该改善的？

【Orlov】义乌的确存在问题，那就是办签证的问题。

【BTV】是不方便吗？

【Orlov】对，很不方便. 我们不得不每一到两个月就去续签一次。你知道的，这里外国人很多，但是无论他们来义乌时间是长是短，都要经常去续签。

【BTV】就是说无论你们住多长时间，签证的时间都是一样短，你是想延长签证的时间，是吗？

【Orlov】是的。实际上，政府可以依据外国人来义乌的原因，决定签证时间的长短。有时候我想办三个月的签证，但是他们就给我办了一个月。

【BTV】你会长期在这里发展你的公司吗？

【Orlov】这也说不定。至少10年之内我还是会留在义乌发展的。

【BTV】非常感谢你接受我们的采访。希望你在义乌能够生活愉快。当然，你的建议对改善义乌城市建设有很大的意义。

【Orlov】不客气。

团队成员：刘李，尚梦丹，刘璐

So Said, So Done

By Shang Mengdan Supervised by Yu Xuyan & Cai Liang

A great portion of foreign businessmen in Yiwu are from the Middle East. When a man with a typical European look came to the gate, I was deeply attracted. Wearing a tee shirt, a pair of jeans and slippers, he didn't carry a bag or bring a translator. He stepped evenly. After a series of observations, I guessed that he might come to the Yiwu International Trade City to buy some goods, so I quickly decided to interview him. Different from other foreign businessmen whom I had asked, he was more than willing to do my interview. After conversing, I knew that he was the head of a foreign trade company near Futian Market. After the interview, I came to know an honest Ukrainian businessman who practices what he preaches.

Orlov mentioned his unhappy experiences with local businessmen. They always prolong delivery time to which both sides agree. The concept of punctuality reflects the differences between Chinese and Western culture. I read a story in the newspaper that said if you ask overseas drivers who serve Chinese tourists in Europe, "What is your deepest impression of Chinese tourists?" 90% of them will answer that Chinese are the least punctual tourists. There are five reasons to explain this: vanity, arrogance, sluggishness, intentional ideas, and force majeure. The reasons are facetious except for the last one. These ideas make them believe, "Being late shows I am the most important", "I would rather have someone wait for me than wait for them" and so on. Though unpunctuality is a minor bad habit, it reflects a variety of deep-rooted bad habits of the Chinese people. The tourists going abroad represent a small part of Chinese people; however, they are windows for foreigners to know about China. In contrast, being punctual is already rooted in Western culture. According to a book, entitled *Be a Punctual Person*, punctuality is a quality to which Westerners generally pay attention. There is a saying in German, "Punctuality is the politeness of kings." In my opinion, being punctual is an important indication of honesty.

In modern society, many people break their promises sometimes. Having integrity, aligning what one says with what one does, should be a major value, thus one can win respect from others. Moreover, doing what one says should be the principle of one's actions.

In the long run, as a businessman, if you are not honest, you will gradually lose your customers. People like to cooperate with trustworthy people. Therefore, when I asked Orlov how to deal with the problem about prolonged delivery time, he said that it was okay the first time, but he would not work with them after that. Thus it can be seen that businessmen should be brave enough to shoulder the responsibility of their words and behavior, and they should stress credibility and keep their word. It is important to businessmen and also to all of us.

By interviewing Orlov, I realized more about the differences between Chinese culture and Western culture. Yiwu is famous all over the world for its Futian Market with excellent quality, reasonable price and great variety of goods. If local businessmen in the Futian Market welcome visitors from all over the world in a more rigorous way and with an honest attitude, the commodity market will embrace a better future!

言出必行

文：尚梦丹　指导老师：喻旭燕　蔡　亮

在义乌，来商贸城做生意的大多数外国人都来自中东。当这个典型的欧洲人踏进一区大门时，我立刻被深深吸引住了。休闲T恤，牛仔短裤，一双拖鞋，没有带包，也没有带翻译，走路速度不紧不慢，于是我猜测他可能是来义乌商贸城采购的。我立刻上前采访他，与前几天碰到的几个外籍商人不同的是，Orlov非常乐意接受我的采访。原来Orlov是福田市场附近一家外贸公司的老板。通过采访，我见识了一位崇尚诚实守信，言出必行的乌克兰生意人。

谈到和当地人做生意的经历，Orlov表示，虽然已经与商家谈定了送货时间，但是仍旧会发生商家推迟送货的不愉快经历。守时观念的不同反映了中西文化的差异。我曾经在报纸上看到过一篇报道：如果你在欧洲询问为中国游客开车的当地司机："中国客人给你留下的最深印象是什么？"90%的回答是中国人不守时。分析迟到的原因，有以下五点：虚荣、傲慢、懒散、蓄意而为以及不可抗力。除了最后一点，其余四点都很滑稽可笑。综合而成的结论是"后到才表示自己的重要"、"来得晚的人，必然是重要角色"、"宁可让别人等我，不可我等人"，等等。不守时只是个小毛病，它却反映了中国人的种种劣根性。出国旅游的人只是中国人中的一小部分，但却是外国人看中国的窗口。相比之下，守时观念已经植根于西方文化。有一本书名为《做一个守时的人》，书中这样描述：守时是一种素质，西方人一般都讲究遵守时间。德国也有一句话："守时是王者之礼。"在我看来，守时也是诚信的重要表现。

在现代这个社会，很多人经常言而无信。诚信守诺应成为主要价值观，从而赢得他人的尊重。此外，言行一致更应成为做人的准则。

从长远来看，不诚信的生意人终将失去顾客。人们都喜欢与可靠的人合作。当问及Orlov怎么处理商家送货推迟的问题时，他的回答是，如果一次这样没关系，但是次数多了可能就不会与之合作。可见，作为一个生意人，一定要勇于对自己的言行负责，生意人讲究的就是一种信誉，讲究的就是说过的话要算数。不仅做生意应当讲究信誉，我们做任何事情都要说到做到，要勇于担当。

此次对Orlov的采访让我对中西方文化差异有了更深刻的了解。义乌以其物美价廉、品种齐全的福田市场享誉全球。如果在经营之道上，能以更加严谨的作风和诚信的姿态迎接八方来客，必将创造一个更加辉煌的未来！

第三章

Love in Yiwu:
Love Brings Me back Home

情定义乌：义乌有爱，心有了家

导言

义乌本是中国大地上一座再普通不过的小城，可是，在历经了岁月的洗礼之后，她却一跃成为沟通中外经济的国际商业枢纽。这一巨大变革要归功于义乌市政府和义乌人民大胆地抓住机遇试点改革。当然，义乌经济的发展也离不开义乌外籍商人。他们奔波于国际市场，建立起国际贸易交流平台，同时也为义乌美好蓝图画下不可或缺的一笔。在这群外籍商人里有这样一群人，他们从初识义乌到熟悉义乌，从驻足义乌到扎根义乌，从选择义乌到恋上义乌。他们不再匆匆在各国奔波，他们不再只是把义乌当成临时停靠点，他们不再感到漂泊于异乡。在这里，他们有了牵挂，有了家；在这里，他们体验着不同的文化，尝试着逐渐融入成为其中一员。他们为义乌带来的不仅是经济的发展，更有文化的交流。这些都是中国走向国际市场不可或缺的要素。

本章中的几位外籍商人多数已在义乌生活了许多年，他们见证并陪伴着义乌一路成长。他们在义乌有了自己的公司、自己的贸易点，从自己国家吸引了越来越多的顾客来到义乌。他们促进了中外经济沟通交流，加快了义乌发展的步伐。同时，他们在义乌有了自己的中国妻子和可爱的混血宝宝。不同文化碰撞出的火花也为他们的生活带来了无穷的乐趣。对于生意，他们有着自己的感悟。他们认为生意固然重要，但陪伴家人的时间却万万不能因此而减少。金钱有价，但亲情却是无价的。肤色有异，国籍不同，但有价值的生活理念是无国界的。这些义乌外籍人士已然为他们的第二个家——义乌在国际市场的持续发展做出了巨大贡献；同时也为中国继续开拓国际市场奠定了坚实的基础。

Bady

Bady: My Indissoluble Bond with Yiwu

我和义乌的不解之缘

Bady is from Algeria. He is thirty years old. He came to China with his uncle and then started his business in Yiwu in 2005. Bady owns a company where there are many Chinese employees. As the company gradually grows, he gains the benefit for both his career and family. He married a Chinese girl, and they had their cute Chinese-Algerian baby. Having lived in China for nearly eight years, Bady has a deep understanding of Chinese culture as well as the means of doing business in China. As for his attitude towards life, he is quite distinct from others as he thinks more highly of health and family rather than money. So Bady is a common but special foreign businessman in Yiwu.

Bady 来自阿尔及利亚，今年 30 岁。2005 年他跟随叔叔来到中国义乌做生意，开了一家自己的公司，雇用了很多中国员工。随着公司的不断壮大，Bady 事业爱情双丰收。他与一位中国女孩喜结连理，又共同孕育了一个可爱的混血宝宝。在中国待了 8 年之久，Bady 深谙中国经商之道，也对中国文化有着深刻的见解。Bady 有着不同于一般商人的生活态度，他认为健康和家庭远比金钱重要得多。这就是 Bady，一个平凡而又特殊的义乌外籍商人。

My Indissoluble Bond with Yiwu

By Bady

Transcript of the Interview:

【BTV】Excuse me. Nice to meet you. We are college students from Ningbo Institute of Technology, Zhejiang University. We are now studying businessmen in Yiwu. Can you spare half an hour for our interview?

【Bady】Sure, please.

【BTV】My name is Cookie. What is your name?

【Bady】Bady, B-A-D-Y, Bady.

【BTV】Wow, interesting. It sounds like "body". Where are you from, Bady?

【Bady】Algeria, in North Africa.

【BTV】It is far from China. How did you come to Yiwu?

【Bady】My uncle took me here in 2005. He was a client here and worked with Chinese. He took me here and asked me to make my own choice to make a living, that is, whether to do business individually or run a company. Then I chose to set up a company and start my business step by step. Since then, my life is closely connected with Yiwu.

【BTV】You have been here for a long time. What attracts you most in Yiwu?

【Bady】My business and also my wife.

【BTV】Your wife?

【Bady】She used to be a translator in my office. She is a Chinese girl. We got married last year.

【BTV】Wow, what is the difference between Chinese girls and girls in your own country?

【Bady】They are all the same. No difference but just language and the culture.

【BTV】So are there any difficulties in communicating with your wife?

【Bady】Sometimes. We don't communicate very smoothly. She doesn't speak my language really well. I don't speak Chinese well. But actually it is not so difficult.

【BTV】Algerians also speak Arabic, right?

【Bady】Yes, Arabic is our first language, the second one is French, and English is the third language. I can also speak some Chinese. I think English is very very easy to acquire, but it is difficult to learn Arabic and Chinese.

【BTV】Have you been living here in Yiwu for the entire eight years?

【Bady】All the time here.

【BTV】So what's your business? Would you tell me something about your company?

【Bady】I have a very big office here with 15 translators. We have nearly 200 regular customers, who come from Algeria to buy products from me and then sell them in our own country.

【BTV】That's great. And have you come across difficulties in your business?

【Bady】I think no difficulties. It runs smoothly.

【BTV】Always smoothly?

【Bady】Yes. The company is good and the taxes here are lower thanks to the policy. The taxes are really high in my country.

【BTV】That's wonderful. So why did you choose Yiwu as the place to start your business?

【Bady】Because of the big market. And people from Algeria all come here to buy from me. They have kept buying from me for nearly eight years since I set up my company.

【BTV】Do you mean there are many businessmen who come from your country?

【Bady】No, not many. A lot of customers but just a few businessmen, maybe 15 or 20.

【BTV】Having a lot of customers really helps your company, right?

【Bady】Not all the time. I mean there is a special month for Algerians just like Chinese New Year. For Algeria people, during that month, they don't work. Every one of them stays at home and eats. We also have another more important festival in our country which is hard to be explained in English. Then, we have parade and eat beef at the festival.

【BTV】Which country do you think has the largest number of people in Yiwu?

【Bady】I am not sure. There are many kinds of people here from all over the world. Maybe most of the foreigners are from Pakistan and some countries in south Africa.

【BTV】There are really so many foreign businessmen. What advantages do you think Yiwu can provide you businessmen?

【Bady】The market. The markets here are concentrated. There are many big markets in Yiwu with a full range of products, so it is convenient for us to purchase and do business. You know, there are also many restaurants and hotels here in Yiwu for foreigners. The hotels are cheap, and the restaurants offer me food for nearly eight years. And the prices of many products in Yiwu are much lower than those in my country, so we purchase from here and sell in Algeria.

【BTV】The products here are cheap but how about the quality?

【Bady】Actually, not so good. I can understand from the low price. It will be much better if good price accompanies good quality.

【BTV】Yes. That is correct. So the products have been at low prices all the time?

【Bady】No, there are some changes. It is more expensive now. In 2011, the economic crisis of Europe affected the economy of many countries in the world, so the value of Euro goes down and RMB is going up. The influence manifests itself slowly but gradually changes the Yiwu market. Sometimes it doesn't have any influence on the rich people but it really makes a difference to the ordinary people.

【BTV】Right. There is now a popular saying among Chinese that the prices of all materials are going up except the salary. It is not so easy for us Chinese to buy a house due to the high price.

【Bady】I know. The housing price especially in some big cities such as Shanghai, Beijing are really sky-high, so is it in Yiwu.

【BTV】Then how about in your country? Are the houses expensive there?

【Bady】No, not expensive. But I decide to live here, so I need to buy a house in Yiwu. You know. It is difficult for us foreigners to buy a house not because of the price but the policy. So thanks to my wife, she doesn't need to be limited by the policy of Yiwu government when buying a house.

【BTV】Different places have different policies, so what other cities have you been to in China apart from Yiwu?

【Bady】Many. I have been to Kunming, Guangzhou, Beijing and Hangzhou.

【BTV】Guangzhou is also a modern city for business. What do you think is the difference between Yiwu and other business cities?

【Bady】Yiwu is the best because it has not only the convenient market but also low prices. And the food is delicious here. They prepare the food which satisfies my taste. And the restaurants, hotels here are much cheaper. For example, a room in the hotel in Guangzhou is 500 yuan but it is only 100 or 200 yuan in Yiwu. Maybe it is also because Yiwu is a small business city.

【BTV】Have you found any other cities that are much better than Yiwu for business?

【Bady】No.

【BTV】No? Okay. So what do you think of the Yiwu people?

【Bady】You know, there are good people and bad people in every place. It is the same in Yiwu. Most people here are kind and friendly.

【BTV】And what other aspects don't you like in Yiwu?

【Bady】Maybe the traffic. In Yiwu, almost each family has two cars on average. But Yiwu is such a small city, so the streets are always full of cars. The traffic is always heavy, so it is really dangerous for people to cross the road. In some places, there are no traffic lights.

【BTV】It is a problem. The drivers won't stop when there are pedestrians crossing the road. Maybe it is because they are trying to save time to do business. Well, how about the food here? Do you like Yiwu food?

【Bady】I can eat but only a little of Chinese food. In my country, we have chicken and potatoes. In fact, the rice in China is nice. It's my favorite. But the dishes are sometimes too spicy and sometimes too light. I don't know. My wife wants me to join them and entertain myself with Chinese food. But it takes some time, I think.

【BTV】So where do you have your meals? Cook at home or go to restaurants?

【Bady】Go to restaurants. There are no cooking utensils for me to cook my food, and my wife doesn't cook.

【BTV】Okay, maybe you could eat rice with meat, such as beef and chicken. And would you mind sharing something with us about your company?

【Bady】Okay, we have big offices here in Yiwu and all of my employees are Chinese.

【BTV】What are your standards for hiring Chinese staff?

【Bady】It depends. My wife will give the first interview, and then our company will train the candidates. After one or two months' training, we will decide which one to be the staff of our company.

【BTV】So do you have some suggestions to graduates who want to be hired by foreigners?

【Bady】It also depends. If you want to be a secretary, you need to be skillful in the basic computer software. And if you want to be a translator, it is not enough for you to master the foreign language well. You are required to know how to do business, too. But in any case, you should be fluent in your foreign language. Just work hard.

【BTV】That's interesting. Translators are also responsible for doing business for the company.

【Bady】Yes, but don't worry. It is not difficult. Our company will teach them and train them.

【BTV】I can't agree more. It is better for us to learn more to make us more competitive. Life is a struggle. Recently, our president mentioned the "China Dream" that all Chinese can realize their dreams through their own struggle and hardwork. Would you mind sharing your Yiwu Dream with us? For example, do you expect your company to become the biggest company in Yiwu?

【Bady】No, it is not my dream. Of course, I hope my company will be running smoothly all the time. But I would rather be a good husband and a good father. You can get lost money back but never the family. Business is important but health is the most important, right?

【BTV】Yes, you are right. Thank you very much for accepting our interview. Your suggestions are very meaningful to our project. I wish you a nice stay in Yiwu. I wish you good heath, a happy family and a successful business.

Group Members: Zheng Yuan, Lin Mengmeng, Luo Qian

叙事记录

【BTV】您好，打扰了，我们是来自浙江大学宁波理工学院的学生。今天我们正在进行有关义乌商人的调研活动。您能否抽出半个小时，让我们对您做个采访呢？

【Bady】好的。

【BTV】您好，我叫 Cookie，您呢？

【Bady】我叫 Bady。

【BTV】您的名字真有趣，乍一听还以为是 body（身体）呢。对了，您来自哪个国家？

【Bady】我来自阿尔及利亚，在非洲北部。

【BTV】那儿离中国很远呢，您为什么选择来义乌？

【Bady】2005 年的时候我叔叔带我来到中国。当时他来义乌采购，和中国商人打交道。他带我来到这儿，让我自己做选择，是自己做个体生意还是开公司。我最后决定开公司，开始一步步慢慢地经营。从那时起，我就与义乌结下不解之缘。

【BTV】您已经在义乌待了这么长时间了。您觉得什么最吸引您呢？

【Bady】我的生意吧，还有我的妻子。

【BTV】您的妻子？

【Bady】嗯，我的妻子。她之前在我的公司当翻译，是个中国女孩，我们去年结婚了。

【BTV】很幸福呢！您觉得中国女孩和阿尔及利亚女孩有什么不同吗？

【Bady】没有，都差不多。真要说不同，就是语言和文化吧。

【BTV】您和您的妻子在交流上有困难吗？

【Bady】有时候有点困难。我们的交流并不是很流畅。她阿拉伯语说得不太好，我中文说得不太好。不过，总的来说，困难不是很大。

【BTV】阿尔及利亚人说的是阿拉伯语，对吗？

【Bady】是的，阿拉伯语是我们的母语，第二语言是法语，第三语言是英语。我也会说一点中文。我觉得英语是非常容易学的一门语言，而阿拉伯语和中文都很难学。

【BTV】您在中国整整 8 年了，这 8 年您都在义乌生活吗？

【Bady】是啊。

【BTV】请问您从事什么样的业务？能介绍一下您的公司吗？

【Bady】我在义乌有个很大的办公地点，公司里有 15 个翻译，还有两百多个老客户。这些客户都来自我的祖国阿尔及利亚。他们来我的公司采购义乌商品，然后回国销售。

【BTV】真是不错。那您在生意上遇到过什么困难吗？

【Bady】没有吧，挺顺利的。

【BTV】一直都很顺利吗？

【Bady】是啊，公司运营良好，这儿的税也比较低，这都多亏了义乌的政策。在我们国家，税可就高多了。

【BTV】那很不错。您为什么选择在义乌创业？

【Bady】因为义乌拥有广阔的市场。从阿尔及利亚来的商人都是从我这儿采购的，自从我成立公司的那一天起，他们就一直是我的固定客源，整整 8 年了。

【BTV】也就是说你们国家有很多人来这儿经商？

【Bady】商人不多，顾客比较多。商人大概也就 15 到 20 个。

【BTV】一直有这么些客源，您的公司一定收益良多。

【Bady】他们也不是整年都来。阿尔及利亚每年都有一个特殊的月份，就像中国的新年一样。在那个月里，他们不工作，只待在家里弄点吃的。当然除了这个节日我们还有一个更重要的节日，我不知该如何用英文来表述，一般我们会通过游行、吃牛肉来庆祝。

【BTV】那么您认为到义乌来的外国人中来自哪个国家的人最多呢？

【Bady】我不太确定，这儿的外国人太多了，来自世界各地。我想或许大多来自巴基斯坦或者非洲南部的一些国家。

【BTV】外国商人确实很多啊。就您而言，您觉得义乌为外籍商人们提供了什么样的有利条件？

【Bady】义乌的市场。义乌的各大市场都比较集中，而且货品齐全，有利于我们采购和经商。同时，义乌有许许多多的餐馆和旅馆为外商们提供服务。这儿的旅店价格公道，8年来，我经常光顾这儿的餐馆。还有，义乌的商品比我们国内的商品要便宜很多，所以我们来这儿进货然后在自己国家销售。

【BTV】价格很便宜，那质量呢？

【Bady】质量一般，但是能理解，毕竟价格低，要是既能价格低又能质量好就再好不过了。

【BTV】嗯，也对。那这几年商品的价格一直都这么便宜吗？

【Bady】有变化。价格在逐渐上涨。2011年那场欧债危机影响到了整个世界的经济。欧元贬值，人民币升值。这一点一点地在影响着义乌市场。可能对很多富人来说没有太大影响，但对普通人来说影响就大些了。

【BTV】是啊。现在中国流行着一种说法，那就是所有东西都在涨价，只有工资不涨。现在，中国人买房真是越来越难了。

【Bady】我听说过。特别是在一些大城市，比如北京、上海的房价就特别高。其实义乌的房子也很贵。

【BTV】你们国家的情况怎样，那里的房子贵吗？

【Bady】不贵的。但我打算以后就住在中国了，所以就要在这儿买房。但外国人在义乌买房并不容易，不是因为价格而是因为很多政策的限制。幸亏我的妻子是中国人，不用受这些购房政策的限制。

【BTV】不同的地方政策也不同。除了义乌您还去过中国的哪些城市呢？

【Bady】挺多的，昆明、广州、北京，还有杭州。

【BTV】广州也是一个有名的商业城市。您觉得义乌和其他商业城市相比有什么不同？

【Bady】我觉得义乌是最好的，它不仅有便利的市场还有价格低廉的商品。而且，这儿的食物真是美味啊，很满足我的味蕾。这儿的餐馆和旅店的消费也挺低的。比如：同样是住旅馆，在广州一晚需500元，而在义乌只需一两百元。也许因为义乌只是个小城市吧。

【BTV】就经商而言，您觉得有没有哪个城市比义乌更好的？

【Bady】嗯，没有。

【BTV】没有？那您觉得义乌人怎么样？

【Bady】客观地讲，每个地方都有好人和坏人，义乌也是这样。这儿大多数人还是非常友善热情的。

【BTV】那义乌还有哪些地方您不太喜欢的呢？

【Bady】或许是交通吧。在义乌，几乎每个家庭都有两辆车。义乌这个城市不大，车一多道路自然就拥挤了。车流量一大，行人过马路就很危险，况且有些地方根本没有红绿灯。

【BTV】这的确是个问题。每次行人过马路的时候，车辆都不愿意停下来让行人先通过。可能这些人都要赶着做生意，耽误不得。那这边的食物呢，您喜欢吗？

【Bady】有些中国菜我能吃一点儿。在我们国家，一般都吃鸡肉和土豆。其实中国的米饭挺好吃的，是我的最爱，但中国的菜常常不是太辣就是太清淡。我也不确定，我妻子总想让我多多享用中国菜，但我觉得自己可能还需要适应一段时间。

【BTV】您平常在哪儿吃饭？出去吃还是在自己家里做？

【Bady】出去吃。家里没有合适的厨具来做我的家乡菜，而且我妻子也不会做饭。

【BTV】好的，也许您可以米饭就肉吃，比如牛肉和鸡肉。您愿意和我们说些关于您公司的情况吗？

【Bady】可以啊。我们有很大的办公场所，我的员工都是中国人。

【BTV】贵公司对中国应聘者有何要求？

【Bady】视情况而定吧。首次面试由我妻子把关，之后公司会对应聘者进行培训。经过一到两个月的培训之后，我们再决定他们的去留。

【BTV】对于那些毕业后想去外企工作的中国学生，您有什么建议吗？

【Bady】各个岗位要求不同。比如应聘秘书，你就需要熟练运用基本的电脑软件。要当翻译，那你不仅要熟练掌握外语还要会做生意。无论如何，熟练的外语能力是必需的。希望他们加油努力！

【BTV】翻译还要会做生意？这挺有意思的。

【Bady】是啊，但是其实不需要担心，这不难，而且公司会进行培训的。

【BTV】这点我非常同意。学得越多就越有竞争力。我们需要为生活不断奋斗。前段时间我们的主席提出了“中国梦”，就是中国人民可以通过不断努力奋斗最终实现美好的梦想。您能和我们说说您的义乌梦吗？比如您希望您的公司发展成为义乌最大的公司吗？

【Bady】这不是我的梦想。当然我希望公司能一直这么顺利地经营下去，但我更希望做一个好丈夫、好父亲。钱失去可以再赚,但家人却不可以忽略;生意固然重要,但健康才是根本,不是吗?

【BTV】您说得很对。感谢您能接受我们的采访,您的建议很有意义。希望您在义乌生活美好,也祝您身体健康、家庭美满、工作顺利!

团队成员:郑媛,林萌萌,罗倩

Capital of Commerce: a Vivid Oriental Pearl

By Zheng Yuan　Supervised by Zhang Jingyan & Cai Liang

The first time I arrived in Yiwu, I found it was quite different from what I had imagined. It lacked the luxury of commercial cities. The houses there seemed to have been built hundreds of years ago and experienced a lot so that they all seemed to be worn-out. The traffic there was so poor that the roads were very crowded with many cars. It was so hot there that the pedestrians passed by in a hurry. That was my first impression of Yiwu. It was such a crowded small town with hot weather, so how could such a small place be so well-known around the world as an international commercial center? With strong curiosity, I began an interesting journey in this charming city to uncover this mystery.

At the beginning of our activity, we arrived at the commercial center of Yiwu. It is better to see for ourselves rather than to hear from many others. We finally visited the heart of Yiwu. There are long rows of booths connected to each other, which are divided by the different types of goods that each row of booths sells. If you want to figure out the mystery of the success of Yiwu, the International Trade City should be your first and best clue. There is hardly a city which has such a big-scale market inside or outside China. It not only has a majestic appearance, but also has various kinds of goods displayed on the counter. You can buy everything you want there, anything that you can think of, but sometimes you may complain that the markets are too big for you to walk around. After you have walked quite a long way to the end of a long corridor, another one will appear in front of you again. That's why the foreign businessmen choose Yiwu to do their business: thanks to the big market and the variety of goods and the convenience Yiwu offers them.

Everyone enjoys themselves picking souvenirs and gifts in this well-known market due to the low price and the abundant types. It is not so easy for us to have a chance to interview the foreign businessmen because they are all occupied with their business and hurrying about. Sometimes they don't even want to do a questionnaire. In addition, there are few foreigners in the morning. They will not go to the market until one or two o'clock in the afternoon because of the differences in rest time. I still remember how my kind interviewee, the handsome thirty-year-old Algerian man, made a joke about himself when he said that he was such a crazy man that he was sober late at night but sleepy in the day, sleeping in the morning and getting up in the afternoon. Then, he liked to thank his Chinese wife's tolerance of the cultural difference between them. When afternoon comes, the number of foreign businessmen grows in the market. We keep coming across foreign businessmen now and then. Most of them have a translator with them. An interesting phenomenon is that the translator in Yiwu should be qualified in business as well as foreign languages. Usually, they are required by their bosses to conclude a business transaction by themselves. Where there is a need, there is a market. Many foreign companies have training classes for the translators on business in order to meet the demand. All the businessmen coming here make good deals in the market due to the price, which is also one of the major attractions of Yiwu.

It is very tiring to walk through such a vast market, and the Yiwu government has already noticed the problem and come up with a wise approach which is to offer free bus rides to and from the market to drop off and pick up the busy businessmen at these endless rows of booths. Meanwhile, many vendors with their carts of food and drinks will appear inside the market. When they are hungry or thirsty, there is no need for them to spend lots of time finding a restaurant. They can just buy the food from the vendors anytime they see them. It is very convenient for them to stop a vendor, eat fast food, and then continue their way. After all, "time is money", especially for businessmen. Every little convenience helps them do business, and that is where the charm of Yiwu lies.

When night falls in Yiwu, my favorite time comes. It is exciting to find that it looks quite different from the daytime. The pedestrians do not hurry along with serious expressions; the temperature is not so high. There are still many people on the road, but they are all relaxed with a smile on their faces as they slow their paces. Foreigners with various skin colors sit in the coffee bars, smoothie bars and lounge bars. In such a casual and comfortable atmosphere, we find it easy to seize the opportunity to ask for interviews, and these kind foreign friends accept our invitations straightforwardly. In Yiwu, in just one block, we could find many restaurants especially designed for foreigners. These restaurants are the resorts for foreigners. If one is in a remote place, one will always suffer from troubles about food. Many foreigners cannot get used to Chinese food, so these foreign restaurants here just satisfy their taste. No matter where they are from, in

Yiwu, they can find the taste that belongs to them and get their favorite food. It is also the charm of Yiwu. Meanwhile, the hotels here are cheaper but just as comfortable as those in their own countries, which is another charm of Yiwu. After a busy day, foreigners like to relax in the lounge bars, which is quite different from Chinese people. All of these conveniences greatly satisfy their needs, and they are not alone because there are many other fellow businessmen. Yiwu makes them feel at home. That's why they like to come here regardless of the long distance. Is there anyone who doesn't like to feel at home?

Actually, they still come across troubles in this place. The traffic is convenient but too many cars cause problems; the international market is so charming, but it would be much better if tax policies could be adjusted. Then it would facilitate trade and build friendlier relations among them. Nowadays, Yiwu has become a well-known international market for small commodities, which benefits not only Yiwu but China and the rest of the world. We all know that there are still problems waiting to be solved by the joint efforts of the Yiwu government and people. Some policies could be implemented to improve the traffic and adjust the taxes. What matters most is to enhance the citizens' quality of life and improve the city's appearance as well as develop the economy in order to bring about a bright future to Yiwu as a perfect commercial capital.

Yiwu is a relatively unknown small city, but it is also an international bond of exchange between China and the world. Many people come here because of its name, its convenience and its considerable charms. If you are a businessman, come here, and Yiwu will give you many opportunities for trade; if you are not a businessman, come here and slow down your hurried pace to experience the fascinating exotic nightlife of Yiwu. Therefore, it is Yiwu, the capital of commerce for the Chinese and the vivid oriental pearl for the world.

商业之都——璀璨的东方明珠

文：郑　媛　指导教师：张静燕　蔡　亮

初到义乌，这个城市与我想象中的不太一样。它没有一般商业都市的豪华，却有着像是历经了数百年的风雨冲刷的沧桑。错落的楼房在路边排开，许多墙上都留有斑驳的岁月痕迹。大大小小的车辆来来往往，为原本就并不宽阔的道路添上了几分拥堵。艳阳高照，炙烤着大地，街上行人来去匆匆。这就是我对义乌的第一印象：一个炎热拥挤的小城。为什么一个本应籍籍无名的小城能够成为沟通中外经济的国际商业枢纽呢？怀揣着满满的好奇心，我在这个神秘而又充满魅力的城市开始了一番有趣的探秘之旅。

活动伊始，我们来到了义乌的商业中心。百闻不如一见，在高楼大厦林立的市中心，我们终于见到义乌的心脏——那连在一起的几片商业街区，是按照销售产品的种类来划分的。要来义乌探寻经商秘籍，首选就是这里的国际商贸城了。义乌有如此庞大的市场，这在国内乃至世界也是少有的。商场外观宏伟不用说，商品更是琳琅满目。柜台上各式各样的商品，只有你想不到，没有你买不到的。明亮干净的直廊好不容易走到尽头，拐角又是另一条长廊，似乎要走很久，才能把这儿逛遍。这就是为什么那些外籍商人长途跋涉来到这个小城的原因之一吧，便利的购买来源、数不尽的商品让人挑花了眼。

人人都说来义乌就要带回一些纪念品，因为在这个闻名遐迩的国际小商品市场，商品种类丰富，价格也便宜。商场内来往的外籍商人很多，大都行色匆匆。莫说采访，有些连做一份问卷调查的时间都没有。因为中国人和外国人有着不同的作息时间，所以外籍商人一般都在下午一两点才会到商场进行采购。记得我的采访对象，那个三十而立的阿尔及利亚帅哥笑着称自己太疯狂，总是白天疲倦，半夜清醒，言辞之中非常感谢他的中国妻子愿意和他磨合这个文化冲突。酷热的中午过后，商场中的外国人逐渐多了起来，总是迎面便是三三两两一群，他们大部分都带着一个翻译。在义乌当翻译，光会翻译是不够的，还得帮助老板谈生意，这是件有趣的事情。经常会有很多外籍老板单独让翻译负责一笔生意，谈下业务。当然他们也有针对翻译的相应商业培训。真是哪里有需求，哪里就有市场，这也是时势所趋吧。因为这诱人的价格，来这里采购的商人都是成批购买，这也是吸引他们到来的原因之一。

在偌大的商场里不断穿行，总是十分考验脚力的。义乌市政府早就考虑到了这一点，在各大商场之间设立了免费巴士，穿行于商场之间。商场之中有推车叫卖的小商贩，小车子里有便餐和饮料。人们不需要走很远找餐馆解决伙食问题，在谈生意的时候直接拦下餐车，吃份便餐便可继续了。这些都省了很多时间。时间就是金钱，有时候一个城市的魅力就在于这些小细节。

等到夜幕降临，义乌又是一幅全然不同的面貌了。我最喜欢夜晚的义乌。人们不再行色匆匆、表情严肃，骄阳也已歇下。行人依旧来来往往，不同的是，他们放慢了步伐，放松了心情，脸上都带着笑容。路边的咖啡馆、奶茶吧、休闲吧，坐满了不同肤色的外国人，他们都以一种悠闲的姿势斜靠着，面容轻松自在。这样的氛围当然也很适合闲聊、适合交朋友、适合采访。这些友善的外国朋友爽快地接受了我们的邀约。光是一条街上，我们就路过好多家外国餐厅。这些都是义乌外籍商人休闲的好去处。在异国他乡，饮食常常会有很多困扰，许多外国人都不习惯中国食物，而这些外国餐馆恰好满足了他们的味蕾。无论他们来自哪里，这里都有属于他们口味的餐馆，这也是义乌的迷人之处。包括大大小小的旅馆，很多也都价格实惠、环境舒适，相较他们国家便宜许多。在忙碌了一天之后，许多休闲吧是外籍商人最喜欢的地方，这也是他们与中国人的不同之处。这些饮食住宿的便利都让外商的需求得到了很大的满足，再加上他们能在义乌找到自己的同胞或具有相同文化的人，这些都给他们带来了家的感觉，所以他们都愿意从世界各地来到这儿。毕竟，谁不喜欢往“家”跑呢？

有时他们在这个“家”里也会遇上一些困扰。比如交通虽然便利，但车辆太多；国际小商品市场是如此吸引人，但如果中国和他们国家的关税政策能稍微调整一下，那么两国之间的贸易往来将源源不断，友好邦交也会更加稳固。现今的义乌已然发展成为中外闻名的国际小商品市场，惠及义乌、惠及中国，也惠及整个世界。但是这里仍存在瑕疵，需要义乌市政府和义乌人民的共同努力来完善。义乌市政府可以出台一些政策改善交通、调整关税，最重要的是在注重经济发展的同时，也要注意义乌城市面貌，进一步提高公民素质风貌，建立一个更完美的商业之都。

这是个籍籍无名的小城，这也是个沟通中外经济的国际枢纽。因为它的便利，因为它无微不至的周到细节，许多人慕名而来。如果你是商人，那么来义乌看看，这里有很多商机；如果你不是商人，那么也来看看，放慢你匆匆的步伐，体验一下义乌热闹且具异国风情的夜景。这就是义乌，中国人眼中的商业之都，外商眼中的东方明珠。

Ahmet Turan

Ahmet Turan: Dreams in China

我的梦，在中国

Ahmet Turan is from Turkey and has been in China for more than seven years. He runs his own business in Yiwu with branches in both Shaoxing and Hong Kong. Ahmet is a person with sharp ideas and creative thoughts, and he, who married a Chinese girl, has his own dreams in China. He has a dream for a better family, for a better world; there is no war and everybody is in peace.

阿曼特·特朗，来自土耳其，在中国已经待了7年之久。他在义乌拥有自己的公司，并且在绍兴和香港开了分公司。阿曼特是一个很有想法并且富有创新思想的人。他娶了一个中国姑娘为妻，并且拥有自己的中国梦。他希望他的家庭更加美满、世界更加美好；他希望战争停止、世界和平。

Dreams in China

By Ahmet Turan

Transcript of the Interview:

【BTV】Thank you for your great support to our project. I hope we can have a nice talk. We know that you were interviewed last year by our classmates, and you're very interested in our project. First, would you mind giving us a brief introduction of yourself?

【Ahmet】Yes. My name is Ahmet. I'm from Turkey. I've been here for about seven years.

【BTV】That's quite a long time. How about your company?

【Ahmet】My company was also set up seven years ago.

【BTV】Is your company in Yiwu?

【Ahmet】Yes. In Yiwu and Hong Kong.

【BTV】Why did you come to do business in Yiwu? Which aspect of Yiwu attracts you most?

【Ahmet】For business. I mean, just for business. If Yiwu didn't have Futian Market, I would not be here.

【BTV】So how did you find out about Yiwu?

【Ahmet】Actually, I followed some of my friends. They did business earlier than me. I got married in Hong Kong. It's about ten years.

【BTV】Is your wife a Chinese woman?

【Ahmet】Yes. She is from Hong Kong. Before I came to Yiwu, I was in Hong Kong. We traveled from Hong Kong to Turkey, so I developed some relationship with China. When I came to Yiwu for the first time, some of my friends suggested that I stay here. That's why I'm here now.

【BTV】Do you have any children?

【Ahmet】Yes, a girl and a boy.

【BTV】What about your family? Are they also living in Yiwu?

【Ahmet】Sometimes. But they are in Hong Kong most of the time.

【BTV】They must travel from Hong Kong to Yiwu a lot so it must be a little bit difficult for you to be a father.

【Ahmet】Difficult. I know that. It's difficult to be a father, a husband, a son, and it's also difficult to be a friend and a boss.

【BTV】And we know that Yiwu is a small city. What do you think of the traffic in Yiwu?

【Ahmet】Honestly, I think the traffic in Yiwu should be improved. Some people just don't obey the rules. Especially some drivers, they don't have any rules in mind. They just drive in whatever way they want. I have a car, and I drive very carefully. Sometimes, for example, when I drive across the road, and see some old people or some ladies with babies in their hands, I just wait until they pass. However, the cars behind me will always honk their horns. They don't care about other people. And of course, there are still some nice people who obey the rules. Yiwu is special; Yiwu is different from any other cities in China.

【BTV】Since you live in Yiwu, do you have your own house?

【Ahmet】No, I don't have a house for my own because the price of houses is very high here. You need a lot of money to buy a house, which I can use to buy my company two nice office rooms. So I don't need to buy a house. I just rent one.

【BTV】You are so smart and tactful. Do you like the local food?

【Ahmet】Yes, Yiwu is a good place for food. We are Muslim, and there are a lot of Muslim restaurants here. They are suitable for us. You know, Yiwu boasts two things, food and Futian Market.

【BTV】Then these are two things that attract you most?

【Ahmet】Yeah, these two things keep us here.

【BTV】Let's talk about the investment environment here. We know that there are a lot of foreigners, like you, who stay in Yiwu, doing business. There are a lot of companies in this building. Could you tell us something about your business?

【Ahmet】Yes, I do trading business here. There are many different lines of business. We deal with what our customers ask for, and we search it from the market, not only in Yiwu, but also in other provinces of China.

【BTV】Then why are you staying in Yiwu?

【Ahmet】Yiwu is like a center, you know. We also do a lot of business in other places in China. For example, my staff person Fiona, she will go to Guangzhou to look for containers, and there are many other people like me: We are in Yiwu, but our business is everywhere in China.

【BTV】Do you do international trading too?

【Ahmet】Yes, our business is global.

【BTV】Like what?

【Ahmet】Like kitchenware. We also do trading in Keqiao, Shaoxing. I have a partner in Keqiao, who is also from my country. You know that, day by day, business and other related areas are becoming more difficult. It is changing everywhere, not only in China. You must be more and more professional. In Yiwu, most of the companies are not very professional.

【BTV】What is business like in Yiwu?

【Ahmet】Not like that in Shanghai, Guangzhou, Ningbo, where there are many big and professional companies. In Yiwu, many who have some small money, come and do quick business. But actually not everyone can do international business.

【BTV】Why not?

【Ahmet】Because it's not easy to do international business. You need to have responsibility, you need to take every detail into consideration, and you must think about all steps in business, like risks. Some people try to do this kind of business; when there is a risk, and a lot of problems arise, they just run away. But I like everything done legally. In about seven years, I do my business, and I try to do everything right. For example, I pay my tax. But some people here, they don't care about rules. So I think the government needs to solve this kind of problems. It is a very important thing.

【BTV】It is an issue that has to be taken care of correctly. What has the Yiwu government done?

【Ahmet】They are changing their policies, day by day. And the rules for companies have been greatly changed. I hope things will be different and better. It will protect both our Chinese friends and us foreigners. And I think two-side benefits are more important. They must make sure that everything is in control, and it is better.

【BTV】It's like a win-win situation.

【Ahmet】Yeah. In Yiwu, people are from all over the world, and this makes Yiwu a complicated place where everybody must obey the rules. I must also obey the rules because I run my business here. It is like if people believe you, even when there is no document, they will believe you, they trust you and they do business with you and help you. So you must be good to them.

【BTV】One good turn deserves another. Does your company have any problems currently?

【Ahmet】Sometimes, of course, we will have problems. You know that Yiwu is actually a place where many problems can be solved.

【BTV】What do you mean?

【Ahmet】I mean, if you are in Yiwu, it means that you have problems and come here to solve them because in Yiwu there are many customers, many products, many companies. So you have to be careful. If not, you would meet a lot of problems here.

【BTV】What do you think of the investment environment in Yiwu?

【Ahmet】On the whole, Yiwu is a great place to do business, but sometimes I come across some people who lie to me. When they say "okay, no problem", they don't take it seriously. I love people who have responsibility, and "trust" is the most important thing in business. In Yiwu, you have to do check work frequently because maybe, at any time, suddenly, anything could happen. Some companies that really think about their future and want to become bigger and stronger will do everything right, and they are really good companies.

【BTV】Yes, I think if we only care about the short-term profit, we would not gain much. Would you mind talking about your employees? What do you think of them? And, what are your standards for hiring Chinese staff?

【Ahmet】They should not only care for the "immediate interests". I think this is the most important problem in China. Not only me, everybody have this problem now. Because conditions change, everything changes in China now. They have to think about the future, not just "the present".

【BTV】Many people just do the opposite. They see the opportunity and jump into it, but they do not even think about what to do next. Should the local government have some preferential policies to support foreign-funded enterprises?

【Ahmet】Just like what I've told you. Every day it changes. In July, the government changed their rules for foreigners. But more things should be done. I mean, people who want a better Yiwu have to be together and support each other.

【BTV】You're definitely right. Have you ever heard of the term "China Dream"?

【Ahmet】No. Tell me about that.

【BTV】It seems that everybody talks about it. The "China Dream", put forth by Chinese President Xi Jinping, is to build a moderately prosperous society and to realize national rejuvenation. Do you have your own dreams in Yiwu and in Turkey?

【Ahmet】Yes. Actually, I have dreams everywhere I go, not only here or in my own country. I have a dream for a better family, for a better world. The war stops and everybody is in peace.

【BTV】That's quite a great dream. People all over the world dream about that. What is your company's blueprint?

【Ahmet】Many companies here are exporting things from China to other countries, like Turkey and Europe, but I find China a large market, and I plan to import to China. I want to have my own brands in China, and I want to sell Turkey ice creams in China. There are way too many things that can be done in China, but we must focus. If one cannot focus on his business, he cannot get a good result.

【BTV】You are right. Do you have any suggestions for me as an English major student?

【Ahmet】Don't think negatively. For example, when you look into a glass with half water, don't care too much about the empty part, see the full space. Then you will be happier, and you should try to help people and try to make your family and your friends happy. Sometimes we do have problems, but it is life, isn't it? If you are always in felicity, you cannot understand the meaning of happiness. If you are always healthy, you will not cherish your health.

【BTV】I see. Thank you very much for your suggestions. I wish you a good time in Yiwu.

【Ahmet】Thank you.

Group Members: Wang Yujia, Pan Jingjing, Li Miao, Wang Jinging

叙事记录

【BTV】非常感谢您对我们这个项目的支持，希望我们交流愉快。我们了解到我们的同学曾在去年采访过您，您对我们这个项目也很有兴趣。首先，您是否介意向大家介绍一下自己呢？

【Ahmet】可以。我叫 Ahmet，是土耳其人。我来义乌已经 7 年了。

【BTV】7 年的时间不短了。那您的公司呢？

【Ahmet】我的公司就是在 7 年之前成立的。

【BTV】您的公司就在义乌吗？

【Ahmet】是的。我同时也在香港注册了公司。

【BTV】您为什么选择到义乌创业？义乌的哪一方面最吸引您？

【Ahmet】为了生意。我的意思是，生意把我带到了义乌。因为义乌有福田市场，所以我选择了义乌。

【BTV】那您一开始是怎么了解到义乌的？

【Ahmet】其实，最初我是跟随我的几个朋友一起做生意的，他们起步比我早。我十年前在香港结了婚。

【BTV】您的妻子是中国人吗？

【Ahmet】是的，她是香港人。在来义乌之前，我生活在香港。我们经常在香港跟土耳其之间来回。就这样，我跟中国产生了一些情愫。当我第一次来义乌的时候，我的朋友们建议我留在这儿做生意，这就是我选择义乌的原因。

【BTV】您有孩子吗？

【Ahmet】有一个女孩和一个男孩。

【BTV】您的妻儿也住在义乌吗？

【Ahmet】有时候。但是他们大部分时间都住在香港。

【BTV】那他们一定经常在香港跟义乌之间来回吧！您作为一个父亲，真不容易！

【Ahmet】是啊，为人父，为人夫，为人子都很不容易；同样的，交朋友，做老板也都不容易。

【BTV】我们都知道义乌是个小城市，您觉得义乌的交通怎么样？

【Ahmet】老实说，我觉得义乌的交通在很大程度上需要得到改善。有些人不太遵守交通规则，一些司机不太礼让，照着自己的方式开车。我有自己的车，但我每次开车都很小心。如果马路上有老人或者抱着孩子的妇女穿过，我会停下来等他们通过以后再开车。但是在我后面的车子会一直按喇叭，他们根本不顾及别人。不过当然了，这里还是有很多遵守交通规则的好人。义乌是个很特殊的地方，她有别于中国的其他任何城市。

【BTV】既然您住在义乌，您有自己的房子吗？

【Ahmet】没有，我没有在义乌买房子。因为义乌的房价实在太贵了，买一套房子需要很多钱。我可以用这些钱为我的公司买两间很棒的办公室。所以我不需要自己买房子，只要租住就行了。

【BTV】您的想法很明智。您喜欢义乌的食物吗？

【Ahmet】很喜欢。义乌的食物非常不错。因为我们是穆斯林，在义乌有很多穆斯林餐厅，所以很适合我们。你知道吗？义乌拥有两样法宝：食物跟福田市场。

【BTV】这两样东西最吸引您吗？

【Ahmet】是的，这就是义乌的魅力。

【BTV】现在让我们来说说义乌的投资环境吧。这里有许多像您这样的外商在做生意，这座大厦里面也有很多公司。您可以告诉我们您的业务范围吗？

【Ahmet】好的。我是做贸易的，产品涉及范围很广。我们的顾客需要什么，我们就提供给他们什么。我们通常会在市场上寻找货源，不仅仅在义乌找，而且也会在中国的其他省市找。

【BTV】那您为什么选择待在义乌呢？

【Ahmet】你知道吗，我们可以以义乌为中心，将生意辐射到中国其他地方。比如说，我的员工 Fiona，她马上就要去广州寻找货柜。在这里有很多像我这样的人，我们待在义乌，但是我们的生意遍及全中国。

【BTV】那您也走国际路线吗？

【Ahmet】是的，我们的贸易是全球化的。

【BTV】请您举个例子。

【Ahmet】比如厨房用具。我们同时也在绍兴柯桥做生意，在那里我有一个生意伙伴，他也是土耳其人。你知道，日复一日，贸易和其他行业一样会面临新的挑战。每个地方都在变化，不只在中国，因此你必须变得越来越专业。但是在义乌，许多公司都不怎么专业。

【BTV】那您是怎么看待义乌的商业的？

【Ahmet】义乌不像上海、广州、宁波那样有很多专业的大公司。在这里，很多人有一点点资金就来做生意。但其实并不是每个人都能做国际贸易的。

【BTV】为什么呢？

【Ahmet】因为做国际贸易是件很不容易的事情。你必须拥有很强的责任心，你需要关注所有的细节，并且要考虑到做生意的每一个步骤，包括风险在内。很多人试着去做这类生意，其间肯定会遇到许多问题和风险，很多人选择一走了之。但是我喜欢做合法的事情。在我做生意的 7 年来，我努力让我做的每件事情都符合规定，比如说我会如期缴税。但是有些人并不遵守这个行业的游戏规则。所以我觉得政府也需要在这个问题上下点功夫。这是很重要的。

【BTV】这确实是一个需要被正视的问题。那么义乌市政府采取了什么措施？

【Ahmet】他们经常调整政策，与公司相关的政策发生了很多变化。我希望制度会朝好的方向发展。政府的政策改变，不仅会更好地保护中国人的利益，同时也使像我这样的外国人的利益得到保护。我觉得双方受益是很重要的。政府需要掌控管辖范围内的所有东西，社会会因此变得更加美好。

【BTV】这将会是一个双赢的局面。

【Ahmet】是的。在这里，人们来自世界各地。对于义乌来说这是一个很复杂的环境，所以每个人都应该遵守这里的规定。我也必须遵守规定。这样的话，别人就会信任你，就算没有白纸黑字的文件，他们还是会信任、帮助你并且跟你进行生意上的往来。当然你也要如此对待别人。

【BTV】这就叫好人有好报啊。您的公司有没有遇到过什么困难？

【Ahmet】当然有时候会遇到难题。不过义乌就是个解决难题的地方呀。

【BTV】您为什么这么说呢？

【Ahmet】我是说，如果你在义乌，说明你有一些问题需要解决。因为义乌就是这样，这里有许多消费者，有许多生产者，有许多公司。当然你也要更加谨慎。如果你掉以轻心，你也会碰到不少麻烦。

【BTV】那您觉得义乌的投资环境怎么样？

【Ahmet】总的来说，义乌是个做生意的好地方。但是有时候我也会碰到不守信用的人，当他们说“好的，没问题”的时候，他们并不真的这么认为。我喜欢有责任感的人，而且信任是生意往来中最重要的东西。在义乌你需要时常检查所做的工作，因为在任何时候都可能会有意想不到的事情发生。当然我也碰到过这样的公司，他们认真考虑自己的未来，希望自己变得越来越强大，努力做好每一件事情，这样的公司会有很好的发展前景。

【BTV】是的。如果只在乎眼前的利益，就不可能会有很大的收获。您介意说说您的员工吗？您觉得他们怎么样？您雇用中国员工的标准是什么？

【Ahmet】他们不应只考虑短期利益。我认为这是中国目前存在的最大问题。不仅是我，每个人都有这个问题。因为各种条件都在变化，中国社会日新月异。员工们必须考虑到未来的发展，而不是单单考虑现在。

【BTV】很多人往往反其道而行之。他们一看到机会就想迫不及待地抓住，却并不去想下一步会怎么样。那么当地的政府有没有出台一些支持外资企业的政策呢？

【Ahmet】正如我跟你说的那样，世事万变。7月份的时候政府对于针对外商的政策做出了一些调整，但是其实政府要做的还有很多。我的意思是，人们如果希望拥有一个更加美好的义乌，就应该团结在一起并且相互支持。

【BTV】您说的完全正确。您有没有听说过“中国梦”？

【Ahmet】没有。你跟我说说。

【BTV】大家都在讨论中国梦，这是习近平主席提出来的。实现中华民族伟大复兴，是中华民族近代以来最伟大的梦想。您在义乌或者土耳其有没有自己的梦想呢？

【Ahmet】当然有。其实在我到过的每个地方都有我的梦想，不仅仅在义乌或在自己的国家。我希望我的家庭更加美满、世界更加美好；我希望战争停止、世界和平。

【BTV】您的梦想很伟大，这也是世界人民的梦想。您对公司未来有何规划？

【Ahmet】在这里有很多公司做出口生意，比如出口到土耳其和欧洲。但是我认为中国是一个巨大的市场，我打算做进口生意。我想在中国拥有自己的品牌。我甚至希望在中国销售土耳其的冰淇淋。在中国能做的事情实在是太多了。但是有一点很重要，我们必须要专注于一件事情。如果一个人不能专心地做一桩生意，那他很难得到好的结果。

【BTV】是的。您对于我这样一个英语专业的学生有何建议？

【Ahmet】要有一颗乐观的心。比如说，当你看到一个盛了半杯水的玻璃杯时，不要太在意空的那一半，你要看到有水的那一半，那样你会更快乐。同样，你应该试着去帮助他人，努力让你的家人和朋友快乐。有时候我们是会遇到一些困难，但是这就是生活。如果你总是处于幸福的环境，你就不会深刻理解到什么是幸福。就像当你一直都很健康，你就不会太注意健康问题一样。

【BTV】我明白了。谢谢您的建议！希望您在义乌生活愉快。

【Ahmet】谢谢。

团队成员：王宇佳，潘晶晶，黎苗，王菁璟

Good People Meet Good People

By Wang Jingjing Supervised by Zhang Jingyan & Cai Liang

On the morning of July 4, 2013, we met Ahmet for the first time while we three were becoming dejected and despondent, thinking maybe we were hopeless about getting any in-depth interviews. Then, at a corner junction in the International Trade City, we saw an honest man who seemed to be from the Middle East. We decided to try our luck. His hospitality surprised us and moved us.

Then, he promised that we could give him an in-depth interview. He also gave his business card to us so that we could make an appointment. We were still quite doubtful with the miserable experience before (other groups have the same tragic experience). We could not feel at ease until the interview really took place. It was simply mission impossible!

Finally, we went to see him at six thirty on the evening of July 6th in his office. He met us in person and then, upstairs, began an intimate conversation with us. He was warm and generous, speaking with fervor and assurance. When it comes to life in Yiwu, Ahmet said it is mainly devoted to business and trade. It is hard to enjoy life because every day is very busy, even on the weekends. The best way to relax is to do some sports in the gym with friends occasionally.

Further in the conversation, we knew that Ahmet had been in China for seven years. His wife is from Hong Kong, so he can speak simple Chinese. They met in his hometown in Turkey. While in Turkey, he worked for the government. Later, some of his friends began to do business in China and suggested that he come to China. They first came to Hong Kong, then moved to Shenzhen. When a number of his business friends came to Yiwu, he moved to Yiwu, too. At present, his wife is in Hong Kong. She is going to give birth to their second child. Ahmet felt that, although in the past two years, his business is quite difficult, the future is still bright. Yiwu is very suitable for commercial activities, and he himself suitable for doing business. In addition, it is from business that he derives the great joy of success.

Ahmet also showed us his work schedule, which is a pile of self-binding white paper, one page after another, filled neatly with every plan and schedule.

After one is completed, he just ticks it off. His desk is very tidy. Serious work and careful organization, no wonder he is successful.

Later, Ahmet also told us that although he is busy, he still maintains a healthy lifestyle. He never stays up late and is used to getting up early and going to bed early. He likes to go to the office as the first thing in the morning to finish his work with a fresh mind. Enjoying the feeling of satisfaction, he can take a rest in the afternoon or go to the gym for a workout with his friends. At night, he likes to go home early. He is a nonsmoker because he thinks that smoking would do harm to his health. Nor does he go to the bar because he thinks coming back home drunk will make his family members feel burdened and unhappy.

Finally, when we asked about the key to success in business, Ahmet became serious and said that good family members, true friends instead of just playmates, and a healthy body are the keys to success. He also said a classic thing—believe me, and believe yourself; good people meet good people, and bad people meet bad people.

After the interview, I was so moved and so happy. I believe that his business in Yiwu will become better and better, and I hope that expatriates in Yiwu will make a greater contribution to the economic development of China.

人以群分,物以类聚

文:王菁璟　指导教师:张静燕　蔡　亮

初见Ahmet,是在2013年7月4日的早晨。正当我们一行三人都垂头丧气,以为深入采访无望的时候,在国际商贸城的一个转角路口,我们看到一个憨厚的中东人迎面走来。我们抱着试一试的态度迎了上去,他的热情友好远远出乎了我们的意料,同时也让我们深深感动。

记得那天,他随即就答应我们可以对他进行深入采访,时间再约,还把名片给了我们。因为前几天有被老外爽约的经历(别的组也有相同的悲惨经历),我们有些怀疑,没有真的碰面,我们难以安心。我们觉得这简直是不可能完成的任务啊!

正式与他见面是在7月6日晚上的六点半。我们三人来到他的办公室,他亲自下来迎接我们,上楼之后,我们便开始了亲切的交谈。他热情大方,侃侃而谈。说到在义乌的生活,Ahmet表示,他的生活主要是以商业贸易为主,基本只有工作,没有什么享受可言。因为每天都是劳碌奔波,没什么空闲工夫,有时候甚至连周末时间都要搭进去,偶尔下班的时候和朋友一起去体育馆就是最好的放松了。

在进一步的交谈中,我们了解到,Ahmet已经在中国待了7年。他与妻子在他的家乡土耳其相识,因为他的妻子是香港人,所以他会讲简单的中文。在土耳其的时候,他在政府部门工作。后来他的一些朋友都来中国做生意,并且建议他也来中国发展。他们先到香港,然后去了深圳。后来一些生意上的朋友来到了义乌,他也就搬到义乌来了。目前,他的妻子在香港待产,他们的第二个孩子将要出生。虽然在过去的两年里,他的生意相当艰难,但是他坚信未来的发展前景还是相当光明的。义乌是一个非常适合从事商业活动的城市,而且他觉得自己也非常适合做生意,同时也很喜欢做生意,更重要的是,他能在生意中获取成功的喜悦。

Ahmet还向我们展示了他的工作日程表,那是一叠自行装订的白纸,一页一页紧密却整齐地写满了每天的计划与日程,每完成一样就勾掉一样。他办公桌上的摆放也相当整齐。这真是一个做事认真、细致又有条理的人,难怪他能够取得成功。

后来,Ahmet还跟我们说,他虽然很忙但还是保持着健康的生活方式。他从不熬夜,习惯于早睡早起。他喜欢一大早来到办公室,用一上午的时间做完工作,享受这份满足感,下午就可以休息一下,和朋友一起去体育馆锻炼身体。晚上,他喜欢早点回家去陪伴家人。他不泡酒吧,也不抽烟,因为他觉得这有害于健康,而且喝醉酒后回家会给家人带来负担，也会使他们不愉快。

最后，当我们问到事业成功的关键时，Ahmet认真地说获得成功的要素有三：家人和睦、朋友真诚、身体健康。他还说了一句相当经典的话：相信自己，相信别人；好人总能遇见好人，而坏人总会遇到坏人。

采访结束以后，我感触很深，也很开心。我相信他在义乌的生意会越来越好，同时也希望在义乌的外籍人士能为中国的经济发展做出更大的贡献！

Nigel Cropp

Nigel Cropp: My Yiwu Dream Works

义乌,我的梦工厂

Nigel Cropp, from London, England, has a nice Chinese name, Taishan. He loves Chinese food very much. He simply came to Yiwu in winter eight years ago with heavy luggage and a dream. He thought that Yiwu was a traditionally oriented small town with old buildings, canals and bridges. However, when he arrived in Yiwu, he surprisingly found Yiwu to be a rather busy international small commodities city. Although he was a little disappointed, he told himself, "When in Rome, do as the Romans do", and soon he married a Yiwu woman. He then established both his enterprise and family in Yiwu and lives a happy life!

奈杰尔·克罗普来自英国伦敦,有一个非常好听的中国名字:泰山。他是一个非常喜欢中国美食的英国人。八年前的冬天,奈杰尔背着行囊,带着梦想来到义乌。他曾经一度以为义乌是一个"小桥流水"般的东方小镇,来到义乌后才发现这是一个喧闹的国际小商品城市。尽管有点小失望,但"既来之,则安之",不久他就娶了一位义乌媳妇,还在义乌建立了自己的事业,生活真是"乐不思蜀"!

My Yiwu Dream Works

By Nigel Cropp

Transcript of the Interview:

【BTV】Thank you for your participation. Let's have a free and open interview.

【Nigel】Okay.

【BTV】First, please briefly introduce yourself.

【Nigel】Okay. Hum, I'm from the UK. I first came to Yiwu in 2005. Actually I heard about Yiwu during my four years stay in Australia, and I wanted to come to China to have a look. And so I bought a ticket to Shanghai and from Shanghai to Yiwu. With an expectation of Yiwu as a small town with old buildings, canals, bridges, I want to come here, but when I arrived, it was different.

【BTV】Were you disappointed?

【Nigel】Hum... Not that disappointed, a little bit, a little bit disappointed. When I first came to Yiwu, I did a teaching job in Weibo, an English training school. After about a week's teaching in Yiwu, I discovered Yiwu was a business place, and there were many opportunities in 2005. At that time, when I frequently walked around Huangyuan Market, Binwang Market and Futian Market, I had an idea that it was not a time of teaching in trading, but trading. While I was teaching English, I found a very interesting phenomenon that many teachers also did business in their spare time. During my first year in Yiwu, I met my wife who had a booth in the Futian Market and we started our Chinese business. Now, I'm still teaching some of my former students. I found Yiwu a very unique city.

【BTV】Then for you, Yiwu has been changing since you came here.

【Nigel】Sure. Yiwu is changing fast, very fast.

【BTV】Can you explain some of these changes?

【Nigel】Hum, the city layout, buildings, especially buildings. I used to live in "Yuan Ding Xin Cun" (the Yuanding Residential Area), "Dan Xi Bei Lu" (North Danxi Road), near "Xiu Hu Zhong Xue" (Xiuhu Middle School).

【BTV】Wow, your Chinese is so good!

【Nigel】Haha... Not very good. I used to think "Yuan Ding Xin Cun" was a common residential area, but now there is a newly built park since the city is becoming bigger and bigger. It's really growing, growing, growing. My customers also see the changes because they come back every six months. I try to tell them there are how many buildings, hotels, restaurants, etc. But it changes quickly, really quickly! It's amazing!

【BTV】Yeah, I see, the whole city is rushing forward very fast. I assume your wife is a local Yiwunese, right?

【Nigel】Yeah. "Yiwu Nong" (Yiwu local dialect, which means Yiwu local citizen).

【BTV】Do you learn Chinese from her?

【Nigel】No, she can speak good English, and she speaks Chinese very fast, so we communicate in English. If she speaks Chinese, I always misunderstand her. It's very frustrating.

【BTV】It can be very interesting I think. Well, when you communicate with her or your customers in daily life, do you have any problems like cultural shock?

【Nigel】No, no trouble. Like in India, Pakistan, and many other neighboring countries, I find my feet in China well, so there is actually no cultural shock. And I'm very interested in Chinese culture and Chinese history, so I'm so embraced, flexible, and I felt no cultural shock.

【BTV】No cultural shock? That's amazing! It's a big advantage for you, and I think one of the reasons is that most of your customers are foreigners. Do you often serve your customers by yourself?

【Nigel】Yes, mostly.

【BTV】Wow! I think you are a responsible boss. If you serve your customers by yourself, you have to spend a lot of time and energy. Is this restaurant your main business?

【Nigel】My main job is trading, exporting. This restaurant is just my hobby.

【BTV】It's really a big hobby! I learned from Yiwu Business Newspaper that your wine pub will be open for business on the second floor. Will it?

【Nigel】Hum, not on the second floor. It's also in this street near here. The second floor is for parties, office parties, and business parties.

【BTV】At that time you may become busier and busier.

【Nigel】Yeah, much busier.

【BTV】Then how do you spend your spare time?

【Nigel】Err... I join parties, ride bicycles, play tennis, play football, go to the gym.

【BTV】Cool! Do you usually invite your friends to join in your activities?

【Nigel】Sometimes I invite them to the bar to have some drinks.

【BTV】Chinese friends or foreign friends?

【Nigel】Both.

【BTV】I have noticed that right now is not busy. Which period is the busiest time of a year?

【Nigel】September, October and November.

【BTV】And which period is not so busy?

【Nigel】April, May, June, July and August because people don't come in this weather, and Europeans and Americans have their summer holiday.

【BTV】Next let's talk about something serious. Have you heard about the "Pilot Reform" project?

【Nigel】"Pilot Reform" project?

【BTV】Yeah, it's a kind of policy from which many businessmen may benefit.

【Nigel】What's it for?

【BTV】It simplifies the procedures for businessmen to start their business in Yiwu. It's not easy for me to explain in detail. Since you haven't heard of it, let's talk about something else. How about food? I know you love Chinese food, and you can name many dishes in Chinese.

【Nigel】Hum... "Fan Qie Chao Dan" (Scrabbled Egg with Tomato), "Dan Chao Fan" (Fried Rice with Egg), "Gong Bao Ji Ding" (Spicy Diced Chicken with Peanuts).

【BTV】Wow! Fabulous! I have a question. You are from the UK, but why do you operate an Italian restaurant rather than an English one?

【Nigel】Because English food is not so delicious. But Chinese food is very famous in the world.

【BTV】Haha... Yes, Chinese food is diversiform. Besides, it's quite hard for a Chinese chef to give a perfect name for every delicacy. Every name has its different profound meaning, so the food may sound more special. Your restaurant is named "Divino". It's an Italian word. Why did you choose this name? Could you tell us more about it?

【Nigel】Actually it's a hard thing to open a restaurant and choose a name. It's difficult. It means "divine" in English. This restaurant has a good location. There are three hotels nearby.

【BTV】Yeah, it's very peaceful around here and makes one feel really comfortable.

(Nigel's daughter entered.)

【BTV】Your daughter is very lovely! Do you educate her in the Chinese way or Western way? Homework in China is like a burden for children. Has your daughter ever complained about it?

【Nigel】Every day. They have too much homework. In my country, children at that age can play football after school, but here they have to do their homework. There is no excuse.

【BTV】Every day? How do you usually get her to study?

【Nigel】Well, my wife just tells her to sit down, and she does her homework.

【BTV】The traditional Chinese way.

【Nigel】Yeah, Chinese way is more strict.

【BTV】That's right. What are your standards for hiring staff? In other words, can you give us some advice if we want to work for you?

【Nigel】It depends on your experience, English speaking skill, appearance, friendly attitude, and out-going personality, etc.

【BTV】Okay. Recently, the hot topic in China is the China Dream. Would you like to share your Yiwu Dream with us?

【Nigel】Hum... When I first came to Yiwu, I don't have any idea of it. But now I'm more localized. I have my business; it's a very great place to do business. I don't have any barriers. It's quite easy. But in England, it's difficult. There are many laws, many barriers.

【BTV】So it's hard to do business in England. Why?

【Nigel】So many taxes. Actually, taxes in England are quite high. However, flats in England are very cheap. But in Yiwu, in China, they're expensive!

【BTV】Yeah, I can't agree more. The housing prices are still rising in China. Furthermore, I have heard that people in Yiwu regard luxury cars as a symbol of success.

【Nigel】Yeah, very strange. They spend a lot of money on cars, but not so much money on housing. Unlike the Englishmen, they spend a lot of money on house, furniture.

【BTV】Since you live in Yiwu, how do you think of Yiwu and its local people?

【Nigel】Most of the local people are friendly, and I have tried to get along well with them. As for the services, some are good, while some are not so good.

【BTV】Which trade do you engage in? Jewelry? Clothing?

【Nigel】Jewelry, accessories, and nightgowns, and now I have a clothing factory in Jinyun, Lishui.

【BTV】Since the competition is so fierce, how do you win?

【Nigel】The biggest advantage is that I'm a foreigner.

【BTV】Yeah, but there are so many foreigners.

【Nigel】Err... But not so many westerners. Most of them are from India, South Africa, and the Middle East. My customers come here to speak to westerners. It's my biggest market.

【BTV】How about management? How do you manage your staff?

【Nigel】I have good staff. Girls work better than boys, but troubles for girls are that when they are 25 or 26, they may get married, and then have a baby. However, boys are lazy.

【BTV】Well, I think you are so busy, and it's high time we finished our interview. Thank you sincerely for your time. We wish you a nice stay in Yiwu.

Group Members: Li Xinxin, Lou Yibo, Yao Xing, Xie Zhiyou

叙事记录

【BTV】谢谢您的参与。现在开始我们的采访吧，我想我们的谈话可以自由一点。

【Nigel】好的。

【BTV】首先，请您做一个简单的自我介绍吧。

【Nigel】好的。我是英国人，2005年来到义乌。在澳大利亚工作的4年期间，我了解到了中国，了解到了义乌，于是我就想来中国看一看。后来我就买了一张飞机票，先到上海，再从上海坐火车到义乌。我一直以为义乌是一个到处可见古老建筑、小桥、流水的小镇，但是，当我来到义乌，我发现这里和我的想象完全不一样。

【BTV】您觉得失望吗？

【Nigel】嗯，没那么失望，有一点点失望，一点点。我刚到义乌的时候在韦博英语培训学校做英语老师。教了大约一个星期左右，我发现义乌其实是一个东方的商业基地，尤其是2005年的时候，这里充满了机遇。那时候，我经常在篁园市场、宾王市场、福田市场附近徘徊。后来我就萌生了一个想法：这已经不是教授如何做贸易的时代，这已经是亲历亲为的时代了。在我教英语的时候，我发现了一个很有趣的现象：老师们都在业余时间经商。在义乌教英语的头一年里，我邂逅了我现在的妻子，她在福田市场有一个摊位做生意，后来，我们开始了我们共同的事业。我现在还在给以前的一些学生上课。我觉得义乌是一个非常特别的城市。

【BTV】所以对您来说，义乌从您来到这儿的时候，就在一步步地改变。

【Nigel】当然，义乌发展得很快，非常快。

【BTV】您能和我们分享一下这些变化吗？

【Nigel】在城市布局、建筑方面，尤其是城市建筑变化很大。我之前住在园丁新村，丹溪北路，在秀湖中学附近。

【BTV】哇！您的中文讲得真好！

【Nigel】哈哈，不是很好。我以前觉得园丁新村非常普通，但是现在随着城市的不断发展，那里建了一个公园，一切都在发展！我的顾客每半年来一次，他们也感受到了这些变化。我总想告诉他们这里有多少建筑，多少宾馆和餐厅，但是它们发展得太快了！让人吃惊！

【BTV】哦，是啊，整个城市都在快速奔跑着。我猜想您的妻子是义乌人，是吗？

【Nigel】是的，“义乌侬”（义乌方言，意思是“义乌人”）。

【BTV】那么，您在跟她学中文吗？

【Nigel】没有，她英语讲得很好，中文又讲得太快，所以我们用英语交流。如果她讲中文，我就会误解她的意思，这会让人很苦恼。

【BTV】我想这样的生活一定非常有趣。当您在和妻子或客户交流的时候，有没有遇到过文化差异问题？

【Nigel】没有，我觉得我就像置身于印度、巴基斯坦以及其他与中国相邻的国家之中一样，对中国的文化非常适应，所以也不会有文化差异的困扰。而且我非常喜欢中国文化和历史，我知道怎么变通。所以我觉得自己被接受、被包容，完全没有感受到文化冲突。

【BTV】没有文化冲突？真让人惊讶！这可是您的一大优势啊！我想，这和您的顾客大部分都是外国人有关系吧。您通常亲自招呼您的顾客吗？

【Nigel】通常会的。

【BTV】哇！您一定是一个极有责任心的好老板。我们都知道，如果您要亲自招呼客人，那是很费时间和精力的。那么这家餐厅是您的主业吗？

【Nigel】我的主业是外贸，进出口贸易。这家餐厅只是我的一个爱好。

【BTV】这真是一个很大的爱好！我从《义乌商报》上了解到您要在这边的二楼建立一个红酒吧，是吗？

【Nigel】不是在二楼，红酒吧也在这条街上，在附近。二楼是用来举办派对的，如一些办公派对，商业派对等。

【BTV】到那个时候，您可能会更忙了。

【Nigel】是的，会越来越忙。

【BTV】那么，您是怎么安排您的业余时间的？

【Nigel】我会参加一些聚会，骑自行车、打网球、踢足球、去健身房。

【BTV】真丰富！您会经常约您的朋友一起参加活动吗？

【Nigel】有时候我会约他们一起出来喝几杯。

【BTV】通常是中国朋友还是外国朋友？

【Nigel】都有。

【BTV】我留意到这个时段的客流量不是特别大。那么一年中的哪几个时间段是最忙的？

【Nigel】九月，十月，十一月。

【BTV】哪几个月是淡季？

【Nigel】四月，五月，六月，七月，八月。因为客人不会在这种天气跑过来，而且欧洲和美国那边都放暑假了。

【BTV】接下来让我们讨论一个稍微严肃一些的话题。您听说过“改革试点”工程吗？

【Nigel】“改革试点”工程？

【BTV】是的，这是一种惠及很多商人的政策。

【Nigel】这个政策的目的是什么？

【BTV】这个政策简化了在义乌经商需要办理的手续。要我详细解释倒有些难度。既然您没有听说过这个政策，我们就聊点别的吧，聊点更轻松的话题……说说美食怎么样？我知道您喜欢吃中国菜，而且您能用中文报出很多菜名。

【Nigel】番茄炒蛋，蛋炒饭，宫保鸡丁……

【BTV】哇！太厉害了！我有一个问题，您来自英国，但是您为什么要经营一家意大利餐厅呢？

【Nigel】因为英国食物不好吃，不过中国菜在世界上非常有名！

【BTV】哈哈，是啊，中国菜系非常丰富。其实中国厨师取菜名也是非常有讲究的，每道菜都赋予了非常深刻的含义，让人品尝起来别有一番风味。您餐厅的名字叫“谛诺”，这是意大利语。为什么要选择这个词呢？能说说您所赋予的含义吗？

【Nigel】说实话，经营一家餐厅、给餐厅起名都非常困难。这个词的英文意思是“非凡,恩赐”。这家店的位置非常有利,附近有三家旅馆。

【BTV】是的,这里的环境非常安静,让人觉得特别舒服!

(奈杰尔的女儿走过来了。)

【BTV】您的女儿真可爱。您教育女儿是用中国的方法,还是西方的方法?中国的家庭作业对于小孩子来说是一个很大的负担,您的女儿向您抱怨过这些吗?

【Nigel】天天抱怨。他们的作业实在太多了。在我们国家,同龄的孩子们放学后可以一起踢足球,但是中国的孩子只有做作业,没有任何借口。

【BTV】每天?那么,在她抱怨完之后,您是怎么让她静下心来做作业的?

【Nigel】我的妻子会让她坐下来把作业完成。

【BTV】这是中国传统的教育方式。

【Nigel】是啊,中国式教育非常严格。

【BTV】是的。我想知道,对您来说,您在雇佣员工时有哪些要求?换句话说,如果我们想到您那里去工作,您能给我们一些建议吗?

【Nigel】这取决于你的经验、英语交流水平、外貌、友好的态度以及外向的性格等等。

【BTV】明白了。最近在我们中国有一个热门词汇叫“中国梦”。您能与我们分享一下您的“义乌梦”吗?

【Nigel】在我刚到义乌的时候,我并没有任何的计划。但是这片土地对于我来说,越来越亲切了。在这里我拥有属于自己的事业,这是一个经商的好地方。在这里,我没遇到什么阻碍,事业运行得很顺利。但是在英国经商就要难得多,那里有很多法律,有很多阻力。

【BTV】在英国经商非常不容易?为什么呢?

【Nigel】有太多的税!英国的税非常高,不过英国的房子很便宜,义乌的房子太贵了!

【BTV】是的,我非常认同您的看法。中国的房价连年攀升,越来越高。另外,我还听说,义乌的商人把开豪车看作是事业成功的一个标志。

【Nigel】是的,非常奇怪,他们花大笔的钱购置豪车,而花在房子上的却并不多。像英国人,他们大多数的钱是花在房子和家具上的。

【BTV】自从您来义乌之后,您对义乌和义乌人的印象怎样?

【Nigel】义乌当地人大多数都很友好。我尝试着和他人友好相处。至于服务设施,有些挺好的,有些不是特别满意。

【BTV】您具体从事哪方面的贸易?珠宝还是服装?

【Nigel】珠宝、饰品和睡衣。我在丽水缙云有一个服装厂。

【BTV】现在市场竞争那么激烈,您认为您的竞争优势在哪里?

【Nigel】我觉得我最大的优势就是我是一个外国人。

【BTV】但是义乌到处都是外国人。

【Nigel】嗯，是的，但是西方人并不多。他们大多数来自印度、南非、中东地区。我的客人会来这里和西方人交流，这是我最大的市场。

【BTV】在管理方面，您是如何管理您的职员的？

【Nigel】我有一群好员工。女孩子做事通常比男孩子强，但是，女孩子在她们二十五六岁的时候要结婚生子，这是比较麻烦的问题，但是男孩子又比较懒。

【BTV】嗯，我想您一定非常忙，是时候结束我们的采访了。非常感谢您抽空接受我们的采访，希望您在义乌生活愉快！

团队成员：李新新，楼一博，姚星，谢之悠

Impression of Yiwu

By Li Xinxin Supervised by Zhang Jingyan & Cai Liang

My impression is that Yiwu should be prosperous and lively just like Shenzhen and Xiamen, not only as a special economic zone, but also the first and sole national level comprehensive reform pilot county-level city in China, though it is a small county. A city gathering businessmen from all over the world should be a place bristling with tall buildings and resounding with the voices of feasting and revelry. However, when my teammates and I arrived in Yiwu, these thoughts were challenged.

Yiwu, the Paradox

A brief stay in Yiwu for three days and nights enables me to know this city more profoundly. Although Yiwu is not a large city, you cannot cover half of the market in a week. Although there are no skyscrapers, the Yiwu Television Center which will be 160 meters high is about to be constructed. Although Yiwu doesn't look like a busy city since there are only a few people on the streets during the day, you may find that your eyes lie to you when you enter the small commodity markets. There are so many businessmen coming and going, arriving and leaving. When evening rolls around, the waysides become especially noisy. Foreigners are common in the streets: Some are drinking alcohol, some are enjoying coffee, some are sipping tea, and some are smoking. What a leisurely life!

Yiwu is truly a great national small commodity market! With three days' rough knowledge, I decide the layout of the market is orderly as well as disorderly. Orderly because one kind of commodity is found in one row of booths. Disorderly because there are multifarious commodities, such as baby products, toys, digital products, machines, etc. Moreover, all the signs of shops in Yiwu are labeled both in Chinese and English, and most foreign businessmen are from the Middle East, so Arabic is also very common. Also, we can see various foreign restaurants all round.

Yiwu is a combination of the East and West. Chinese are practical and think more about profit. However, foreigners are more carefree and pay more attention to the quality of life. We can see that almost all the Chinese restaurants in Yiwu are fast food restaurants. Just as their name suggests: "busy customers", every customer eats very fast because they are busy with their trading. As for foreign restaurants, there are more coffee shops, tea restaurants, dessert shops rather than KFC and McDonald's. At nightfall, you rarely see Chinese people sitting in a cane chair sipping tea whereas foreigners sit together drinking and talking.

Day and Night

Day is distinct from night in Yiwu. Yiwu is busy during the day, but the night is freer and more relaxing. Yiwu businessmen know how to enjoy life by unwinding in the evening after a day's exhausting work. The working hours in Yiwu are from 8 a. m. to 5 p. m. The small commodity markets start to become lively at about 9 a. m. , especially in Yiwu International Trade City; but you can hardly feel this kind of energy outside the markets. You wonder where these people are while you are walking on the streets. Only when you enter the markets, will you feel the energy of this young city and see so many international businessmen hurrying on their way. At 4 p. m. , the roads become noisy again because people are getting off work. At dusk, there is the scene of foreigners talking and laughing in groups under colorful neon signs. How I envy their life!

Further Investigation

I knew Taishan from *Yiwu Business Newspaper*. His English name is Nigel Cropp. Attracted by its fame, he came all way from England to Yiwu. I managed to look for Nigel's Italian restaurant named "Divino" in order to interview him.

Nigel's restaurant is located near the beautiful Xiuhu Park under the ancient Da'an Temple Tower in a very comfortable neighborhood. In the interview, I learned that Nigel's initial impression of Yiwu was an ancient small town with old buildings, canals and bridges. He said he did not like big cities like Beijing and Shanghai. When he first heard about Yiwu, he tried to find this city on the map, but he couldn't, so he thought it was a traditional orient county. This really interested us.

Nigel did not start out as a businessman. When he first came to Yiwu, he worked as an English teacher in Weibo English training school. After about a week of living in Yiwu, he discovered that Yiwu was more a city right for doing business than teaching. Only by doing business, can he earn real money, so he started his own business in Yiwu, and he also married a beautiful Yiwu woman.

Yiwu people like luxury cars, and they regard a luxurious car as a symbol of success, which really confuses Nigel. Rather than buying luxury cars, he'd prefer to spend money on buying a big house.

As for the future, he hopes that he will live a happy life with his family and that his business grows and grows.

In Yiwu, the base fare of a taxi is quite low. I wonder if it's because of the rapid pace of Yiwu life, which makes people rely heavily on taxis. Yiwu people are clever and warm-hearted. Almost every Yiwu businessman can speak basic English or Arabic. Furthermore, they always help newcomers warmly.

Yiwu is a young city which lacks the conditions for development required by classical economic theory. While depending on the function of markets, an open government policy and innovation, Yiwu is promoting the harmonious development of its economy. It's a miniature of the thirty years of reform and opening up of China. The great potential for Chinese development as well as the profound wisdom of a grass-roots economy are the solid foundation to develop the Chinese economy.

义乌印象

文:李新新　指导教师:张静燕　蔡　亮

在我的脑海中,义乌虽然是一个小县城,但是作为一个经济特区,作为全国首个也是唯一的一个县级市国家级综合改革试点城市,也应该具有几分深圳、厦门那样的繁华、热闹;作为一个集聚了五湖四海的商人的城市,无论如何也应该是一个高楼林立、灯红酒绿的地方。但是,当我和我的队友们踏上这方土地的时候,现实中的义乌印象着实挑战着我想象中的城市景象。

义乌——矛盾的结合体

在义乌短短的三天三夜,这座城市的气息感染着我的每一个细胞。义乌虽然不大,但是你用一周的时间都未必能够走遍半个市场;义乌虽然没有特别突兀的高楼大厦,但是,一座160米高的义乌广电中心即将拔地而起;义乌虽然表面看起来并不繁忙,甚至大白天走在街头人烟稀少,但是走进各大市场,你会发现眼睛跟你撒了个大谎,市场里人头攒动,摩肩接踵,到了晚上,街上更是热闹非凡——喝着酒,享受着咖啡,品着茶,抽着香烟的老外随处可见,生活悠闲至极!

义乌不愧是一个国际化的小商品大市场！三天简单的接触,我发现义乌的街面结构可以说非常整齐,但又可以说有几分凌乱。整齐的是一种小商品经常会占领几条街,商人采购起来十分方便;凌乱的是小到婴幼儿产品、布偶玩具,大到各种数码产品、机械器材应有尽有、种类繁多！而且,义乌所有店面的招牌都是中英文标注的。由于外籍商人大多来自中东地区,阿拉伯语也非常常见,各国异域餐厅更是普遍。

义乌是中西的结合体。中国人比较实在,更讲究实际利益;而外国人更悠闲,更注重生活品质。在义乌,我们可以看到的中餐厅几乎都是快餐店。正如他们的店名“匆忙客”所示,客人匆匆来,又匆匆去,奔波于交易。当然外国餐厅也有常见的肯德基、麦当劳,但更多的是咖啡厅、茶餐厅、甜品屋,等等。到傍晚,鲜有中国人坐在路边藤椅里品茶,倒是随处可见外国人围坐一处喝咖啡谈笑。

白天黑夜,天差地别

义乌的白天与黑夜带给人们的感觉是截然不同的。如果说白天的生活节奏是忙碌的,那么,晚上的生活则是舒缓轻松的。义乌商人很懂得享受生活,经过一天的工作忙碌,晚上的时间会留给自己放松身心、品味生活、享受生活。

义乌的工作时间是早上八点到下午五点。义乌的小商品市场在九点多开始热闹起来,尤其是国际商贸城,但这种热闹通常很难在市场外面体会到。走在街上,你会奇怪这座城市的人都到哪里去了？只有进入商贸城，你才能真正体会到这座年轻城市的活力，看到行色匆匆的国际友人来回忙于采购。到了下午四点半，街道开始拥堵，因为大家都纷纷下班回家了。傍晚时分，五颜六色的霓虹灯开始闪烁起来，路边渐渐形成了一道道靓丽的风景线，外国人一小桌一小桌三五成群地围坐着喝茶聊天，让人好不羡慕！

深入探访

通过《义乌商报》，我对“泰山”有所了解。他的英文名叫奈杰尔·克罗普，是一个千里迢迢从英国慕名而来的商人。我抱着试试看的心态找到泰山开的“谛诺”意大利餐厅，并对他进行了采访。

泰山的餐厅坐落在美丽的绣湖公园旁，古老的大安寺塔下，环境非常舒适。我在和泰山的交流中发现，在泰山最初的印象中，义乌是一个“小桥流水”般的古镇。他说，他不喜欢北京、上海这样的大城市。在第一次听说义乌的时候，在地图上找不到义乌，所以他以为义乌是一个传统的东方小城。这让我们感到十分有趣。

泰山并非一到义乌就从事商业。刚到义乌的时候他在韦博英语培训学校做英语老师，过了一段时间以后才发觉在义乌更适合做小商品生意，这样他才能赚更多的钱。于是他慢慢地创立了自己的事业，还娶了个义乌媳妇，在义乌过得如鱼得水。

义乌人很喜欢豪车，觉得豪车是事业成功的一个标志。泰山对此表示不能理解，他说义乌的房价很贵，还不如把买车的钱用在营造一个温暖的家上。

对于未来，泰山表示希望家庭幸福，事业上有进一步的发展！

在义乌，出租车的起步价很低，我猜想或许是因为忙碌的生活节奏，使义乌人更依赖快捷方便的出租车吧。

义乌人聪明热情，几乎每个义乌商人都会用基本的英语口语或是阿拉伯语进行交易。对于外来者，他们热心地给予指导和帮助。

义乌是一个后发地区，缺乏经典经济理论所普遍要求的发展条件，但它依靠市场主体有为和政府开明、创业创新，促进了经济社会的和谐发展。它是中国改革开放30年发展历程的一个生动缩影。中国发展模式的广阔空间和巨大潜力以及“草根经济”的敏锐嗅觉和深远智慧，正是中国经济高速发展的坚实基础。

我们的团队和泰山的合影

Ghansham

Ghansham: Live Life to the Fullest

随心，随性

Ghansham, a retired Indian businessman, is a kind and elegant gentleman. He came to Yiwu in 2005 for his own trading business. When we first met him, he was helping in his son's Indian restaurant, Swad-E-Hindustan. In this fast-paced commercial city, there is something different between this man and other foreigners. Now he is no longer working for money. At this stage of life, he has his own plain but unique life attitude. He enjoys every one of his simple and guileless days in Yiwu.

Ghansham，一个已经退休的印度商人。他友好平和，颇有绅士风度。自2005年来到义乌以后，他一直从事贸易工作。我们与他见面时，他正在他儿子经营的印度餐厅Swad-E-Hindustan里帮忙。在这个商业化、快节奏的城市中，他与其他的外国商人有所不同：如今的他不再为钱而工作，更多的情况下，他有着属于自己的独特朴实的生活态度，享受着简单而又平凡的每一天。

Live Life to the Fullest

By Ghansham

Transcript of the Interview:

【BTV】Good evening, Sir! We are students from Ningbo Institute of Technology, Zhejiang University. We are now working on a project about businessmen in Yiwu, so I wonder if you would like to participate in this project and agree to our interview.

【Ghansham】Yes, that's all right. You can sit there at the table to have some dinner first and then we can start the interview.

【BTV】Thank you very much! First of all, would you please introduce yourself?

【Ghansham】Okay. First I'm a businessman, and I came here in 2005. For one reason, my daughter was living here in Yiwu, and my little son was working here. For the other reason, my wife passed away, so my daughter told me that I would come to work here and live with her. Second, one of my sons, he was working in Shanghai, China, then. Now he is with me here. He is the boss of this restaurant.

【BTV】He's the boss here, what about you?

【Ghansham】My son is in charge of this restaurant, so I'm not doing anything. In 2005, I came here to do some trading business. I simply bought commodities from some markets, some factories, and sent them to the addresses given by my customers in other countries. Working like this, I did my business of trading.

【BTV】All the time you did it that way?

【Ghansham】Yes, in the morning and early afternoon, when the markets were open, I did my business; after four o'clock, five o'clock, six o'clock, when the markets are closed, I just get free. So sometimes I came here to give some help before I slept.

【BTV】I think I've got it. Is there anything you can tell us about the trade you have engaged in?

【Ghansham】My English is very good, so I take my advantage. When I first arrived, I went to Futian Market and all the people were working there. All the Chinese sellers were trying to bring the foreign customers to their stores. In doing so, they were actually trying to bring up the business. I was just looking there in the market. I was so impressed, and then I went to do some trading business as well, to collect some items from many other countries, get the item from the market and send them abroad.

【BTV】So you bought things here and exported the commodities to your country, India?

【Ghansham】No, I have many different customers. They do not only come from India. Some of them are from New Zealand, some from Australia, some from Africa and so on.

【BTV】They are from all over the world. There are all kinds of customers here.

【Ghansham】When I'm in the Futian Market, I could tell who are the local customers from Yiwu, and I made dealings with them one to one.

【BTV】What do you think of Futian Market?

【Ghansham】Futian is an excellent market. I have never seen such a big market in my life. It is maybe the biggest market in the world. Every day new things emerge in the market. It is developing fast. Anyway, I like it. There are so many markets in India as well, but none of them is like this one.

【BTV】You know, there are many different types of items in the market: toys, jewelry, clothes. Which ones did you mainly deal with?

【Ghansham】Whatever the customers wanted, whatever they needed. We did the export. In other words, I traded everything. I also worked as a translator for a period of time. And now I barely do any trade business.

【BTV】So now you help your son with his restaurant, right?

【Ghansham】Now I'm 62 years old, and in India, when we are older than 60 or 65, we get retired. We just stay at home, get money from the bank. The government pays us.

【BTV】You have been here for almost ten years. Do you still remember your initial impression of the city when you first came?

【Ghansham】When I first came to Yiwu, I found this place a very nice city, and I had no problem here with the Chinese people and the foreigners.

【BTV】No problem at all?

【Ghansham】No problem. Because you see, in my language, if I'm nice, then

I will consider you also a kind person. If I am evil, it means in my eyes you are also bad. It's a saying from our language.

【BTV】Oh, I see.

【Ghansham】If I see any bad things done by you, I will not learn these from you. I collect from you your strengths and treat you like anyone else. I only absorb good things. Therefore, I have no problem in Yiwu.

【BTV】This philosophy is really good. Impressive!

【Ghansham】What's more, I'm very happy here.

【BTV】So you have many friends here?

【Ghansham】Yes, some customers and some businessmen come here. They are all my friends. Now you come to my place. You see, I'm making you a friend.

【BTV】Yeah, we are already friends.

【Ghansham】Yes, everybody is my friend. Now Vishnu (a God in Hinduism) serves as my business guide. People come here. They're kind to me, and I am kind to them.

【BTV】You are so nice! How is the business going in this restaurant?

【Ghansham】Actually, now it's the big hour. The business is good here, because most of the customers are foreigners. Sometimes, Chinese people also come.

【BTV】How do you spend your time when you are free?

【Ghansham】I go to some parks, gardens, somewhere nearby.

【BTV】Binwang Garden?

【Ghansham】Yes, it is. Binwang has some gardens there.

【BTV】You like them, right?

【Ghansham】Yes. And I go to my house and I pray to God.

【BTV】Pray to god?

【Ghansham】Yes, I go to the garden, pray and take a walk. It's very nice.

【BTV】Have you ever thought of settling down here in this city?

【Ghansham】Yes, I will stay here. My son is here, my daughter is here, so my family is here. Yiwu is my home.

【BTV】Have you adapted yourself to the lifestyle here?

【Ghansham】Yes, I like it. In India, we sleep at twelve o'clock, but in China, everybody sleeps at ten to eleven o'clock, and dinner time is at six o'clock or seven o'clock. I change my everyday work hours like a Chinese people. As you can see every country has their culture. I've been here for eight years, I have already changed. Now I'm not an Indian, I'm a Chinese.

【BTV】Have you ever met any confusions or difficulties that you can't solve?

【Ghansham】The only problem is that I can't speak Chinese, so I have trouble in communicating with the local residents.

【BTV】Why don't you learn some Chinese?

【Ghansham】I'm eager to learn Chinese, but I cannot get any teachers. For many times, I asked my friends to come here to teach me some Chinese, but everyone is busy nowadays. Nobody has free time. Of course I can spend money on it, if somebody can teach me Chinese, no matter how much it would cost.

【BTV】Maybe you should go to a school to take some Chinese classes.

【Ghansham】There is no such school here in Yiwu, and there should be one. There are so many schools here, but most of them are designed for the Chinese to learn English. There are Chinese schools all over India, in Mumbai, New Delhi, Kolkata, Bangalore. People can learn Chinese almost everywhere, but here, there is not a single school to teach foreigners Chinese. I hope there will be one.

【BTV】Since your children have to take care of their own business, do you feel bored at home?

【Ghansham】Bored? Of course not! I wake in the morning, wash, take a bath, go to the park, and pray to God. Although this is what I do every day, I never feel bored. There are papers like *China Daily* of English version in the hotel near there. I read newspapers every day, not only news about China and India, but also news about any other countries. *China Daily* is good. I know a lot of news in China from it. Even when I go to Hangzhou, to Hong Kong or to Indian cities, there are English newspapers available on the airline.

【BTV】You know in China, when parents get old and are unable to work, their children should support them and take good care of them. Do the Indian people do the same?

【Ghansham】In India, in this modern era, daughters are married to their husbands' houses. This is what we call "Ila", and we don't get anything from our daughters. However, our sons must look after us. Normally, most of the sons, after they're married, take good care of their parents when their parents are old.

【BTV】That's similar to China. Yiwu has been called another name, "Wushang", which means "the wounded ravens" in English. The name comes from an ancient legend about a dutiful son named Yan Wu. What he did for his seriously ill father moved the ravens and the ravens hurt themselves trying to help Yan Wu and his father. To this day, the filial spirits have remained as a kind of folk legend in Yiwu, which has been passed down through generations since then.

【Ghansham】It's interesting. Thank you for telling me this great legend. I am very lucky that I'm not doing business for money. I have so many friends with me. My family is here and my God is here. My son can take care of me. I pray to God. I trust my God. My God is here. If there are any problems, I pray to God. God will take care of me as well. I like my life.

【BTV】I can tell you are enjoying your life here. Do you know something about the China Dream, the one like the American Dream?

【Ghansham】Sounds great! Can you tell me more about it?

【BTV】The China Dream was put forth by Chinese President Xi Jinping to build a moderately prosperous society and realize national rejuvenation. Can you tell us something about your Yiwu Dream?

【Ghansham】I dream that God will give my son good life, good wife, good family, and good business in China. And as God guides me, I dream this country to be nice, to grow and grow. Because I live and work here, my everything is here. I like China much more than any other countries.

【BTV】I hope your nice dream will come true as soon as possible! It's so kind of you to take your time to participate in our interview. Thank you so much!

【Ghansham】That's all right, you're welcome.

Group Members: Lou Yibo, Li Xinxin, Xie Zhiyou, Yao Xing

叙事记录

【BTV】晚上好，先生！我们是来自浙江大学宁波理工学院的学生，现在我们正在进行一个关于义乌商人的调查项目。不知道您能否腾出时间接受我们的采访？

【Ghansham】当然可以。你们可以坐在那边的餐桌边先品尝一下我们这里的食物，然后就可以开始采访了。

【BTV】真是太感谢您了。您可以先简单地介绍一下自己吗？

【Ghansham】可以。首先我是一个商人，2005 年来到义乌。当时，我的女儿在这里生活，我的小儿子在这里工作。在我妻子去世之后，我女儿就让我来到这里和他们在一起生活。另外，我的其中一个儿子，他那时在上海工作，现在已经回到义乌，和我生活在一起。他是这家餐厅的老板。

【BTV】原来是这样，您的儿子才是这家餐厅的老板，那么您的工作呢？

【Ghansham】正因为他是这家餐厅的老板，所以我在这里不需要做什么事情。从2005年开始，我就开始在义乌做外贸。简单说就是从工厂、市场采购一些货物和商品，然后根据顾客指定的地址，将它们出口到别的国家去。这就是我做生意的方式。

【BTV】您一直都从事这个工作，从来没有改变吗？

【Ghansham】是的。上下午市场开门营业期间，我都在市场工作。在下午的四、五、六点钟市场歇业之后，我就空闲下来了，就会到这儿来帮点忙。

【BTV】原来如此。您能和我们讲讲您的贸易工作吗？

【Ghansham】我英语讲得不错，这是我的优势。在我刚刚到达义乌的时候，我去了福田市场，在市场里我看到所有的人都在认真工作，在交易。所有的中国本地卖家都努力争取将外商带进自己的店里，以此促进贸易。这些景象给我留下了非常深刻的印象。受此影响，我也决定像他们一样从事外贸工作了：在市场里面采购各个国家需要的商品然后将他们运送到国外。

【BTV】您在义乌购买然后出口到印度？

【Ghansham】不只是印度。我的顾客来自五湖四海，有新西兰的、澳大利亚的，还有非洲的，等等。

【BTV】哦，他们来自世界各地。在义乌，各种各样的顾客都有。

【Ghansham】我在福田市场的时候，我能够判断出哪些是义乌本地客商，然后我找到他们并和他们进行一对一的交易。

【BTV】您觉得福田市场怎么样？

【Ghansham】福田市场是一个十分出色的市场，我的一生中从来没有见过这么巨大的市场。这是世界上最大的小商品集散地，每天都有新的事物出现在市场里。它正在迅速发展！总之我喜欢这里。虽然在印度也有很多的市场，但是没有一个市场的规模像福田市场这么大。

【BTV】福田市场里面有很多商品的分类，比如说玩具、珠宝、衣服……您主要是经营哪种商品？

【Ghansham】这主要取决于顾客的需求。我主要是做出口贸易的，商品种类不限。我还做过一段时间的翻译。现在贸易方面的工作已经几乎不做了。

【BTV】您现在主要在餐厅帮忙，是吗？

【Ghansham】现在我已经62岁了。在我们印度，活到60、65岁的时候，我们就应该退休了。退休之后我们就一直待在家里，从银行领取政府给我们的养老津贴。

【BTV】您在义乌差不多有10年了。您还记得您最初来到义乌时，对这个城市的印象吗？

【Ghansham】我觉得义乌是个相当出色的城市。当时，无论是中国人还是外国人，我和他们打交道时都没有碰到过任何的麻烦。

【BTV】完全没有吗？

【Ghansham】是的，完全没有。你看，在我们印度语里面，有这么一句话——若其身善则视他人者善，若其身劣则视他人者劣。这是一句印度谚语。

【BTV】我想我懂了。

【Ghansham】我的待人态度就如同一句中国谚语“取其精华，去其糟粕”。因此，我在义乌并没有遇到什么困难。

【BTV】这个处世哲学真的很好。让人印象深刻！

【Ghansham】还有呢，我在这里过得非常愉快！

【BTV】您在这里有很多朋友吗？

【Ghansham】有。一些市场上的顾客、一些商人来到这里，他们都是我的朋友。现在你到了我这儿，也会成为我的朋友。

【BTV】的确，我们已经是朋友了。

【Ghansham】是的，所有人都是我的朋友，毗湿奴（印度教的神明）为我指引了方向。人们来到这里，他们只要对我友善我就会报以友善。

【BTV】您真是太好了！这个餐厅的生意怎么样？

【Ghansham】事实上现在就是餐厅的高峰期。这里的生意挺好的。光顾这里的顾客大都是外国人，当然，有时候也有中国人。

【BTV】您是怎么打发您的业余时间的？

【Ghansham】我会到附近的公园、花园里去走走。

【BTV】您指的是宾王花园吗？

【Ghansham】对呀，就是宾王，那里有很多的花园。

【BTV】您很喜欢那里吧？

【Ghansham】嗯，除此之外我还在家向我的神明祈祷。

【BTV】祈祷？

【Ghansham】对，我去花园走走、祈祷、散步，就是这样，挺好的。

【BTV】您是否打算在这个城市定居下来？

【Ghansham】是的。我的儿子在这儿，我的女儿在这儿，我的整个家庭都在这儿。义乌现在就是我的家。

【BTV】您适应这儿的生活方式吗？

【Ghansham】是的，我很喜欢。在印度，我们晚上要到 12 点才睡觉，但是在这里，几乎所有人都在 10 点到 11 点上床了。而且他们的晚饭时间在六七点左右。每个国家都有每个国家的传统。我来这里已经有 8 年了，我把我的作息时间改成了中国人的作息时间。这里改变了我，与其说我是个印度人，不如说我已经是个中国人了。

【BTV】到现在为止，您在生活方面有没有遇到过什么难题，或是让您感到困惑的事情？

【Ghansham】唯一的遗憾是我不懂中文，所以和当地人交流不方便。

【BTV】您为什么不学一些中文呢？

【Ghansham】事实上我挺想学中文的，但是我找不到一个好的中文老师。有好几次，我请我的朋友来教我中文，但是现在大家都很忙，没有人有这么多的空闲时间。我很愿意花钱请老师来教我中文。

【BTV】也许您应该去学校参加中文学习。

【Ghansham】可惜义乌并没有教外国人中文的学校，我们需要这样的学校。这里有很多学校，大多数是教中国人学英语的。在印度的孟买、新德里、加尔各答、班加罗尔等城市都有教中文的学校。希望义乌也能建立这样的学校。

【BTV】您的子女都在义乌有自己的事业，您一个人在家会感到无聊吗？

【Ghansham】无聊？一点儿也不！我每天早上起床、洗漱、洗澡、去公园、做祷告。虽然每天如此，我一点儿也不感到无聊。对了，附近有一个宾馆，那里有英文版的中国日报，我每天都去看报纸。我不仅仅关注中国和印度两个国家，各个国家的新闻我都看。China Daily（中国日报）不错，我可以了解到很多中国的新闻。在去印度各个城市、杭州和香港的航班上，都能读到英文报纸。

【BTV】您知道吗，在中国，当父母老了失去工作能力之后，他们的孩子应该承担起赡养父母的义务并照顾好他们。在印度也有这样的习俗吗？

【Ghansham】在印度，在这个现代社会，女儿们会嫁到她们丈夫家里去，我们管这个叫作“Ila”。我们不向女儿索求什么东西，但是我们的儿子必须照顾好自己的长辈。一般情况下，大多数的儿子们在结婚之后都会照顾好年迈的父母的。

【BTV】这和中国还是很相似的。义乌曾经又名“乌伤”，意思是“受伤的乌鸦”。这个名字源自于一个名叫“颜乌”的孝子的传说，他对病重父亲的孝顺感动了乌鸦，使那些乌鸦们不惜受伤为其治病。从此，“孝子”文化在义乌作为一种民间传说代代流传，直至今日。

【Ghansham】非常有意思，谢谢你告诉我这个传说。我觉得自己非常幸运，不必为了赚钱而工作。我身边有这么多的朋友，我的家庭，我的神明都在这里。我的儿子会照顾好我，我向我的神祈祷，我的神也会眷顾我。我很享受我的生活！

【BTV】您确实非常享受这儿的生活！您听说过中国梦吗？和美国梦类似的中国梦？

【Ghansham】听起来很不错，能解释一下吗？

【BTV】中国梦是习近平主席近期提出来的，是全面建设小康社会，实现中华民族伟大复兴的梦想。您在义乌有什么梦想？能跟我们一起分享吗？

【Ghansham】我希望神能够给我的儿子美好的生活，优秀的妻子，美满的家庭和顺利的事业。我的神指引着我！我希望这个国家能够变得更加美好、繁荣、强大！我的所有都在这里，我对于中国的感情远远大于对其他任何一个国家的感情。

【BTV】祝愿您的美好梦想早日成真！您能够参与我们的采访真的是太好了，非常感谢您！

【Ghansham】嗯！别客气。

团队成员：楼一博，李新新，谢之悠，姚星

Make Every Day Count

By Lou Yibo　Supervised by Zhang Jingyan & Cai Liang

As a local Yiwu citizen, I have been living in this city for over ten years. However, in our latest investigations of the expatriate businessmen in Yiwu this summer, I got another chance to gain a deeper understanding of Yiwu in a completely different way.

As we all know, Yiwu is a small city at the county level, but it owns the largest trading market in the world. Meanwhile, it is the number one distributing center of small commodities in the world, drawing businessmen and corporations from hundreds of countries. This is a rapidly developing commercial city. However, in such an environment, there is a man, trading and living here as everyone else, who stands out from others. We sense that his lifestyle and his attitude towards life are not the same as those of others.

We found him, our interviewee, in an Indian restaurant named Swad-E-Hindustan near the commercial area. His name is Ghansham. As a kind and elegant gentleman, he came from India about nine years ago and is 62 years old this year. He could be regarded as one of the first groups of business foreigners who came to Yiwu seeking commercial opportunities. Our original plan for the interview was to limit questions to their opinions of or suggestions for the markets. However, after just a few words from Ghansham, I found him quite different from other businessmen in Yiwu. He maintains a low-key life style, and he does his best to be guileless. Instead of being interested in questions about the investment situation nowadays or the potential for the future or some other similar questions, he is much more concerned with his own life.

During our forty-minute interview, we learned that he came to the city for family reasons. Foreigners seldom come to this city for this reason. After he moved here, he started doing foreign trade for a time. Then he spent more time running and managing this Indian restaurant together with his son. Nothing has changed much since then. He is satisfied with his family life. Within a fixed daily rhythm of life, he has his own faith in his God. He enjoys every day of his simple, plain and ordinary life. If I did not hear it myself, see it with my own eyes, it would be difficult to imagine that there is an elderly man, who comes far away from India, lives such a cozy, pristine, and, of course, happy life in such a fast-paced city which is full of competitive business.

Getting up, washing, working, reading the newspaper, going to a nearby park, taking a walk, meditating, praying, what seems so simple indeed enriches his beautiful everyday life. A fixed time, place and schedule never make him feel tedious at all. When asked about if he had ever felt bored, he immediately denied it. He said that though maybe he had no other things to do, unlike those people who go to disco or have overnight parties, and in addition, he is a vegetarian, however, he just did not, does not, and will not feel bored. One of his utterances impresses me even today: "I keep myself busy." Maybe from our point of view, we think that what he is doing might be too simple and too leisurely. However, for him, all those little things are precious treasures in his life.

When it comes to the questions about life or the business in Yiwu, I asked if he had encountered some difficulties, setbacks, or something that he was not satisfied with, or if he had any suggestions for the city's improvement. His answer was no. "Everything here is very good. I really like here." We can see that he has been completely integrated into this city where his life is rooted. In his words, "Now I live here. I am a Chinese already."

Moreover, when we mentioned something about the China Dream in our interview, we found that almost all the expatriates have a poor understanding of it. After all, the new term China Dream was defined and put forward only recently. Similarly, when Mr. Ghansham talked about his dreams, he said that his dream was very simple: He hoped God was able to give his son a good future, a kind wife, and a wonderful family life. Additionally, he hoped that China will develop much more and progress further. Perhaps this is exactly Mr. Ghansham's own little China Dream. It is simple, indeed.

In this conversation, I could not help but think of some Chinese elderly people of the same age and their living conditions. Because from what Ghansham has told us, he is living a life which is more or less similar to or exactly the same as some of the Chinese retirees.

In China, the care of elderly parents and "empty nesters" are major social issues. So I asked Ghansham some relevant questions. Today, many Chinese elderly are confronted with loneliness, getting no support from their sons and daughters. To our surprise, Ghansham never feels lonely. He keeps a low profile all the time. He is good at making friends, treating people with a kind heart. On the question of the support from his family, he also never has any troubles. He told us how the children in India support their parents. In India, most of the sons are able to take very good care of their fathers and mothers. In China, he and his son live a quite good life in peace and harmony. In my opinion, regarding the care of elderly parents, supporting and respecting the elderly are virtues that Chinese and Indians share.

In this forty-minute interview, we learned much and were genuinely moved by his special and kind attitude towards life. Investigations from another perspective, like from Ghansham's, also provide me an alternative way to see Yiwu.

Maybe in such a place where everyone is chasing money and his own interests, we forget something indeed, something, compared with this competition, which is much more important. We work and earn money endlessly for a better life, but we finally forget our original intention: to enjoy life. Here in Yiwu, we also find an elderly man, Mr. Ghansham with his characteristic working habits and his happy life with his low profile and elegance. Maybe we should remind ourselves from time to time, at an appropriate time and at an appropriate place, to slow down, to relax, to find our happiness, to enjoy every simple day.

让生活绽放光彩

文：楼一博　指导教师：张静燕　蔡　亮

作为一名义乌本地人，我已经在这个城市里生活了十几年。今年暑期我参与了在义乌的外籍商人调研活动，这次活动在另一个层面上给了我一次深入了解我的家乡义乌的机会。

正如大家所知，这个仅为县级规模的小城市拥有着世界上最大的交易市场，它同时也是全球最大的小商品集散地，聚集着来自世界各地上百个国家的商人和公司。这是一个正在高速发展的商业化城市。然而就在这样的环境下，有一位同样在此经商、生活的外籍商人，在他的身上我们领略到了一种截然不同的生活方式和态度。

我们是在商贸区附近一家名叫做 Swad-E-Hindustan 的印度餐厅里找到这位采访对象的。他叫 Ghansham，今年 62 岁，来自印度。他早在 9 年之前就已经来到这里，可以说是最初几批来到义乌寻找商机的外籍人士之一。我们原先的采访方案为外籍商人在义乌的各种有关商业的问题以及他们对贸易或是义乌市场的各种看法或建议。但是，在短短几句话的交谈之后，我们便发现他与其他商人的不同之处：他一直保持低调和朴实——对于更加商业化的诸如对于国际商贸城的投资前景和发展空间之类的问题，他不太感兴趣。相反，他把关注点更多地放在自己的生活上。

在长达四十分钟的采访中我们了解到，他最初是出于家庭原因来到这个城市的(很少有外国人是为这个原因来义乌的)。随后一段时间里他从事外贸生意，到后来他用更多的时间和儿子一起经营管理这家印度餐厅。他满足于自己的生活和家庭，有着固定的生活节奏，有着自己的信仰，他享受着这里每一天简单而又平凡的生活。若不是亲耳所闻，亲眼所见，很难想象有这么一个来自于远方印度的老人，在这么一个快节奏、充满着竞争的商业城市中如此安逸、质朴、快乐地生活着。

起床、洗漱、工作、看报纸、去附近的公园散步、静坐、祈祷，这些事看似简单但是对他而言都在充实着美好的日常生活。固定的时间、地点以及事件从未让他感到过乏味。当我问他是否曾感到过无聊的时候，他立即否认。他说他虽然没有其他事情可以做，也不像别人一样有着去迪斯科和派对之类的爱好，而且他还是一个素食主义者，但他并不感到无聊。他的一句话让我至今记忆犹新：“我会让自己充实起来。”可能在我们看来这些也许会太过平淡，但是对他而言，这一切都是属于他自己的宝贵财富。

当谈到在生活或经商时，是否曾经遇到过一些困难挫折，是否有什么不满或者需要改进的地方的时候，他的回答也是否定的。“在这里的一切都很好，我很喜欢这里。”可以看出他已经完全融入了这个城市，在这里扎根生活。以他的话说就是：

“现在我也算是个中国人了。”

另外说到“中国梦”这个话题，我们发现大多数外国人对于这个新名词都知之甚少。在Ghansham先生和我们聊到他的梦想的时候，他说他的梦想很简单——希望神能够给他的儿子一个好的前程，一个善良的妻子，一个美满的家庭。还有一点，就是希望中国能够更加富强、发达。也许，这就是Ghansham先生自己的小小“中国梦”吧。就是如此，简单、实在。

这样的交谈中，不禁会让人联想到和他同龄的中国老人的生活状况。因为在他所言之中，他的生活多多少少都与中国的老人有些相同或是相似之处。

在中国，父母的赡养问题和一些类似于“空巢老人”的问题是比较重要的一个社会问题。于是我也问了他一些相关方面的信息，类似于如今很多中国老人所面临的孤独、无人赡养等问题。出乎我们意料的是，他从未感到过孤独。他低调，善于交朋友，对人保持着友善之心。在子女赡养的问题上，他也未曾有过任何麻烦。他提到在印度，大部分的儿子们都能够很好地照顾自己的父亲和母亲。在中国，他和自己的儿子也过着和睦美好的生活。孝敬长辈、赡养老人是我们两个民族共同崇尚的美德。

在这短短四十分钟的采访时间里，我们收获良多，并对他独特的生活方式感同身受。同时，这次活动也使我们得以从一个另类的角度来观察研究义乌。

也许在这么一个人人都忙于金钱、追逐利益的城市里，我们确实是忘记了一些别的东西，一些相比起来更加重要的东西。我们为了享受生活而工作，但我们最终还是忘记了我们的初衷，一味地为了金钱而不断奋斗。在这里，同样是在义乌，Ghansham先生特有的安居乐业的生活态度以及低调优雅的处事风格，也许能够提醒我们应该适当地缓下自己的节奏，去细细品味生活。

Bouda

Bouda: To Be with You, Yiwu

义乌,与你共同成长

Bouda, who comes from Egypt, has lived in China and run his own business for nine years. Owning a clothing store in Yiwu, he enjoys the peaceful environment in China and wants to expand his business. To him, optimism and diligence are the key points to his success. He likes this city and wants to develop and share his own happiness and troubles with her. He believes that all the problems will be solved, and he will live a happy life with his beautiful Chinese wife in Yiwu.

布达,来自埃及,在义乌拥有一家服装店。他定居中国,已在义乌经商9个年头了。在中国这个比较安定的环境里,他打算扩大自己的店铺和事业。在他看来,乐观和勤劳是事业成功的关键。他已经喜欢上了义乌这个城市,想和义乌一起成长、一起发展,分享喜悦与困难。他坚信所有的困难都能得到解决,他和他美丽的中国妻子将会在这个城市拥有一个美好的未来。

To Be with You, Yiwu

By Bouda

Transcript of the Interview:

【BTV】Good afternoon, Bouda. Thank you for agreeing to our interview. We are from Ningbo Institute of Technology, Zhejiang University. Can you tell us how long you have been in China?

【Bouda】I've been in China for nine years since 2004, and now I've been to many cities. Before I was working for a British company in China. After that I quit my job, started to do my own business trading, but not all the time in Yiwu. I also go to other cities on business. Now I am doing trading and some other things. So what else do you want to talk about?

【BTV】How is your business?

【Bouda】It's okay, but this kind of business is seasonal, depending on when the foreigners will come to purchase from me. Nowadays because it's the holy month for Moslems, there are not too many people coming. Just wait a little while, and after that, I think at the end of this month, the business will certainly become better. This is the point.

【BTV】Can you tell us more about your business? what's your products?

【Bouda】Man-clothes, anything related to man-clothes, the accessories.

【BTV】From the labels, I learn the clothes are manufactured in Jinhua.

【Bouda】Yes, Jinhua, and all over China.

【BTV】Then, you go to the factory directly?

【Bouda】Yeah.

【BTV】Do you have other shops in Yiwu?

【Bouda】No.

【BTV】Do you have any further plans? Like expanding your store?

【Bouda】Sure. It depends. I cannot decide now. It depends on what my plan is and also the market because the latter is changeable. You cannot decide what you are going to do. After one year maybe you can have the blueprint for the next few years, but not now. I cannot tell you exactly what I'm going to do because I have no plans now.

【BTV】Have you been to Ningbo?

【Bouda】Ningbo? Not yet. I'd like to go there, but no chance yet. Most of the time now, I'm looking for employees. It's not easy. Unbelievable situation in China.

【BTV】What kind of employees do you prefer?

【Bouda】Females. Because they have more patience to customers than boys. Boys may be a little bit lazy; they're more likely to get angry. You know different customers have different attitudes. Some of them may be aggressive, so you have to be patient. Females are the best for this kind of jobs.

【BTV】Which age group do you think is better?

【Bouda】Around twenty. During this age is okay. Favorable if they are educated.

【BTV】Would you prefer local Yiwu people to those from other parts of China?

【Bouda】No, I'm not specifically asking for local people. If they're local, it is okay, but it's not easy. Most of the local people are rich. Then people from other cities of China, because their parents, sisters and brothers may have worked for a long time, most of them also lead a rich and comfortable life.

【BTV】I notice most of the customers here are foreigners, so do you expect that your staff can speak English fluently?

【Bouda】Not necessarily fluently, but can communicate. This is very important. Not all the Chinese can speak English fluently to communicate with the customers.

【BTV】What are the differences in doing business between Yiwu and your motherland?

【Bouda】Okay, let me tell you something about doing business in my country. Doing business in Egypt, the traders are easy to get loans from banks. You know, it's like borrowing money from the bank. In China, no, not allowed, because I'm a foreigner. I have no right to do that, to borrow money or obtain credit from banks. It's not very flexible for foreigners especially in China. Another thing, foreign currency exchange like sending money or receiving money in China is controlled by the government. Foreigners are limited to $50, 000 transaction a year. So this is a little bit too tight, very small amount. You know some foreigners are dealing with billions or millions in China, but they can't send or exchange the money flexibly from or to China. It's easy for Chinese people, but for foreigners they're always not allowed. Just only the government puts restriction on them, so this is a part of the problem. But in Egypt the foreign exchange is more flexible for foreigners than that in China. Uh, that's it, so I think in the future... how to say, most people are now using many illegal ways to send their money to China because they have no other choices, you know, and this has caused lots of troubles for them. It's a problem for the government to solve to make the city more attractive.

【BTV】Yeah... Got it. Let's talk about other things. How about "cultural shock"? Have you experienced cultural shock?

【Bouda】I'm already in China for nine years, so I can say I can communicate with most of the Chinese people. Also, my wife is a Chinese. I know a lot about the Chinese culture and thoughts of many talented Chinese people.

【BTV】Well, we know you have different religious belief from the people here.

【Bouda】Yeah, some people here are Muslim, and some are Christian. You know China has many religions, but on the whole Confucianism is the main culture in China.

【BTV】What do you think of the Confucius culture?

【Bouda】How to say... I know something about it... It's good for life, so in my belief, it's good as culture, but as religion I can't quite accept.

【BTV】Do you know anything else about Confucius?

【Bouda】No, this is all I know. Actually, I'm not very knowledgeable about this.

【BTV】Okay, since you've been here nine years, you must be familiar with the local people. What do you think of them?

【Bouda】Okay! Let me tell you one thing. It's not easy to judge people in China in different places, and you can say we are living in the whole world with angels. But, you may meet good people; you may also meet bad people, especially in Yiwu. Why? Because Yiwu is a market, and in the market people deal with money, so you can see many good people and also many bad ones. But in my opinion, it depends on the people who you are meeting, how well they are educated, and how good they are.

【BTV】As you know, people here used to be quite poor. I mean, they had to go out to do small business with others, and gradually Yiwu became the largest commodity market in China.

【Bouda】Right.

【BTV】What makes Yiwu successful in your opinion?

【Bouda】Well, first of all, Yiwu people are talented. They like to do business, deal business with other people, and accept other cultures.

【BTV】You mean they are open-minded?

【Bouda】Yes!

【BTV】Yiwu is a pilot city for China's economic reform, right?

【Bouda】Yes, the central government also supports it.

【BTV】Do you benefit from any policies issued by the government?

【Bouda】Um... I'm not dealing with the government too much about this kind of policies, but to foreigners they're not so open.

【BTV】Another interviewee told us that the foreigners are not encouraged to buy houses here. Is that true? Any restrictions?

【Bouda】How to say, for example, I cannot buy a house by credit, only in cash, and this is too much money for foreigners. Like if you pay one million or two million, how about your business? You freeze almost all your money in buying an apartment, so you cannot do your business. How can you manage this? It's not easy for foreigners to do so, especially if you are running your money like this, the fund chain will be broken. It will be stuck, and your business will stop. But if the government encourages foreigners to buy houses with the guarantees of the good reputations of a company, or staying in China without any kind of criminal records or other problems, that'll be the best solution. So it is a problem worth reconsidering by the government. The foreign policy in Yiwu is expected to be more flexible.

【BTV】Can you tell me what attracted you most to do business here? Why did you choose this place?

【Bouda】Let me tell you why. Now the world is quite changeable, but China is a relatively peaceful country. You can see many problems in the whole world. Some people, especially the businessmen, would like to protect their families and their business, so China is a good destination for them. This has also helped boost Chinese economy. If I can move with my family, I can bring my children to stay in a safe place, why not?

【BTV】The peaceful environment attracts you.

【Bouda】Yes, right. Who likes wars?

【BTV】What is the biggest problem confronting you nowadays? The currency?

【Bouda】It depends on the whole economic situation of the country. Yes, the changing currency does affect overseas business.

【BTV】Any influence on your store?

【Bouda】Yes, the influence will be fewer foreigners coming, which means not too much business done. It's like this way, more foreigners, more business; fewer foreigners, less business. This kind of things is quite normal.

【BTV】Oh, I see. Do you have any dreams or plans about your business in Yiwu?

【Bouda】Um, sure. I expect my business to become bigger and do more projects in China. You know everyone wants to expand his business because business is like a baby: You take care of it, it grows up; you care less, it breaks down. So it's a little bit hard, very tough but you must do your best.

【BTV】Yes. "No pains, no gains". Well, thank you so much for the interview, and we wish you a nice stay here in Yiwu! Thank you again!

【Bouda】No problem, anytime.

Group Members: Li Miao, Wang Yujia, Pan Jingjing

叙事记录

【BTV】下午好，Bouda。首先感谢您接受我们的采访，我们是浙江大学宁波理工学院的学生。请问您来中国有多久了？

【Bouda】我 2004 年来到中国，至今有 9 年了。之前我在一家英国公司工作，去过中国很多其他城市。后来我辞掉了工作，开始自己做生意，但也并不一直待在义乌，有时也会出差去外地。现在从事贸易工作以及其他一些业务。

【BTV】您的生意怎么样呢？

【Bouda】还行。我的生意有很强的季节因素，关键看顾客什么时候来。最近是伊斯兰教信徒的斋月，所以来的人不是特别多。再过一段时间，大概到本月末生意又会好起来。

【BTV】您经营哪一类产品？

【Bouda】男士服装，包括与男士服装有关的配件和其他产品。

【BTV】从商品标签上我们注意到生产地是在金华。

【Bouda】是的，在金华，也包括中国其他城市。

【BTV】那么，您是亲自去生产商那儿采购吗？

【Bouda】是的。

【BTV】您在义乌还有其他分店吗？

【Bouda】没有，就这一家。

【BTV】您目前有什么规划吗？比如多开几家分店？

【Bouda】是的。但也要看情况，我现在还不能十分确定。得看我的计划和市场的变化，因为市场太多变了。或许等一年以后市场稳定之后能有所决定，现在的话，还不确定。

【BTV】您去过宁波吗？

【Bouda】宁波？还没有去过。但我很想去，只是还没有机会。现在我大多数时间都在招聘员工。不太好找，呵呵，有点令人难以相信！

【BTV】那您需要什么样的员工呢？

【Bouda】主要为女性。相比男孩子而言，她们对待顾客更有耐心，男孩子比较懒惰，更容易发怒。而不同的顾客会有不同的态度，有些可能脾气不大好，那你就得耐心点。所以女性更适合这个工作。

【BTV】您认为员工在哪个年龄段比较合适？

【Bouda】20 岁左右。这个年龄是最好的，当然受过教育的更好。

【BTV】对于员工您是倾向于义乌本地人还是外地人？

【Bouda】没有特别要求本地人来做这个工作。如果是本地人的话，当然很好，但是这样的员工不好找。许多本地人都比较富有，包括一些来自于中国其他城市的人，由于他们的父母和兄弟姐妹已经工作很长时间了，他们的生活也很宽裕。

【BTV】我们注意到您的大多数客户都是外国人。那么您要求您的员工能讲流利的英语吗？

【Bouda】不要求特别流利，能对话、沟通就可以了，这是很重要的。毕竟并不是所有的中国人都能用流利的英语对话。

【BTV】您认为在义乌做生意和在您自己国家做生意有哪些不同之处？

【Bouda】嗯，让我来解释一下吧。在埃及做生意的话，从银行贷款会比较容易。在中国，就不那么容易了。因为我是外国人，从银行借钱，或是从事跟信贷有关的活动，会受到限制，这对外商来说是比较不方便的事情。另外就是，外汇交易，比如引进外资或对外投资会受到限制。中国政府规定外商每年只能有五万美元的资金进出，这个数额实在太少了，微乎其微。你知道在中国外商交易额差不多有数百万甚至数十亿美金，他们却不能方便地使用或转换这些资金。当然，对于中国本国公民来说，这些困难就不存在了。而在埃及的话，因为我是埃及人，在这方面几乎没什么问题，埃及的外汇政策要比中国灵活得多。我认为政府未来的计划重点应该是……怎么说呢，因为现在有些人用非正规途径把钱转到中国，这是会产生很多问题、造成许多麻烦的。这也确实是个值得探讨并解决的问题，在这方面政府应该有所作为。

【BTV】是的，这确实得解决。我们谈谈其他话题吧。在中国您有什么文化上的不适应吗？

【Bouda】我在中国已经9年了，我和大多数的中国人交流非常顺畅。加上我的妻子也是中国人，所以我知道的中国文化还是很多的，也了解很多中国智者的思想。

【BTV】嗯，看得出您的宗教信仰和中国人不同。

【Bouda】是的，这里有些人是穆斯林，有些人是基督教徒。你也知道中国有许多的宗教派别，但我认为对中国人影响最深的还是孔子的儒家思想。

【BTV】您对儒家思想是怎么看的？

【Bouda】怎么说呢，我有所了解。我认为作为一种文化它是有利于生活的，但是作为一种宗教，我对它不是很认同。

【BTV】看来您对孔子本人也有所了解？

【Bouda】不，我了解得不多，仅此而已了，呵呵，我没有深入地研究过。

【BTV】您在中国待了9年，谈谈您对当地人的认识和了解吧。

【Bouda】好吧。是这样的，中国幅员辽阔，不同地方的人你是不能轻易评价的，只能说这个世界充满了天使。但是，你可能遇到好人，也有可能遇见不那么友善的人，尤其是在义乌这个地方。为什么呢？因为义乌是个国际小商品市场，人们都做着各种各样的贸易，都在和钱打交道，因而你就有可能碰到好人也有可能碰到坏人。但是在我看来这取决于你和什么样的人打交道和他们所受的教育。

【BTV】有道理。我们都知道义乌人以前非常贫穷，所以不得不出门做些小生意。他们各自结伴，渐渐地，义乌这个地方变成了中国最大的小商品市场。

【Bouda】对，是这样。

【BTV】那么您认为是什么促成了义乌的成功呢？

【Bouda】成功首先是由于当地人的勤劳，而且他们有做生意的天赋，他们能够接受并容纳不同的文化。

【BTV】您是指开放的心，包容的心？

【Bouda】是的。

【BTV】义乌是中国改革试点城市，对吧？

【Bouda】是的，中央政府支持的。

【BTV】政府的优惠政策有让您从中受益吗？

【Bouda】嗯……我不怎么和政府打交道，只是觉得政府对外商不太开放。

【BTV】我们从其他外商那里了解到中国政府对外国人在义乌买房有所限制。是真的吗？有哪些限制呢？

【Bouda】嗯，这样说吧，我不能通过贷款买房，只能用现金支付。这笔金额对我们来说还是很大的。比如你花一两百万现金去买房，那你的生意怎么办？几乎所有的钱都冻结在房款里了，因此会导致周转不灵。要处理好这个问题对我们来说不是那么容易的。如果你真的这么做了，那么企业流动资金链将会断掉。如果中国政府能出台一些政策，允许外国企业通过良好信誉或其他条件担保买房，或者说通过看他待在中国期间是否有犯罪记录等来评判是否予以贷款，那是最好的。所以，这也是值得政府思考和解决的问题，政策应该变得更加灵活。

【BTV】那么您觉得义乌最吸引您的地方是什么？为什么选择来义乌？

【Bouda】当今世界风云变化，而中国呢，又是一个比较和平、环境相对安定的国家。现在世界上不少地区都有冲突、战争等问题，而作为一个商人首先要保护好他的家人和生意免受干扰，所以中国才成为他们的目的地。这对中国经济的增长也起到了很大作用。有稳定而合适的经济环境，又可以照顾家人，何乐而不为呢？

【BTV】所以说是安定的社会环境和投资环境吸引了您。

【Bouda】我明白了，谁都不喜欢战争。

【BTV】当前您所面临的主要困难是什么？汇率的变化？

【Bouda】这得看国家的整体情况而言。不过汇率的变化对海外贸易确实有很大影响。

【BTV】对您的经营有哪些影响呢？

【Bouda】来店里的外国顾客减少了，没有很多的生意可以做，这些都是很大的影响。外国顾客多，生意好；外国顾客少，生意不好，非常简单的道理。

【BTV】我明白了。最后想问问您，您在义乌有自己的梦想和计划吗？

【Bouda】当然，我想把店面扩大，把生意做大，另外在中国做一些其他的项目。因为做生意就像照顾小孩，你悉心照料，生意会越做越好；如果你疏忽大意，最后也只有破产。所以，是有那么一点困难，比较艰苦，但做了就必须努力把它做好。

【BTV】是的，有付出才有收获。十分感谢您今天接受我们的采访，祝您在义乌生活愉快！再次表示感谢！

【Bouda】不客气，谢谢你的祝福。

团队成员：黎苗，王宇佳，潘晶晶

Yiwu, Wonderful Because of You

By Li Miao　Supervised by Zhang Jingyan & Cai Liang

The July sun scorches the whole city. Various kinds of cars go to and fro on all main roads. The streets are crowded with businessmen from all over the world. As you pass them, you will hear different languages. They walk with different gestures, talking earnestly about something. This is Yiwu, which gathers merchants from more than 200 countries into this place in order to carry on the running of the international small commodity economy. Yiwu, famous for its small commodity markets, emerges from this fertile land on the east coast of China with brilliant rays, illuminating the other parts of its motherland, affecting every corner of the world.

When I first came to Yiwu, the first image of this city was of its large potential. Though it's not that big, everything looks in order. In the international business district, all sorts of people are talking, making gestures as one order after another is placed, and piles of business transactions are finished. Yiwu owns the world's largest small commodity market. This is amazing and attractive, also it is the ultimate factor to attract foreign investments. As we know, in 2010, Yiwu reported the highest number of exports in history. Though European and American markets have shrunk, the Middle East and African markets are growing strongly. As the international oceanic shipping prices keep falling, the route to the Middle East becomes very popular.

From our interview, we learned that many foreign investors have stayed in Yiwu for quite a few years, many for 10 years or more. They operate their own businesses in Yiwu and also have their own families. They are witnesses to the development of Yiwu city. They grow with Yiwu. My interviewee is an Egyptian businessman called Bouda, who deals in clothing. He also has his own shop. Together with his Chinese wife, they settled in Yiwu. In his eyes, Yiwu is a wonderful city. He thinks Yiwu is quite welcoming. But with the development of the economy, problems also emerge. He points out some problems that have bothered him and wants them to be discussed and resolved.

Bouda stated that the government has put too many restrictions on the capital carried by foreigners, which makes the raising of capital for trading more difficult. Furthermore, the government does not allow foreign investors to get loans from local banks. These two limitations greatly impact Bouda's business. They mean that it will be more difficult for his clothing business to expand. Certainly money is one of the most important factors for the survival of an enterprise.

In addition, the inflation of RMB, the devaluation of dollar, and the instability of the exchange rate will inevitably lead to an increase in the cost of production. It also means that the funds from abroad will shrink. But I think this loss is unavoidable. Bouda, however, has decided to stay in China and run his own business with his Chinese wife.

What leads to the success and prosperity in Yiwu today? From Bouda, we know the business boom in Yiwu comes from the fact that the local people started to do business at a very early stage of Chinese economic reform. They started doing small business, slowly accumulated experiences and capital, and made progress step by step. Yiwu people are geniuses at doing business. They have both talent and diligence.

In Yiwu, you can also feel its inclusiveness and openness. An inclusive and open heart makes people of different colors, people of different languages and different cultures settle in one place. Therefore, more and more businessmen come here with their families, to inject fresh blood and add vitality to Yiwu and to China.

In my opinion, although Yiwu's business journey started early, and Yiwu's foreign culture flourishes, it is still a young city, like a child. Maybe the only difference is that this child is much more mature than its peers. Yiwu is continuously developing, making progress without stopping, and tempering herself perpetually. With the speeding up of social modernization, much should be improved and changed in Yiwu. In pursuit of this goal, the interdependence between the rising economy and culture can never be neglected. They both allow Yiwu to be one of the most outstanding cities in China.

Blessing Yiwu, blessing China!

义乌，因你而精彩

文：黎　苗　指导教师：张静燕　蔡　亮

七月的阳光炙烤着这座城市，各条交通要道上大大小小的车辆来来往往。街道上多是行色匆匆的商人，从他们身边走过你会听到各种不同的语言，看到他们边走边用不同的手势比画着，商量着什么。这就是义乌，集全球多达两百多个国家的商人于一地，共同商议并运转着国际小商品经济。义乌这个国际小商品市场，在东部沿海这片富饶的土地上，发光发亮，辐射中国大地，影响五湖四海。

初次来到义乌，我对这个城市的第一印象就是潜力非凡。城市虽不大，但一切看起来都井井有条。在国际商贸区里面，琳琅满目的商品，各色各样的人群，交谈着，勾画着，一笔又一笔的订单在这里拿下，一桩又一桩的生意在这里谈成。义乌拥有全球最大的小商品市场，这便是一块吸金石，也是外商外资在此聚集的最终因素。2010 年时，义乌出口量已创新高。在欧美市场有所萎缩的情况下，义乌小商品对中东、非洲市场的出口却在强劲增长。在国际海运价格普遍下降的情况下，义乌小商品出口的中东航线变得十分受欢迎。

从我们的采访中可以了解到，许多外商来到义乌已有好几年了，有些已经待了 10 年或更久。他们在义乌经营着各自的事业，也成立了各自的家庭，他们几乎是义乌城市变迁的见证人，他们也同义乌一起成长。我的采访对象名叫布达，是一位来自埃及的服装外销商。他拥有一家自己的店铺，和他的中国妻子一起安家于义乌。在他眼中，义乌是个神奇的城市，她包罗万象，海纳百川，但随着义乌经济的不断发展，一些问题也浮出水面。他指出了困扰着他的几个问题，希望得到解决并有所改变。

布达提出政府对外商所能携带的资金的限额过高，不利于外商融资；而政府又不允许外商向本地银行贷款。这两项条件的制约对布达来说影响最大。这意味着他的服装生意要扩大生产会有困难，因为资金的确是一个企业生存最重要的因素之一。

另外人民币的升值、美元的贬值以及汇率的不稳定因素难免会导致生产成本的增加。这也意味着外商从国外带到国内的资金缩水了。在我看来这是一个难以避免的损失。但是，布达还是决定继续待在中国，和他的中国妻子一起打理好自己的生意。

是什么促成义乌现今的成功和繁荣呢？从布达那里我们了解到义乌繁荣景象的原因。那是因为义乌人在很早的时候就已经开始做起了生意，从做小买卖开始，慢慢积累下经验和资本。这是一步一步踏踏实实走出来的脚印。义乌人还有的，就是做生意的天赋，先天天赋再加上后天的努力，离成功也就更近了。

在义乌，你还能感受到的就是包容和开放。只有拥有一颗包容和开放的心，才能集不同肤色的人群、不同语言和文化的人们于一地。所以，越来越多的商人们带着他们的家人来到中国，来到义乌，给义乌注入了不同的血液，为中国增添了不少的活力。

在我看来，义乌虽然经商较早，接触外来文化较多，但她还是如同孩子一般，只不过这个孩子比其他同龄人要成熟许多。义乌还在不断地发展，不断地进步，不断地打磨自己。随着整个社会现代化进程的加快，义乌还有许多地方值得改善和提高。经济的雄起也需要文化的力量做后盾，双管齐下，才能让义乌成为中国一张最出色的名片。

祝福义乌，祝福中国！

第四章

Dream in Yiwu:
Cultural Bond that Links You and Me

筑梦义乌：
义乌梦，文化情

导言

义乌经济的发展，是中国 30 多年改革开放历程的写照，从一个贫穷落后的小县城发展成为了一个知名的国际贸易城市；义乌城市的发展梦想，折射出了中华民族伟大复兴的灿烂光芒。这座城市，寄托了来自五大洲朋友的梦想，他们不远万里、携妻带子，或从这里开始人生的第一次拼搏，或在这里扎根筑梦，实践人生的目标。在逐梦的过程中，他们与义乌结下了不解情缘，在他们眼里，中国的历史、文化是绕不开的话题，"美好"、"朋友"是他们经常使用的词汇。

本章中重点采访的五位外商，尽管来义乌的途径各不相同，但因为热爱中华美食和中国文化，视义乌为第二故乡，在义乌经商的过程中，渐渐融入义乌，深深扎根于义乌，他们的生活充满乐趣，事业蒸蒸日上。他们中有人已经在义乌生活、经商了十多年，亲眼看见义乌市场从小到大，变田野为高楼。有人曾经游玩过中国各地的城市，但是义乌得天独厚的投资环境使他最终定居在这里；有人最初来中国是为了求学，但对经商产生了浓厚的兴趣，在义乌一待就是五年，并深深爱上了这个城市和城市里的人们。比如苏丹人里达作为义乌苏丹商会的前主席，带领着苏丹商人在义乌开辟出了一条成功之路。

义乌，是一个梦开始的地方，也是很多人圆梦的地方。因为对贸易事业的追求和执着，他们寻梦到此；因为对中华文化的认同和向往，他们扎根于斯。

Muhammad Haroon Bashir

Harry: Honesty Is the Best Policy

事业之梦，诚信铸就

Muhammad Haroon Bashir, also called Harry, comes from Pakistan and has been in Yiwu for more than five years. He likes living with local residents because he thinks, "If people don't live here, they will not know what happens here." Yiwu is a big market, which gives him a chance to realize his personal values. He takes a sincere attitude to his Mian Trading Company which provides good services and high quality stationery to customers. We were impressed by his unique insights, personal charisma and great love for Yiwu.

穆罕默德·哈伦·巴希尔，又名哈里，是一个在义乌待了五年之久的巴基斯坦人。他喜欢与当地的老百姓生活在一起，因为在他看来："如果你不住在这里，你将无法深入了解这个城市。"义乌是一个巨大的市场，给了他实现个人价值的机会。他秉承真诚的工作态度经营着他的米尔贸易公司，为顾客提供优质的服务和高品质的办公用品。采访时，他独到的见解、亲和的个人魅力和对义乌的热爱给我们留下了深刻的印象。

Honesty Is the Best Policy

By Harry

Transcript of the Interview:

【BTV】Hello, nice to meet you. We are students from Ningbo Institute of Technology, Zhejiang University. This is our service-learning project. We know that you are very busy, so thank you very much for agreeing to our interview. First, would you please introduce yourself?

【Harry】Okay, I am from Pakistan. I am living in Yiwu for more than five years. I am here running a trade company. We provide service for customers, like Portuguese, Cubans. It is a good choice for me to come here to do business. When I completed my college study, I chose to be a businessman. I also enjoy my business because I think I got lots of experience from it. It's my hobby, and I like this kind of career. I do business with different kinds of people, and Chinese are very hospitable.

【BTV】You have been here for almost five years. Do you still remember the first time you came to Yiwu? What was your first impression of Yiwu?

【Harry】I felt so confused and nervous the first time I came here because I could not speak Chinese. I tried my best to adapt myself to the new places and met new people with different languages, so it was very difficult for me to stay here, to live here, especially when I went outside. I needed to take a taxi, but I could not speak Chinese, and the driver also couldn't speak English. Everything was new for me because of different country, different people and different culture.

【BTV】Since everything is different in Yiwu, I wonder if you have ever experienced culture shock in Yiwu. What are the cultural differences between your country and China?

【Harry】Great differences. First of all, the language, people's thinking and religion are obviously different, but I think the nature is the same, especially since Pakistan and Chinese are very good friends, so we have a good friendship with China, with the government. What's more, the food, the dressing, the living styles are all very different, for example the lunch time. Most Chinese have lunch at eleven or twelve o'clock, but in my country we usually have lunch at one o'clock. Another thing is that we start our work at 10:00 a. m. and end the work at 8:00 p. m. , but here we start our work at 8:00 a. m. and the market is closed at 5:00 p. m.

【BTV】As you have mentioned, food is one of the great differences. Do you like Chinese food?

【Harry】I like Chinese food very much, especially seafood and Chinese vegetables.

【BTV】Have you ever been to Ningbo which is famous for its seafood?

【Harry】I went to Ninghai last weekend. This was the first time I had been there and I did drive. My stay there is just one day, so I had not enough time to enjoy this place. I wish I can go there again to taste the delicious seafood and have a look at the sea.

【BTV】You have already had many experiences since you came to Yiwu. What is the most unforgettable memory?

【Harry】I have many good memories. When I came here in 2008, the Olympic Game was held in Beijing. When the Beijing Olympic started, people were anticipating for the open ceremony by watching television and big screens, so I was also very excited on that day because I watched it with some of my Chinese friends in Yiwu.

【BTV】I can see you are adaptable, easy-going and willing to make new friends. I suppose you have made some Chinese friends.

【Harry】Yes, I have many Chinese friends because I am doing business with them. My friends always help and support me with my business. I also have many friends whom I go with to the gym, and running, sometimes playing snooker. They are very nice, and we have our friendship since I came here. We read, go for places and sometimes go to other cities for traveling.

【BTV】Can you share with us some experience when you went out with your friends?

【Harry】Yes. The first place I went out of Yiwu was Hangzhou. I cannot forget the scenery the first time I saw the West Lake and Xixi Park. I traveled all the day and stayed there one night. I enjoyed that travel very much.

【BTV】Have you ever learned Chinese?

【Harry】I cannot read and write, but I can speak a little, not too much, only business language.

【BTV】Do you think it is helpful?

【Harry】Yes, of course. I think it is very good for the people who can speak Chinese to do the business. I think people should learn Chinese if they want to stay here for a long time, and I also wish I have time to join some institutes to learn Chinese.

【BTV】Maybe you can learn it in your leisure time. What do you usually do in your spare time?

【Harry】I like sports, and I also play with my friends. We go out for traveling, especially in holidays. I like traveling too much. While in Yiwu, we usually go to the gym and play snooker or badminton.

【BTV】Compared with other cities, what advantages do you think Yiwu has? Why did your company start business in Yiwu?

【Harry】Yiwu is good for business. My company started business from 2005, eight years ago, but I joined this company in 2008. Our company is not an investment company. Our company is a comprehensive trading office, so we can provide services to the customers from different countries who can't speak Chinese or don't know how to go to Futian Market to find the goods.

【BTV】Is your main company in Pakistan or just here?

【Harry】Our main company is in Pakistan and the branch is in Yiwu.

【BTV】What's your business mainly about?

【Harry】We do many kinds of business, especially the stationary, you know, about pens, ballpoint pens, pencils in schools. We provide whatever our customers need as long as we can find them in the Futian Market.

【BTV】What do you think of the Futian Market?

【Harry】It is a very big market, and I never see another market like this in my life. All kinds of things collect in one roof. We don't need to go outside, only in the market, and we can go to other districts. It is a big market for all kinds of products with good quality and good style. You can easily find everything you want, so it is very easy and convenient for purchasing there.

【BTV】What do you think of the local residents in the Futian Market? Are they your friends or competitors?

【Harry】Many local people have their shops in that market. We buy products from them and have very good business relationship with them. However, we cannot say all the businessmen are the same. Some are very, very good, but I also had some unpleasant experiences. They showed me this quality, but later they sent another quality to me. It is not only about the local businessmen, but also about the people from different countries. But we should say this sort of people is few, not so many.

【BTV】As for the customers, what do you do to make them believe that your company can provide the desirable products for them?

【Harry】Yeah, it's a nice question. We do the trade business, so the first thing is quality, how to provide the high-quality products in a friendly environment. We try our best to provide high-quality products and excellent services at the same time. Customers can trust what we are saying because we do the same. We keep our promise in our dealing. If we promised to sell the products of high quality, and we must give them this quality, so keeping the promise is the most important thing in the business.

【BTV】Your principle is quite similar to an old Chinese business rule: honesty is the best policy. Compared with other trade companies, what are the strengths of your company?

【Harry】We don't have too many problems from 2008 to now. Our company is going better, and our business is day by day going up. To some degree, I can consider that our company has the good quality: honesty; we don't believe doing the cheating. If we cheat once and make profit from it, customers will never believe us, so it is actually harmful to the company. Our company holds the belief that we should do the long-time business with honesty.

【BTV】There was an economic crisis in 2008. Did your company suffer from it?

【Harry】Yes, it is a world effect and all the world has the crisis in the business, but I haven't seen too many times happened in China. I think China is a lucky country. Here the business is going stable, but we had some crisis in our country, and people struggled through one year or two years.

【BTV】Are there any problems that your company currently faces? If so, what are they?

【Harry】Not only my company, all foreign companies in China faced the problem about the taxes and visa. One kind of new tax was sent to us recently, but we were not informed before. Luckily now we have already solved this problem.

【BTV】What policies do you think the local government should take to support companies like yours?

【Harry】First, it would be great if the government would give us some small delay to live here because it is troublesome to renew every year's visa. We hope we can be granted a long-time visa if we have a good business and obey all the rules here. Second, as a businessman, I hope I can get the information about new policies and other activities directly and clearly.

【BTV】Can you give some suggestions to those who also want to start their business in Yiwu?

【Harry】I think, first of all, the new people should read the policies clearly and learn how to start business. Secondly, they should learn Chinese which will be helpful for their business and life here. If they don't live here, they will not know things that happened here. Thirdly, they should follow the rules, not only about the new people, but also about the old people, because we are living in another country and these can provide us some protection.

【BTV】Do you know about the American Dream that was popular in the last century? People wanted to pursue freedom, independence and make more money in America. Many foreigners went to America to do business because they thought America could give them a chance to make their personal dreams come true.

【Harry】Yes, a lot of people from my country also went to America to do their business last century, and they had a good business. But this century is not for America, it's for China. There is only one problem that we live here.

【BTV】What is it?

【Harry】Only the visa problem. I am staying here more than five years and our company is doing business here more than eight years. The old people and the new people here are the same in the sense of the visa, in the sense of the government. You know, if people have been in America for more than five years, the American government will give some identification cards. I want to stay here for a long time. It would be more convenient if I can validate my visa every three or five years. I think it is a new world here in China, so people should come here and do their business here. It is better than go to America.

【BTV】Your China Dream in Yiwu is to solve the visa problem and do more business in the big market.

【Harry】Yes.

【BTV】Thank you again for taking time to answer our questions. We hope you have a nice stay in Yiwu.

Group Members: Yao Xing, Xie Zhiyou, Lou Yibo, Li Xinxin

叙事记录

【BTV】您好，很高兴见到您。我们是来自浙江大学宁波理工学院的学生。这是我们学校的服务型学习项目。我们知道您很忙，所以非常感谢您在百忙之中抽出时间接受我们的采访。首先，您能做一个简单的自我介绍吗？

【Harry】好的。我来自巴基斯坦，在义乌生活五年多了。我在这里经营着一家贸易公司。我们为顾客，像葡萄牙人、古巴人，提供优质的服务。我觉得来义乌经商是个明智的选择。当我完成了大学学业，我就加入了商人的行列。我也很享受这份事业，从中获得了很多经验。这也是我的一个爱好，我喜欢这项事业。我与各个国家的人做生意，而且中国人十分友好。

【BTV】您来这里已经有五年了，还记得第一次来义乌的情景吗？能否向我们描述一下对义乌的第一印象？

【Harry】我第一次来义乌时感到十分的困惑和紧张，因为我不会说中文。我努力适应新的环境，与说不同语言的人们打交道。留在这儿，生活在这儿，对我来说有难度。特别是当我要出去的时候，需要乘坐出租车，但是我不会说中文，司机也不会说英语。每一件事物对我来说都是全新的，因为这是不同的国家，不同的民族，不同的文化。

【BTV】在义乌这个全新的环境里，我想知道您是否感受到过文化冲击。您的国家和中国之间有哪些文化差异？

【Harry】差异挺大的。首先，语言、人们的思考方式以及宗教差异显著，但是我认为本质都是一样的，特别是巴基斯坦人和中国人是很好的朋友，我们和中国及中国政府有深厚的友谊。此外，食物、衣着和生活方式也大为不同，比方说午饭时间。大多数中国人在 11 点或者 12 点吃中饭，而在我们国家要到下午 1 点钟才吃。还有就是我们在早上 10 点开始上班，晚上 8 点结束一天的工作，但是在这儿我们早上 8 点上班，下午 5 点市场就关门了。

【BTV】正如您所提到的，饮食习惯差异很大。那么您喜欢中国的食物吗？

【Harry】我非常喜欢中国食物，特别是海鲜，还有中国蔬菜。

【BTV】您去过宁波吗？宁波的海鲜很出名。

【Harry】上周末我去了宁海。这是我第一次驱车去那儿。我只在那儿待了一天，所以没有足够时间去欣赏美丽的风光。我希望能再次去那儿享受美味的海鲜以及辽阔的大海。

【BTV】您来义乌以后收获了很多人生体验，那么最难忘的回忆是什么？

【Harry】我有很多美好的回忆。2008 年我来这里，恰巧奥林匹克运动会在北京举办。人们在电视机、大显示屏前很兴奋地期待着开幕式。那天我也异常兴奋，因为我和一些中国的朋友在义乌一起观看了开幕式。

【BTV】看得出来，您适应性强，容易相处，而且乐于结交新朋友。我想您一定有不少中国朋友吧。

【Harry】是的。我有很多的中国朋友，因为我和他们有生意往来。他们总是在生意上给我帮助和支持。同时我也有很多生活中的朋友，这些朋友和我一起去健身房，跑步，有时候一起玩斯诺克。他们非常友好。自从我来到这里，我们就建立了深厚的友谊。我们一起读书、一起玩，有时候一起去其他城市旅游。

【BTV】您能和我们分享一下与朋友出去旅游的经历吗？

【Harry】好的，我旅游去的第一个城市是杭州。我无法忘记自己第一次见到西湖和西溪湿地的画面。我在那儿玩了一天一夜，非常尽兴。

【BTV】您学过中文吗？

【Harry】我不会读和写，但是我会说一点，不是很多，也只是商务中文。

【BTV】您认为中文对您有帮助吗？

【Harry】是的，那当然了。在这儿做生意，会讲中文可以说是如鱼得水。我认为外国人如果想长期待在这里的话应该学习中文，我也希望自己能加入一些语言机构学习中文。

【BTV】也许您可以在闲暇时学中文。上班之余您还会做些什么呢？

【Harry】我喜欢运动，经常和朋友一起玩。我喜欢和朋友一起出去旅游，尤其是在节假日。我非常喜欢旅游。平时在义乌，我们经常去健身房，玩斯诺克或者打羽毛球。

【BTV】与其他城市相比，您觉得义乌有什么优势？为什么会选择在义乌开始自己的事业？

【Harry】义乌很适合做生意。我的公司是 2005 年，也就是八年前开始创业的。我是在 2008 年加入这个公司的。我们的公司不是一所投资公司，是综合性的贸易公司，向顾客提供优质的服务，帮助那些不会说中文，或者不知道怎么去福田市场寻找所需商品的顾客。

【BTV】你们的总公司在巴基斯坦还是这儿？

【Harry】我们的总公司在巴基斯坦，这里是我们的分公司。

【BTV】公司主要经营哪些业务呢？

【Harry】我们做很多类型的生意，特别是办公用品，包括在学校里使用的钢笔、圆珠笔和铅笔等。只要能在福田市场里找到，顾客需要什么，我们就提供什么。

【BTV】您认为福田市场如何？

【Harry】这是一个很大的市场，我从来没有见过这么大的市场。全部的产品都在一个屋檐下。我们不需要走到外面，直接在市场里穿行，就可以到达别的区域。这个大市场提供各种各样、品质样式俱佳的商品。你可以很容易地找到你需要的商品，所以在这里采购非常方便。

【BTV】您怎么看待在福田市场经商的当地人，他们是您的朋友还是竞争对手？

【Harry】很多当地人都在市场里有自己的商铺。我们向他们购买商品，与之建立了密切的业务关系。但不是所有的商人都是一样的。大多数人非常友好，但是我也有过一些不愉快的经历。他们给我看的是这样的商品，而发货的时候却是不一样的质量。这些行为当地商人有过，各个国家的商人也有过。当然这样的人是少之又少的少数。

【BTV】对于顾客，您如何使他们相信贵公司提供的商品就是他们想要的商品？

【Harry】嗯，问得好。我们做的是贸易，所以最重要的是质量——如何在友好的环境下真诚地提供高质量的产品。我们尽最大的努力同时提供高质量的产品和服务。顾客可以信任我们所说的话，因为我们言出必行。我们在贸易中信守承诺。如果我们约定出售优质产品，我们就会提供高质量产品。所以信守承诺是经营之本。

【BTV】您说的原则与中国古老的商业原则很接近——诚信为本。与其他类似的贸易公司相比，贵公司的优势在哪里？

【Harry】从2008年至今，我们公司没有太大的问题。我们公司的发展越来越好，可以说蒸蒸日上。某种程度而言，我觉得是因为我们公司有好的品质——真诚；我们拒绝欺骗的行为。欺骗一次也许能获利，但是顾客再也不会相信我们了，所以这实际上是对公司有害的。我们公司坚持以诚信做长期生意。

【BTV】在2008年发生过一场金融危机，贵公司是否也受到冲击？

【Harry】这是全球效应，全球商业都经历了危机。但是在中国我看到的次数不多。中国是一个幸运的国家，经济稳定。但是在我们国家就有一些危机，人们陷入其中可能要一两年才能摆脱。

【BTV】贵公司当前是否面临困难，如果有，是什么样的困难呢？

【Harry】不仅仅是我们公司，所有在中国的外资企业都面临着税收和签证的问题。最近，我们被告知要缴纳一种新的税，但是之前我们并不知情。幸运的是，现在我们已经解决这个问题了。

【BTV】您认为政府需要提供怎样的政策来支持类似贵公司的企业？

【Harry】第一，如果政府能延长我们在这里居住的时间，那就太好了，因为每年更新签证是一件很麻烦的事。如果我们在这里有好的生意，并且遵守相关规定，希望政府能给我们更长时间的签证。第二，作为一个商人，我希望能够及时、清楚地得知关于新政策和其他事项的信息。

【BTV】对于想在义乌创业的商人，您能否给提供一些建议？

【Harry】我认为，首先，这些新人应该读懂这里的政策，并学习如何创业。其次，他们应该学习中文，这对他们的工作和生活很有帮助。如果不住在这里，他们将无法深入地了解这里。最后，他们应该按照规则办事。这对新人和之前来的人都适用，我们生活在别的国家，这可以提供一定的保护。

【BTV】您知道20世纪流行的美国梦吗？人们想要在美国追求自由、独立，获得更多的财富。很多人去美国经商，因为他们认为美国可以给他们实现个人价值的机会。

【Harry】是的，我们国家很多人在20世纪前往美国创建他们自己的事业，而且事业有成。但是21世纪不再是美国的，而是中国的。但我们居住在这里有一个问题。

【BTV】是什么问题？

【Harry】是签证问题。我在这里已经待了五年了，我们公司创业至今也有八年了。就签证而言，对政府来说，我们这些老一辈的人和初来乍到的人是一样的。你知道，如果人们在美国居住五年以上，美国政府将会给他们相应的身份。我希望长期待在这里，如果每三年或者五年更新签证，那就会很方便。我认为新的世界在这里，在中国，所以人们应该到这里来开始他们的事业，这比去美国更好。

【BTV】或许这就是您在义乌的中国梦——解决签证问题，在中国这个大市场开创事业。

【Harry】是的。

【BTV】谢谢您抽出时间来接受我们的采访。我们希望您在义乌生活愉快。

团队成员：姚星，谢之优，楼一博，李新新

On Our Way to Success

By Yao Xing Supervised by Wu Danping & Cai Liang

It is the second time that I have taken part in this service-learning project during the summer holiday. I had many experiences with the project, not only about Yiwu, a fascinating city appealing to different people from all over the world, but also about myself. This project witnessed my personal growth from a freshman to a junior student.

With the process of social development, many cities in China are changing rapidly, especially in the coastal areas, such as Shenzhen, Shanghai and Ningbo, and even the inland cities, like Yiwu. Yiwu is an amazing city that I get to know it many years ago because she is famous for her big market which is beyond one's imagination. The first time that I entered into the market, it was hard for me to find my way from section one to section two even though these sections are combined. Finally, thanks to the signs, I found my way to the different sections. When I walked into the toy section, I was totally shocked because there are so many different kinds of products in one category. For instance, the material of the products is from stuffed to plastic; the shape of the products is from square to irregular; the purpose of the products is from exclusively for children to those for special holidays. In this market, you can find everything you want and many products which you could not even imagine. Maybe this is the strength of the market that appeals to a large number of people from all over the world. When we did the research in this market, people of different skin colors are walking around us. Some are black while some are white. Some look like Chinese, but actually they come from other countries such as Japan, Singapore, Vietnam and so on.

Although the market is huge, the design is almost perfect which allows the customers to purchase products easily and provides shelter from the strong sunshine and the heavy rain. Although the market was built in the 20th century, it has a wide variety of goods in the latest styles to meet the customers' needs. Although this market is in Yiwu, a small county in Zhejiang Province, it attracts people from different countries who not only purchase goods, but also sell goods in this market. As far as I am concerned, the above advantages characterize the

Yiwu Market and appeal to people at home and abroad.

My interviewee is a handsome Pakistani named Muhammad Haroon Bashir. His friends call him Harry. His unique insights, personal charisma and great love for Yiwu impressed me deeply. Unlike most other expatriates who are in favor of living together with companions because of the same language and hobbies, Henry has been living in Yiwu for five years, and he likes to be friends with the local residents, greeting them warmly and chatting with them casually. He believes, "If people don't live here, they will not know what happens here."

Foreigner as Harry is, he possesses the qualities that Chinese admire, namely, the pursuit of harmony and honesty. As an old Chinese commercial principle goes, honesty is the best policy, which can be traced back to *Zhouyi*, "Decent people behave honestly to realize their achievements." This virtue of honesty has passed down until today. Harry's belief in honesty counts for his success. China is a big market, especially in Yiwu, which gives him the chance to fulfill his personal goals. He takes this sincere attitude toward work when running his Mian Trading Company which provides good services and high-quality stationery to customers. Now his company is growing day by day. I sincerely hope he will have a bright future in Yiwu.

It is the second time that I have been a member of the summer project, "Beyond the Voices". From a freshman to a junior, I have had many experiences to enhance my education such as communication skills, professional knowledge, and the more important things, confidence and growth. I still remember the situation when I participated in this project for the first time. When I was assigned the interview, I could do nothing but turn to the upperclassman for help. He told me, "Don't worry! Just believe yourself, and you can do it." To be frank, I was worried that I would make many mistakes during the interview because I had no face-to-face communication experience with foreigners, not to mention the interactive interview which would last for more than ten minutes. Finally, the interview was finished, but roughly.

Before our group came to Yiwu, I spent much time elaborately composing the outline and designing the meaningful questions with the aim of having a perfect interview. During the interview, I communicated with Harry fluently especially when we came to some interesting topics. I also got much important information from his talk. After the interview, I still keep in touch with Harry to refine points in the interview. The three years of studying English at NIT has given me confidence. Although this interview was not perfect, it was much better than last time.

I was lucky to work on the project in Yiwu. To the foreigners, this project lets them know that we respect and care about their lives, their investment and their dreams in China. To the students, it is not only an excellent platform to practice English and broaden our horizons, but also a precious chance to enrich our life experience by applying knowledge to practice. All in all, confidence means power, and if we have enough confidence, we can show our abilities better.

成功路上，事在人为

文：姚　星　指导教师：吴丹苹　蔡　亮

这是我第二次参加暑期社会实践活动——"用声音叙事"。在这个项目中，我收获了很多的经历，不仅认识了义乌，这座吸引着海内外商业人士的魅力城市，也锻炼了自己——这个项目见证了我从大一到大三的个人成长。

伴随着社会的进步，在中国很多城市飞速发展，呈现出日新月异的面貌，其中有像深圳、上海、宁波这样的沿海城市，还有一些则是内陆城市，如义乌。我很多年之前就知道义乌这座神奇的城市了，因为她有一个超乎你想象的大市场。当我第一次踏进这个市场的时候，尽管每个区都是连在一起的，但还是很难找到从一个区到另一个区的通道。最后，要感谢指示牌使我发现了去往不同区域的道路。当我踏进玩具区域的时候，我彻底被震撼了，因为尽管是同一种类，产品却是多样的。例如，商品的材质从棉质到塑料，各式各样；商品的形状从方形到不规则形；商品的用途也是从只限儿童玩耍到为一些重要的节假日准备。在这个市场里，你可以找到任何你想要的，以及那些你压根就没有想到的东西。当我们在这个市场里做调查问卷的时候，有着各种肤色的人在我们四周。有黑皮肤的，有白皮肤的；有的看起来很像中国人，但是事实上他们来自不同的国家，像日本、新加坡、越南，等等。

尽管这个市场很大，但是它的设计近乎完美，使顾客能够轻易地购买商品以及避免强烈阳光和暴风雨；尽管这个市场建造于20世纪，但是它提供种类繁多、最新款式的商品来满足消费者；尽管这个市场坐落在义乌，浙江省的一个县级市，但是它容纳着来自不同国家的人们。他们有些在这里采购，有些在这里经营着自己的商铺。就我个人而言，这些优势是义乌市场的三大特色，吸引着五湖四海的人士。

我的采访对象是一位名叫穆罕默德·哈利·巴斯尔的巴基斯坦英俊小伙子，他的朋友们都叫他哈里。他独到的见解、亲和的个人魅力、对义乌的热爱给我留下了深刻的印象。哈里来义乌五年了，有别于大多数外国人，他喜欢与当地的老百姓生活在一起。我们可以想象在异国打拼的人大多喜欢和自己的同伴生活在一起，因为有共同的语言和生活喜好。哈里很特别，他喜欢与当地的老百姓为邻，热情地打招呼，随意地聊天。就像他曾经说过的："如果你不住在这里，你将无法深入了解这个城市。"

尽管他是外国人，他却拥有中国人所崇尚的品质——追求和谐，讲究诚信。中国有一条古老的商业原则——诚信为本。中华民族的诚信思想最早可以追溯到《周易》："修辞立其诚，所以居业也"，认为君子说话、理论都应该诚实不欺，真诚无妄，才能建功立业。诚实的美德传承至今，而哈里的经营理念恰巧与之对应，我想这是他取得成功的重要原因。中国是一个巨大的市场，特别是义乌；义乌给了他实现个人价值的机会。他秉承着真诚的工作态度经营着他的米尔贸易公司，为顾客提供优质的服务及高质量的办公用品。如今他的事业蒸蒸日上，在这里，我真诚地祝愿他在义乌有一个美好的未来。

义乌之行是我第二次参加“用声音叙事”实践活动，从大一到大三，我收获了交流技能和专业知识，更重要的是自信和成长。我仍旧记得大一时第一次参加活动的情景。当接到采访任务的时候，我压根招架不住，只能向学长求援。他对我说：“不要担心，只要相信你自己，你可以做好的。”坦白地说，我还是很担心，生怕在采访的过程中出很多的差池，毕竟我没有多少与外国人面对面交流的经验，更不用说超过十分钟以上的互动访谈了。最终，我粗糙地完成了那次采访。

此次来义乌之前，我花了几天的时间精心撰写采访提纲，设计提问，做足功课。这次采访顺利多了，我与哈里相谈甚欢，从中获得了很多重要的信息。采访结束后，我还和哈里进行过后续联系核对采访内容。这三年的英语学习生涯，给了我一些展示自己的自信，尽管访谈不是很完美，但是好于之前。

很幸运我能参加义乌的调研项目。对于在义乌的外商而言，此次活动使得他们知道我们尊重并关心他们在中国的工作、生活和梦想。对于学生而言，这是一个锻炼交流技能、开拓视野的广阔平台，是增加我们的社会经历从而学以致用的绝好机会。总而言之，自信是力量，如果我们有足够的自信，那么我们将会更好地展示我们的能力。

Mamadou Sall

Mamadou Sall: Grow, Thrive and Achieve in Yiwu

成长,壮大,成功——扎根义乌

Mamadou Sall is from Senegal and has been doing business in Yiwu for almost 12 years. He founded his own company in 2000 in Yiwu because of its good investment environment. His main business is textiles. In addition to his business here, he has many branches in Africa and exports textiles to different parts of the world. In fact, he is not only a successful president of his company but also a kind father in his harmonious family. He loves Chinese food and culture and feels himself a part of Yiwu. Nowadays, his roots are in Yiwu, and he leads a happy life.

Mamadou Sall 是一个在义乌经商将近 12 年的塞内加尔人。2000 年,Mamadou 受义乌良好投资环境的吸引前来创办公司。公司的主要业务是纺织品出口,目前已取得了不俗的成绩。与此同时,他在非洲有多家分公司,产品出口到世界各地。事实上,Mamadou 不仅是一名成功的公司总裁,也是一位慈祥的父亲,拥有和睦幸福的家庭。他热爱中华美食、中国文化,觉得自己已经融入义乌。现在,他深深扎根于义乌,生活充满乐趣。

Grow, Thrive and Achieve in Yiwu

By Mamadou Sall

Transcript of the Interview:

【BTV】Hello, Mr. Mamadou Sall. Thanks for your agreeing to our interview. It is our honor to have the opportunity to interview you. We are from Ningbo Institute of Technology, Zhejiang University. As a part of our service-learning course, our research will serve as a bridge between overseas-funded enterprises and local government. We aim to explore how overseas-funded enterprises of small and medium-size develop in Yiwu and what major difficulties and problems they may confront during their current development. First, would you please introduce yourself briefly?

【Mamadou Sall】Well, my name is Mamadou Sall. I am from Senegal. I have been in Yiwu for almost 12 years since I founded a company in 2000. My company is exporting textile. In fact, I have companies in China and Senegal. My main business is textile, and our products are exported to several countries. At the same time, I have two sons and a beautiful wife.

【BTV】I have some information about your company. Can you tell me why you chose textiles as your main business instead of toys or jewelry?

【Mamadou Sall】As a matter of fact, I have done it for six years in Senegal and gained a lot of valuable experience. The most key point is that there is a big market in China, so I chose it.

【BTV】To which countries or areas do you export your products?

【Mamadou Sall】I have a company in Yiwu and my homeland respectively. Meanwhile, there are plenty of branches in Africa. Our company always exports products to Africa and Middle East.

【BTV】Your homeland is far from Yiwu. Why did you choose to settle down and do business in Yiwu?

【Mamadou Sall】Because Yiwu is a good city that gathers different people all over the world. It provides a very good environment for foreigners to meet different friends and do business with partners. The most important thing is that it has one of the biggest international markets in the world. Compared with my country, I prefer Yiwu market.

【BTV】I believe you have been to some big cities in China, like Shanghai, Beijing, Guangzhou and so on. Compared with these big cities, what advantages does Yiwu enjoy?

【Mamadou Sall】Yeah, Shanghai, Beijing, Guangzhou may have a prosperous economy now, but I see there are a great many of foreigners and existing potential opportunities in Yiwu. What's more, it is the biggest exporting market in the world.

【BTV】I am happy to hear that you think highly of Yiwu. What attracts you most in Yiwu?

【Mamadou Sall】I come to Yiwu for investment environment. What's more, I really enjoy Chinese food, and living in Yiwu is also a brilliant choice because I can eat different kinds of food, like Arabic food, Italian food and so on. That's great.

【BTV】You have been in Yiwu for 12 years and achieved great success both in business and family. Do you remember your first impression of Yiwu?

【Mamadou Sall】Oh, it is positive. I thought it was a good city. As we can see, Yiwu has been thriving quickly. It becomes more open and prosperous. I really love it!

【BTV】In which aspects has Yiwu changed since you came here?

【Mamadou Sall】Great changes have taken place in the 12 years. Buildings, governments, policies, life standard and environment all have a new face.

【BTV】As a successful businessman, you have been to many countries and gained much life experience. Did you have any culture shock the first time you came to Yiwu?

【Mamadou Sall】Of course, I think the main problem is language. To be honest, many people doing business here come from all over the world. As a foreigner, language may cause some communication problems and misunderstandings in the life, and lots of Chinese cannot speak fluent English.

【BTV】How do you overcome the problem?

【Mamadou Sall】I have some staff who speak good English and handle the problems well.

【BTV】Have you ever studied Chinese?

【Mamadou Sall】Of course. In fact, my son is brought up in Yiwu, so he speaks perfect Chinese. My son is very young and smart, so there is no problem for him to learn new things. I have learned a little from him, but I am so busy that I have not enough time to learn it. What a pity!

【BTV】You mentioned that you have been running your company here for 12 years and have many employees. What are your standards for hiring staff?

【Mamadou Sall】I prefer to employ staff who can stay longer and learn new things quickly. Maybe they first came here without perfect English. That's okay. The key point is that they have enthusiasm to learn it. It is better to hire people who can speak English well, and it will solve some unnecessary problems.

【BTV】What is your main responsibilities in the company?

【Mamadou Sall】I am the president in my company. I don't have to do the trifles. I have many good employees. I am in charge of the company and give orders.

【BTV】As you have mentioned, you are in charge of the company and give orders. Are there any communication problems between you and your employees?

【Mamadou Sall】Not at all. We are a big family. We all have enough experience and know how to manage the company. It is easy for us to communicate with each other.

【BTV】Yiwu is known for its market. Meanwhile, there is fierce competition in the market. Have you considered how to gain advantage in the competition?

【Mamadou Sall】I think the key point is innovation. Innovation is very important. We should pay attention to what customers need and want. Besides, we have to see ourselves in new perspective and keep up with the times.

【BTV】It is universally known that the financial crisis in 2008 affected a lot of companies. Was your company influenced seriously?

【Mamadou Sall】Yeah, certainly. I think almost every company felt that serious impact even its aftermath.

【BTV】As a matter of fact, many companies have even gone bankrupt. How did your company survive in the crisis? What measures did you take?

【Mamadou Sall】It is difficult for everyone. We have to think everything carefully and deliberately. In order to win the advantage, we have to minimize the expenditure, and during the hard time, we must hold on our belief and never lose heart.

【BTV】Every company has its bottleneck period. What is the biggest challenge for your company at present?

【Mamadou Sall】I think innovation is a very urgent task. We should change our pattern and design according to customers' demand, and we must focus on time and market. Only new and fashion products can attract our customers.

【BTV】You have been doing business for 12 years and contacted all kinds of customers. Is there any difference between Chinese and foreign customers?

【Mamadou Sall】Yeah, there is an obvious difference between them. What impressed me was that Chinese cared about the quality most, so our company will especially pay attention to the quality so that we can appeal to more customers in the future.

【BTV】You are occupied with working every day. I wonder if it is complicated to balance your job and family. How do you manage it?

【Mamadou Sall】Eh, in fact, I am really busy, but I often spend more time with my family as much as possible even when I am tired, and my wife lives in Yiwu with me, and one of my sons studies in the USA. We usually have a family day.

【BTV】Your son lives in the Unites States. Do you find it difficult to communicate with him?

【Mamadou Sall】No, nowadays IT has developed a lot, so we could chat with each other anytime. We usually share our news and life on the Internet when we are free.

【BTV】What do you do in your spare time?

【Mamadou Sall】I often spend time in staying with my family and friends. Sometimes, I will see some customers.

【BTV】I think friends are very important to everyone. Have you made some new friends in Yiwu?

【Mamadou Sall】Of course, I make a lot of friends, including Chinese and Arabic partners.

【BTV】Your company is established in Yiwu and has achieved great success. Can you tell us some details about the blueprint for your company in the future?

【Mamadou Sall】I hope my company will become better and attract more customers. Besides, I want to export products to various countries. Nowadays, our main aim is Africa. Maybe Europe is also a good choice.

【BTV】Problems are unavoidable when you are running a business in a foreign country. What kind of services and policies would you like to get from the Yiwu government?

【Mamadou Sall】Government's support is very significant. I hope the barrier like high tax can be removed. In addition, the government can formulate some policies and laws to improve the investment environment, so it will benefit us a lot.

【BTV】This year, the China Dream is a buzzword. Do you have your own Yiwu Dream?

【Mamadou Sall】Yeah, I anticipate that there are more opportunities and potential in Yiwu. At the same time, investment environment can be improved. I feel that I am a part of Yiwu. I really love here!

【BTV】Okay, we have a deeper understanding about Yiwu and your life from the interview. I am pleased to have the chance to talk with you! Thank you very much!

【Mamadou Sall】It's my pleasure.

Group Members: Xie Zhiyou, Lou Yibo, Yao Xing, Li Xinxin

叙事记录

【BTV】您好，Mamadou Sall 先生。非常感谢您能够接受我们的采访。我们是来自浙江大学宁波理工学院的学生。作为服务学习交流的项目之一，我们的调查将会起到连接外资企业和当地政府沟通桥梁的作用。我们旨在探求外资中小型企业如何在义乌发展，以及他们在发展过程中遇到的主要困难和问题。首先，能否请您简单地自我介绍一下？

【Mamadou Sall】好的，我叫 Mamadou Sall，来自塞内加尔。从 2000 年我来义乌创办公司到现在将近 12 年了，公司主要出口纺织品。事实上，我在中国和塞内加尔都有公司，经营纺织品为主，我们的产品出口到各个国家。我有两个儿子和一位美丽的妻子。

【BTV】我之前已经对您的公司有些许了解，我很想知道为什么您不选择玩具或者珠宝，而是选择纺织产品作为您的主要业务？

【Mamadou Sall】事实上，我在塞内加尔做纺织生意将近 6 年，积累了很多宝贵的经验。最重要的是中国有很大的市场，所以我选择纺织产品。

【BTV】您的产品出口到哪些国家和地区？

【Mamadou Sall】我在义乌和我的家乡都有公司。同时，在非洲也有很多分公司。我们的产品主要是出口到非洲以及中东。

【BTV】我们知道您的家乡距离义乌十分遥远，您为什么选择义乌安定下来做生意呢？

【Mamadou Sall】因为义乌是一个很好的城市，它聚集了来自世界各地不同的人。义乌给外国人提供了很好的环境和不同的人做生意，结交不同的朋友。最重要的一点是义乌拥有世界上最大的国际市场。和我的祖国相比，我更青睐义乌的市场。

【BTV】我相信您一定去过中国的一些大城市，像上海、北京、广州等。和这些大城市相比，您觉得义乌有什么优势呢？

【Mamadou Sall】是的，上海、北京、广州现在经济繁荣。但是我看见很多外国人在义乌，而且义乌拥有潜在的机遇。另外，义乌是世界上最大的出口市场之一。

【BTV】很高兴您对义乌如此高的评价。您觉得义乌最吸引您的地方是什么？

【Mamadou Sall】我来义乌是因为义乌良好的投资环境。另外，我十分喜欢中国美食。我觉得在义乌生活是一个很明智的选择，因为在这里我可以品尝到不同的美食，包括阿拉伯美食、意大利美食，等等。那对于我来说实在是太棒了。

【BTV】您来义乌有12年了，现在事业有成、家庭幸福，还记得对义乌的第一印象吗？

【Mamadou Sall】我对义乌的第一印象是十分不错的。我觉得这是一个很美丽的城市。众所周知，义乌发展十分迅速。义乌现在变得更加开放而且繁荣。我十分喜欢义乌。

【BTV】自从您来到这里，您觉得在哪些方面义乌有了深刻的变化？

【Mamadou Sall】义乌在很多方面都改变了很多。包括建筑、政府机关、政策、生活水平、环境都有了全新的面貌。

【BTV】作为一位非常成功的生意人，您去过许多国家，见多识广。那么，在您刚来到义乌的时候，是否有过文化冲突的经历？

【Mamadou Sall】当然，我觉得最主要的问题就是语言。说实话，很多生意人来自世界各地。作为一个外国人，语言可能在生活上会造成很多交流问题和误会。而且很多中国人不能够讲流利的英语。

【BTV】您是如何克服这个问题的呢？

【Mamadou Sall】我有很多员工，他们可以说一口流利的英语并且处理问题得当。

【BTV】您有没有学过中文呢？

【Mamadou Sall】当然有。事实上，我的儿子是在义乌长大的，所以他可以说一口流利的中文。我的儿子挺聪明而且年轻，所以他学东西很快。我也从他身上学了一点中文，但是我平时十分忙碌，没有足够的时间去学习中文。这是十分遗憾的事！

【BTV】您刚刚提到了您在义乌待了12年并且拥有了很多的员工。我想了解您招聘员工的标准是什么？

【Mamadou Sall】我更喜欢聘用那些可以长期待在这里并且学东西很快的人作

为员工。也许他们一开始来这里并不能说一口流利的英语，那没有关系。最重要的是一点是他们必须有热情去学习一项新事物。当然最好能够聘用拥有一口流利英语的员工。因为这样也可以解决一些不必要的麻烦。

【BTV】您在公司的主要职责是什么？

【Mamadou Sall】我是这家公司的总裁。我不需要去做很多琐碎的事情。我有很多优秀的职员。我只要掌管公司运作，并且给予指令就可以。

【BTV】就像您提到的，您掌管公司运作，下达指令，那么您和员工之间会存在沟通问题吗？

【Mamadou Sall】一点也没有。我们像一个大家庭一样。我们都有足够的经验而且知道怎么去管理公司。我们沟通起来没有障碍。

【BTV】义乌以市场出名。同时，在市场上也存在十分激烈的竞争。您是否思考过您为什么能在激烈的市场当中占有一席之地呢？

【Mamadou Sall】我认为最主要的一点是创新。创新是非常重要的。我们需要去关注消费者需要什么和想要什么。另外，我们必须正确看待自己和紧跟时代潮流。

【BTV】众所周知，2008年的金融危机给许多公司造成了影响。您是否感到了金融危机强烈的影响呢？

【Mamadou Sall】是的，当然。我想几乎每个公司都感觉到了金融危机的严重影响，甚至受到它余波的影响。

【BTV】事实上，不少公司已经宣布了破产。您的公司是如何在金融危机中幸存下来的？采取了哪些措施？

【Mamadou Sall】对于每个人来说，这是一个难关。我们需要仔细思考每一件事情，深思熟虑。为了能够在竞争中赢得优势，我们需要减小预算与成本。在那段艰难的时间里，我们必须坚持我们的信念，决不能丧失信心。

【BTV】每一个公司在一段时间内都有一个瓶颈。目前来说，您的公司面对的最大的挑战是什么？

【Mamadou Sall】我认为创新是一个艰巨并且紧急的任务。根据消费者的需求，我们需要改变我们的模式以及设计。而且我们必须要关注市场和时代潮流。只有新的和时尚的产品才能够吸引我们的消费者。

【BTV】您在这里做生意已经12年了，也和各种各样的客户打过交道。中国客户和外国客户是否存在某些差异呢？

【Mamadou Sall】是的，他们之间存在一个很明显的差异。最令我印象深刻的是中国人总是最在乎产品的品质。所以我们公司特别注重产品的质量，以此来吸引更多的客户。

【BTV】您每天忙于工作。对于您来说平衡工作和家庭是否是一件困难的事情？您是如何做到的？

【Mamadou Sall】嗯，事实上，我平时很忙碌。但是我尽可能抽时间和我家人待在一起，即使我很疲惫。我的妻子现在和我一起居住于义乌，我的一个儿子在美国读书，我们经常有家庭日。

【BTV】您的儿子在美国，你们之间是否会存在隔阂呢？

【Mamadou Sall】其实没有。现在IT发展十分迅速，所以我们可以随时同彼此聊天。我们经常会在有空的时候通过互联网来分享我们的生活以及新鲜事儿。

【BTV】您空闲时间会做些什么呢？

【Mamadou Sall】我经常和我家人以及朋友在一起。有时候会见一些客户。

【BTV】我觉得朋友对每个人来说都很重要。您有没有在义乌交到新朋友呢？

【Mamadou Sall】当然，我在这里交了很多朋友，包括中国人，以及阿拉伯人。

【BTV】您的公司在义乌创建，而且经营得很成功。能和我们谈谈您对公司未来的蓝图有何规划吗？

【Mamadou Sall】我希望我的公司可以发展得更好，而且能够吸引更多的客户。另外，我也希望能够将产品出口到不同的国家。如今，我们的主要目标是非洲，也许欧洲是将来不错的选择。

【BTV】在异国他乡经商难免会碰到一些困难。您希望义乌市政府能够为你们提供什么样的政策和服务呢？

【Mamadou Sall】政府的支持是十分重要的。我希望像高税率这些障碍可以解决。另外，政府可以推行一些政策和法令改善投资环境。这样会为我们提供许多便利。

【BTV】今年，中国梦是热门话题。您是否有您自己的义乌梦呢？

【Mamadou Sall】是的，我希望在义乌能够有更多的机遇和潜能。同时，投资环境能够进一步改善。我已经觉得我是义乌的一分子了。我太爱这里了！

【BTV】好的，通过采访，我们对于义乌和您的生活有了更深的了解。我很高兴能够有机会和您交谈。十分感谢您的配合！

【Mamadou Sall】这是我的荣幸。

团队成员：谢之悠，楼一博，姚星，李新新

The City of Dream and Hope

By Xie Zhiyou　Supervised by Wu Danping & Cai Liang

With the thriving development of the economy, how to gain an advantage in the market and gain as much profit as possible is one of the most serious problems for all businessmen. At the same time, as the competition is becoming fiercer, more foreigners choose to become a part of the Chinese market. I am very lucky to have such a wonderful opportunity to communicate with various foreign businessmen in this activity. What I have learned is beneficial to me.

Mamadou Sall is from Senegal and has been doing business in Yiwu for almost 12 years. He founded his own company in 2000 in Yiwu because of its good investment environment. His main business is textiles. In addition to his business here, he has many branches in Africa and exports textiles to different parts of the world. In fact, he is not only a successful president of his company but also a kind father in his harmonious family.

During our conversation, the key word was innovation. Compared with other foreign businessmen, Mamadou Sall thinks innovation is a very important method to gain profit and to earn a good reputation in the market. There is a huge difference between Chinese businessmen and him. According to our traditional beliefs, many businessmen try to improve their efficiency or collaborate with others when they are in trouble. However, they ignore the significance of innovation all the time. Mamadou Sall always makes changes to cater to different customers. What surprised me was that their company chose to package the products in a way to satisfy different customer's needs. That explains his success. During our interview, I noticed a striking difference between Chinese businessmen and foreign businessmen in how they keep the balance between life and career. Most Chinese businessmen will choose to devote themselves to work even in their free time. They always bury themselves in looking through files and having meetings all day. In order to make as much money as possible, they sacrifice their family and hobbies. However, this is not the case with Mamadou Sall. He is not only a very successful businessman, but also a good father and husband. He is very serious about his business, but he will spend as much time as possible with his family and friends. He will chat with his son and hold a family day if he is free. It cannot be denied that success is very significant to us, but how to maintain the balance between the family and work is still a tough task for everyone. If someone can balance these things well, he will lead a happy and bright life.

In the past I did not have enough chances to talk face to face with foreign businessmen, or to have a good understanding of their lives. Due to this project, I found that more and more foreigners are coming to Yiwu. As a matter of fact, they see the potential of Yiwu and cherish its opportunities very much. They begin to learn Chinese customs, including Chinese, Chinese market principles and Chinese customers' requirements. The foreigners realize that the Chinese have begun to attach importance to quality, so they decided to improve the quality of the products and meet the Chinese customer's needs. It is inevitable that they will meet severe problems in business, but they are positive and never lose heart. Although they are new to Yiwu, they are enthusiastic, diligent, innovative and trying to make a home in Yiwu.

In fact, I really appreciate being a part of this team. Thanks to this project, I not only learned much and had wonderful experiences, but also changed my former ideas about Yiwu. Compared with some big cities like Shanghai, Beijing, and Guangzhou, Yiwu is a small city, so I never thought that it would be a good choice to do business. However, everything is changing. Yiwu's market attracts plenty of people and investors. In addition, precious potential and chances are waiting for us in the future. I used to think Yiwu lacked some key qualities, including a nice environment, enough financing, and supportive policies. What surprises me is that the market has become increasingly active, and the local government supports middle-sized and small companies in many ways. In addition, the transportation, the environment, the competence of the residents have improved considerably. Yiwu has taken on a new look and welcomes more people to begin their business career and family life.

During this project, I attained some precious experience and memories which will accompany me forever and lead me to a bright future.

梦想之城，希望之都

文：谢之悠　指导老师：吴丹苹　蔡　亮

随着经济的繁荣发展，对于所有的经商者来说如何在市场上获取优势和获得较大利润是一个非常严峻的问题。同时，市场竞争愈发激烈，更多的外国人选择加入中国市场。我十分荣幸通过这个活动有机会去和不同的外国经商者进行沟通交流，这次所学也将令我受益终生。

Mamadou Sall 是一个在义乌经商将近 12 年的塞内加尔人。2000 年，Mamadou 受义乌良好投资环境的吸引前来创办公司。公司的主要业务是纺织品出口，目前已取得了巨大的成功。与此同时，他在非洲有多家分公司，产品出口到世界各地。事实上，Mamadou 不仅是一名成功的公司总裁，也是一位慈祥的父亲，拥有和睦幸福的家庭。

在我们的谈话中，创新无疑成了关键词。跟其他外国商人相比，Mamadou Sall 认为创新是获取利润以及营造良好的企业声誉和形象的重要途径。同时，他和传统的中国商人相比存在着很大的不同点。在我们的传统观念里，当面临困境，很多中国商人会尝试提高自身的工作效率或者是与其他企业合作。然而，他们一直忽视了创新的重要性。Mamadou Sall 总是会根据不同客户的需要进行改变与创新。最让我惊讶的一点是他们公司会根据客户的需求采用专门的包装，我想这就是他成功的原因。在我们的采访过程当中，我注意到了中国商人和外国商人存在很大差异，那就是如何在生活和工作之间保持平衡。即使在空余时间，很多中国商人也会选择全身心投入工作。他们经常会忙于浏览文件，没完没了地开会。为了赚更多金钱，他们会牺牲自己的家庭和爱好。然而，Mamadou Sall 并非如此。他不仅是一个很成功的商人，而且是一个很优秀的父亲和丈夫。他对工作兢兢业业，但是会尽可能多抽时间陪伴家人和朋友。在空余时间，他会和他儿子聊天并举办家庭日。不可否认成功对于我们很重要，但是对于每个人来说如何平衡家庭和工作仍然是一个挑战。如果一个人可以平衡两者，那么他将拥有一个美好的未来。

过去，我并没有很多机会和外国商人近距离接触，或者是对他们有深入的了解。通过这次活动，我发现越来越多的外国人涌入义乌。事实上，他们预见了义乌的潜力，也十分珍惜机会。他们开始学习中国习俗，包括中文、中国市场规则，还有中国客户的需求。外商敏锐地意识到中国人开始注重品质，所以他们决定提高他们产品的品质以满足中国客户的需求。在贸易活动中不可避免会遇到很多严峻的问题。但是他们积极面对，从不丧失信心。虽然他们在义乌刚刚起步，但是他们热情、勤劳、有创新精神并且想要扎根于义乌。

事实上，我非常感谢这次能够有机会成为这个团队的一员。通过这次活动，我不仅学到了知识和经验，而且改变了对义乌旧有的看法。和上海、北京、广州等城市相比，义乌是一个小城市，所以我从来没有想过义乌适合做生意和发展经济。然而，万物都会改变。义乌市场吸引了大量人群和投资者。另外，义乌的未来存在很多珍贵的机遇和潜力。曾经我以为义乌缺少很多重要因素，包括良好的投资环境、足够的资金和好的扶持政策。让我最惊讶的是义乌市场变得越来越活跃，当地的政府也在很多方面给予中小型企业支持。另外，交通设施、城市环境、市民素质都有了很大的提升。义乌焕然一新，敞开怀抱欢迎更多的人来经商创业、安家落户。

在这次的活动中，我获得了很多宝贵的经验和记忆，这些财富都将伴随我终生并且在未来起到指引作用。

Rida

Rida: Yiwu, the Conversion of a City

义乌，繁都的华丽转身

Rida whose full name is Murtada Ahmed Hamid is a Sudanese of wisdom and insight. He has been living in Yiwu for ten years. He and his wife enjoy the life in China very much. They traveled and experienced many cities in China, but he finally decided to settle in Yiwu for its excellent investment environment. After years of struggling, he owned the company named Sally Company Ltd. He is also the former chairman of the Sudan Chamber of Commerce in Yiwu, leading Sudanese businessmen in Yiwu to open up a path to success.

里达全名叫穆尔塔达·艾哈迈德·哈米德，是个充满智慧和远见的苏丹人。他和他的妻子很享受在中国的生活，已经在义乌居住了十年，曾经游玩过中国各地的城市，但是义乌得天独厚的投资环境使他最终定居在义乌。经过多年的打拼，他成立了自己的公司，取名为莎莉有限公司。作为义乌苏丹商会的前主席，他带领着苏丹商人在义乌开辟出一条成功之路。

Yiwu, the Conversion of a City

By Rida

Transcript of the Interview:

【BTV】Thank you for agreeing to our interview. First, would you like to briefly introduce yourself?

【Rida】My name is Rida. I come from Sudan. I have been living in Yiwu for ten years.

【BTV】Yiwu is not a large and famous city like Shanghai or Guangzhou. How did you find out about Yiwu?

【Rida】I started to know Yiwu long time ago, and it was my first visit in China. I came here just to meet some friends, and my wife has been in China for a long time. She first came to China at the age of eight as an exchange student with an acrobatics troupe with 50 other people, and my son studied Chinese at Zhejiang University. He speaks good Chinese, and now he is a Chinese teacher in Sudan.

【BTV】Wow, your family has a long story in China. I suppose you must have made many Chinese friends here. Have you participated in social or cultural activities in the local community?

【Rida】Yes. Actually every time I have more and more friends. Because I have been living here for a long time, I make many Yiwu friends and also other business friends.

【BTV】Have you learned of traditional Chinese festivals or customs from your Chinese friends? Are there any similarities between Chinese culture and Sudanese culture?

【Rida】I know a lot of Chinese festivals like Chinese New Year and Dragon Boat Festival, and they eat mooncakes on Mid-Autumn Day. Actually, we have two or three Muslim celebrations in our country, and one is called Ramadan which lasts from morning to evening, and my wife and I don't eat or drink and only have one meal in the morning.

【BTV】Have you experienced any cultural shock in Yiwu?

【Rida】I first came here in 2003. At that time, I know very little about

Chinese, and all my staff are Chinese. But to my surprise, most of them can speak English. My wife can speak good Chinese, but we mainly speak English with our partners.

【BTV】Where do you usually go when you are free in Yiwu?

【Rida】When I am free, I like to go walking along the riverside and go shopping, but I prefer to walking because it can help me lose weight and keep healthy.

【BTV】You have been to many places in China and know much about China. What do you think of the transportation in Yiwu?

【Rida】The transportation in Yiwu is convenient, and it's easy to transfer from one place to another place by taxi or bus or even train. There are a lot of trains to other provinces in China, but the taxi drivers in Yiwu are not so proficient and honest. When I take a taxi in Shanghai, I just need to tell him about the destination, and they offer good service, but in Yiwu, things are not always going like that.

【BTV】What do you think of the investment environment in Yiwu?

【Rida】I think Yiwu is a business city, and it is one of the biggest markets in the world. Most factories in China supply goods to Yiwu, and from my view, compared with Guangdong Fair which is also a big market, Yiwu is more famous for producing daily-use items than any other cities in China, and it is a good market for everyone because most of the people are mainly looking for daily useful products.

【BTV】In your opinion, what factors contribute to the success of Yiwu?

【Rida】I think the government is important. The government of Yiwu is more flexible than other governments to make an active market. They encourage the foreigners to do the business, and they give the licenses and residence permits and free advertisements to foreigners to do business.

【BTV】I suppose Yiwu's good investment environment attracted you to live and work here. Is there anything else that appeals to you?

【Rida】Yes. Before I come here, there are a lot of Sudanese people living in Yiwu. This is the major reason I live here. With Yiwu people and my Sudanese friends, I feel that I am at home. I choose Yiwu, and I prefer to say that Yiwu is my second hometown.

【BTV】Can you tell us some details about your business?

【Rida】Yes. My business was trading business, but two years ago, I changed my business, and now I am specialized in complete production line for different things such as plastic, and I have two staff. They come from Jiangdong, and they help me deal with business of the company.

【BTV】Can you share with us how you motivate your staff?

【Rida】By increasing their salaries and satisfying their demand, and I will be concerned about their thoughts about the company. It is generally the essential way to encourage people to do good business and to do good jobs. Also, they care about my business and success. We are a group, and we are successful together.

【BTV】You sound like a kind boss. It is, of course, unavoidable to have dealings with Chinese people in China. Are there any differences in doing business with Chinese and other foreigners?

【Rida】Of course it's different. China or Yiwu market is for wholesale market while our market is for detailed sale. Most of the people from my country prefer to do business in Yiwu because they can buy different goods from Yiwu. But some people are looking for the factories to apply to be agents, and some other bosses are looking for some components for different items, so they go to Futian Market to buy small components. When my friends or my customers come to China, I take them to different factories to compare the quality and price and choose one of them. So, our business cooperates with factories, not with Futian Market.

【BTV】Does your company confront any difficulties?

【Rida】At present, there is no big difficulty in my company because the government considers about everything and makes it easy to do business in Yiwu.

【BTV】As we all know, the financial crisis in 2008 was quite serious. Was your company influenced?

【Rida】Yes. My business was affected by this in 2008. However, we see that Chinese economy is strong and stable. We got involved in much trouble at that time, but we get through it, and we solve most of problems now.

【BTV】I heard that foreigners can only send back \$50,000 to their country. Do you think this is a problem?

【Rida】Before it was a problem, but now there is another way: Hong Kong license. We send our money to Hong Kong so that we get more money changed to dollars. However, the disunited rule in Yiwu market brings us problem. We like to cooperate with the Chinese market, but most of the factories don't like RMB, so we transfer money like this. But some markets like Futian Market prefer RMB than dollar, so the customers who come to Chinese market are limited. I think all the markets in China should be on the way to solve the problem.

【BTV】What aspect does the government need to improve for the development of investment in Yiwu?

【Rida】The first problem is about the money we referred to before. Second, many countries have cheaters. I advise the businessmen in Yiwu don't meet with these people. These cheaters make a lot of trouble in China and any other countries. And I'd like to encourage my country to stimulate Yiwu government to make policy to support people to do business and to study what kind of policy makes business easier.

【BTV】I think that will be a useful suggestion for our government. Have you heard of the China Dream? Now it's a hot topic in China.

【Rida】Although I didn't know much about it, I think China Dream is to make the people's dream come true. And it will soon be realized because the economy in China is strong. We like to follow the policy and the way in China. And China is a good teacher. All the countries have to follow China to do business and to make the economy well.

【BTV】It's true that good business depends on good policy. Anyway, do you have any Yiwu dreams? What is the blueprint for your company for the next five years?

【Rida】I plan to go back to my country. Maybe my son will come to China and take over from me.

【BTV】Finally, can you describe the local residents in Yiwu using a couple of adjectives?

【Rida】Yiwu people are very lucky because the government takes care about jobs. You see, people in Yiwu before were poor, and now the market increases the business. Most people in Yiwu now are rich. They follow the policy of Yiwu government to make the business more successful.

【BTV】I wish you a nice stay in Yiwu, and thank you very much for agreeing to our interview. Your suggestions are very meaningful for improving the image of the city.

【Rida】You are welcome.

Group Members: Zhu Jiangshan, Qian Chen, Chen Jialu, Cen Ye

叙事记录

【BTV】感谢您接受我们的采访。首先,可以给我们做一个简短的自我介绍吗?

【Rida】我的名字叫里达,来自苏丹。我已经在义乌生活了十年。

【BTV】义乌不如上海和广州那些大城市出名,请问您是如何知道义乌这个地方的?

【Rida】我很早以前就知道义乌。我到中国的第一站就是义乌。我来这里是为了见朋友。而我的妻子在义乌待了很久,在八岁的时候,她和另外的五十个人作为杂技团的交换生来中国学习。我的儿子在浙江大学学过中文。他的中文很好,现在在苏丹教中文。

【BTV】哇,您的家庭和中国很有渊源。既然您在义乌待了这么长的时间,您肯定在这儿结交了不少中国朋友吧?您参加过当地社区的社会文化活动吗?

【Rida】是的。每一次我参加此类的活动都能交到很多朋友。因为我已经在义乌生活了很长一段时间,所以我有很多义乌的朋友和其他生意场上的朋友。

【BTV】您知道中国的某些传统节日和习俗吗?您认为苏丹文化和中国文化有什么相似之处?

【Rida】我确实知道很多关于中国的节日,比如春节和端午节。而且我知道中国人在中秋节的时候还会吃月饼。在我们国家,我们每年都有两到三个穆斯林庆祝活动。其中一个活动叫斋月,从早晨到傍晚,我和我的家人都是不吃不喝,我们只在清晨时分吃一顿饭。

【BTV】不同国家的文化之间存在差异。您在义乌碰到过文化冲突吗?

【Rida】我来中国的时候是2003年。那时我对中文一窍不通,而我的员工都是中国人。令我很惊讶的是,他们都会说英语。我的妻子中文说得很好。但我们基本上都是用英语和我们的合作伙伴交流。

【BTV】您空闲的时候最喜欢去哪里?

【Rida】我有空的时候就喜欢沿着河岸散步或者去购物。但是我更喜欢散步,因为它可以帮助我减肥并且保持健康。

【BTV】您曾去过中国的很多不同地方,对中国了解颇多。您觉得义乌的交通状况如何?

【Rida】义乌的交通很便利。从一个地方到另一个地方很容易,可以乘出租车、公交,甚至火车,很多火车通往中国的其他省份。但是义乌的出租车司机还不够敬业、诚恳。当我在上海乘出租车的时候,只需告诉司机去哪儿,那些司机就可提供良好的服务。但是在义乌这个地方,情况时好时坏。

【BTV】从投资环境方面来看,您觉得义乌怎么样?

【Rida】我觉得义乌是一个商业城市。它是世界上最大的贸易市场之一。大多数中国的工厂都会给义乌供应货物。个人而论，我觉得广交会虽然也很大，但是义乌市场提供的日用品名声更大。对大家来说它是一个很好的市场，因为大多数商人都在寻找日常有用的产品。

【BTV】您认为是什么造就了义乌的成功？

【Rida】我认为政府的作用不容小觑。义乌市政府比其他政府更加开明。他们给义乌市场注入了新鲜的血液，鼓励外国人在义乌经商，并给予营业执照和居住许可证。与此同时，他们通过免费的广告来推广义乌市场，使义乌企业更加成功。

【BTV】我想是义乌良好的投资环境吸引您来义乌生活和工作。除此之外，还有什么其他的原因吗？

【Rida】有的。在我来义乌之前，这边居住着很多苏丹同胞，这是我愿意在中国长久发展的主要原因。有了义乌和苏丹朋友的陪伴，我觉得如同在自己家一样。更确切地说，义乌是我的第二故乡。

【BTV】能和我们详细谈谈您的生意状况吗？

【Rida】好的。我以前是做外贸生意的。但是两年前，我的业务发生了改变，我现在拥有完整的生产线可以生产不同的东西，比如塑料制品。我有两名来自江东的员工，他们在帮我打理公司的事。

【BTV】那么能告诉我们您是如何激励您的员工更有效率地工作吗？

【Rida】我给他们加薪并且适时满足他们的需求，同时我会关心他们对公司的想法和意见，这是常规的也是最主要的鼓励员工认真工作的方式。同时，他们也时刻关心我的生意成功与否。我们是一个团队，荣辱与共。

【BTV】您真是个仁慈的老板。您经常跟中国人做生意，那么，中国人和外国人做生意有什么区别呢？

【Rida】当然很不同。义乌市场是批发市场而我们国家的市场却是零售市场。我们国家的大多数人更喜欢在义乌做生意，因为他们可以从义乌购买不同的货物。然而有一些人直接找到厂家，申请代理开店。而其他一些公司的老板需要一些货物的零件，所以他们去福田市场购买一些小部件。每当我的朋友或我的客户来中国的时候，我会带他们到不同的厂家比较产品的价格和质量，然后选择其中的一款。所以我们的业务是和厂家合作，而不是福田市场。

【BTV】请问您公司目前面临的主要困境是什么？

【Rida】目前，我们公司暂时未遇到很大的困难。因为义乌市政府已经考虑得很周到了。

【BTV】众所周知，2008 年金融危机非常严峻，您的公司有受到影响吗？

【Rida】是的。在 2008 年我们公司确实受到了影响，然而我们看到中国的经济是强劲和稳定的。虽然当时我们陷入了重重困境，但是我们公司现在已经从金融危机中恢复过来。

【BTV】听说外国人被允许带回本国的资金不能超过50000美元，您如何看待这个问题？

【Rida】在此之前，这是一个问题。但是现在我们有了解决的方法。我们可以开通香港离岸账户，这样可以汇出更多的美金。然而义乌市场未统一的规则使我们犯难。我们愿意配合中国市场，但是现在大多数工厂都不愿以人民币交易，所以我们用这种方式汇钱。但是有一些市场比如福田市场更喜欢用人民币交易。因此，到中国来做生意的客户被限制了，所以我认为中国市场应该解决这个问题。

【BTV】您认为义乌市政府应该改善哪些方面以促进义乌投资的发展？

【Rida】第一点是关于之前我们提到的结售汇的问题。另外一点是，许多国家都存在着诈骗分子。我建议义乌商人不要与这些人打交道，这些诈骗分子在中国和其他国家制造了很多麻烦。我也希望我的祖国能促使义乌市政府出台有利经商的政策，并研究出何种政策能使商务活动更便利。

【BTV】我认为您的建议对我们政府很有用。请问，您听说过"中国梦"吗？这个话题在中国很热门。

【Rida】尽管我对此不是很了解，但是我想中国梦就是让人们的梦想成真。我想这个梦想在不久的将来肯定会实现。因为中国有如此强大的经济做后盾。我们乐于遵循中国的制度和方式。中国是一个好老师，所有的国家都应学习中国的经验使经济繁荣昌盛。

【BTV】的确，没有好的政策是做不成贸易的。那么，您有"义乌梦"吗？我指在未来五年里关于公司未来蓝图您有何设想？

【Rida】我打算回到自己的国家。我的儿子可能会来中国接替我。

【BTV】采访的最后，您能用一些词来描述一下您眼中的义乌人吗？

【Rida】义乌人是非常幸运的，因为政府关心就业。你看，以前义乌人很贫穷。而现在的义乌市场却是一派欣欣向荣的景象。如今大多数的义乌人都很富有，他们遵循义乌市政府的政策，生意兴隆。

【BTV】祝您在义乌心想事成。非常感谢您接受我们的采访，您的建议对提高城市形象有重要意义。

【Rida】不客气。

团队成员：朱江珊，钱晨，陈佳露，岑烨

Rida and His Family in Yiwu

By Zhu Jiangshan   Supervised by Wu Danping & Cai Liang

I have never set foot in such a place as Yiwu where one word can incisively and vividly describe my first impression of it: international. My heart is full of curiosity and desire to explore this unfamiliar city since I first came here. Following the team, I walked down the street and observed the diverse people who have different colors of skin, different clothing, different diets and different cultures. These people add passion and enthusiasm to Yiwu and create the diversity of the international city.

Yiwu, the world's largest small commodity distribution center, is known as "an ocean of small commodities and a paradise for shoppers". With China's reform and opening-up, Yiwu followed the strategy of the local government by "promoting the business and developing the city" and found its distinctive way to fast development. At that time, Yiwu was surrounded by small commodity factories and crowded with merchants. The energetic market gradually became a distribution center which now enjoys great prestige all over the world.

However, I had never really felt the spirit of this commercial city until I went to a small night market when busy workers and the people who stay at home in the air-conditioning by day come out into the street at night. Our team went to a nearby night market in order to find interviewees. People from different countries moved back and forth in the small streets and enjoyed the lively city. Walking down the street, our eyes were full of beautiful and inexpensive things as well as delicious snacks which constantly attract our taste buds. This was the first time I experienced the charm of the city.

The interview with Rida was not as easy as I had expected. As the former Chairman of the Sudan Chamber of Commerce of Yiwu and a successful businessman, Rida is always busy with his work. However, I gained much from this hard-won interview. The deeper the conversation with Rida went, the more one found how this intelligent Sudanese businessman and his family were closely connected with China. His wife came to China at an early age as an exchange student with an acrobatic troupe. When I asked how her Chinese was, the wife laughed and told me that she used to speak Chinese well because she had a

Chinese nanny from whom she often had the chance to learn Chinese. Moreover, their son who once studied Chinese at Zhejiang University has become a Chinese teacher in Sudan. Meanwhile, Rida told me that he and his family love China. They not only do business here but also have been to many other cities in China. During the last ten years of doing business in China, he had made many Chinese friends and come to know much about Chinese festivals and customs. Yiwu has brought him success in business and has become his second hometown at the same time.

When it comes to the International Trade City, he pointed out that the Yiwu market enjoys a great advantage as a large wholesale market for daily-use products, which is rare in his own country. At the same time, he also speaks highly of the Yiwu government, which actively encourages foreigners' investment by offering favorable support in daily life and policies that support business. Yiwu residents' living standards have improved so much as they followed the government's policy to make their fortunes. Meanwhile, he hopes that the government of Sudan could take China as an example and encourage the local government to help businessmen create more opportunities to develop trade. Concerning the issue that foreigners are limited in the amount of money that they can send back to their homeland, he states his viewpoint and proposes that the government should work to solve the problem.

Although Rida did not say too much about the future, I still sensed Rida's rigorous and meticulous attitude from his busy schedule. Even on Ramadan, such a special time when Muslims fast from sunrise to sundown, they did not halt the pace of the work. I suddenly realized that behind the success was the hard work and great efforts, which is absolutely what we need when pursuing our dreams. Taking a steadfast and diligent attitude to learning is what we should do now after which we can obtain the qualification to compete with thousands of young people pursuing dreams like us.

Dreams cannot make themselves come true. Only with great effort can we realize our dreams. Yiwu is not only the miracle place where Rida fulfills his dreams but also the paradise for so many other dream chasers!

情系东方，梦圆中国

文：朱江珊　指导教师：吴丹苹　蔡　亮

之前从未踏上过义乌这片热土，一个词可以淋漓尽致地描述我对它的第一印象：国际化。初来乍到的我，对义乌这座陌生的城市充满着未知的好奇和探索的欲望。跟随着团队的步伐，走在义乌宽敞的大道上，看到来来往往的人形形色色，他们拥有不同的肤色、不同的着装、不同的饮食习惯、不同的文化。他们给义乌这座城市注入了激情和活力，造就了这个多元的国际化都市。

作为全球最大的小商品集散中心，义乌被冠以"小商品海洋，购物者天堂"的美名。改革开放以来，义乌坚持和深化"兴商建市"发展战略，走出了一条富有自身特色的区域发展之路。商人们蜂拥而至，一时间，各地的小商品都集中到了义乌，义乌市场逐渐强大，最终形成一个集散中心，在全国乃至全球都赫赫有名。

而真正了解到义乌这座都市的商业化，是从并不起眼的小夜市开始的。夜幕降临，白天忙于工作的人和待在家里避暑的人都走出办公室和家门来到大街上。为了寻找采访对象，我们团队来到附近的一个夜市。不同肤色的人穿梭在小街上，夜市无疑是热闹繁华的。沿街走来，琳琅满目、物美价廉的小商品已使我们目不应接，各种美味的小吃又不断地在挑逗我们的味蕾。这是第一次我切身体验到这座城市的魅力。

与里达的碰面，可谓是好事多磨。作为苏丹商会的前主席和一名成功的商人，里达的行程总是排得很满。但是来之不易的两次采访使我收获甚多。越是与里达深入交谈，你越会发现，这个充满智慧的苏丹商人以及他的家庭和中国之间有着千丝万缕的联系。他的妻子很早就踏足中国，少年时代就作为杂技团的交换生来中国学习。当我问及她中文讲得如何时，她笑称自己以前讲得很好，因为来中国学习时身边有个中国保姆，常常有机会学习讲中文。而他们的儿子也曾在浙江大学学习中文，现在已是苏丹的一名中文教师。里达告诉我，他和他的家人很喜欢中国，他们不仅在中国经商，而且还游玩过很多中国城市。在十年的中国经商之旅中，他结交了很多中国朋友，也知道很多关于中国的节日和习俗。义乌带给他贸易成功的同时，已然成了他的第二故乡。

当我们聊到义乌商贸城时，他说，义乌市场最大的特点在于它是大型的日用品批发市场。在这边进货成本更低，能够使利益最大化。而这样的市场正是他们自己国家所匮乏的。同时，他也高度评价了义乌市政府对于义乌的成功所发挥的作用，义乌市政府积极鼓励外商的投资，在生活和贸易政策上给予大力支持。义乌的居民以前并不富有，但他们遵循政府的政策致富发家。他很期待苏丹的政府能够向中国学习，激励地方政府，为商人发展贸易提供更多的机会。并且，他对于外币结售汇使外国人经商受到限制的问题提出了自己的看法和办法，并倡议政府颁布一些政策来解决这个问题。

对于未来，里达并没有做出太多的期许，但是，从里达与其妻子忙碌的背影中，我仍然感受到里达对于工作的严谨和一丝不苟的态度。即使在斋月如此特殊的日子里(穆斯林的斋戒月，从日出到日落停止一切饮食、性事等活动。通常人们在天晓前吃“封斋饭”，在日落时以食物或饮料开斋，即“开斋小吃”)，他们也没有停下工作的步伐。我忽然体会到，那些光鲜的成功背后其实是很多不为人知的艰辛和努力。而这种肯做肯干、吃苦耐劳的精神正是我们每一个拥有梦想的人应该学习的。我们当下所要做的就是踏踏实实、勤勤恳恳地学习，然后才有资格去和千千万万同样怀揣梦想的年轻人去角逐。

梦想不该只是梦，奋力地追逐方能梦想成真。义乌这片神奇的热土是里达圆梦的地方，更是千千万万追梦者的天堂！

Subhi

Subhi: Yiwu, My Second Home

义乌,我的第二故乡

Subhi Daglish comes from Jordan, a country in the Middle East. He is a businessman with humor and hospitality. He came to China 18 years ago and has a Chinese name, Su Baihe. Before he came to Yiwu, he had been to Guangzhou. On his friend's advice, Subhi came to Yiwu in 2004. His company exports gifts, furniture and stationery to the Middle East. He knows much about Chinese culture and history. Subhi has many friends in Yiwu, enjoys every moment here, and considers Yiwu as his second home.

苏布希·达格里什来自中东国家约旦,是一个幽默、热情的商人。他的中文名字叫苏百贺。18 年前他来到中国,在来义乌之前曾去过广州。2004 年,在朋友的建议下他来到了义乌。他的公司主要出口礼品、家具、文具一类的商品到中东国家。他很了解中国的历史文化。苏布希在义乌拥有很多的朋友,他十分享受在这里生活的每分每秒,已经把义乌当作了他的第二故乡。

Yiwu, My Second Home

By Subhi

Transcript of the Interview:

【BTV】Hello, we are the team, "Beyond the Voice", and come from Ningbo Institute of Technology, Zhejiang University. Thank you very much for agreeing to our interview. Would you briefly introduce yourself first?

【Subhi】My name is Subhi Daglish, and my Chinese name is Su Baihe. I am from Jordan, a country in the Middle East.

【BTV】Actually I do not know the Middle East very well. Could you tell me something about it?

【Subhi】Okay, the Middle East is a very important area for oil, but all these areas have wars, especially in the last two years. You can hear something about the war or conflict in Egypt, Tunisia, Libya, Iraq, and Syria, so although there are chances in the Middle East, they still come here to do business.

【BTV】How did you hear about Yiwu in your country?

【Subhi】I found out about Yiwu in Guangzhou. It was 1999, and some friends told us that there is a small commodity market in Yiwu, and people do business, and small businesses there can fill one overseas shipping container with various items. Then we asked our friends in Guangzhou if they knew where it was, but they didn't know. Actually even many Chinese didn't know Yiwu at that time. At last we found it.

【BTV】What was your first impression of Yiwu?

【Subhi】At that time, Yiwu was very small indeed. The four new markets were not here. Also there was nothing from the East Hotel to far north. Only farms, so we thought it may not be easy to do business in Yiwu.

【BTV】When did you start your business in Yiwu?

【Subhi】I came to Yiwu in 2004, and I was impressed by the large variety of goods in the market, the familiar Muslim food in restaurants, and the fast development of the city, so I established an office to do business.

【BTV】What are the differences between Guangzhou and Yiwu in terms of buying goods?

【Subhi】When you go to Guangzhou, the factory or the shop asks you how many containers you want, but in Yiwu, they ask you how many types of goods you want. This is indeed different and easy because in this way, the buyer can collect many items in one container and can immediately send this to the customers in his country.

【BTV】Is this the main reason you chose Yiwu? How about the quality of the goods in Yiwu?

【Subhi】You are right, and we have little worry about the quality because most of the goods are made in Yiwu. The goods are always what we want and easy to sell out in our country to make a profit.

【BTV】That explains why so many people begin their businesses here, right?

【Subhi】Yeah. More foreign buyers who had been to Guangzhou before now come to Yiwu. Maybe they find the same item but with a lower price, or if it is more expensive, they do not need to have many containers, just one or two containers are enough. In Yiwu, it is easier. They ask me for each item, sometimes each design instead of the number of containers.

【BTV】Will you encourage your friends to start businesses in Yiwu? If so, what will you say to your friends about Yiwu?

【Subhi】Sure I will. Everybody asks me about Yiwu, and I advise them to come here to do business. I tell them about the products in Yiwu, and it is very easy for everybody to do business here because you can put many items in one container. The delivery time is very short for all these things.

【BTV】Which do you prefer, quality or the price?

【Subhi】Quality is important; also the price is important. The most important thing is to buy something you can sell out in your country, not buy something very beautiful and expensive, but nobody buys it. In this way, it is not business. People can evaluate quality and price, and they may evaluate how much it costs to produce this product and if it is practical.

【BTV】Can you tell us your standards for hiring staff?

【Subhi】There are two conditions: first, he/she should graduate from university; and second, he or she should be fluent in English. Age is not important.

【BTV】Are the staff in your company Chinese or foreigners?

【Subhi】My staff are Chinese for sure. I do not need to employ foreigners.

【BTV】Do you have some suggestions for the college students who want to start their own business?

【Subhi】I know, in China, they are very ambitious. First of all, the first three months after their graduation, they should work in any company. After three months, they should go to another company to have a better job. They should be moving from one company to another. Then, they have experience. After that, maybe they open their own office and do their own business. They are very ambitious because there are many opportunities for young people to start their own business.

【BTV】How much do you know about Chinese culture?

【Subhi】I know much about China. For example, the long history, and the ancient Silk Route from Xi'an to the Middle East. I have been to Xi'an several times. The relationship between China and the Middle East is very long in both business-relations and culture-exchange relations.

【BTV】How much do you know about the history of China in the last century?

【Subhi】I know something about the new China history. The revolution of Mao Zedong united all China greatly. The revolution was also very correct at that time, which makes it easier for Chinese people themselves to exchange with other countries in business and culture.

【BTV】What are the differences between China and the Middle East?

【Subhi】Now in the Middle East, we are unlucky. We did not have such a revolution to unite all our countries, but China is united, so people from south to north, from east or west can travel and trade easily without a visa, without a passport. Also in China, the language is the same. People all speak Mandarin Chinese. The development in China makes the security. We feel safe when we are in China. It is essential to be safe and secure in order to do business and to develop the country.

【BTV】Did you meet language barriers in Yiwu when you first came here?

【Subhi】When I came to Yiwu the first time, I could speak some Chinese, so I did not have this problem.

【BTV】You learned Chinese in your country?

【Subhi】No, I learned Chinese in "People's University of China". This means that I learned Chinese from the people in China, from you, from him, from everybody. It is all the "People's University of China".

【BTV】You are so humorous. You can speak Chinese and know much about the history, so it must be easy for you to do business and live in Yiwu. Do you like Chinese food? If so, what's your favorite?

【Subhi】I like Chinese food very much, almost everything. First of all, I like the roasted Beijing Duck. It is very delicious. Second, some vegetarian food like tofu. Tofu is also called "Chinese cheese", and I also like the foreign restaurants here. In Yiwu, there are many cafes. Sometimes I will go with my foreign friends.

【BTV】Have you had the experience of celebrating traditional Chinese festivals?

【Subhi】I celebrated the Spring Festival with my Chinese friends, also the National Day, and the National Day is set up to memorialize the establishment of the People's Republic of China.

【BTV】How do you spend your spare time in Yiwu?

【Subhi】Playing mahjong with my Chinese friends. I have made many Chinese friends in Yiwu now.

【BTV】What do you think of the local people? Are they easy to get along with?

【Subhi】Very friendly. I do business and talk with Yiwu people every day, and I play mahjong and cards with my friends in Yiwu.

【BTV】Could you use one word to describe Yiwu?

【Subhi】This makes me paint one very big picture: beautiful Yiwu. I enjoy my life, I love China and I consider Yiwu as my second home.

【BTV】Thank you very much for doing the interview. We wish you a nice stay in Yiwu.

【Subhi】Oh, thank you.

Group Members: Luo Yiyuan, Shen Danni, Yang Xiajian

叙事记录

【BTV】您好！我们是"用声音叙事"活动小组，来自浙江大学宁波理工学院。非常感谢您接受我们的采访。请您先做一下自我介绍好吗？

【Subhi】我叫苏布希·达格里什，中文名叫苏百贺，来自中东国家约旦。

【BTV】事实上我不怎么了解中东这个地区，您能和我说说吗？

【Subhi】好的。中东是一块石油资源非常丰富的地区。但是这几年，那边有较多的战争。你可以听到一些在埃及、突尼斯、利比亚、伊拉克和叙利亚等国发生的战乱。所以，即使在中东有很多机会，大家仍然到中国来做生意。

【BTV】在约旦，您是怎么知道义乌的呢？

【Subhi】我是在1999年广州交易会上知道义乌的。一些朋友告诉我们在义乌有一个小商品市场。人们在那里做生意，各种类型的小商品可以装满整整一个集装箱。我们问了在广州的朋友是否知道义乌在哪里，但是他们并不知道。事实上在那个时候，甚至很多中国人也不太了解义乌。最后，我们还是找到了义乌。

【BTV】您对义乌的第一印象如何？

【Subhi】在那个时候，义乌是一个小城。这四个市场当时不在这里的。从东方大厦向北的地方本来什么都没有，只有农田。所以我们觉得在义乌做生意会有点难。

【BTV】那您是什么时候开始在义乌做生意的呢？

【Subhi】在2004年的时候我来到义乌。市场里商品种类繁多，餐馆里有熟悉的穆斯林清真食物，城市飞速发展，这一切给我留下了深刻印象，所以我在这里成立了办事处开始做生意。

【BTV】广州交易会和义乌的市场在采购方面有什么差异？

【Subhi】当你在广州交易会的时候，那些工厂和商铺会问你需要多少集装箱的货量。而在义乌，他们问你需要多少种的款式，做生意方式更简单，采购者可以选购各种各样的商品装入一个集装箱，然后马上发货给自己国家的客户。

【BTV】这是您选择义乌的主要原因吗？那么义乌商品的质量怎么样？

【Subhi】你说得对。对质量问题我们不怎么担心，因为大部分商品都是在义乌制造的。这些商品通常是我们所需要的，在我们国家卖得很好，有钱可赚。

【BTV】正因为如此，越来越多的人来义乌做生意，是吗？

【Subhi】是的。越来越多去过广州交易会的外商都来到了义乌。可能在这里他们找到一模一样的商品，而价格更低；或价格稍贵，但是不需要买很多集装箱的量，只要一两个集装箱的量就足够了。所以在义乌做生意更简单。他们问我需要什么商品，什么款式，而不是需要几个集装箱。

【BTV】那您会介绍您的朋友来这边做生意吗？如果是的话，您会怎么介绍义乌？

【Subhi】当然会。每个朋友都问我有关义乌的事，我也建议他们到这边来做生意。我会告诉他们义乌的商品，而且做生意门槛不高，因为在这里你可以采购一集装箱的商品，而且发货的速度非常快，等等，诸如此类介绍。

【BTV】您更注重于质量还是价格呢？

【Subhi】质量很重要，当然价格也很重要。但是对于我来说最重要的是所进的货可以卖得出去。有些东西虽然漂亮、昂贵但是没有销路，我也不会进货，否则就做不成生意了。人们可以自己评估商品的质量和价格，评估成本以及实用与否。

【BTV】能谈谈您雇佣员工的标准吗？

【Subhi】我有两个条件，一是大学毕业，二是英语流利。年龄不重要。

【BTV】那您的员工是中国人呢还是外国人？

【Subhi】都是中国人，我不需要去雇佣外国人。

【BTV】对于大学生创业您有什么建议吗？

【Subhi】我知道在中国，大学生们有很大的抱负。首先，在毕业后的头三个月内，他们应该找家公司工作。三个月之后，他们可以去别的公司找更好的工作。他们可以不断跳槽以积累工作经验。之后，他们就可以自己创业了。他们很有抱负，现在有很多的机会可助力他们自主创业。

【BTV】您对中国文化的了解有多少呢？

【Subhi】我对中国有较多的了解，例如，悠久的历史和从西安到中东的丝绸之路。我去过西安很多次。中国和中东的贸易关系和文化交流都是非常悠久的。

【BTV】那您对中国二十世纪的历史有了解吗？

【Subhi】我知道一些新中国的历史。毛泽东的革命很好地将全中国团结在一起。这一革命在那个时候是非常正确的，因为只有全中国团结在一起才会使中国人民更好地进行贸易上及文化上的交流。

【BTV】您觉得中国和中东有哪些不同的地方呢？

【Subhi】在中东我们很不幸。我们没有那样的革命来统一我们的国家。而中国是统一的，从南方到北方，从东部到西部，来自不同省份的中国人可以不用签证和护照就轻而易举地进行交流。同时在中国，语言也是统一的，大家都说普通话。中国的发展造就了稳定的国内环境。在中国，我们会觉得很安全，这是贸易开展、国家发展所必不可少的。

【BTV】在您第一次来义乌的时候有没有遇到一些语言上的障碍呢？

【Subhi】在我第一次来义乌的时候，我就会说一些中文，所以我没有这方面的困扰。

【BTV】那您是在您自己的国家学的中文吗？

【Subhi】不是的。我在“中国人民大学”学的中文。我的意思是我是从中国人，从你，从他，从其他人那里学习中文的。这就是所有中国人的大学。

【BTV】您好幽默。您会说中文，了解中国的历史，在义乌做生意、生活可以说是如鱼得水。我很想知道您是否喜欢中国的食物？最喜欢什么菜？

【Subhi】我非常喜欢中国的食物，差不多都喜欢。我最喜欢的是北京烤鸭，味道好极了。还有一些素菜，比如说豆腐。豆腐也叫作中国奶酪。我也很喜欢这里的外国餐厅。另外义乌有很多的咖啡店，有时候我会和我的外国朋友一起去。

【BTV】您有庆祝中国传统节日的经历吗？

【Subhi】我和中国朋友一起欢度春节和国庆节，国庆节是用来纪念中华人民共和国成立的日子。

【BTV】在义乌您是怎么度过您的空闲时间呢?

【Subhi】和我的中国朋友打麻将。现在我在义乌结交了很多的中国朋友。

【BTV】您觉得义乌当地人怎么样? 他们好相处吗?

【Subhi】非常友好。我每天都和义乌人做买卖、聊天,有空的时候还和我的义乌朋友们打麻将、打牌。

【BTV】您可以用一个词来描述义乌吗?

【Subhi】这让我的脑海里出现了一张宏图——美丽义乌。我很享受在中国的生活,我喜欢中国,我把义乌当作我的第二故乡。

【BTV】谢谢您接受我们的采访。祝您在义乌过得开心。

【Subhi】谢谢。

团队成员:罗一圆,沈丹妮,杨侠剑

Small City, Big World

By Luo Yiyuan Supervised by Wu Danping & Cai Liang

As an English major in college, I am greatly interested in foreigners. I want to know what they think about the world, what they think about China, and what they know about Yiwu. Luckily, I have the opportunity to take part in the project "Beyond the Voices: Yiwu, Here I Am". Thanks to this project, I have come to know some foreigners who do business and live there. From the foreigners' great passion for Yiwu, I know what great changes this small city has brought to its people. During the interview, Su Baihe, a Jordan gentleman, described Yiwu and everything he knows about Yiwu vividly. His love for Yiwu inspires me to have great expectations for Yiwu's prosperity in the future.

Yiwu, with Guangdong Province and Fujian Province to the south, is located in the middle of Zhejiang Province. The Shanghai economic development zone is to the north of Yiwu, and Ningbo harbor is to the east. Moreover, it is a city built on a market. Developing from a small city into the biggest market in China known to foreigners, Yiwu has witnessed earth-shaking changes. It was for this simple reason that I am eager to know what foreigners think about it.

In the process of interviewing, I learned that as a typical foreign businessman, Su Baihe is much attached to China and Yiwu. He has been living in Yiwu for about ten years and has witnessed the great changes. When he came to Yiwu for the first time, what he found was that from the East Hotel to up north was farmland. However, the farmland has been replaced by tall buildings in recent years. He could not restrain his excitement the moment that he began to talk about Yiwu with me. Yiwu is apparently his second home where he communicates with people in Chinese, celebrates the traditional Chinese festivals with his friends, and tastes Chinese traditional food. He even knows how to cook Chinese meals. Moreover, what impressed me most was when he told me humorously that he learned Chinese in "the People's University of China". This means that he learned Chinese from the ordinary people in China. All these details revealed his fascination with Chinese culture and food and his satisfaction with his life in Yiwu. Furthermore, he not only knew about the Silk Route but also knows the modern history of China. He knew that it was Chairman Mao who led the people to the founding of the People's Republic of China. Everyone could see his admiration for the fast development of China and his longing for the stability and unity of the countries in his Middle East.

After the interview was finished, his fluent Chinese, together with his sense of humor and the outgoing and confident smile, lingered in my mind. Compared with other people who do their business abroad, Su Baihe adjusted himself well to the life here. I wondered why he loves China so much and what made him settle down in Yiwu. It was not only because Yiwu has the unique market but also his fondness for everything in Yiwu. From Guangzhou to the Yiwu Market, and from knowing a little Chinese to a good command of Chinese, he must have devoted many efforts to his trade. I was deeply moved by his persistence in his business and his attachment to Yiwu. Su Baihe's success can be attributed to his positive attitude towards life and his unceasing enterprise, which greatly inspired me.

I used to be inferior, passive and afraid of making any mistakes. On the first day of our project, we were faced with many troubles, including a group member losing his backpack, foreigners refusing to answer questionnaires, no proper interviewees, and so on. With the encouragement of my group members, I began to take the initiative to talk with foreigners, telling myself that I should stick to the efforts, and it does not matter to lose face. I would like to mark it as the first step of my success. A few days later, we began to find some clues. We knew the areas where we could meet foreigners and the most proper time to ask for an interview. Once we came across foreigners who turned to us for help, although we did not know much about the market, we still tried our best the whole afternoon to help them find the products that they want. Another challenge we were faced with was the interviewees' strong accent. The foreign teachers at school usually come from England and America, so we are used to standard English. When talking with foreigners from the Middle East, I could barely understand what they were saying. In order to solve this problem, our group members gathered together to discuss the pronunciation differences of Middle East people. You cannot imagine how happy I was when all the recording materials were sorted out. My heart was filled with the sense of achievement. Thanks to this project, I not only got to know Yiwu's potentials and bright prospects but also realized that we should adjust our minds and stick to our efforts when confronted with challenges.

小城市，大世界

文：罗一圆　指导教师：吴丹苹　蔡　亮

作为一名英语专业的大学生，我对外国人很感兴趣。我想了解他们眼里的世界，了解他们眼里的中国，了解他们眼里的义乌。幸运的是，我有机会参加“用声音叙事：义乌，我来了”这一实践活动。通过这次活动，我结识了很多在义乌工作、生活的外国人，并且从他们对义乌的热爱中看到了义乌城市发展给义乌人带来的巨大变化。在这次采访期间，苏百贺，一位约旦商人，生动地描述了他对中国了解的点点滴滴。他对义乌的热爱激发了我对义乌未来发展的无限憧憬。

义乌地处浙江中部，南接广东和福建，北边是上海经济区，东邻宁波港。义乌是一座建在市场上的城市。从一个无名小城，到现在中国最大的小商品市场，为外国人所熟知，义乌发生着惊天动地的变化。正是因为这个原因，我才更想知道在外国人眼中的义乌。

在采访苏百贺的过程中，我了解到这位典型的外商对中国、对义乌感情深厚。他在义乌居住了10年，见证了义乌这些年巨大的发展。他初见义乌时，从东方大厦向北的地方只有农田，而如今，广阔的田野早已被林立的高楼大厦所取代。在向我描述这一切时，他仍掩盖不住内心的激动。义乌已然成为他的第二故乡。在这里，他用中文与人交谈，和中国朋友们一起欢度中国传统节日，品尝中国食物，还会做中国菜。最让人印象深刻的是，他幽默地称自己在“中国人民大学”里学中文——他跟中国的老百姓学中文。点点滴滴无不流露出他对中国文化和饮食的喜爱，对义乌生活的满足。他不仅知道中国古代的丝绸之路，还了解中国近代史，知道毛主席领导中国人民建立了新中国。言谈中他流露出对中国社会快速发展的羡慕和对中东祖国能够早日安定统一的期盼。

采访结束后，苏百贺流利的中文，幽默、开朗且自信的笑容一直在我的脑海里萦绕。相比较很多在异国他乡打拼的人，他完全适应这里的生活。我一直在思考是什么让他对中国如此喜爱，是什么让他决心定居义乌。这其中离不开义乌得天独厚的市场优势，更因为他热爱这里的一切。从广州交易会到义乌的商贸城，从只会一点点中文到现在完全可以用中文交流，可以想象他付出了许多。他对事业的执着，对义乌这片热土的喜爱感动着我。苏百贺的成功源于他有很好的心态去面对生活，不断进取，这一点令我深受启发。

一直以来，我都不太自信，比较被动，害怕出错。从实践开始的第一天，我们就开始遇到各种各样的困难，包括组员丢包，外国人拒绝填写问卷，找不到合适的采访对象等。在队友们的鼓励下，我放下思想包袱，主动与外国人交谈，告诉自己坚持不懈，不要怕丢面子，终于走出了成功的第一步。在几天的调研后，我们摸索出了一些规律，知道了外商主要的集中区域，知道他们在什么时间段更乐意接受采访。我们也遇到了向我们求助的外国人，虽然不了解市场布局，我们还是用一下午的时间尽力帮助他们寻找所需的物品。外国人的口音是我们在采访中碰到的另一个难题。学校里的外教大都是英美人士，我们比较习惯于他们的标准英语。而采访中东地区的外国人时，我常常听不懂他们所表达意思。为此，队员们聚在一起，讨论中东人士的发音规律。当完整的录音稿被整理出来的时候，那种欣喜和成就感难以忘怀。通过这次实践，我不仅认识到义乌的潜力和前景，同时也领悟到很重要的一点，在面临挑战时要调整好心态，并且坚持不懈地努力。

Manson

Manson: Fall in Love with Yiwu

义乌情,中国梦

Manson, who comes from Iran, is a manager of Yiwu Elya Trading Company. He came to China for study first, but later he got interested in doing business. He has been living in Yiwu for about five years. He fell in love with this city because of its culture, history as well as the people.

Manson来自伊朗,是义乌市婀雅贸易公司的经理。一开始他来中国是为了求学,后来对经商产生了浓厚的兴趣。他已经在义乌待了五年,并深深爱上了这个城市,喜欢这儿的文化、历史还有义乌人。

Fall in Love with Yiwu

By Manson

Transcript of the Interview:

【BTV】First, thank you for your kindness to help us do the interview. We are students from Ningbo Institute of Technology, Zhejiang University, and we are conducting a research about foreign companies and foreign businessmen in Yiwu. Would you please introduce yourself?

【Manson】OK. My name is Manson, and first I went to China to Wuhan University for studying MBA, but later I didn't follow my education. I came for business.

【BTV】I see. Where are you from?

【Manson】I'm from Iran. Do you know Iran? It is far from China.

【BTV】Yeah, I know. It is famous for oil.

【Manson】Iran has more than four thousand years' history.

【BTV】And China has more than five thousand years' history.

【Manson】Hah-hah, Iran has lots of historical bridges and towers and ancient mountains. These days we have improved everything.

【BTV】How long have you been in Yiwu? Do you like the Chinese food? Any favorite dishes?

【Manson】I have been here for five years, and I like Chinese food. Actually I like all the delicious food, such as Iranian food and Italian food. My favorite Chinese dish is Suan Cai Yu.

【BTV】Suan Cai Yu? I like it too. It is very spicy and hot. The meat is delicious and fresh.

【Manson】I think Chinese people don't like too much pepper or salt, but Sichuan dishes are an exception, and I think it is great.

【BTV】You have a warm and friendly smile, so you must be popular with the people around you. Have you made any Chinese friends, and what do you think of the local people in Yiwu?

【Manson】To be honest, I like people here. They are very hospitable and nice. When I get lost in my hometown in Iran and ask someone to show me the way, they just point one direction, and I have to find the way by myself, or maybe I have to ask another person when I stop at the next crossroad, but in China, people show you the way around until you find your destination. It is quite different.

【BTV】I am proud of being a Chinese. Did you meet cultural differences here? Can you share some experiences with us?

【Manson】Sure. You know, there is something I can't understand. Chinese people like to talk loudly in telephone and ignore the people around them, like they are chatting cross the street. The environment is a little bit noisy, and many people like smoking. They smoke one after another. I'm afraid it can lead to cancer and other serious illness.

【BTV】I don't like smoking, either. Thanks to the new rules, smoking in public places is forbidden nowadays. Have you participated in some social or cultural activities in the local community?

【Manson】Not yet. But I like exercise if I really have the time. Businessmen should be fresh; they can't keep working all the time. They need to have a rest.

【BTV】You chose Yiwu to start your business. Can you tell me what aspects of Yiwu attracted you most?

【Manson】As we all know, Yiwu has a good market, an international market. The goods here have good quality, and the price is lower than Guangdong. The diverse range of goods can meet a variety of needs. The markets are well organized; everything collects in one place. We can find the places we want to go to very easily. If I am purchasing in Guangdong, I have to go to one market and another, but they are far from each other. They are in different parts of the city. Yiwu is more convenient to do my own business.

【BTV】You mean the market in Yiwu can shorten the distances so as to save more time to do your business.

【Manson】Yeah, you are a good translator.

【BTV】Thank you. I know you have a company in Yiwu. Can you tell us more details about your business?

【Manson】Well, we send some special products to airport; that is, we play a role as a conveyor, making a bridge between foreign and Chinese business.

【BTV】Why do you choose "Elya" as your brand name?

【Manson】Because I like it, and it is easy to remember.

【BTV】How many employees are there in your company?

【Manson】Thirteen.

【BTV】What education have they received? How many of them have attended college?

【Manson】Er, let me see, maybe three of them graduated from college.

【BTV】How do you communicate with them? Any trouble in communication?

【Manson】We communicate with each other in English, and we communicate well.

【BTV】Do you have any suggestions for our college students who want to work in the foreign companies?

【Manson】I would rather they are hired by Chinese company because China has a bigger market. If they master several kinds of foreign languages, they will enjoy more advantages. Anyway, dealing with people is a challenge since different people have different attitudes. Some people get angry very easily while some people are always smiling, like me.

【BTV】You seem to be such a kind, patient, and outgoing person, and you are very friendly even to new friends like us. Your personality must be an advantage in doing business. As for the ways of doing business, do you find any differences between Yiwu and your hometown?

【Manson】Chinese people have connection with other people. They have relations to other countries. You can see that everything has a logo "made in China". In Iran, customers are Iranians, but in Yiwu, customers come from all over the world. China has a bigger market than my country.

【BTV】Would you tell us what kind of difficulties you have met in developing your business?

【Manson】Well, everything is smooth except for one thing. When we export goods, it is difficult for us to deal with passport, and I do hope that some policy can help us solve this problem.

【BTV】The efficiency can be improved if the problem is solved. From your words, I can see you have a good impression of Yiwu, right? How long will you stay in Yiwu?

【Manson】Yes, you know me. I like Chinese history. I really would like to learn your language if I have time. I like China. Maybe I will work here for a long time since I have a company here.

【BTV】What are your future plans for your company?

【Manson】You know, it is a long way to go to develop the company. Getting enough financing is the first step, so we can scale up our volumes. Next, with the further expansion of the company, I have to employ more talents. I have to work harder and harder, but I'm sure that in the near future it can turn to be something.

【BTV】I hope so. Well, it is well known that talent is crucial for companies. Do you have any requirements on the choice of talent?

【Manson】You know language is crucial. They need to master several languages. It will accelerate the development, and they have to understand the cultural differences, which will be very helpful. Wait, one important thing is the person should be outgoing, willing to communicate with others, modest to accept others' suggestions.

【BTV】We all know in the fierce market competition to retain talent is of major importance. What do you think of it?

【Manson】Well, maybe their first consideration is the pay and benefits. Besides, we have a series of personal training systems. It can help them increase self-worth and foster personal competitiveness in employment. For example, we will send them to a short-term training class abroad. As for the external conditions, we are making good office environment and working atmosphere.

【BTV】Woo, it would be very nice to be your staff. Tell us your dream?

【Manson】Yes, I have a dream. I want to have a good life. I want to have my company bigger and bigger, but I know I have a long way to go, and another thing, I want to improve my Chinese. It will be helpful for my business. I like Chinese history, and I like collecting china. It gives me more information about knowing the Chinese history.

【BTV】As a businessman, how do you contribute to society?

【Manson】Society is a big family, so it needs everyone's contribution. Although I just can do little, I will try my best to do whatever I can.

【BTV】Okay, these are all of my questions. Thank you for your participation. I believe you can make your dream come true, and I hope you will have a better life in Yiwu. See you.

【Manson】I was happy to talk with you. See you.

Group Members: Huang Shuang, Zhu Xiaotong, Zhao Yating

叙事记录

【BTV】首先，谢谢您能接受我们的采访。我们是浙江大学宁波理工学院的学生，正在做一项关于在义乌的外企和外商的调研。您能先介绍一下自己吗？

【Manson】好的，我叫 Manson，刚开始我来中国是为了去武汉大学攻读 MBA，但是后来我没有继续我的学业，而是开始自己做生意。

【BTV】原来是这样，您来自哪里呢？

【Manson】我来自伊朗。你们知道伊朗吗？伊朗离中国很远。

【BTV】我知道，那里的石油很有名。

【Manson】伊朗有着四千多年的历史。

【BTV】中国可是有上下五千年的历史哦！

【Manson】哈哈！伊朗有许多历史名桥和高塔，还有许多名山，现在我们的每个方面都有所进步。

【BTV】您来义乌多久了？您喜欢中国的食物吗？最喜欢什么菜？

【Manson】我来义乌有五年了，挺喜欢中国的食物。事实上我喜欢各种美食，比如伊朗的食物、意大利的食物。我最喜欢的中国菜是酸菜鱼。

【BTV】酸菜鱼！噢！我知道了，我也很喜欢它，那个很辣，鱼肉非常美味和新鲜。

【Manson】我觉得中国人好像不喜欢菜里放很多的辣椒和盐，但是四川菜是个例外，我觉得那样很美味。

【BTV】您有非常热情友好的笑容，所以您一定很受人欢迎。在义乌你有没有结识中国朋友，您对义乌当地人印象如何？

【Manson】说实话，我挺喜欢这里的人，他们都很热情友好，如果我在自己家乡迷路了，我去向别人问路，他们只会给我指一个方向，然后我就要继续自己找路，可能在下个路口又不得不问另外一个人。但是在中国，人们会帮我带路直到我找到目的地。这是非常不同的。

【BTV】因此我很自豪我是一个中国人。您在这边遇到过什么文化差异吗？能跟我们分享一下你的经历吗？

【Manson】当然有。你知道，这儿有些事我不太理解。中国人喜欢在打电话的时候大声说话，忽视周围的人，就像是两个人在街头聊天一样，环境就会有点吵闹。另外很多人喜欢抽烟，会一支接一支地抽，那会导致癌症和其他严重的疾病。

【BTV】我也不赞同抽烟。现在有了新的规定，公共场合禁止吸烟。您去参加过当地社区组织的社会文化活动吗？

【Manson】还没有。但是如果我有时间的话，我很喜欢运动。商人应该保持精力充沛，他们不能一直工作，他们也需要休息的。

【BTV】您选择义乌开始自己的生意，义乌最吸引你的地方是什么？

【Manson】众所周知，义乌有一个很好的市场，一个国际市场。这里的商品质量都很好，价格要比广东便宜，小商品品种丰富，可以满足各种需求。市场组织得很好，每样东西都会归类在一个特定的地方。我们可以很容易地找到要去的地方。如果我在广东采购的话，我必须要从这个市场跑到那个市场，而市场彼此之间离得很远，它们在一个城市的不同地方。相比较而言在义乌做自己的生意要方便得多。

【BTV】所以您的意思是在义乌的市场做生意可以缩短行程，从而节约更多的时间，是吗？

【Manson】是的，你说得对！

【BTV】谢谢。我知道您在义乌开了一家自己的公司，您能跟我们讲讲您公司的经营状况吗？

【Manson】好的，我们把一些特定的产品运送到机场，或者说我们扮演传送带的角色，为外国和中国的企业搭建桥梁。

【BTV】那么您为什么会把"Elya"作为你的商标名称呢？

【Manson】因为我很喜欢这个名字，简单容易记。

【BTV】请问您的公司有多少员工呢？

【Manson】13 个。

【BTV】他们的教育程度如何？

【Manson】我想一下，可能有三个是大学毕业的。

【BTV】您如何与他们交流？有交流困难吗？

【Manson】我们用英语交流，沟通很顺利。

【BTV】对于现在像我们这样的大学生，如果希望在外资企业工作，您有什么好的建议吗？

【Manson】我还是觉得他们在中国的企业工作比较好，因为中国市场潜力更大。如果他们掌握了好几种外语，那就更具有优势。无论如何，与人打交道是一项挑战，因为不同的人做事有不同的态度。有些人很容易生气，然而有些人脸上总是挂着微笑，就像我一样。

【BTV】在我看来，您是一个和善、有耐心，而且非常外向的人，对于像我们这样初次见面的人也非常热情友好。您的性格一定会有助于您的事业发展。就做生意的方式而言，您觉得义乌和您的家乡有什么不同呢？

【Manson】中国人会和许多人有联系，他们和其他国家也建立了关系，你可以看见每件商品都会标上"中国制造"。然而在伊朗的话，顾客都是伊朗人，在义乌有来自世界各地的顾客，中国市场比我们的市场大得多。

【BTV】您在事业发展过程中有没有遇到什么困难呢？

【Manson】除了一件事，其他都挺顺的。当我们出口商品的时候，对于我们来说办理通行许可证比较麻烦。我非常希望有政策可以帮助我们解决这个问题。

【BTV】如果这个问题能够解决,效率就更高了。从您的话语中,我感觉您对义乌的印象很好是吗?您会在义乌待多久呢?

【Manson】是的,我很喜欢中国历史,如果有时间我想去学中文。我很喜欢中国,我应该会在这边工作很长一段时间,因为我有公司在这儿呢。

【BTV】那么您的公司发展蓝图是什么呢?

【Manson】你们知道的,要发展公司的话我还有很长的一段路要走。得到足够的融资是第一步,这样我们才可以扩大规模;接下来,公司扩大了,我就必须再招聘更多的人才。我必须很努力地工作,但是我相信在不久的将来公司会发展得很好。

【BTV】我也希望如此。众所周知,人才对于企业来说是至关重要的一环。您在人才的选择上有什么要求呢?

【Manson】你知道语言是关键,他们需要掌握好几门外语,这样会加速发展。他们还必须去了解不同的文化差异,那会很有用。等一下,很重要的一点是这个人必须是很外向的,乐意与他人交流,能够虚心接受他人的建议。

【BTV】我们都知道在激烈的市场竞争中,怎样留住人才是一个非常重要的问题,您是如何看待这一问题的呢?

【Manson】可能他们最先考虑的会是薪水报酬吧,另外,我们有一套员工培训方案,这能帮助他们提高自我价值,培养工作中的竞争意识。举个例子,我们会送他们去进行短期的海外培训。至于外部条件,我们一直都在营造好的办公室环境和工作氛围。

【BTV】做您的员工真幸福!告诉我们您的梦想好吗?

【Manson】是的,我有梦想,我想要有好的生活,我想要把我的公司变得越来越大,但是我知道我还有很长一段路要走。还有一件事,我想要提高我的中文水平,那将会对我的生意大有帮助,我很喜欢中国的历史,我也很喜欢收集中国的瓷器,这为我了解中国的历史提供了更多的信息。

【BTV】作为一名商人,您觉得应该通过什么方式来回报社会呢?

【Manson】社会是一个大家庭,需要每个人做出贡献,尽管我能做到的不多,但我会尽我所能做我应该做的。

【BTV】好的,这些就是我所有的问题,感谢您的配合,我相信您能够梦想成真,也希望您在义乌会有一个更好的生活,再见!

【Manson】和你们谈话我也很开心,再见!

团队成员:黄爽,朱小曈,赵雅婷

Wonderland: Yiwu

By Huang Shuang Supervised by Wu Danping & Cai Liang

It has been more than one week since I came back from Yiwu, the place for summer social practice. However, I shall never forget such a bitter and sweet experience.

Before going to Yiwu, my teammates and I were too excited to fall asleep. We were longing to visit the well-known trading city with a fabulous international market and businessmen from all over the world. I had imagined that foreigners with different skin colors were waiting to chat with us. However, it was very different from what I had expected. When I arrived, I realized that it was not easy at all to find a suitable interviewee.

The first businessman whom we interviewed was from Iran. His name is Manson. The handsome young man has a good sense of humor, which made the atmosphere relaxing and harmonious. When asked why he came to Yiwu for business, Manson explained to us how wonderful the Yiwu market is. The goods here have good quality, and prices are lower than that in Guangdong. The market is well organized. Everything is in one place. He could find the places that he wants to go to very easily. If he is in Guangdong, he has to go to one market after another, and the markets are far from each other. Yiwu is more convenient for doing his business. As for his impression of the Chinese people, he gave us an example of how hospitable the Chinese people are. Actually, Manson himself has very good communication skills. He is talkative, friendly, adaptable and open-mined. To our great surprise, he told us that he likes Chinese history very much, and he has been collecting chinaware for many years. It is acknowledged that China has a charming and glorious history, no wonder even people from other countries fall in love with it. We took photos with him when the interview came to an end, and later we found his brilliant and confident smile in almost every picture, which impressed everyone.

The second foreign businessman told us that he is from Iraq, and he came to China three years ago because of the war. He lives in Yiwu with his whole family and runs a grill house. As I looked around, I found several young ladies smile peacefully, and two lovely babies were staring at us curiously. We invited the whole family to take photos with us, including father, mother, grandmother as well as children. Compared with his hometown, Yiwu may not be the best place for him, but it is a second home to him. He lives here, appreciates the hospitality that the local people show to his family, and learns and absorbs the cultural tradition and language. In the daytime, he runs the restaurant with his family. When night falls, he can chat with his family in the square freely, enjoying the peaceful and cozy life. I came to realize the preciousness of peace and stability. Our older generations had experienced the ordeals of war, natural disaster and social instability, but nowadays we are lucky to have such a carefree life. Although we live in a stressful and competitive society, there is no gunfire, no cruelty, and no discrimination. Leaving his motherland may not be his best option, but I am sure that the longer he lives in China, the more he will love China.

Recalling the amicable people whom we interviewed, although they do not know each other, coming from different countries with different cultures, they all fell in love with Yiwu after they settled down. This is the reason that Yiwu attracts people from home and abroad, leading them to this new land and a new start in life. I am also moved by their passion to learn the Chinese language and Chinese traditional culture. It is not only the pride of Yiwu, but also of the whole of China.

Meanwhile, I began to think about why Yiwu developed at such a magical speed. This inland city does not have seaport advantages or rich natural resources and was once even backward and poor. I once went to Yiwu with my parents more than ten years ago. At that time, it was just a little county. The streets were narrow, and the market was crowded and poorly equipped. There were not many foreigners. It has changed so much. Modern buildings are everywhere, and the market is well organized and well furnished. The shop owners bargain with foreign businessmen in English. When night falls, people sit in the coffee bars and relax.

Yiwu is the first county that was approved as an International Trade Comprehensive Reform Pilot City in China, but I do not think this is the main reason. The people's innovation and enterprise changed the town into a prosperous city. No matter how busy a day the businessmen might have had, they were willing to help us with our project. When it comes to their impressions of the city, they all speak highly of Yiwu. This explains the attraction and glamour of Yiwu. Yiwu's success could not have been achieved without its unique business environment and particularly the industriousness of the local people. I am proud of being a Zhejiangese, and I believe we can work more miracles here.

伊朗大哥哥的笑容

左一：黄爽（采访） 中间：Manson

右一：赵雅婷（记录） 摄影：朱小曈

奇妙宝地义乌

文:黄　爽　指导教师:吴丹苹　蔡　亮

距离去义乌进行暑期社会实践已经过去一个多星期了,但是我永远不会忘记这段喜忧参半的宝贵经历。

去义乌之前,我和我的队友们都兴奋得难以入睡,我们都很渴望去参观这个闻名遐迩的贸易城市,那里有极好的国际商城,还有来自世界各地的外国商人。我想象着肤色各异的外国人正在那里等着我们去交谈。但事实并非我所想象的那样,当我到达那里的时候,我发现寻找合适的采访对象并不是一件简单的事儿。

我们采访的第一位外商来自伊朗,名叫 Manson。这位年轻帅气的小伙子很有幽默感,这使我们的整个交谈氛围放松而融洽。当被问到为什么来义乌做生意的时候,他向我们解释说义乌有一个非常完美的市场,商品质量都很不错,价格也比广东要低。市场规划得很好,每类商品都会集中在一个区域。他能够很容易找到想去的地方。如果他身在广东,他就不得不从一个市场穿梭到另一个市场,而市场彼此相距遥远。义乌给他做生意提供了更多便利。在谈到对中国人的印象的时候,他给我们举了个例子来说明中国人是非常热情的。事实上 Manson 本身具有很强的沟通能力。他健谈、友好、适应性强,而且善于接受新鲜事物。最让人惊讶的是,他告诉我们他非常喜欢中国的历史,他一直在收集中国的瓷器。举世公认中国有非常迷人辉煌的历史,难怪外国朋友们都会爱上它。在采访接近尾声的时候,我们和他合了影。在整理照片的时候,我们发现在每张合影中,他的脸上都露出了灿烂自信的笑容,这一点给我们留下了深刻的印象。

我们采访的第二名外商告诉我们他来自伊拉克,三年前他为了躲避战乱来到中国。现在他和他的整个家庭都居住在义乌,经营着一家烧烤店。当我环顾四周,发现两个非常可爱的小宝宝正好奇地盯着我们看,几位年轻妇女脸上都挂着笑容。在我们的邀请下,这个大家庭包括奶奶、爸爸、妈妈和孩子们,很友好地与我们合影。义乌可能无法和他们的家乡相比,但这是他们的第二个家,他们在这里生活,感受着当地人民对他们的友好,了解和学习着这里的语言和文化。白天一家人经营着烧烤店,当夜幕降临,他们就可以围坐在广场上一起聊天,享受这平静、温馨的生活。这让我感悟到了和平与安定的可贵,我们的祖父辈们曾经饱受战争、自然灾害和社会动荡之苦,我们很幸运生活在一个和平年代。尽管有压力和竞争,但是没有战火,没有暴行,没有歧视。远离祖国是这个伊拉克家庭的无奈之举,但是我相信他们在中国待得越久,他们就会越发喜欢上中国。

回想起我们访问的这些友好的外商,虽然他们互相不认识,来自不同的国家,接受着不同文化的熏陶，却都在来到义乌之后爱上了这个城市，这就是义乌的魅力所在。这种魅力可以让他们远渡重洋在这个原本陌生的城市里重新开始生活，开启新的人生。他们对中文的热爱、对中国传统文化的痴迷让我们这些中国人感动着，骄傲着。这不仅是义乌人的骄傲，更是我们所有中国人的骄傲。

与此同时，我不禁开始思考义乌为何有如此神奇的发展速度。这个内陆城市没有港口优势，也没有丰富的自然资源，甚至一度处于落后贫穷的局面。十几年前，我和我的父母来过义乌，那时义乌还只是一个小县城，街道狭窄，市场拥挤，装潢也不好，那时候没有像现在这么多的外国人。但是现在有了天翻地覆的变化，到处都是现代化大楼，市场规划有序、干净整洁，店主人用英文和外商进行讨价还价。夜幕降临，人们都坐在咖啡厅里休息。

义乌是中国第一个国际贸易综合改革试点县级市，但我觉得这不是主要原因，是当地人的开拓创新和锐意进取才将义乌发展成了一个繁荣的大都市。不管外商朋友的一天有多繁忙，他们都很乐意帮助我们做调查。当谈到对义乌的印象时，他们都予以高度赞扬，这就是义乌的魅力所在。义乌的成功离不开这个城市独特的商业环境，更离不开义乌人的发愤图强。作为一个浙江人，我很骄傲自己能够生活在这片土地上，我也相信我们能在这里继续创造奇迹。

第五章

Construction of Yiwu: It'll Be Better with Me

共建义乌：义乌有我更精彩

导言

义乌的贸易非常发达，作为国际小商品城，这里汇集了浙江省约三分之一的资金流。资金流、商品流、信息流等交叉混合，吸引了很多外地人来创业经商，也成就了很多人的梦想。

然而初到义乌，你也许会失望，因为义乌与很多小县市并没有多少不同：拥挤混乱的交通，参差不齐的建筑……与她“世界第一大市场”的称号形成了很大的反差，但是世界公认的这个称号一定不是空穴来风，请与本章的队员一起，逐梦义乌，探索如何更好地建设这座传奇般的城市。

义乌是如何发展起来的？很多农民在农业较差的自然条件下，只好外出经商，摇拨浪鼓卖糖，政府和义乌人“敢为天下先”，在很多地方都在驱赶“马路市场”的时候，政府考虑接纳他们并使之能够生存下来。20 世纪 80 年代初，义乌在全国率先放宽个体户工商登记，允许农民经商，允许开放城乡市场。放开手脚经商的农民如鱼得水，纷纷加入经商队伍。这期间，部分经营户通过经商初步完成了资本的原始积累，买进机器办起加工厂，形成了“前店后厂”工商一体的家庭经营模式。

义乌在浙江中部乃至长三角的物流地位日趋凸显，但与此同时义乌的城市文化服务水平已经不能满足日益增长的经济发展水平。据粗略估计，义乌现在常住人口有两百多万，外来人口超过了一百多万，作为一个县级市这个人口规模的确是非常大。贸易日益国际化、市场化以后，物流业、会展业的国际化对外语服务、网络服务等要求越来越高。人口增加引发了交通、环境、生活习惯、治安管理等问题，越来越多的外籍人士在购房、签证、投资以及对政府政策的了解和执行过程中的沟通问题也越来越紧迫。在本章，义乌外籍人士在义乌追寻着自己的梦想，也为更加精彩的义乌献言献策，小到城市英汉双语指示牌的提议，大到促进交流、平等互惠、相互信任以及权利保护政策等。

相信中国的青年和外籍商人能与勤劳、智慧、有创意的义乌人民和政府共同努力，建设一个更为精彩的义乌！

Zack

Zack: We Have Whatever You Want

多彩义乌，应有尽有

Zack is a friendly Englishman. Three years ago, he started his business in Yiwu. He says, "You can find anything you want in Yiwu." Now, he comes to Yiwu regularly because his friend and partner lives here. He thinks Yiwu is a big factory, an international factory. During the interview, we were impressed by his vitality and great sense of humor.

扎克是一位友善的英国人。三年前，他来到了义乌并开始了他的事业。如今，他在这里已经有一家属于他自己的公司。他说："在这里，你可以找到任何你想要的东西。"现在，因为他有一个长期住在义乌的好友兼合伙人，他只要定期来到这里"视察"就可以了。在他眼里，义乌是一家大工厂，一间国际性的工厂。言谈间，他的活力和幽默感给我们留下了深刻的印象。

We Have Whatever You Want

By Zack

Transcript of the Interview:

【BTV】Hello, nice to meet you!

【Zack】Hello, nice to meet you, too.

【BTV】We are from Ningbo Institute of Technology, Zhejiang University. Can we ask you some questions?

【Zack】Yes, that's okay.

【BTV】How long have you known Yiwu?

【Zack】About three years.

【BTV】Why did you come here?

【Zack】For business.

【BTV】So which trade do you engage in?

【Zack】Accessories, that's my trade.

【BTV】Accessories? That is very beautiful.

【Zack】Yeah, you know, it's cheap and it changes quickly. All girls and women like to buy accessories. This was a good choice.

【BTV】Yes, sure was. There are many accessory factories here. Have you been to any other cities in China?

【Zack】Yes, Guangzhou and Shanghai.

【BTV】Since you have been to Guangzhou, do you think Yiwu has some special things that Guangzhou does not have?

【Zack】Yes, special people here, nice people here.

【BTV】How long have you been here?

【Zack】This time, I have been here just for one week now. I've been before, you see, I have an office here.

【BTV】Do you have any communication problems with the local people?

【Zack】Yes, most people here cannot speak English.

【BTV】Yes, we need to improve that. Do you know the history of Yiwu?

【Zack】I don't know.

【BTV】Do you think the transportation is convenient here? Which one is more convenient, a bus or a taxi?

【Zack】We don't use taxis. We have a motorcycle.

【BTV】You have a motorcycle here? Do you live here?

【Zack】We have a company, so we don't use taxis often. Sometimes. I can't speak Chinese, you see.

【BTV】Do you think the security here is good?

【Zack】Yeah, no problem here.

【BTV】Any suggestions to improve the image of Yiwu?

【Zack】Maybe you should improve the English signs here because English is international. Just like Britain and America. You should use more English, but everything here is Chinese. I have been to many other cities around the world, and they have the local language and English signs, because English is international. You know, if I seek Chinese for some business, I don't know where to go and what the signs are saying. I can only go where somebody tells me. If I am riding, the sign in Chinese does not work for me. Maybe there is already the place, you know, but I don't know because I can't read Chinese. Sometimes, people tell me to go there, and then there I go. I can't look for it myself because I can't read Chinese. So you know, they need to improve the signs. Many foreigners come here and they only go where somebody tells them to go.

【BTV】Yes, I get that.

【Zack】So if you want to have an international market, you need to improve English. English is very important. Almost everyone in an international city speaks English. Such as cities in America, Australia and Pakistan.

【BTV】English is an international language.

【Zack】Yeah, an international language, so I would hope local people could speak English. You know, I have been to Shanghai, and many people there speak English because English is international.

【BTV】Yes, it is very important to learn English well. I think everyone will speak English in the future.

【BTV】What do you usually do in your spare time?

【Zack】I often go to the restaurants.

【BTV】How do you like the food here?

【Zack】You know, Chinese food is very good. It tastes very good, and most importantly Chinese food is full of nutrition. It is not like KFC or other fast foods. They are not fried. You know, when you catch a cold, just a bowl of porridge can make you get better. That's really delicious. Many Chinese students studying overseas will seek Chinese food.

【BTV】Yeah, Chinese food tastes good. Many foreigners like to eat it very much. We are very happy that you also like it. Is there any entertainment in your daily life?

【Zack】I will go to the supermarket.

【BTV】When you meet difficulties in your business, to whom do you turn for help?

【Zack】We are okay because we have a partner here who speaks Chinese, and we have an interpreter.

【BTV】Your partner is a Chinese?

【Zack】No, he speaks Chinese. He lives here most of the time. Sometimes maybe six months and sometimes maybe longer than six months.

【BTV】How do you understand the sentence, "an ocean of small commodities and a paradise for shoppers"?

【Zack】I do not think it is the "paradise for shoppers". I would not use that word. This is not for shoppers, and I would say "for the world business".

【BTV】Can you use a word or a sentence to describe Yiwu?

【Zack】Hot, very hot here.

【BTV】Doesn't the air conditioning here work?

【Zack】No. It's not that. The air conditioning here is very good, but it's very hot outside. The wind here is too weak.

【BTV】Can you use other words?

【Zack】Good for business.

【BTV】Why do you think it is good for business?

【Zack】Because you can find everything here in Yiwu.

【BTV】Is it a business city?

【Zack】Yes. You know, when I go to the UK, they ask me, "What is your factory?" Then I would say Yiwu.

【BTV】Do you know of the policy put forward by the government recently to improve the business environment here?

【Zack】That's fine. I like it.

【BTV】Yes, that's really good. We hope that the policies will help you in your business. How will you introduce Yiwu to your friends?

【Zack】A factory, a big factory, a big international factory.

【BTV】Do you know of other cities similar to Yiwu?

【Zack】No，I don't know. I think Yiwu is unique. You can't find another city similar to it. You know，it is for business. It is not for travel. If you want to travel here，you have nothing to see. Yiwu is the business center of the world. We can buy everything here.

【BTV】You can buy everything!

【Zack】We have whatever you want.

【BTV】Thank you again for making time for the interview. We wish everything good for your company.

【Zack】Thank you!

Group Members：Zhao Yanyan，Chen Yuan，Si Wenjun

叙事记录

【BTV】您好，很高兴认识您。

【Zack】你们好，我也很高兴认识你们。

【BTV】我们是来自浙江大学宁波理工学院的学生，我们可以问您一些问题吗？

【Zack】好的，没问题。

【BTV】您知道义乌多久了？

【Zack】大概有三年了。

【BTV】您为什么要来义乌？

【Zack】因为生意。

【BTV】那么，您从事哪个行业呢？

【Zack】我从事饰品业。

【BTV】饰品？很漂亮的东西啊！

【Zack】是的，你知道的，饰品很便宜、很好看，并且更新得快。年轻女孩和中年妇女都会买，这一行是个不错的选择。

【BTV】是的，这个选择不会错，这里有很多生产饰品的工厂。您去过中国的其他城市吗？

【Zack】是的，广州和上海。

【BTV】那么，与广州相比，义乌有什么特别的地方吗？

【Zack】是的，这里的人比较特别，这里的人很好。

【BTV】您来这里多久了？

【Zack】这次我来这里有一个星期了。我以前来过这里，你们知道的，我有公司在这里。

【BTV】您与当地居民有沟通问题吗？

【Zack】有啊！这里的居民很多都不会说英语。

【BTV】是的，这是我们需要改进的地方。那您知道义乌的历史吗？

【Zack】不清楚。

【BTV】这里的交通还便利吗？公交车方便还是出租车方便？

【Zack】我们不坐出租车，我们自己有摩托车。

【BTV】您有摩托车？您住在这儿？

【Zack】我们有公司在这里，所以我们一般不坐出租车。你们知道的，我不会讲中文。

【BTV】您觉得这里的治安怎么样？

【Zack】这里的治安没问题。

【BTV】对于提升义乌的形象有什么建议吗？

【Zack】也许你们可以增加这里的英语标识，因为英语是国际化的语言，像英国、美国都说英语。你们应该使用更多的英语，但是这里的东西都是中文的。我曾经去过世界上的许多其他城市，他们的指示牌是用当地的语言与英文写的，因为英语是国际化的语言。你们知道的，如果我要和中国人做生意，我不知道要去哪里，也看不懂路上的指示牌。我只能去那些别人告诉我的地方。如果我骑摩托车出门，中文的路标我看不懂，即使我已经到了目的地，我也无从得知。有时候，别人告诉我去哪儿我就去哪儿，我自己找不到地方，因为我看不懂汉语，所以这里的指示牌有待改善，很多外籍人士来到这里却只能去别人告诉他们的地方。

【BTV】是的，我明白。

【Zack】所以，如果你们想要成为国际性的市场，你们需要提高英语水平。英语很重要，国际化的都市几乎人人都会说英语，比如美国、澳大利亚和巴基斯坦的许多城市。

【BTV】英语是国际性的语言。

【Zack】是的，国际性语言。所以我希望义乌的人能说英语。我以前去过上海，那里很多人都会说英语，因为英语是国际性的。

【BTV】是的，学好英语非常重要，我想，在不久的将来每个人都会说英语了。

【BTV】您空余时间经常做什么？

【Zack】我会去一些餐馆。

【BTV】您认为这里的食物怎么样？

【Zack】很好，中国的食物很好吃而且很有营养。中国的食物不像肯德基和其他一些快餐，它不是油炸的。你们知道的，当你感冒的时候，喝一碗白粥就会让你感觉好多了，那真的很美味。有很多在外求学的中国留学生都会在当地寻找中国食物。

【BTV】是的，中国的食物真的很美味，有很多外籍人士都喜欢吃，我们很高兴您喜欢。那您在日常生活中有其他娱乐活动吗？

【Zack】我会去逛逛超市。

【BTV】您在生意上出现问题时，您会向谁寻求帮助？

【Zack】没遇到什么问题，我们在这里的合作伙伴会讲中文，而且我们公司有自己的翻译员。

【BTV】您的合伙人是中国人吗？

【Zack】不是，他会说中文，他大部分时间都住在这里，有时可能住6个月，有的时候可能会更久。

【BTV】您是怎么理解“小商品海洋，购物者天堂”这句话的？

【Zack】我觉得用“购物者的天堂”不足以描述这里，因为这里不仅仅是买东西的地方，说这里是“世界生意人的天堂”更合适。

【BTV】您能用一个词或者一句话来形容义乌吗？

【Zack】热，这里非常热。

【BTV】是这里的空调不好用吗？

【Zack】不是，市场内的空调还好，就是外面太热了，因为没有风。

【BTV】您还可以用哪句话来形容义乌呢？

【Zack】很适合做生意。

【BTV】您为什么觉得义乌适合做生意？

【Zack】因为这里应有尽有。

【BTV】您认为义乌是个商业城市吗？

【Zack】是的，你知道的，我在英国的时候，他们就会问“您的工厂呢？”我就回答说义乌就是我的工厂。

【BTV】您知道政府近几年推出的政策吗？用来改善这里的经济环境的。

【Zack】那个很好，我喜欢那种政策。

【BTV】是的，相关政策真的很好，我们希望它能在生意上帮到您。您会怎么向您的朋友介绍义乌？

【Zack】一间工厂，一间大工厂，一间国际性的大工厂。

【BTV】您知道其他一些与义乌相似的城市吗？

【Zack】我不知道。我认为义乌是独一无二的，你找不到一个与它相似的城市。义乌是为了商业而存在的，它不是旅游胜地。如果你想到义乌旅游，你看不到很美丽的风景。义乌是世界的商业中心，在这里，我们可以买到任何想要的商品。

【BTV】确实如此。

【Zack】只要你想要，我们就有。

【BTV】再次感谢您抽空接受采访，我们祝愿您的公司在未来更上一层楼。

【Zack】谢谢！

团队成员：赵艳艳，陈圆，斯文俊

Cultural Construction of Business City Yiwu

By Zhao Yanyan Supervised by Nan Erli & Cai Liang

When someone mentions Yiwu, most people will associate it with Futian Market. Almost everyone has heard the saying, "an ocean of small commodities and a paradise for shoppers". It took Yiwu about ten years to become an international trade city. People here built a new market about seven years ago. The new market is bigger than the old one and still expanding today. Many people have heard about the market, but few know its origins, including the local people. I have heard about "trading something sweet for the feather", but that is all I know about the origins of Yiwu's market. The land in Yiwu used to be so poor that the local people had to get the feather by giving something sweet to people from the outside world. Local people used the feather to make the land fertile. Someone may ask, "How could Yiwu build this market while other cities could not, such as Ningbo? Ningbo is a port city. Therefore, it was more suitable than Yiwu, wasn't it?" The words of the workers in the market gave the answer, "Yiwu developed its business first and then it's market."

During this interview, Zack, a warm-hearted foreign businessman gave us many suggestions to improve the image of Yiwu. He felt that more local people and businessmen should speak English. In addition, he believed that the road signs in Yiwu should be in English as well as Chinese. He has a motorcycle in Yiwu, but he has trouble finding his way because he cannot read the Chinese on the signs. During the interview, Zack constantly mentioned that English is an international language. We understand that English is really important, and we must learn English well. Zack also stated that so many expatriates come to Yiwu to develop their business because they can buy anything in Yiwu.

However, we also found some shortcomings in Yiwu, which is really important to us. The awareness of our shortcomings can give us ideas to improve, right? As a native, I am very happy that so many expatriates come to Yiwu for business. However, it also causes some problems. With the development of the economy, the number of workers from other cities is rising. Yiwu is a small city, so it is likely to become overcrowded. More and more cars and people appear on the roads. At rush hour, the buses are full of people, especially the buses to and from the market. Once someone said, "Many local people live off the market. If the market disappeared, a lot of people would lose their jobs." It's true that the disappearance of the market means unemployment for a large number of people. However, the growing number of migrant workers is a challenge to Yiwu's administration. The growth of the population puts pressure on the local environment. It is more difficult to keep this city clean. Most importantly, the workers from other cities have influenced the local customs.

The summer social practice, "Beyond the Voices: Yiwu, Here I Am", was more difficult than I had expected, but we have learned many things. Through our interviews and questionnaires, we have put together a wealth of information about such things like the development of the market. As far back as I can remember, I have known that there is a commodity market and Binwang Market and that different districts sell different things. Later, the International Trade City opened. Almost all goods were moved there except for clothing. This made things more convenient for businessmen. Now Yiwu has become the place for experimental reform in China designed to promote the development of the market. In addition to the economic development, tourism is also being developed. There used to be few tourist attractions, only several former residences of celebrities and a Forest Park, and it is inconvenient to go there. Now, Futian Market has turned into an attraction in Yiwu. The number of visitors going there is constantly growing. We met some tourists during our interview. Futian Market sets up a special shopping center for the tourists in order to let travelers buy their ideal things. Also, there is a special office for them, too. In addition, there is a small movie theater with quite advanced technology. I heard that it once welcomed a president. As a native of Yiwu, I am very proud of my hometown. I hope that the cultural construction of Yiwu can develop into something even better than "a paradise for shoppers".

商海义乌，文化为舟

文：赵艳艳　指导老师：南二丽　蔡　亮

当有人提到义乌的时候，很多人都会想到小商品城。很多人都听说过“小商品海洋，购物者天堂”这句话。义乌花了近十年的时间发展成了国际商贸城，大概在七年前，义乌人建了一个新的市场，这个新的市场比旧的大了很多，至今仍在扩建。也许有很多人听说过这个市场，但是没有多少人知道它的起源，就算是当地人，知道的也很少。我曾经听说过“鸡毛换糖”这个词，但我并没有深入了解过。因为义乌的土地很贫瘠，所以当地居民外出用糖换取鸡毛，再用换来的鸡毛来肥沃土地。也许有人会问：“为什么义乌可以建造这个市场，而其他城市却没有，比如说宁波？宁波是港口城市，比义乌更适合，不是吗？”市场的工作人员是这样回答的：“义乌是先有市，再有场。”

在这次采访过程中，热心的外籍商人扎克给了我们很多改善义乌面貌的建议。他说如果有更多的当地居民和商人会说英语就更好了。另外他建议指示牌最好用英汉双语写。他在义乌有自己的摩托车，但是因为他不识中文路标，常常迷路。在这次采访过程中，我们还发现扎克经常提到“英语是国际性的语言”，可见，英语非常重要，我们必须学好英语。扎克还说义乌能吸引这么多外籍人士在这里做生意就是因为在义乌他们可以找到任何他们想要的东西。

通过这次采访，我们发现了义乌的一些不足之处，这对我们来说非常重要。只有了解到自己的不足之处才有办法改善，不是吗？作为一名义乌人，我很高兴有这么多外籍人士到义乌来做生意。不过，在这发展的过程中也出现了不好的地方。随着经济的发展，外来人员越来越多，义乌本来就是个小地方，所以越来越拥挤。路上的车辆越来越多，人也越来越多，每到上下班时间，公交车上就挤满了人，尤其是途经市场的公交车。曾经有人说过，很多义乌人都是靠着市场生存的，没有这个市场，很多人会失业。是的，如果市场没有了，确实会有很多人失业，但是外来务工人员的增多对市政管理是一项挑战。人口增加也对环境构成了压力。保持城市卫生更加困难。更重要的是，外来人口也在不断影响着义乌的传统习惯。

这次“用声音叙事：义乌，我来了”暑期社会实践活动比我预想的辛苦，但是我们学到了很多。经过辛苦的采访、填写问卷，我们搜集了很多信息，比如说市场的发展过程。自我记事起，义乌就有小商品城，有宾王市场，不同的地方卖不同的东西。后来有了国际商贸城，除了服装外，几乎所有的商品都移到了那里，这给商人提供了便利。现在，为了进一步发展市场经济，义乌被列为改革试点。除了商业得到了发展，义乌的旅游业也发展起来了。过去义乌的旅游景区不多，我知道的只有几个名人故居和森林公园，而且交通非常不便。现在，国际商贸城成了义乌的另一道风景，到这里旅游的人也逐渐增加。在我们的采访中就碰到了好多游客。市场还专门为这些旅游者设立了购买点，让游客可以购买自己喜欢的东西，还有专为游客服务的办公室。市场内还有采用先进技术的迷你影院，听说，那里还招待过某个国家的领导人。作为一名地道的义乌人，我感到很骄傲。我希望义乌能在“购物者的天堂”的基础上有更全面的发展。

Adnan Swidan

Swidan: Equality—Born for Business

自由竞争:为商业而生

Adnan Swidan comes from Libya. He has two offices in China, and his offices are called "AS" after his initials. He has a dream that he hopes we are "the same": His country and China can become brothers, and people from each country can visit each other without a visa. He has been in China for five years, is very kind and enjoys himself in Yiwu.

Adnan Swidan 来自利比亚,他在中国有两个办公室,根据他名和姓的首字母命名为"AS"。他有一个梦想:他希望我们都是一样的,他的国家利比亚和中国可以亲如兄弟,两国人民互访可以不需要签证。他在中国已经五年了,他为人友善,非常享受在义乌的生活。

Equality—Born for Business

By Swidan

Transcript of the Interview:

【BTV】Excuse me, we are students from Ningbo Institute of Technology, Zhejiang University. We are doing a study to discover the reasons why foreigners choose Yiwu to do business and the major problems they may confront here in Yiwu.

【Swidan】Okay, that sounds great!

【BTV】How long have you been in China?

【Swidan】I have been in China for five years.

【BTV】When did you come to Yiwu?

【Swidan】Two years ago. I have two offices in China. They are called "AS". One is in Guangzhou and the other in Yiwu.

【BTV】Have you been to other cities in China?

【Swidan】Yes, many.

【BTV】Guangzhou?

【Swidan】I've been to Wenzhou, Guangzhou, Shanghai, Nanjing, Beijing, and so on.

【BTV】Okay, so many cities. How do you know Yiwu?

【Swidan】I know Yiwu because all people know about it around me, and it is near many cities which have factories, you know. And it has many taverns.

【BTV】What is your first impression of Yiwu?

【Swidan】That Yiwu has many hotels is the impression I got first. Then it impressed me with so many Arabians, you know. And the deepest impression is the Futian Market which may be known as "Big Market Futian".

【BTV】Yes, Yiwu is called "small city, big market".

【Swidan】Yes, yes! And for foreigners, there are so many factories and Futian Market, so they can stay in Yiwu if they want to find any factories, you know. So many machines are from Ningbo, and it is very convenient.

【BTV】You mean to procure machines from Ningbo is very convenient?

【Swidan】Yes, I have been to many cities, such as Wenzhou, Guangzhou, etc. Yiwu is a very convenient place to do business. You don't have to go here or there to gather the materials or machines you need.

【BTV】Have you noticed any changes in Yiwu?

【Swidan】Oh, yes. The market is becoming bigger and bigger. When I just arrived here, the Futian Market was not so big. And the Binwang Market was busier, but now the Binwang Market is closed, and we are all doing business in Futian Market. It is also called International Trade Market. The number of markets in Yiwu is increasing, and we do business more easily than before.

【BTV】What is the difference between buying goods in Guangzhou and buying them in Yiwu?

【Swidan】Goods in Yiwu are mostly made by themselves and richer in variety, but in Guangzhou, they are large in quantity but not so in variety. The price in Yiwu is relatively lower, too.

【BTV】Have you encouraged your friends to start a business in Yiwu?

【Swidan】Sure. Whenever I was asked about Yiwu, I would advice them to come here to do business. Yiwu has many chances for everyone, and you have many choices here.

【BTV】How do you talk about Yiwu to your friends?

【Swidan】I told them Yiwu had a big market and many kinds of products, and it was very easy for everybody to do business. Here you can put different items in one container. The delivery time is very short. All things like that.

【BTV】Do you know Yiwu is the only place for our National Experimental Reform in China?

【Swidan】No.

【BTV】Okay, because of the big market and so many foreigners involved in Yiwu, the government decided to give and create some favorable policies for Yiwu. By the way, how do you usually spend your free time in Yiwu?

【Swidan】I sometimes do some physical exercises in a gym, sometimes do nothing and sometimes have a cup of coffee or milk.

【BTV】Do you like Chinese food? Have you ever tasted dumplings or noodles?

【Swidan】Actually, many foreigners are not used to Chinese food, which is much different from our food, you know.

【BTV】Yes.

【Swidan】I see many dishes of Chinese food don't have many spices, and the taste is very light, not very rich.

【BTV】Do you often cook at home?

【Swidan】No, I always dine at restaurants. We are so busy that we have no time eating at home.

【BTV】What do you think of the difference between Yiwu and other cities?

【Swidan】Yiwu is more convenient for the foreigners. Here many people can speak English, you know, but in many other cities, it isn't easy to find people who can speak English.

【BTV】Yes, there are many foreigners in Yiwu. Maybe you can find people from your hometown by chance.

【Swidan】Yes, I found business comes easier here in Yiwu, you know. I show them a sample, and they can find the products for me quickly.

【BTV】Do you have your own company?

【Swidan】My own company? What is the meaning?

【BTV】Are you a boss or just an employee here?

【Swidan】Oh I see. I have some customers from Fujian and also an office in Yiwu. As I have shown you, I have some business in Fujian.

【BTV】You also do business for people from your own country?

【Swidan】Yes, I collect products in China and take them back.

【BTV】Have you had cultural shock experiences in Yiwu? Any interesting stories that you would like to share with us?

【Swidan】Really, in China, the machines for trade are almost the same, but different in price and quality. In Yiwu, we can find one market after another, which makes it easy to get some products and have many choices, but in my country, there is usually only one market for certain products and at the same price. In China some people like expensive goods while some like cheap ones. Likewise, in my country, some people like high quality, some, middle quality and some rather low quality. Most Chinese like walking, but foreigners like sleeping.

【BTV】Yes, in China many women like shopping, especially of my mother's age. They go around the market, compare prices, and finally take the product with high quality and low price. This is their manner of shopping.

【Swidan】Yes, many foreigners like delaying. They are likely to postpone the things they need to do today to tomorrow while Chinese people are likely to finish today's things today.

【BTV】You mean they are very punctual?

【Swidan】Not exactly. Actually, some Chinese businessmen always tend to be late. Sometimes, they may show up at half past three for an appointment at three o'clock. Or they promise you to finish the work on Friday, and they maybe still can't finish it at that time.

【BTV】I'm so sorry. Have you encountered any other problems in China?

【Swidan】You know, I have been to India and Iraq. China is different from them. China is stronger and bigger, which makes people all like China better, but the rate of RMB exchange is up. Five years ago, when I came to China, the rate is 1 : 1, but now is 1 : 6. And it is not easy to exchange our country's money to RMB.

【BTV】Where are you from?

【Swidan】I'm from Libya. The things in China are not cheap now.

【BTV】Yes, ten years ago, when I was a child, I could buy many things with one yuan, but now one yuan can buy few things. Money is worth less.

【Swidan】Yes, businessmen's life is harder and harder. Many foreign businessmen in China now maybe are not earning money. Instead, they are losing their money, and now taxes are higher and are of more kinds.

【BTV】Yes. Not only you but also our parents think doing business is harder and harder. Have you ever heard of the China Dream?

【Swidan】China Dream? Can you explain it to me?

【BTV】Yes, the China Dream is to make Chinese people live a better and better life and have a brighter future. What is your own dream?

【Swidan】I hope Chinese people and people of my country are like people from one country, you know, like brothers and sisters, this is my dream. Chinese people will not have to get a visa to visit my country, and vice versa because visa is not easy to get. Many people failed to come to China because of the difficulty of getting a visa.

【BTV】In what way do you think it is difficult to get a visa?

【Swidan】First, the policy. Many people want to come to China for work, but they can't get the visa. Second, the cost. Getting the visa is very expensive and troublesome. In many countries businessmen can get one visa and that visa can allow him to visit many countries, which is more convenient.

【BTV】What kind of products do you sell?

【Swidan】Big machines, you know, big machines are all from Ningbo, and we have some factories in Ningbo, some in Wenzhou and Hangzhou. We buy goods in China and sell them in my own country.

【BTV】So you are selling many kinds of products, not only one?

【Swidan】Yeah, but the prices are little higher than before.

【BTV】Have you ever thought about settling in Yiwu? Say getting married with a Yiwu girl or buying a house or a car?

【Swidan】Buying a house? It is not easy for us foreigners, you know.

【BTV】Yes, now the prices of houses are higher and higher.

【Swidan】No, not for the money but for the policy. I want to buy, but it's difficult. I have already bought a car.

【BTV】How about the weather here in Yiwu?

【Swidan】The weather is hot.

【BTV】It's hotter than your country?

【Swidan】No, not hotter than my country, but my country is close to the sea.

(He shows his photo: a long beach, blue sky and his car near the sea.)

【BTV】That's great.

【Swidan】This photo was taken when I went back during the Chinese Spring Festival.

【BTV】It is beautiful! I hope I will be able to visit your hometown one day.

【Swidan】Welcome! You will see many different things.

【BTV】Can you give us some suggestions about Yiwu?

【Swidan】I hope there would be fewer cars.

【BTV】Yiwu is so small, but almost every family has at least two cars. At four or five o'clock, the rush hour, when people all leave their work to go home, the traffic is terrible.

【Swidan】Yes, that's true.

【BTV】Can you give us some advice about our interview?

【Swidan】Nice to meet you!

【BTV】Nice to meet you, too. You're so humorous. We hope you will have a good life in Yiwu, and your business will be better and better.

【Swidan】Can you see my car? It is over there.

【BTV】It looks very nice.

【Swidan】And here is my business card.

【BTV】Thank you. See you!

【Swidan】See you!

Group Members: Luo Qian, Zheng Yuan, Lin Mengmeng

叙事记录

【BTV】打扰一下，我们是浙江大学宁波理工学院的学生。现在我们正在做一项调研，了解外商选择义乌来发展的原因和他们在义乌经商时可能会面临的问题和困难。

【Swidan】这听起来很不错。

【BTV】请问您在中国多久了？

【Swidan】我在中国已经五年了。

【BTV】那您何时来义乌的呢？

【Swidan】两年前。在中国我有两个办公场所，都叫 AS，一个在广州，一个在义乌。

【BTV】除了义乌，您还去过中国的其他城市吗？

【Swidan】是的，去过很多。

【BTV】广州？

【Swidan】不仅仅是广州，我还去过温州、上海、南京和北京等城市。

【BTV】哇，您去过中国很多地方啊！那您在国外是怎么知道义乌这个城市的？

【Swidan】我是因为我周围的朋友都知道义乌这个地方，并且义乌所在的位置与许多有大型工厂的城市很近，你知道的，这对我来说非常重要。义乌还有许多旅馆。

【BTV】您对义乌的第一印象是什么？

【Swidan】首先义乌有很多宾馆，其次这里很多阿拉伯商人，印象最深的是福田市场，你知道的，就是那个最大的福田市场。

【BTV】是的，义乌被称为“小城大市”。

【Swidan】对外国商人来说，这里有这么多工厂和国际大市场。想要物色合适的工厂，就可以在义乌找到。你知道的，宁波有很多大型的机器，从宁波到义乌是非常方便的。

【BTV】你的意思是从宁波采购这些机器到义乌非常方便？

【Swidan】是的。我前面说过我去过很多城市，如温州、广州等，在义乌做生意非常方便，不用跑东跑西就能买到你想要的材料或者机器。

【BTV】您认为义乌有哪些变化？

【Swidan】我刚来义乌的时候，福田市场还没这么大。那时还有宾王市场，非常繁荣，现在已经关掉了。现在我们都在福田市场做生意，很方便。它被称为“国际商贸城”，有了它，我们找样品更容易了。

【BTV】那您觉得在义乌采购和在广州有什么不一样？

【Swidan】义乌的商品大多是自产自销的，种类较多，而广州的数量大但种类不太多，而且义乌的更便宜。

【BTV】您向您的朋友介绍过义乌吗？

【Swidan】当然了，只要问起关于义乌的事，我都建议他们到这儿来做生意。这儿有很多商机，我们自己也有很多选择。

【BTV】那您是怎么介绍义乌的呢？

【Swidan】我向他们介绍这里的市场，也告诉他们义乌的商品，也会说在义乌做生意对每个人都很容易。你可以采购一集装箱的商品，而且发货的速度十分快，诸如此类。

【BTV】您知道义乌是目前国家改革开放的唯一试点吗？

【Swidan】不知道。

【BTV】因为义乌的市场这么大，并且有这么多的外国商人，所以国家决定给义乌一定的优惠政策。顺便问一下，您在义乌的业余时间一般怎么过？

【Swidan】有时我去健身房健身，有时就啥事也不做，有时来这里喝杯咖啡或牛奶。

【BTV】您喜欢吃中国食物吗？如饺子、面条。

【Swidan】事实上很多外国人都不习惯中国食物，这和我们的食物有很大的不同。

【BTV】是的。

【Swidan】我觉得很多中国的食物调料加得不多，味道不够重，都太淡了。

【BTV】那您常常在家里自己做饭吃吗？

【Swidan】不，我经常下馆子，我们都太忙了，没有时间在家里做饭。

【BTV】您觉得义乌和中国其他城市有什么不同？

【Swidan】对外国人来说，在义乌比在其他城市更加方便，许多人会讲英语，你知道的，在其他城市很难找到会讲英语的人。

【BTV】是的，义乌有很多外籍商人，很可能你在大街上就能找到自己的老乡。

【Swidan】嗯，而且在义乌我发现生意来得特别容易，只要我将样品拿给他们看，他们很快就可以帮我找到相同的产品。

【BTV】您有自己的公司吗？

【Swidan】自己的公司？什么意思？

【BTV】就是为您自己做生意还是为其他人跑生意。

【Swidan】我是为自己做生意的，我有些客户来自福建，我在义乌有自己的办公室，你知道的，我在福建也有一些业务。

【BTV】您还为自己国家的人在做生意吗？

【Swidan】是的，我在中国采购产品，然后带回自己国家的市场上去卖。

【BTV】您在中国遇到过“文化休克”吗？有没有一些特别印象深刻的故事？

【Swidan】有啊。其实在中国我认为大家的机器几乎都是一样的，但他们的产品价格是不一样的，质量也各不相同。例如在义乌，我们发现一个市场接着一个市场，这对我们来说找产品非常方便，而且我有很多选择，在我的国家某些东西只能在某些特定的市场才能买到，而且价钱统一。在中国，人们有的喜欢高档货，有的喜欢地摊货。在我们国家也是如此，有人喜欢质量好的，有人喜欢质量中等的，还有人喜欢质量一般的。中国人大多喜欢走走逛逛，我们外国人却比较喜欢睡觉。

【BTV】是的，在中国很多像我妈妈那个年龄的妇女都喜欢逛街。她们看中一样东西，会将整个市场逛遍，再货比三家，选出质量好价格便宜的那家，再决定把它买下来。

【Swidan】是的，而且很多外国人喜欢把今天的事情留到明天做，中国人喜欢今日事今日毕。

【BTV】您的意思是他们很守时？

【Swidan】也不全是，一些中国商人喜欢拖延时间，你和他们约在三点，他们可能三点半才来。他们保证了在周五能够交货，但可能要更迟。

【BTV】听到这个实在抱歉。您在中国还遇到过什么问题吗？

【Swidan】你知道的，我曾经去过印度和伊拉克，中国和他们不同。中国比他们更强、更大，这使得人们更喜欢中国，但人民币汇率升高了。五年前我来到中国时比例为 1∶1，现在已经升到了 1∶6，并且在中国将我们的钱兑换成人民币并不是很容易。

【BTV】请问您来自哪里？

【Swidan】我来自利比亚。现在中国的东西也不便宜了。

【BTV】是的，十年前，我小时候，一元钱可以买很多东西，但现在一元钱几乎买不了什么东西。

【Swidan】现在这生意越来越难做了，有些人可能没有挣到钱，反而亏本了。而且现在光税都要交不少钱，税的种类也增多了。

【BTV】是呀，不要说你们了，就连我们的父母都认为生意越来越难做了。您听说过中国梦吗？

【Swidan】中国梦？你能解释一下吗？

【BTV】中国梦就是让中国人民的生活越过越好，有更美好的将来。那您自己的梦想呢？

【Swidan】我希望中国人民和我们国家的人民如一家人一样，这就是我的梦想，中国人到我们国家不需要签证，我们来到中国也不需要签证。因为签证不太好办理，许多人都想来中国，但由于签证问题，他们都来不了。

【BTV】您认为签证的困难有哪些？

【Swidan】首先是政策，有很多人想来中国工作，但因为签证很难申请到。第二是办签证的费用较高。很多国家会给商人办一张特别的签证，有了它，商人们到很多国家就不用再办了，非常方便。

【BTV】您主要销售哪一类产品？

【Swidan】大型机器，你知道的，大型机器很多来自宁波，我们有工厂在宁波、杭州和温州，我们在中国买材料，再带回本国卖。

【BTV】哇，您经营的种类好多呀！

【Swidan】是的，但和之前相比价格也高了很多。

【BTV】那您有在义乌定居的打算吗？比如娶个义乌女孩，买房子或买辆车？

【Swidan】买房子？对我们外国人来说这可不简单。

【BTV】是的，现在房价很高。

【Swidan】不是价钱的问题，是政策问题。我想买但条件受限，车我已经买好了。

【BTV】那您认为义乌的天气如何？

【Swidan】天气太热了。

【BTV】比您国家还热？

【Swidan】那倒没有，但我们国家靠近大海。

（他给我们看了一张照片，长长的沙滩，蓝蓝的天。海边还停着一辆他的车。）

【BTV】真好。

【Swidan】这是我春节期间回利比亚拍的照片。

【BTV】真漂亮啊，希望有一天我能去您的家乡看看。

【Swidan】非常欢迎！你会发现两国之间有很大的不同。

【BTV】您能给我们一些关于义乌的建议吗？

【Swidan】我希望义乌车能少一些。

【BTV】义乌地方很小，但几乎所有人家都有两辆车。一到下午四五点的高峰期，路会特别堵。

【Swidan】是的。

【BTV】您能给我们一些关于我们采访的建议吗？

【Swidan】认识你们很高兴！

【BTV】我们也是，您真幽默。我们希望您在中国的生活越来越好，生意越做越大。

【Swidan】你们看那是我的车，就在不远处。

【BTV】非常好看的车啊。

【Swidan】这是我的名片。

【BTV】谢谢，再见！

【Swidan】再见！

团队成员：罗倩，郑媛，林萌萌

Small City but Big Market: City or Market?

By Luo Qian Supervised by Nan Erli & Cai Liang

Yiwu is a small city but famous for its international market called China Commodity City. This summer holiday I took part in the project "Growing with Yiwu: My Dream in Yiwu" which gave me an opportunity to know Yiwu better.

Located in the central part of Zhejiang Province, Yiwu is connected to Guangdong and Fujian to the south, to the hinterland of the Yangtze River to the west, to China's large commercial city Shanghai to the east and right nearby the Pacific Golden Path. Yiwu has her own airport although it is a small city. Yiwu is not near the sea, neither does it have an open port, but its trade is very busy, which is magic.

Yiwu is famous in China as a commodities center. People from all over the world come to Yiwu City to buy commodities for resale in other parts of China or abroad. The Yiwu market has ranked on the top of the list of the national professional markets in volume of transaction for 22 consecutive years. It has been named the "flagship" of China's market economy, and with a large variety of less-expensive-but-good-quality commodities, the market has become a shopping paradise for tourists.

Yiwu now is the only county-level city for Chinese National Experimental Reform and was named the biggest market in the world by the United Nations and the World Bank. The China National Tourism Administration recognized Yiwu International Market as the first AAAA shopping and tourist city. If you say you are from Yiwu, people will respond that Yiwu is an ocean of small commodities and a paradise for shoppers. Yiwu is a small city but has an international market which is why it is called "A City Built on a Market".

Yiwu has become a strong commercial city. It was built around three large markets: Binwang Market, Futian Market and Huangyuan Market. Futian Market is also called International Trade City. It is divided into five areas, and each area is for different goods, and the environment is very good: All markets are equipped with air-conditioners and are very clean. Binwang Market is closed now because it deteriorated and was not needed after the expansion of Futian Market. Huangyuan Market has five floors, different floors are for different goods, and Huangyuan is a retail market while Futian Market is a wholesale market. The products made in Yiwu are exported to 220 countries.

When walking in the street or market, you can see many foreigners. I met Swidan in a coffee house when he was drinking from his cup at the doorway. He comes from Libya, and he has been in China for five years and Yiwu for two years. He has two offices in China, one in Guangzhou and another in Yiwu. He enjoys his life in Yiwu. Swidan owns a car, and he also wants to buy a house, but it is very difficult for a foreigner like him to do so. Policies covering the purchasing of real estate for foreigners are strict. For example, they must have been in China more than one year, and the down payment for the first apartment is 30% of the total. This is not easy for foreigners like him.

He has been to many cities, such as Wenzhou, Hangzhou and Guangzhou. Compared with other cities, he thinks Yiwu is more convenient. There are many foreigners. Maybe they will meet their fellow countrymen on the streets by chance. He said most business people in Yiwu can speak English. When he was walking in the market, he could hear people talk with foreigners fluently in simple English, and there are many hotels for foreigners, so it is very convenient.

Because he has offices in Guangzhou and Yiwu, he always flies between the two cites. Guangzhou is also famous for its markets. He thinks when one goes to a shop or a factory in Guangzhou, one would be asked how many containers they want, but in Yiwu, one would be asked how many types of commodities they want. This is indeed the difference, and buyers have more choices in Yiwu, so they can put many different items in one container and send the goods to their customers in their country immediately.

Not only foreigners but also the local people are deeply impressed by the rapid development of Yiwu. 20 years ago, because of the location and poor transportation, Yiwu was a poor and small city, and people used sugar to exchange for feather. Then they used the feather to exchange for something that they wanted.

My father actually experienced this transformation. He started to do business 15 years ago. He has witnessed the changes in Small Ware Market, Binwang Market and Futian Market. In my memory, Small Ware Market was very small and dirty. Binwang market was very hot. Now they are all in the Futian Market. The environment is very good, the floor is very clean, and the place is very comfortable in the summer.

During the past 15 years, the living conditions of my family have changed a great deal. Our means of transportation has changed from motorcycle to automobile and our small house to a big apartment. However, at the same time the traffic has become worse. Though Yiwu has a big market, it is a small city after all. With at least two cars for each family, the traffic in this city is rather crowded, especially at rush hour.

Besides, with the development of information technology, online shops like shops on Taobao and TMALL are very fashionable, convenient and cheap. To compete with these shops, the markets of Yiwu are faced with many challenges. Because business people in Yiwu are mostly doing wholesale trade, not retail, most people choose to get on Taobao to buy what they want at prices similar to those in Yiwu. As a reaction, Yiwu has also created an Internet market called Buying in Yiwu. If the local businessmen do not understand how to use the Internet, they will be in a poor situation and will lose many chances. Also, many cities like Guangzhou have built their own markets. Therefore, local people in Yiwu must keep pace with the times. To keep pace with times, the government has created a market for online business and tourism shopping, which is a perfect combination of the physical market and the virtual market.

As far as I am concerned, many places of interest have been destroyed during the development of markets. I hope that while the city is developing its economy, the historic buildings and environment could be protected and the civilization of the city could be developed at the same speed.

小城大市，“城”“市”并肩

文：罗　倩　指导教师：南二丽　蔡　亮

义乌是一个小城市，但是却因小商品城而很有名气。这个暑假我参加了“义乌我来了”调研活动，对义乌有了更深的认识。

义乌市位于浙江省中部，南至广东、福建，西接长江腹地，东靠中国的商业大城市上海，对面就是太平洋黄金通道。尽管义乌是个小城市，但它拥有属于自己的机场。义乌不靠近海边，没有港口，但它的贸易却如此繁华，这真称得上是一个奇迹。

义乌是中国的小商品中心，来自世界各地的人们慕名而来，批发小商品，再将它们销售到中国其他城市或国外。义乌中国小商品城成交额连续22年居全国专业市场榜首，被誉为中国市场经济的旗舰，义乌市场拥有质优价廉的商品，是游客的购物天堂。

现在义乌是第一个也是中国唯一一个县级国家改革试点城市，被联合国和世界银行称为世界上最大的市场。义乌国际商贸城被国家旅游局授予中国首个4A级购物旅游区。如果你对别人说你来自义乌，他们的第一反应就是，义乌是小商品海洋，购物者天堂！义乌是个小城市，但它有一个国际大市场，被称为是一座建在市场上的城市。

义乌已成为了经济强市，主要市场有三个——宾王市场、篁园市场和福田市场。福田市场也叫作国际商贸城，它分为五个部分，不同的区域卖不同的产品，并且里面的环境非常好，都有空调，地面很干净。现在有了福田市场，宾王市场也因为太旧已经关闭了。篁园市场现有五层，不同的楼层卖不同的商品。不过那边零售比较多，福田市场主要是批发的。义乌的产品出口国已多达220个国家。

大街上或市场上，老外随处可见。我遇见Swidan是在一家咖啡店的门口，那时他正在喝咖啡。Swidan来自利比亚，他来中国五年，在义乌已经两年了。他在中国有两个办公场所，一个在广州，一个在义乌。他非常享受自己在义乌的生活，他在义乌买了车，本来他还想买房的，但这非常困难，因为政策规定外籍人士在中国买房子必须满足一定的条件，例如必须在中国住满一年以上，而且第一套房的首付款比例不低于30%。凑够首付款对他这样的外国人而言并不容易。

他去过很多城市，例如温州、杭州、广州……与其他城市相比他认为义乌更加方便，并且这里有许多外国商人，他们很容易就能碰到来自同乡的人。义乌的许多商人会说英语，他说走在市场上，能听见义乌人与外籍商人在用英语进行简单的交流。并且这里有许多旅馆，这对外籍人士来说非常方便。

因为他在义乌和广州都有办公室，所以他经常乘飞机在两座城市间往返。广州也是因市场而出名的。他说在广州，那些工厂和商铺都是问你需要多少集装箱的货物。而在义乌，他们问你的是你需要多少种的款式。这就完全不同了，而且他在义乌的选择更多，由此以来，义乌的采购者可以选购各种各样的商品装入一个集装箱，然后可以马上向他们自己国家的客户发货。

义乌的发展不只让老外感触颇深，义乌本地人有更深的体会。20 年前因为地理位置和交通关系，义乌还是个贫困的小城，大家用糖去换鸡毛，然后再用那些鸡毛换取他们需要的东西。

我爸爸也经历过这些，现在他已经做了 15 年的生意了，他经历了小商品市场、宾王市场和福田市场的变迁。在我的印象中，小商品市场又小又脏，宾王市场很热。现在福田市场的环境非常好，每个市场多有空调并且非常干净，夏天在市场里非常舒服。

在这 15 年里我家生活水平也提高了很多，出行工具从摩托车变成了现在的小轿车，从小楼房搬到了大公寓。但与此同时，义乌的交通状况也变得越来越差了。尽管义乌有个大市场，但它毕竟是个小城市，近几年，几乎每户家庭都有两辆车，一到高峰期，交通就变得非常拥挤。

另外，随着信息技术的发展，在淘宝和天猫的网店购物变成了一种时尚，方便又便宜。义乌的小商品店也因此面临很多挑战。因为义乌的商人大部分是做批发生意的，不零售。淘宝上的价格和义乌批发的价格都很便宜，大多数人就选择在淘宝上买他们需要的东西。现在义乌也创办了一个网络市场，叫做义乌购，如果当地的商户不懂如何使用网络，他们将处于不利的局面，也将会失去很多机会。并且其他很多城市像广州也建立了属于自己的市场。因此义乌的商人必须与时俱进。为了跟上时代的步伐，当地政府为便于客户网上购物和旅游购物，专门开辟了一个新的市场，这样义乌就将实体市场和电子商务结合了起来。

但是，城市的经济建设过程中很多名胜古迹被破坏了，非常让人遗憾。我希望我们在发展经济的同时别忘了保护我们的古建筑和环境，我们的城市文明建设可以跟上经济发展的步伐。

Mohammed

Mohammed: Honesty and Trust Are Our Need

经商之道,“诚”“信”二字

Mohammed, a warm and generous Egyptian businessman, has been in Yiwu for six years. He can speak fluent Chinese. He is responsible for helping his Egyptian company buy jewelry and gifts. Because of his good character, he has made many friends in Yiwu. When he was asked about relevant local policy, he said that he hoped there would be a department dealing exclusively with communication problems between foreign businessmen and local government, facilitating their mutual understanding and the development of trade. He fully demonstrated his faith and wisdom during our interview.

穆罕默德是一个热情大方的埃及商人。在义乌已经六年的他,能说一口流利的中文,在义乌负责帮助埃及公司打理珠宝和礼品生意。由于他性格好,在义乌结交了许多朋友。谈到有关当地的政策时,他表示十分希望有一个部门专门解决外籍商人和当地政府之间的沟通和交流问题,便于促进双方的了解以及贸易发展。他给我们留下了一个诚信、睿智并且大方的外国人的印象。

Honesty and Trust Are Our Need

By Mohammed

Transcript of the Interview:

【BTV】First, Would you please introduce yourself briefly?

【Mohammed】Sure. My name is Mohammed. I am from Egypt. I have been in China for six years till now. I came here to Yiwu to help my Egyptian Company do business in jewelry and gifts.

【BTV】Oh! Six years! No wonder you can speak Chinese so well. Did you learn Chinese from daily life or formal classes?

【Mohammed】I have one Egyptian teacher. She teaches me Chinese, and also I learn from the Internet, sometimes from my Chinese friends.

【BTV】Is language a problem for your life or work here in Yiwu?

【Mohammed】Yes, it is very difficult to find and to communicate with any suppliers well because few can speak English well.

【BTV】How did you hear about Yiwu?

【Mohammed】You know, the world knows China. We also know that Yiwu is the biggest market in China.

【BTV】Which aspect of Yiwu do you like the most?

【Mohammed】Just my business because I do business in jewelry. I only have this business here.

【BTV】What do you usually do in your spare time?

【Mohammed】Every day I have to come back to handle my orders. Almost all my time is spent on my business if I stay here. Sometimes when I am free, I visit some places here in Yiwu and visit friends.

【BTV】Do you participate in local social or cultural activities in Yiwu?

【Mohammed】I usually take care of my business in the mornings or afternoons. Sometimes, I have my dinner outside, and then I go back to my home.

【BTV】Do you go to your Chinese friends' homes to celebrate Chinese festivals together, like Spring Festival, making dumplings and noodles?

【Mohammed】I like that! I like so many things like that in China.

【BTV】Do you like Yiwu food?

【Mohammed】Yiwu food is nice, but I am more used to eating Muslim food, and I also go to Chinese restaurants in my country.

【BTV】Can you cook Chinese food?

【Mohammed】Yeah, I can. I cook it in my country, too.

【BTV】How much do you know about Yiwu culture? Or Chinese culture?

【Mohammed】I know lots of that. Marriage, or helping people and so on. I know something about that because I have a lot of Chinese friends.

【BTV】Was it your friends who invited you to Yiwu to start the business?

【Mohammed】You can say something like that.

【BTV】Can you describe Yiwu and the people in Yiwu with only one word?

【Mohammed】In general, people in Yiwu are different. Many people are very friendly. During lunch time I always come there. I have meals with the boss and employees of this store, and they share their business experiences or interesting stories about China. I really like and trust them.

【BTV】Have you bought something today?

【Mohammed】Sure!

【BTV】What?

【Mohammed】Scarves, watches and wallets. All these accessories are for ladies' everyday use.

【BTV】What do you think of the jewelry?

【Mohammed】About what? About designing, about price or about what?

【BTV】About price.

【Mohammed】The price is a little bit high, but the exchange rate is very important. Now, compared with American dollars, Chinese RMB is going up, which means the business is good for Chinese but not good for us. Because, for example, if you bought something from China in the past, the rate was 1 RMB to 0.75 of our money, but now it is 1 to 0.96. For us, the price is higher, so it is an important thing for Chinese to find some way to ease the situation. Otherwise, the customers will go to another country. Now we have already planned to go to other countries, like India, Turkey, Vietnam and Italy. There the prices of the goods now are very close to those of the Chinese. Therefore, I think if the exchange rate between the American dollar and Chinese RMB continues to rise like that, maybe in five years, it will be very difficult for anyone to buy goods from China.

【BTV】How about the quality?

【Mohammed】Yi Fen Jia Qian Yi Fen Huo! [English: you get what you pay for.]

【BTV】Do you know that local government has a policy aimed to promote international trade in Yiwu? Do you have some advice?

【Mohammed】Yes. I know the Chinese government is trying their best to promote trade. Actually, that is a challenge for us at present because the rules are changing. We just come to China thinking of how to do business, but if the rules change quickly, we'll have to spend much time and energy handling new rules.

【BTV】Okay, any other suggestion?

【Mohammed】We hope the Chinese government would make getting a visa a faster or easier thing. I know they must choose good people and good businessmen to continue doing business in China. However, there are many people who intend to do business here for a long time like us. That'll be great if they can help us with the visa. Maybe a department can be set up to help fix all the problems concerning foreign businessmen. This department could communicate with each embassy from each country. For example, we are from Egypt, and this Chinese department could communicate with the Egyptian embassy and admit the people good at communication to handle problems in the trade between the Chinese and the Egyptians.

【BTV】How do you like the investment environment?

【Mohammed】I think it's okay. Every year it is easy to find quality goods. I think goods, especially jewelry, must be up to date, but this year it's quite difficult to find any new designs.

【BTV】How about the business before this year?

【Mohammed】Before... We just found it a bit hard to find another factory or another supplier to talk about new designs for us, something like that.

【BTV】Will you invite your Egyptian friends to come here for business?

【Mohammed】Sure. I have made comments about the city to them. Though I would like to introduce China to my friends and ask them to come here, sometimes I am still afraid of some Chinese businessmen because some play games with us.

【BTV】What do you mean by "play games"?

【Mohammed】Like when we buy some goods from them, they don't give us the goods with the quality that we ordered. They change the quality or something else. In such a case, we cannot find any Chinese to help us with that. So, we hope the Chinese government could help us and find some ways to fix the problem.

【BTV】How do you usually deal with it?

【Mohammed】I have a very good idea that would help to handle any problems between Chinese and foreigners. I just don't know how to connect with the Chinese government to do that. I have some plans in mind. For instance, embassies from each country and the Chinese government could have a meeting and talk about how to cooperate with each other to deal with commercial dishonesty. We could ask foreigners from each country to report to the Chinese government the list of good businessmen and bad businessmen. The Chinese government, in turn, could report which supplier is reliable and who is not so that both good suppliers and customers are protected. A win-win situation!

【BTV】That sounds great! If you have the chance to talk with the Chinese government, would you want to tell them about that?

【Mohammed】Sure! I want the Chinese economy to grow very well. I am Muslim, and I must be just. I don't like to talk behind others' backs, Chinese or foreigners, so if I have a chance, sure I will tell them China is very good. And I have done that a long time ago.

【BTV】Do you know about the comprehensive international trade reform in Yiwu?

【Mohammed】No, I don't.

【BTV】Would you please let me introduce it briefly?

【Mohammed】Of course.

【BTV】A comprehensive international trade reform is being carried out experimentally in Yiwu, which mainly aims to establish new trade mode, support the development of electronic-commerce, construct a national international trade area and promote import-and-export trade.

【Mohammed】That sounds great! And it will be a great help to domestic and foreign trade.

【BTV】Did the financial crisis influence your business last year?

【Mohammed】No, I feel the business was close to what it had been the past few years.

【BTV】So you earned great profit?

【Mohammed】No. You know, we're looking for jewelry. Fashion changes very quickly. Today's jewelry is fashionable, but maybe after several days it will be out of date. So I won't buy too much. And China's customs charges our company some money. We are charged much more than before. And also it is rather difficult to get inspection certificates from China. So we didn't earn a great profit.

【BTV】What kind of Yiwu people do you want to do business with? Or how do you choose your partners?

【Mohammed】Honest. Honest people. Everything goes well with honest people. Without honesty, even though he or she has goods that I want, I won't do business with him or her! Honesty is number one important.

【BTV】Can you bargain with them?

【Mohammed】Bargaining is easy business. We must bargain! But my associates must also earn profit. If they doesn't have good profits, they won't make new designs for us nor cooperate with us. So I want good profits for both of us, my associates and me. That's fair.

【BTV】Thank you very much!

【Mohammed】You're welcome.

Group Members: Liu Li, Liu Lu, Shang Mengdan

叙事记录

【BTV】您能先简短地介绍一下自己吗?

【Mohammed】哦，当然可以。我来自埃及，我来中国已经六年了，现在在义乌帮助我们公司做珠宝和礼品的生意。

【BTV】噢，六年，难怪您的汉语说这么好呢！您是从日常生活中学的汉语还是上了汉语课?

【Mohammed】我有一个埃及老师，她教我汉语。我也在网上学或者跟我的中国朋友学。

【BTV】语言是您在义乌的生活或工作的一个问题吗?

【Mohammed】是的，因为懂英语的人不多，所以很难找到供应商，找到了也不能很好地沟通。

【BTV】您如何知道义乌的呢?

【Mohammed】中国闻名于世。我们知道义乌是中国最大的市场。

【BTV】义乌最吸引您的是什么?

【Mohammed】生意，因为我做珠宝生意，在这里我只经营这个业务。

【BTV】您通常空闲时做些什么？

【Mohammed】每天我都要回来处理订单。如果我在中国，几乎所有的时间都用在我的业务上了，很少有时间空闲下来，空的话我会去义乌的一些地方见见这里的一些朋友。

【BTV】您会在义乌参加一些当地的社会或文化活动吗？

【Mohammed】通常白天我要打理生意，晚上有时候我在外面吃晚餐，然后回家。

【BTV】您去中国朋友家里庆祝中国的节日吗？比如春节，做饺子或面条什么的？

【Mohammed】我很喜欢这样啊！我喜欢中国很多的东西。

【BTV】您喜欢义乌的食物吗？

【Mohammed】义乌的食物很不错，但我更习惯于穆斯林食品。在埃及我也会去中国餐馆。

【BTV】您会做中国菜吗？

【Mohammed】是的，我在埃及有时也做中国菜。

【BTV】您对义乌文化和中国文化有怎样的了解呢？

【Mohammed】我了解了很多，中国的结婚习俗，助人为乐等，因为我有很多中国朋友。

【BTV】所以是您的朋友邀请您来义乌开始这项工作的吗？

【Mohammed】可以这么说。

【BTV】如果请您用一个词分别形容义乌和义乌人，您会怎么形容？

【Mohammed】总的来说，义乌人挺不一样的，他们非常友好。午餐时间，我总是在这家店与这家店的老板和员工一起吃饭，他们与我分享业务经验或那些有关中国的趣事，我真的很喜欢他们，也信任他们。

【BTV】您今天买到什么东西了吗？

【Mohammed】当然。

【BTV】您买了什么东西？

【Mohammed】围巾，手表和钱包。所有这些都是女士每日必需的配饰。

【BTV】您认为这儿的珠宝怎么样？

【Mohammed】关于什么？关于设计，关于价格或关于其他？

【BTV】关于价格。

【Mohammed】这儿的价格有点高。但是汇率非常重要，现在，相对于美元，人民币正在升值，这对中国人做生意有利，但对我们没有什么益处。因为，如果你从中国买东西，以前是一元人民币兑换 0.75 埃及镑，现在是 0.96 埃及镑，所以这意味着我们买东西价格高了。这是中方要重视的一个问题。否则,客户会去另一个国家。现在我们已经计划去其他国家像印度、土耳其、越南和意大利采购。那里商品的价格现在很接近中国的。所以我觉得如果美元和人民币之间的汇率一直这样下去的话,也许五年以后人们会觉得中国制造的商品真是买不起了。

【BTV】关于质量呢?

【Mohammed】一分价钱,一分货!(他用中文说的)

【BTV】您知道义乌市政府有一个旨在促进国际贸易的政策吗?您有什么建议吗?

【Mohammed】是的,我知道中国政府一直致力于对外贸易的进一步发展。实际上,我们目前觉得困难的就是政府的这些措施,因为政策经常变化,我们要经常思考如何调整,比较麻烦。很多精力和时间都用在这上面了。

【BTV】还有其他建议吗?

【Mohammed】另外我们希望能更快捷地办好中国签证。我知道中国政府须选择人品好和讲诚信的商人继续在中国做生意。我理解,但是他们也必须考虑像我们这样打算长期在这里的发展的人,如果在签证方面更方便的话就太好了。希望专门有这么一个部门帮助外国人解决问题。这个部门能够与每一个国家的大使馆沟通协调。例如,我们来自埃及,中国这个部门可以与驻埃及大使馆沟通,选择一些善于沟通的人来处理两国之间的贸易问题。

【BTV】就投资环境而言,您有什么看法?

【Mohammed】我认为这儿投资环境很好。年年都可找到质量上乘的商品。商品必须不断推陈出新,特别是首饰,但今年新款不好找。

【BTV】之前的业务怎么样?

【Mohammed】之前我们只是很难在市场上找到工厂或供应商和我们商讨新款设计方面的问题。

【BTV】您会邀请埃及的朋友来义乌做生意吗?

【Mohammed】当然,我跟他们说过义乌。虽然我很想介绍一些朋友们来,但是有时我也得小心有一些中国商人,因为他们会耍花招。

【BTV】什么样的花招?

【Mohammed】就像当我们订购一些产品,但发过来的货物跟我们订的不一样,质量或者其他方面有差异。在这种情况下,我们不知道该找谁帮忙。所以我们希望中国政府能够帮助我们应对这样的问题。

【BTV】遇到这种问题您一般怎么办?

【Mohammed】我有一个非常好的想法,旨在帮助解决中国人和外国人之间的许多问题,但是我不知道该怎样去与中国政府沟通。我在想,是不是……每个国家的大使馆与中国政府可以开会交流解决贸易中的商业欺诈问题。可以从每个国家选聘一些外国人，与中国政府合作，列出信誉好的商人和信誉不好商人的名单。同时让中国政府告诉我们哪些供应商信誉良好，哪些供应商信誉不良。这样供应商和客户都能得到保护，双赢！

【BTV】这个主意不错！如果有机会与中国政府对话，您想告诉他们吗？

【Mohammed】当然！我希望中国的经济能有很好的发展。我是穆斯林，公平对我很重要。我不喜欢在背后议论他人，不论是中国人还是外国人，所以如果我有机会，我当然会告诉他们中国很好。而且，我很久以前就这样做了。

【BTV】您知道在义乌有一个全面的国际贸易改革吗？

【Mohammed】不知道。

【BTV】那我可以向您介绍一下这项改革的内容吗？

【Mohammed】欢迎！

【BTV】就是义乌市要开展国际贸易综合改革试点，目的是建立新型贸易方式、支持电子商务发展、建设国家级小商品国际贸易区、发展进出口贸易等。

【Mohammed】听起来不错，对国内外的贸易发展会有很大的帮助。

【BTV】金融危机影响了您去年的业务吗？

【Mohammed】没有，生意与过去的几年差不多。

【BTV】那您赚到了很多利润吗？

【Mohammed】没有。你知道我们是做珠宝生意的，流行趋势的变化非常迅速。有些首饰今天还很流行，也许过几天就过时了，所以我就不会买太多。中国海关要向我们公司收取费用，现在的收费也比以前多好多。申请来自中国的检验证书的过程也比较困难，所以我们没有赚多少。

【BTV】您想跟什么样的义乌人做生意？或者说您如何选择合作伙伴？

【Mohammed】诚实的人。人诚实的话任何事都能做好，如果人不诚实，即使他有我想要的货物，我也不会和他做生意！诚实第一。

【BTV】您会跟他们讨价还价吗？

【Mohammed】讲价不是难事。必须讨价还价！但是对方也要得到利益，如果没有得到利益，他们就不会给我们一些新的设计，也不会跟我们合作。所以我希望我们双方赢利，这样才公平。

【BTV】非常感谢您接受我们的采访。

【Mohammed】不客气。

团队成员：刘李，刘璐，尚梦丹

Honesty and Trust Contribute to Stable Development

By Liu Lu Supervised by Nan Erli & Cai Liang

Before I came to the city, Yiwu was already a renowned name to me: the largest small commodity distribution center. It has political, geographic, and people advantages. Under the socialist market economy, the local government keeps pace with the times by making a special economic policy for Yiwu to realize its smooth and fast development. Next, it has geographic advantage: Yiwu is in the middle of Zhejiang, close to Guangdong and Fujian, the hinterland of the Yangtze River, Shanghai economic development zone and the Pacific Ocean Gold Channel. It extends in all directions. Finally, it has people advantage: as the world's biggest market, it is not only the ideal place to do business for Chinese people but also for foreigners. There is a huge daily stream and turnover, and it is really "an ocean of small commodities and a paradise for shoppers". However, beneath the prosperity, there are many hidden problems.

This summer holiday, I finally set foot in Yiwu, the land that I have been looking forward to for a long time. Through the continuous stream of the crowd, I saw a wide variety of goods which is mind-boggling. By chance, I got to know an Egyptian called Mohammed. He has been in Yiwu for six years and is responsible for helping his Egyptian company buy jewelry and gifts here in Yiwu. To adapt to Chinese society, he has been learning Chinese from an Egyptian teacher. After six years of study and practice, he has gained a good command of Chinese. However, in order to facilitate our students' oral practice, he spoke English in the interview. To tell the truth, his Chinese is better than his English. What a keen and lovely foreign friend!

During the conversation, he showed great enthusiasm for Chinese culture and thought highly of Chinese cuisine. (As he said, he not only likes to eat, but also cooks Chinese food.) Also, he did not hesitate to praise the enthusiasm of the Chinese people. However, Mohammed also criticized dishonest businessmen. Admittedly, Chinese people are famous for their diligence and wisdom, but some people like to use underhand means to earn money. People become angry if they are cheated on workmanship and materials. When the dishonest are happy about their petty profits that they have racked their brains to get, they don't realize that they have lost the immeasurable value of honesty and business opportunities. After all, entertaining guests with trustworthiness can attract more customers and receive more orders!

Despite the prosperity and joy of Yiwu business, Muhammed has still been challenged by the policies made by the government to promote economic development. He found them hard to follow. When many foreign businessmen are longing for visas for long-term stay in Yiwu, doing legitimate business, he hopes that the government would create a special office dealing exclusively with communication between foreign businessmen and local government, facilitating them to agree on the prompt and effective use of local policies to promote the development of trade. To keep up with the trend of "internationalization" and "experimental reform", the Yiwu government established a foreign affairs service platform earlier this year to realize all foreign service projects being authorized by the Yiwu government and make external services more transparent.

After the interview, walking in the streets of Yiwu, we praised the skyscrapers, but also saw their shadows. Someone said, in this age, there is always a "shadowland of development". I agree that the speed of the development of a city can neither be too fast nor too slow. Either leads to a worse future sooner or later. Only with an even rate, can a city develop stably, and honesty and trust are basic rules in fostering that.

稳中求进，诚信为本

文：刘　璐　指导老师：南二丽　蔡　亮

当我还未涉足这片土地的时候，"义乌"之名便如雷贯耳——全球最大的小商品集散中心。说她是天时地利人和，一点也不为过。天时，在社会主义市场经济的领导下，当地政府与时俱进，为义乌量身定做了一套又一套经济政策，实现平稳快速发展。地利，义乌市位于浙江省中部，比邻广东、福建，长江腹地，上海经济区以及太平洋黄金通道，可谓四通八达。人和，作为世界第一大市场，不仅中国人翘首企盼，外国人也为之向往。每日客流量巨大，交易额巨大，真是"小商品海洋，购物者天堂"。但是在这繁华之下，也潜藏着一些问题。

今年暑假，我终于踏上了这片神往已久的土地。穿梭在络绎不绝的人潮中，琳琅满目的商品令人眼花缭乱。在机缘巧合之下，我认识了一个叫穆罕默德的埃及人。他在义乌六年了，负责帮助埃及公司打理珠宝和礼品生意。为了能更好地融入中国社会，他特地拜师学习中文，经过六年时间的学习和实践，他已经能够把中文融会贯通。不过，为了方便我们的口语练习，他特地迁就我们用了英文沟通。说实话，他的英文说得还不如中文流利。真是一个热心又可爱的外国友人！

交谈中，他对中国文化表现出极大的热情，对中国的美味赞不绝口(听说他不但爱吃，还能下厨露上两手)，还毫不犹豫地肯定了大多数中国人的热情。不过，对于部分道德水平有待提高的中国人，穆罕默德也提出了很直率的批评。不可否认，中国人的勤劳智慧有目共睹，但一些人喜欢用不正当的手段来赚钱，货不对板，偷工减料，确实令人反感。当他们为自己通过耍小聪明得来的那些蝇头小利而沾沾自喜的时候，却不知道自己失去可是价值无量的诚信和商机。毕竟，诚信待客，生意才能长久！

义乌繁荣的经济无疑对穆罕默德而言有很大的吸引力，但是政府的一些促进经济发展的政策对他而言却是个挑战，他还不能及时了解这些政策。许多外国商人都渴望长期在义乌发展，合法经营，因此，他迫切希望有一个部门专门解决外国商人和当地政府之间沟通和交流问题，以便他们能够及时了解并有效利用当地促进贸易发展的政策。为了让义乌跟上"国际潮流"，推动"义乌试点"的改革进程，今年初，义乌市政府设立了这个涉外政务服务平台，实现了政府管理权限内所有涉外服务项目的集中以及服务过程的透明。

和穆罕默德的交谈结束后，我们流连于义乌的大街小巷，在赞美仰望高楼大厦的同时，也留意到巍巍耸立之下不易忽略的阴影。有人说在这个时代，城市的发展总会有一个"跟不上节奏之处"。我认为城市的发展速度既不可以太快，也不可以太慢，否则前景暗淡。只有速度适中，城市才能更稳地发展。而实现这一切，诚实和信任是最基本的准则。

Stephen

Stephen: The Wonderland of Yiwu

趣意盎然在义乌

Stephen Little is a businessman from Canada, but Yiwu is the birthplace of his business. His arrival in Yiwu was in December, 2011. Since then, he has commenced on a journey of purchasing in Yiwu. He loves both the people and the customs in Yiwu. Stephen feels his Yiwu life is very interesting every day. As a Canadian, his dream is to found his own factory in Yiwu, and now he is busy chasing his dream!

史蒂芬·里托是一名来自加拿大的商人，义乌是他事业的发源地。2011 年 12 月，他第一次来到义乌并从此开始了在义乌的采购之旅。他很喜爱义乌的风土人情。他觉得他在义乌的每一天都趣意盎然。作为一名加拿大人，他的梦想是在义乌创建属于自己的工厂，而他也正在忙碌地追逐着自己的梦！

The Wonderland of Yiwu

By Stephen

Transcript of the Interview:

【BTV】Hello, Stephen! Thanks for your participation in this survey, which is jointly conducted by the Foreign Affairs Office of the Yiwu Municipal People's Government and Ningbo Institute of Technology, Zhejiang University. Would you mind starting the interview now?

【Stephen】Of course not!

【BTV】What do you think of Yiwu food, or in other words, are you accustomed to the food here?

【Stephen】I am not quite used to Yiwu food. It's very hard for me to adapt to food quite different from that of my own country. I have to eat pizza every day.

【BTV】What do you think of the transportation in Yiwu?

【Stephen】I think it's great because there are so many taxis in Yiwu, and it's pretty cheap to take a taxi.

【BTV】Would you mind sharing some special or interesting experiences that you encountered in Yiwu?

【Stephen】I find every day here is interesting. Yesterday, I met a man, also a foreigner, and we shared some ideas about the new market system in Yiwu with each other, which inspired my insight in business, and the other day, I met a Nigerian lady who wanted to send her son to Canada, my motherland, for education. I promised her that I could help her.

【BTV】Do you have local friends here? Besides the language barriers, have you found any other cultural barriers when you hang out or communicate with Chinese people?

【Stephen】Yeah, I surely have. However, I enjoy the cultural differences. If it's a shock, I will enjoy more. I'll think, "Wow, so different." Then, I tend to ask many questions about the customs every day about everything. Besides the interesting customs, people here are both friendly and humorous.

【BTV】I see you are staying in a hotel. Why don't you buy a house or an apartment here?

【Stephen】I just come here for purchasing. I won't stay long every time. Let me see, almost three weeks each time. So, I don't need a house here.

【BTV】Oh, I see. How often do you come here each year?

【Stephen】I don't come here regularly because I have just started my business two years ago. The first time I came here was in December, 2011. The second time was in March, 2013, and this time was the third time, in July, 2013. And I'll come again in January, 2014. I hope I can come here three times each year in the future.

【BTV】Have you ever been to any other cities in China besides Yiwu?

【Stephen】No, Yiwu is the only city I have ever been to in China, but I hope I can visit other Chinese cities one day. Yiwu is my first station in China.

【BTV】Why did you choose Yiwu to be the first station in China, or in other words, how did you find out Yiwu?

【Stephen】Because I met a man in Yiwu on the Internet a long time ago. He helped me discover new business opportunities here. So, after saving enough money, I then came here to start my business.

【BTV】When we met you at the International Trade Fair this morning, were you doing some purchasing there?

【Stephen】I was searching for items and purchasing, such as jewelry, clothing, toys, and souvenirs. These are the primary commodities of my company.

【BTV】Are there any differences between the markets of Canada and China?

【Stephen】As far as the factories are concerned, we don't have many factories in Canada, but there are a lot in Yiwu. In addition, they are much bigger in size compared with those in Canada. People here know how to make things efficiently and technologically. Most items, imported into my country, come from China, especially from Yiwu, among which there are certain machines to tailor certain things. Most importantly, the labor cost is quite low here.

【BTV】Have you heard about the government's policy to develop the economy and the mutual-trade between different countries?

【Stephen】Oh, I've heard that Yiwu was made a special zone by the government to bring all the businesses around here and promote the economic development of this area. It's a mixture of people from all walks of life. Besides that, there are other good policies. I have benefited a lot from them. For example, most of the fairs are gathered in one place. All the items make it easy to find the one I want. It's so convenient for purchasing here, just too good to be true.

【BTV】You come to Yiwu because you find it a very good city for investment, right?

【Stephen】Yeah, as a very good investment city, Yiwu is the best place to come. Among many factors, the lowest price of products is the major one.

【BTV】Besides the advantages, are there any disadvantages or any suggestions for the markets in Yiwu?

【Stephen】One problem is that the quality of the products is not high enough. But because of that, I can purchase them at a low price, and then get very good profits. So, you see, Yiwu helps me develop business. But for it, I couldn't have started my business.

【BTV】What did you sell when you started your business?

【Stephen】I started with jewelry selling. Jewelry is very profitable. Now, we are also selling clothing and souvenirs.

【BTV】Did you have any difficulties when you started your business here?

【Stephen】Quality is a big problem, as I have mentioned. If you don't know what you are doing, it can be a big problem. For example, after we did some purchasing here, and we sent the goods to Canada, but then we might find that we could not sell them there because no one wanted them. Some items I have purchased don't sell well.

【BTV】Has Chinese language ever been a problem to you?

【Stephen】I have translators here. So, it didn't trouble me a lot. I have tried to learn Chinese, but it's really a difficult language. Learning Chinese costs more time and effort than learning other foreign languages.

【BTV】Do you like the way Chinese people do business?

【Stephen】Yes! Compared with the Canadians, I prefer the Chinese way to do business. Most of the Chinese people treat me more respectfully than Canadians. Also, I find people in China work very hard. They work six days or even seven days a week, just like me. People in Canada are a little lazy. They don't work very hard. They enjoy their life, and think it's enough if they can afford their daily expense, and they think that's all right. In addition, the family culture is considered more important in China than in Canada. You cannot see families spend much time together in Canada.

【BTV】You know China is developing quickly in recent years. Just like the American Dream, China has the China Dream. Do you have a Canadian Dream?

【Stephen】Although Canada and America are much similar, like language for example, Canadians are different from Americans. In Canada, most people don't care much about politics. That's the difference. Canadians prefer an easy life. If there must be a Canadian Dream for me, it must be coming to China for business. I think I have already achieved my dream, and my next dream is to have a factory in Yiwu.

【BTV】Suppose you have achieved your next dream, what would be your standard for hiring staff?

【Stephen】I know the Chinese standards are very different from Canadian ones. The Chinese boss needs the employee to bring more profit to the company. I am not quite sure about my standards, but I'm sure that I'd like to pay them more. I think people don't make enough money here. Most Chinese are offered just two or three thousand RMB each month. I think they deserve more. In the other words, if I pay them more, they'll be happier and work harder. My factory will be more successful.

【BTV】Thank you for your agreeing to our interview.

【Stephen】It's my pleasure.

Group Members: Chen Jialu, Cen Ye, Zhu Jiangshan, Qian Chen

叙事记录

【BTV】您好，史蒂芬！感谢您参加这次由义乌市政府外事办和浙江大学宁波理工学院共同举办的调研活动。现在，我们能开始访谈吗？

【Stephen】当然可以。

【BTV】来了义乌这么久，您适应义乌的饮食吗？

【Stephen】我不太习惯义乌的饮食。对我来说，这儿的食物与加拿大不太一样，我不怎么适应。我只能每天吃比萨饼。

【BTV】您觉得义乌的交通怎么样？

【Stephen】很好啊！出租车很多，费用也不高。

【BTV】您在义乌有什么趣事吗？能跟我们分享一下吗？

【Stephen】我发现在这里的每一天都是趣意盎然的。昨天，我遇到了一位在义乌的外国朋友，我们谈了义乌的市场和经济方面的看法，我很受益。前几天，我遇到了一位尼日利亚的女士。她想把自己的儿子送到加拿大的学校接受教育，我告诉她有困难可以找我帮忙。

【BTV】您的朋友中有义乌土生土长的本地人吗？您在与他们的交往中，有没有文化差异带来的沟通困难？

【Stephen】我当然有义乌朋友了。文化差异带来的沟通困难并没有困扰我，相反，这种文化差异会让我觉得“那么不同，真是有趣！”我对这里的风俗习惯很好奇，常常问好多问题，这里不仅风俗很吸引人，人也很友善，很幽默。

【BTV】您好像在宾馆住，请问您为什么不在这里买房呢？

【Stephen】我来义乌只是短期的采购，每次来这里三个星期，所以在义乌，我暂时不需要有固定的住房。

【BTV】我明白了，那您每年来义乌几次呢？

【Stephen】我并不是定期地来义乌，因为我的事业才刚刚起步。第一次来义乌是在 2011 年 12 月，第二次是 2013 年 3 月，这一次是第三次，2013 年 7 月来的。2014 年 1 月，我会再来义乌。我希望以后能够每年来义乌三次。

【BTV】那您去过中国的其他城市吗？

【Stephen】没有，义乌是我唯一到过的中国城市。但是我期待去中国其他城市看一看，义乌是我在中国的第一站。

【BTV】您为什么选择了义乌呢？您怎么知道义乌这个城市的？

【Stephen】很久以前我在网上认识了一个义乌人，在他的帮助下，我发现义乌充满商机。于是，在加拿大存到足够的费用后，我来义乌开始了我的事业。

【BTV】我们上午在国际商贸城遇到您时，您是在采购吗？

【Stephen】是的，我在买珠宝、布料、玩具和纪念品。这些都是我们公司经营的主要商品。

【BTV】中国市场与加拿大市场有什么不同吗？

【Stephen】就工厂而言，义乌的工厂密集，加拿大的工厂很少。而在规模上，加拿大工厂的规模也不如义乌的大。义乌人知道怎么科学而有效率地制造产品。加拿大的许多商品都是从中国进口的，来自义乌的商品在这些商品中占了很大的比例，包括一些专业的切割、剪裁的机器。最重要的是，义乌劳动力成本低。

【BTV】您听说过义乌市政府为发展经济促进各国间的多元贸易而颁布的政策吗？

【Stephen】我听说义乌被设为试点来带动义乌区域的商业发展。就像是一个大熔炉，囊括了来自各国的各行各业的人。许多其他政策也让我受益良多。比如，义乌的小商铺集中在同一个地方，所有的商品都可以被轻松找到。这里便利得就像是一个采购者的天堂。

【BTV】所以，您来到义乌也是被这里良好的投资环境所吸引是吗？

【Stephen】是的，良好的投资环境让义乌成了我的第一选择。这其中，商品价格低廉是最重要的因素。

【BTV】那么，义乌的市场有什么不足或者如何完善呢？

【Stephen】产品质量不够好是需要重视的问题。但也因为这样，我能以较低价格买入这些产品并赢利。你看，义乌帮助我发展事业，没有义乌我的事业也就无法起步。

【BTV】您一开始做什么生意？

【Stephen】珠宝，珠宝业有很高的利润。现在我也销售布料和纪念品。

【BTV】事业起步的时候，您遇到过什么困难吗？

【Stephen】就如我所提到过的，产品质量使我困扰。你得明确自己到底要采购什么产品到加拿大卖，否则将会很麻烦。比如，有时会发生这样的情况：我在义乌采购好的商品运到加拿大后，没有人感兴趣，卖不动。

【BTV】您遇到过语言上的困难吗？

【Stephen】我有自己的翻译，没有语言困难。我也尝试过学习汉语，不过汉语真的很难，比学习其他外语要耗时间。

【BTV】您喜欢中国人做生意的方式吗？

【Stephen】当然！与加拿大人相比，我更喜欢与中国人打交道。与中国人做生意，我能得到更多尊重。而且，我发现大多数中国人都是工作狂，他们一周工作六天甚至七天。相反，加拿大人比较懒。大多数加拿大人更享受生活带来的乐趣，他们只要求工作所得能够维持日常开销。另一方面，在中国，人们更重视家庭，而在加拿大，人们不常与家人聚在一起。

【BTV】近几年，中国发展十分迅速。就像美国人有美国梦，中国人也有了中国梦。您有加拿大梦吗？

【Stephen】尽管加拿大与美国有许多相似之处，比如语言，但两国之间也有许多差异。加拿大人不关心政治，这就是最大的不同之处。加拿大人更爱从容自在地生活。如果我有加拿大梦，那一定是来中国经商，这是我早就实现了的。我的下一个梦想是在义乌创建属于自己的工厂。

【BTV】如果您成功在中国创建了工厂，您聘用员工的标准是什么呢？

【Stephen】在我看来，中国人聘用员工的标准与加拿大人是有所差异的。中国老板需要的是能够给自己的公司带来更多盈利的员工。我不确定自己聘用员工的标准，但是我想我愿意付给他们更高的酬劳。我觉得这里的人们并没有得到与他们所付出相对等的酬劳。大多数中国人的月工资维持在两三千元的水平。我觉得他们的所得应该更多些。其实换个角度来看，员工得到的更多，他们会过得更开心，与此同时，工作积极性会更高，我的工厂也会更成功。

【BTV】感谢您接受我们的采访。

【Stephen】不客气，这是我的荣幸。

团队成员：陈佳露，岑烨，朱江珊，钱晨

Yiwu: More than the Appearance

By Chen Jialu　Supervised by Nan Erli & Cai Liang

The small commodity market of Yiwu is familiar to all Chinese. The city, which is named after a bird, has a long history and a profound culture. This is the place where the story of the "Yue Hardships" (Namely, the Rebirth of the King of Yue Kingdom). happened, and it now has the most powerful privilege of economic management among all counties in China. As the world's largest commodity distribution center, Yiwu is close to the Pacific Ocean and has been identified as the world's largest market by the United Nations, the World Bank, and other international authoritative organizations. In 2011, Yiwu was made the tenth special economic zone and is also the only city under a national experimental economic reform among all the county-level cities in China.

As a person born in Zhejiang, I have been longing to see the city that represents a special humanistic phenomenon. This summer, I got an opportunity to visit the city because of the survey that we were asked to do. As the bus drove into the city, I shook off my fatigue and stared at the scenery outside the bus, but at first she disappointed me. There was not much difference between Yiwu and the small town I come from. She is also a city with traffic jams and sprawling buildings... I had assumed that she was a city with amazing skyscrapers. However, being identified as the "World's Largest Market", there must be something peculiar behind the characterless appearance of the city, I thought. With such expectation, I started my research trip in Yiwu.

The first place that surprised me in Yiwu was the Yiwu International Market where all the booths are gathered together and booths of the same items are located in one zone. In addition, we could see people in different races and ethnic groups walking through the fairs in a hurry.

Having been refused by many hurrying foreigners, we met our first interviewee, Stephen, a Canadian businessman. He knew of the amazing city from a net pal of Yiwu. In 2011, he came to China, his first trip to an oriental country, and he went straight to Yiwu to do market research. The firsthand experience amazed Stephen much more than just the words he had heard. At the same time, the commercial opportunity behind the featureless appearance attracted him. Taking the city as a commodity supply resource, he decided to settle in Yiwu and set up his own business here. In our interview, Stephen pictured a marvelous Yiwu City from the perspective of a businessman. He said that Yiwu is totally different from Canada. Compared with the few factories in Canada, Yiwu is a city which is strewn with factories. Influenced by the large market here, many local families have certain machines to make certain products and can produce items skillfully. All these superiorities, especially the cheap labor, cannot be found in developed countries like Canada. Meanwhile, sea routes provided by the Pacific Ocean make the export industry in Yiwu tops in China. As a freshman in Yiwu, Stephen said that the cheap transportation in Yiwu also made his early career free from much unwanted trouble. In the streets here, there are taxis ever ready. Compared with the other neighboring cities, taxis here are not only cheaper but also easier to find. Foreign businessmen like Stephen who come to purchase here benefit much from that. Never could Yiwu be so prosperous without the hard-working people. When we came to discuss cultural differences, Stephen sang high praises for the local people. As far as he is concerned, most people in Canada aim to lead a life of leisure. However, he has found many workaholics in Yiwu who are working six or seven days each week trying to accumulate much wealth for their descendants for several generations. To some degree, the differences originate from the differences of different family cultures. Canadians do not think much of family, but Chinese people do, and it is obvious that people in Yiwu attach great importance to family. At the end of the pleasant interview, Stephen told us about his dream—to found a factory of his own in Yiwu.

The second day of our stay in Yiwu, we said good-bye to Stephen, and then a warm-hearted local businessman recommended a second interviewee to us. The passion that person has for Yiwu and China was beyond my expectations and even puzzled me. Nevertheless, after witnessing his busy day, I suddenly realized the fact that all his passion for the city is due to the sense of fulfillment and the good life that he achieved in the city. Another interviewee, however, a Pakistani businessman who has lived alone in Yiwu for years, put forward the only flaw of his pleasant life here. He said that as soon as he learned to speak Chinese, there were few difficulties for his business in Yiwu. The only problem that persecuted him was that he could not live together with his family and let his family enjoy the life here in Yiwu. He wishes that Yiwu government might improve the policy about foreigners' residing in Yiwu.

The night before we left, we touched the heart of the city and realized what made Yiwu distinct from other cities. While it is hot and tense at day time, it is leisurely and soothing at night. The outdoor cafés along the street are filled with people from different countries, who are smoking nargile and hookah. Some are talking and laughing loudly while others are relaxing in the peaceful night. This scene makes the city quite exotic and charming, and the sprawling buildings become special in a positive way.

During that peaceful night, in the car back to home, I stared at the city for the last time. She was still a plain city in appearance, but there was something amazing behind this. I could see foreigners in the cafés, and my memory went back to the time when Stephen and other foreigners were talking with me. The words suddenly dawned on me, "Yiwu, more than the appearance."

A Group Picture with Stephen

义乌，不可貌相

文：陈佳露　指导教师：南二丽　蔡　亮

义乌小商品市场，这个名字对每个中国人来说都不陌生。她是一座以乌命名的城市，历史上，她是越王勾践卧薪尝胆的地方，有着悠久的历史和深厚的文化底蕴；21世纪的今天，她可谓中国权力最大县，有着自由的经济特权。义乌地理位置靠近太平洋黄金通道，是全球最大的小商品集散中心，被联合国、世界银行等国际权威机构称为“世界第一大市场”。2011年，义乌被设立为第十个经济特区，是全国唯一一个县级市国家级综合改革试点。

作为一名浙江人，我对义乌这个名字所代表的特殊人文现象早就充满憧憬。这一次，我终于借着采访之名来到了这里。车子一驶进义乌，我便从旅途的劳顿中清醒过来，睁大了双眼观察车窗外的景色。然而车窗外的义乌，着实让我失望。她与我生活的那个小县市并没有多少不同，拥挤的交通，参差不齐的建筑……我以为我会来到一个满是喧嚣、高楼林立的经济大区。不过，义乌能被公认为“世界第一大市场”一定不是毫无根据的。怀着这样的期待，我开始了义乌探访之旅。

义乌国际商贸城是第一个让我惊叹的地方。在这里，所有的商铺被集中到一起。同类型的小商铺聚拢成一个小区域，随处可见不同种族、不同国家的人们穿梭于各个小商铺。

被许多行色匆匆的老外拒绝后，我们遇到了第一个采访对象——史蒂芬。史蒂芬是名加拿大籍商人。通过一名义乌网友，他了解了义乌这个神奇的城市。2011年，他第一次来到中国，直奔义乌进行了市场调查。亲身经历比道听途说更让史蒂芬感到兴奋，这个城市平凡的外表下巨大的商机让史蒂芬心动，他决定扎根于义乌，将义乌作为货源基地，创办属于自己的事业。采访过程中，史蒂芬向我们描述了一个商人眼中的非凡义乌。这是和加拿大完全不同的世界。相对于加拿大的工厂稀落，义乌是一个工厂密集的世界。受小商品市场影响，土生土长的义乌人，好多家庭有自己的小作坊，拥有专业的商品制造机器和娴熟的生产技术。种种此类的优势，再加上加拿大这样的发达国家所没有的低廉劳动力以及天然的太平洋黄金通道，让义乌的出口产业处于全国顶尖的位置。在初来乍到的史蒂芬看来，义乌的廉价交通费用也为他的事业起步扫去许多不必要的麻烦。义乌出租车很多，相比邻近的其他浙江城市，这里的出租车便宜又好打，最受益的就是像史蒂芬一样来这里采购的外籍商人了。这样出色的城市，自然有出色的人。当谈及中国与加拿大的文化差异时，史蒂芬对中国人的勤奋赞不绝口。他说，在加拿大，大多数人们的目标是过闲适安逸的生活，除此之外，没有更大的野心；而这几年在义乌，他发现义乌有许多工作狂，他们一周工作六天甚至七天，他们渴望赚得几世的财富给后代子孙。从某种程度上来讲，是两国家庭文化的差异带来了这样的不同，加拿大人并不太注重家庭成员间的联系，而在中国，人们看重家庭，义乌就是一个很好的例子。这次愉快的采访要结束的时候，史蒂芬告诉了我们他的梦想——在义乌建一家自己的工厂。

告别史蒂芬的第二天，我们在一位热情的本地商人的介绍下认识了我们的第二位采访对象。这个老外对义乌、对中国的热爱超乎想象，竟让我这本土的中国人都深深困惑。可目睹了他短短几个小时的忙碌后，我突然明白，这个城市成就他们的事业，给予他们富足的生活，怎能不让他们喜爱？另外一位采访对象——一个多年独居在义乌的巴基斯坦商人，他说，会讲普通话后，在义乌做生意并不困难，唯一使他困扰的是家人无法随他一起待在义乌，他觉得义乌市政府应该完善这方面的政策。

离开义乌的前一天晚上，我们走入城市深处，彻底感受了义乌的与众不同之处。白天燥热匆忙的城市，到了晚上一派从容闲适。街道旁的露天咖啡馆坐满了来自异国的人们，他们吸着水烟，有人高声谈笑，有人沉浸于夜晚祥和慵懒的气氛，为这座东方小城抹上绚丽的异域色彩，连前几天觉得杂乱没有章法的建筑都变得可爱起来。在这样的一片和谐里，我们坐在回程的车上，最后望了一眼这座城市，她还是那么平淡无奇。但这一次，又似有什么不同，看着咖啡馆里的外国人，史蒂芬和我们的采访对象又好像在我面前侃侃而谈……我恍然，义乌，不可貌相。

第六章

義烏城の日本人

乌伤城里扶桑人：日籍人士在义乌

导言

义乌，这座堪称“中国经济对接世界市场最快速的动脉血管”、“全球最大的小商品批发市场”的国际化小城，历经30余年的风雨历程，从最早的“鸡毛换糖”发展成为全国第十个“经济特区”，用其实际行动诠释了中国梦。义乌以其独特的文化底蕴和雄厚的商品市场魅力吸引着数以千万来自五湖四海的世界友人前来贸易、观光、圆梦。传承中华民族热情好客传统的义乌人，以开放、包容的胸怀，让四方商客感受到宾至如归，他们在这块沃土的滋养下，有的扎根生长，有的展翅翱翔。

当然，他们中也有我们的隔海邻居——日籍人士。不过，他们与来自欧美的客人有所不同。因为地理位置的先天优势，对他们来说去义乌就好比去了一趟邻居家开的超市，来去方便自如。本章汇集了几位日籍人士在义乌的经历、梦想以及对义乌的印象，其中不乏许多真知灼见。他们用独具魅力的声音，展示着精彩纷呈的文化，展示着他们不懈追求的梦想。他们不是中华儿女却拥有着中华民族艰苦奋斗、自强不息的精神，他们不是中国人却和我们一样孕育着一个中国梦。让我们一起来分享他们的中国梦，用心来倾听他们的声音。

古贺崇嗣

古賀崇嗣:義烏の縁

义乌之缘

古賀崇嗣:九州の福岡県に生まれ、東京で育った。大学を卒業した後、福岡に帰り、両親の花屋を引き継いだ。長期で義烏の「小物卸売り場」から花と関係の材料、籠、リボン、アクセサリーなど大量仕入れる。とてもユーモアのある人である。義烏が大好きだと言った。

古贺崇嗣,出生于日本福冈县,在东京长大,现在在福冈继承家业做花店生意。他长期在义乌采购大量与鲜花有关的材料,像花篮、束带及其附属品。古贺先生十分风趣,他说很喜欢义乌这个地方。

義烏の縁

古賀崇嗣

インタビューの記録

【BTV】こんにちは、浙江大学寧波理工学院日本語科の三年生です。初めまして、どうぞよろしくお願いします。まず、簡単な自己紹介をしてくださいませんか。

【古賀】はい、私は古賀崇嗣です。生まれは福岡県で、東京で育ちました。今福岡で家業の花屋を継いでいます。初めまして、どうぞよろしくお願いします。

【BTV】それでは、本題に入りましょう。古賀さんの義烏に対するイメージを教えてくれませんか。

【古賀】何と言うか、とにかく義烏は大好きです。実際、現地の人と付き合う回数は少ないが、親切な人だと思います。交通は便利だし、特にタイヤが三つある何て言うのか知らないけど、絵にかけます。あれは好きですが、すごく危ないよね。

【BTV】おっしゃる通り、私達も義烏人が親切だと思っています。例えば、日本人の企業家を探した時、地元の人にいろいろお世話になりました。古賀さんは義烏の料理についてどう思いますか。ここの飲食習慣はもう慣れましたか。

【古賀】ええ、大好きですよ。チャーハン、芋を細く切って炒める料理、鍋料理など、いろいろ美味しくて大好きです。でも、完全に慣れたと言えません。中国人はよく「xiang cai」(シャンツァイ)食べているでしょう、あれは無理でそれ以外は大丈夫です。また、ザリガニも駄目なんです。日本人はあまり食べませんが中国に人気があります。

【BTV】それは多分食文化の違いでしょう。そう言えば、義烏の風俗習慣のことについても何か可笑しい或いは不思議なことなど、自分の気持ちの中でどうしても受け取れられないことはありますか。

【古賀】文化や習慣などはまあいいですが、全部答えるのは難しいですね。

【BTV】いくつかの具体的な例でかまいませんよ。

【古賀】例えばここの運転が乱暴でクラクションを鳴らし過ぎですね。人がごみをよく捨てるし、町が汚いし、ぐちゃぐちゃしてその他に、いつも路上に隔離した板のような何か囲んで工事中が見えるようですが日本だったら少ないです。

【BTV】これは確かに、工事用の隔離の板よく見られるから今中国の多くの町は高速発展しているように見えます。

【古賀】いろんな分野も成長しているような気がします。中国の経済がこんなに速いスピードで発展していくには、国民素質も必要です。ともかく、国と国、国民と国民、及び文化の関係も発展途上で、今は日本と中国の関係も工事中、両国の関係はもっと上の方に行ってほしいです。やっぱり、毎日少しずつ成長することを望みます。現在中国はそのように毎日成長して経済、他の分野も日本を追い抜いています。日本は完成した発達国だけれども何でも止まっています。

【BTV】そうだと思いません。日本は科学技術、教育などの分野で世界の先頭に立ちます。それは私たちの国が習うべき所です。では、話題をかえてもいいですか。

【古賀】どうぞ、ご自由にして。

【BTV】古賀さん、どうして取引の対象として義烏を選びましたか?

【古賀】市場「小物卸売り場」があるから、私は花屋さんです。義烏の「小物卸売り場」から花と関係の材料、籠とかリボンとかアクセサリーなど大量に仕入れています。ここの種類が多くて値段がやすいが品質は普通です。だからこそ、私達の仕入れた物は日本で売れ行きがいいです。「小物卸売り場」があるから、それが一番重要な動機だと思います。

【BTV】義烏で仕入れと言えば、中国の他の町と比べると義烏の政府は何かよい政策を提供していますか。

【古賀】何も知りません、君たちは何か知っていますか。

【BTV】私も知りません、義烏で取引することは何かが不便な所がありますか或いは義烏の政府に何の改善する所を要求することがありますか。

【古賀】ええ、こんな悪い点を載せ、みんなに見せるんですか。すごいですね。

【BTV】勿論、ご満足は私達の進む原動力です。ご意見を聞かせてください。

【古賀】それは税関検査するときすごく時間がかかることです。効率的にしてほしいです。花にとって時間が大切なんですが、もし花のパッキング材料は路上で時間がかかると花が萎み落ちになった、どうなるかなあ。もう一つ、毎回自分一人で日本から中国義烏まで往来する時、上海で高速鉄道に乗り換えては何かの面倒なことは感じませんが大量の荷物は面倒臭いね。それで、どうして直接に義烏から日本まで飛行機を飛ばさないんですか。もう一つ、誠実さは非常に大切なものです。商売の活動で誠実で信頼できないとそのような会社はたとえ成立しても成長しません。貿易城の旨が書いているように誠実は金持ちになり、皆が誠実で取引きをしてほしいです。それぐらいいいかな。

【BTV】いいアドバイスですね。ご存知のように最近、中国の大学生の就職問題がますます深刻になっています。日本の大学生は就職問題もありますか。

【古賀】ありますよ。何って言うか、あの学生は仕事を選ぶよね。すごくいい会社に入って高いお金を貰う仕事だけを求めて皆が上の方に行っていますけど、仕事はいっぱいあるから、もし仕事を選ばなければ就職問題何でもないでしょう。それらの日本の大学生はこの問題が分かっていません。

【BTV】それでは、私達のような中国の大学生に対して何かアドバイスをいただけませんか。

【古賀】やあ、どうかなあ。僕は中国の就職問題をよく知らないから、難しいです。でもまあ、あなた達は言葉をしっかり学んで、まず君たちは日本語をうまくしゃべるといいと思いますよ。外国人とぺらぺらしゃべれることですね。ここを案内できる人が少ないので、ここに来てガイドになるのもいいですね。そして、今の大学生は、日本であれ中国であれわがまま過ぎて我慢できないが、大学生としてどんなことでも、中途でやめてはいけません。

【BTV】ご意見をどうも有難うございました。私達は真剣に考えます。ところで、この頃中国で「中国の夢」と言う話題がブームになっていること、ご存知ですか。古賀さんは中国の夢がありますか。

【古賀】実は「中国の夢」なんかこれまでよく分かりませんが中国での夢はあります。中国語をぺらぺらしゃべるが当面の夢です。

【BTV】そう言えば、中国語をしゃべれますね。

【古賀】話せるとも言えません、「ni hao」「bu ke qi」「ce suo zai na li」(こんにちは、どういたしまして、トイレはどこ)など、簡単な言葉です。

【BTV】古賀さんの発音がいいですね。では、中国での長期の夢は何ですか。

【古賀】お金を沢山儲けるとも言っていいでしょう、上海に花屋の支店を作るつもりです。

【BTV】義烏で花屋の支店を作りませんか。どうして花屋を作りたいですか。

【古賀】義烏にまだ早いです。義烏では花の需要はあまり多くありません。君はそんなきれいな花が好きではありませんか。

【BTV】いいえ、私も大好きです。中国で花屋の支店を作るのは古賀さんの「中国の夢」って言えませんか。

【古賀】そう言えます。中国で花屋の支店を作るのも自分の夢です。

【BTV】一日も早く古賀さんの「中国の夢」が叶えられるよう祈っています。そろそろここでしましょう。私達の実践活動を親切にサポートしていただき、お忙しいところインタビューを快く引き受けてくださり、本当にありがとうございました。

【古賀】お疲れ様でした。

团体：侯琳琳，侯朋

叙事记录

【BTV】你好，我们是浙江大学宁波理工学院日语专业大三的学生。初次见面，请多多关照。首先，可以请你先简单地自我介绍一下吗？

【古贺】好的，我叫古贺崇嗣，出生于福冈县，在东京长大，现在在福冈，继承家业做花店生意。初次见面请多多关照。

【BTV】那我们就直接进入正题吧。古贺先生，能谈谈你对义乌的印象吗？

【古贺】我和义乌本地人接触得不是太多，但他们都很友善，总的来说我很喜欢这个地方。义乌交通便捷，尤其是那种三个轮子的交通工具特别多，我不知道它叫什么名字，但我能画出来。我很喜欢坐这种交通工具，虽然感觉很危险但也非常有意思。

【BTV】义乌人确实很友善，在寻找日籍企业家时我们也得到了很多本地人的热心帮助。你觉得义乌菜怎么样，能够适应这里的饮食吗？

【古贺】我个人非常喜欢义乌菜。比如炒饭、炒土豆丝、火锅等。但并不是所有的中国菜我都能够接受，像香菜我一点都不吃。还有小龙虾，我们日本人几乎不吃，但是在中国却很受欢迎。

【BTV】可能是文化差异吧。你对本地的文化风俗或者其他方面有感到不可思议，难以理解或者无法接受的事情吗？

【古贺】在文化风俗习惯方面还好，其他要全部回答有点难啊。

【BTV】举几个具体的事例也行。

【古贺】比如说：在交通方面，这里的车主几乎都不遵守交通规则，喜欢鸣笛。还有很多人会随手乱丢垃圾，街道不整洁。除此之外，好像到处都在施工，可以看到很多地方用施工隔离板围着，这个在日本很少见到。

【BTV】的确如此，中国的很多地方都在快速发展中，隔离板之类很常见。

【古贺】我觉得中国的各个方面都在发展中。经济发展如此快速，国民素质也应该与经济发展相协调。不仅如此，其实国与国之间也是在发展之中，像日本和中国的关系现在就在发展中，我希望两国之间的关系可以向更高层次发展。现在中国每天都在进步，在经济以及其他方面都赶超了日本。日本虽然是发达国家，但是现在各方面好像都处于停滞状态。

【BTV】也不能完全这么说吧，日本在很多方面都是很先进的，像科技、教育等方面，都是很值得我们借鉴学习的。下面我们可以继续义乌这个话题吗？

【古贺】可以。

【BTV】你为什么会选择义乌这个城市作为生意上合作的对象？

【古贺】最主要的原因是义乌的小商品贸易城。你可能知道，我在日本是做鲜花生意的，需要采购大量与鲜花有关的材料，如花篮、束带及其他附属品。这些材料在义乌有很多，而且种类丰富、价格便宜、质量优良，我们在这里进的货在日本都很畅销。

【BTV】说起你在义乌进货，与中国的其他城市相比，当地政府能给你们提供一些政策优惠吗？

【古贺】这个我倒没听说过，好像没有，你知道一些吗？

【BTV】我也不清楚，那你认为义乌在哪些地方存在不足，需要义乌市政府加以改进吗？

【古贺】唉，这个也可以刊登出来吗？这个很有意思啊。

【BTV】是的，你的意见就是我们前进的动力，所以请提出你的真知灼见。

【古贺】那我就直说了。在接受海关检查时，要花费很长时间，希望他们能提高效率。因为鲜花的保鲜期很短，所以希望在过海关时，尽量减少一些时间。除此之外，在运输方面，我每次回日本都要坐飞机或高铁到上海，再从上海飞回日本，这个我倒是没觉得什么麻烦，但是如果是大量的货物也需要这么运输的话就有点麻烦了。为什么不可以开通义乌直飞日本的航班呢？还有一点，诚信也是非常重要的，做生意我们要以诚待人，不然的话，企业就不会发展下去，我觉得要像贸易城精神所说的那样——诚信致富，希望大家要诚信买卖。

【BTV】这些都是好建议。另外，现在中国的大学毕业生就业压力非常大，日本的大学生也有这样大的就业压力吗？

【古贺】这个也是有的。怎么说呢，很多大学生都想选择条件好、工资高的工作，都是瞄准一个职位去的，其实岗位很多，如果他们不挑工作也就没有所谓的就业压力了，只是他们没有意识到这个问题罢了。

【BTV】那你能给我们这样的大学生毕业后找工作提点建议吗？

【古贺】这个怎么说呢，因为我不是很了解中国目前的就业现状，所以有点难啊。不过像你们这样能够流利地说日语，能够自如地和外国人对话就很好。还有可以来义乌做日语向导，这边会日语的向导好像很少。此外，现在的大学生无论是日本的还是中国的都有点任性、娇气，年轻人应该要有持之以恒的精神，做事不要半途而废。

【BTV】谢谢你的建议，我们会认真考虑的。你知道最近在中国有一个关于“中国梦”的话题引起热议，你有中国梦吗？

【古贺】实话说，关于中国梦我不是很了解，不过我有中国梦，短期的中国梦就是希望自己能够说一口非常流利的汉语。

【BTV】这么说，你会说汉语？

【古贺】也算不上会吧，就一些而已。比如：你好，不客气，厕所在哪里等。

【BTV】古贺先生的发音真的很标准。那请问你长期的中国梦是什么？

【古贺】说为了挣很多钱也可以吧，我打算在上海开几家花店。

【BTV】为什么要在上海开花店呢？不打算在义乌开分店吗？

【古贺】义乌的市场对花的需求好像不是很大，开分店还为时过早。你们喜欢这些漂亮的花吗？

【BTV】我们很喜欢的。请问开花店是你的一个中国梦吗？

【古贺】可以这么说，在中国开自己的花店也是我的梦想。

【BTV】那祝你早日实现自己的中国梦。差不多就到这里吧，感谢你对我们本次活动的支持，能够在百忙之中抽空接受我们的采访，非常感谢。

【古贺】哪里哪里，你们都辛苦了。

团队成员：侯琳琳，侯朋

古贺崇嗣、秦书采访结束后与我们的合影

付録:秦書さんへのインタビュー

秦書さんは古賀崇嗣のお得意さんです。初めて秦さんと話し合った時、日本人だと思っていたが、少しあいさつした後、彼は突然中国語を話し出し、びっくりした。秦さんの発音がとても上手だった。中国人であるが、日本語もぺらぺらしゃべれる。その流暢な日本語は私たち日本語科の学生の目標である。しかし、秦さんは大学に入らなかった。19歳の際、ひとりで日本に行った。最初他の人と一緒に商売をし、数年後自分の会社を作った。主に花卉の商売を経営している。秦さんはしばしば中国と日本の間を走り回り、家族も日本に住んでいる。

インタビューの記録

【BTV】:初めまして、私達は浙江大学寧波理工学院日本語科の三年生です。どうぞよろしくお願いします。では、お聞きしたいですが、義烏を知ったきっかけは何ですか。

【秦書】:前の会社の社長が私をここへ連れてきました。

【BTV】:秦さんは、義烏のどんな所が魅力だと感じましたか?

【秦書】:南のほうの中国文化です。昔から流れる歴史を感じます。

【BTV】:具体的に説明してくれませんか、例えば。

【秦書】:場所の名前は全部歴史の中に出てきます。

【BTV】:私たちは義烏に来たばかりです。だから、それをまだ知りません。秦さんの会社は義烏で何年営業していますか。

【秦書】:三年以上です。

【BTV】:秦さんは自分のブランドがありますか。

【秦書】:うち? あるよ、うちのブランドだから、名前は「秦貴」。

【BTV】:いい名前ですね。今の従業員が何人いますか。

【秦書】:六人です。

【BTV】:秦さんの従業員についてどう思いますか?

【秦書】:すごくいいよ、頑張ってるよ、でももうすぐ結婚するからやめるですよ、女性だから、結婚するから子供もつかないできないし。

【BTV】:そうですね、大変ですね。では、なぜ義烏でビジネスを始めましたか。

【秦書】:それはなぜか。運ですね、縁があるから、難しいね(笑う)。

【BTV】:中国従業員の雇用標準は何ですか。

【秦書】:長く続ければいい。

【BTV】:最低年数は。

【秦書】:最低、一年でいい、できれば三年。

【BTV】:今の大学生は就職することについて何か足りないことがありますか。

【秦書】:まあ、落ち着いて働けばいい。ええと、我慢して、今の大学生は我慢しないよ、すぐやめたりするでしょう。それでは、何も手に入らないですよ。我慢して、一年間とか二年間三年間働けば、あのう、勉強できる。

【BTV】:私もそう思います。ところで、秦さんの会社は今どのような難題に直面していますか。ちょっと簡単な例がありますか?

【秦書】:まあ、困っていることは中国人の考え方ですよね。中国人としての考え方と日本人の考え方ですよね。文化と習慣が大分違うから、基準が違う。自分でそれでいいよオッケー、でもお客さんのこと考えてない。で、だからよくあるのが不良品、頭が痛いです。

【BTV】:地方政府は外資系企業に対する支援策を制定していますか。

【秦書】:いい政策なんか、必要がない。ただちゃんとルールつければいい。それは開始企業対して何も付く必要がない。みんな平等だから、同じルールで、みんなちゃんと守ればいい。外資企業中国企業が同じでしょう。だから、そう言う法律とか政策ちゃんと作って　みんな守るといいよ。でも、みんな守ってないでしょう、意味がない、どんないい政策を作っても意味がない。

【BTV】:もし秦さんが義烏の管理者なら、外資系企業をどのように支援したいですか。例えば、資金。

【秦書】:うう、資金じゃないよ。資金が自分で頑張ればいいよ。信頼関係が上がる、アップする、それは一番大事ですから。みんなここに来るように頑張らなければ行けないし、商売は長い、長く長くのことです。利益最大でもらえたいです。

【BTV】:義烏のイメージはどうですか、いいところですか?

【秦書】:いいよ、みんな頑張っているから。

【BTV】:最後の問題、義烏の都市建設はどう思いますか。

【秦書】:足りないことがある。効率がアップする。政府が日本にいってそういうことが読んで来て、この道の作りが考えてもらったらぜったいにいいです。そう、効率がアップするから、みんな来る。そうしないと、これはもう「アウト」、汚いと言うが混乱している。車どのぐらい通っているのか、どの時間通っているのか、全部きちんと調べてから道を作るのですよ、改良したりとか。そう、日本の場合は、ずっと一日中人が道に座って車の数を数える　この時間でなぜ混んでいるとか。で、調べる原因が分かってから、改良する。道作るのは科学です、なんでも効率がアップしないと意味がないね。だから、効率が大事です。みんな遠い場所から来ているから、時間的に一週間とか三日間ぐらい来てるでしょう、効率一番大事なことです。

【BTV】:私達の実践活動を親切にサポートして、お忙しいところインタビューを受けてくださって本当にありがとうございました。

【秦書】:お疲れ様でした。

团体:侯琳琳,侯朋

附录:对秦书先生的采访

秦书先生是古贺先生生意上的合作伙伴。第一次听秦书先生讲话的时候,我以为他是日本人,谁知在几句寒暄之后,他突然说起了汉语,原来是中国人。对于学日语的我们来说,他那一口流利的日语无疑是我们的终极目标。当我询问他是怎么学日语时,他说他没读过大学,19岁就独自一人到日本闯荡,起初跟着老板做生意,后来自己在义乌开了公司,日本也有自己的公司,主要经营花卉生意。他常常在中国与日本两国之间奔波,家人也都住在日本。

叙事记录

【BTV】您好,我们是浙大宁波理工学院日语专业大三的学生。初次见面,请多关照。

【秦书】请多多关照。

【BTV】您是怎样开始知道义乌的呢?

【秦书】以前公司的老板带我来的。

【BTV】那么义乌在哪个方面对您有吸引力?

【秦书】文化,南方的文化,感觉义乌有源远流长的历史。

【BTV】能具体说明一下吗,比如呢?

【秦书】义乌各个景点的命名都与历史有关。

【BTV】哦,原来是这样啊,我刚来义乌,对这个不是很了解。请问您的公司在义乌开了多久呢?

【秦书】三年多。

【BTV】那有自己的品牌吗?

【秦书】噢,有的,叫“秦贵”。

【BTV】这个名字不错,现在公司里有几名员工?

【秦书】有六个人。

【BTV】您觉得自己的员工怎么样?

【秦书】非常好，很努力。但是女性的话，结婚了就不在我这里工作了，因为要照顾自己的孩子，两者不能兼顾。

【BTV】那您雇用员工的标准是什么呢？

【秦书】最好能够长期工作的。

【BTV】那您认为最低的工作年数是几年呢？

【秦书】最低的话一年吧，最好是三年。

【BTV】为什么您会选择在义乌做生意呢？

【秦书】为什么呢？可能是缘分吧，这个很难回答。（笑）

【BTV】您认为现在的大学生在工作中有什么不足之处？

【秦书】求职者最好能定下心来工作，要学会忍耐，不要做一两个月就走。现在的大学生不懂得忍耐，很快就辞职不干，对吧？但是这样什么都学不到，要忍耐，经过一两年的工作经历，才能学到东西。在日企工作没个三年的，基本学不到什么真本事。

【BTV】我也觉得是这样。那么，您公司现在面临的困难是什么，能简单地举例说一下吗？

【秦书】说到困难，可能是中国人的思考方式吧。中日文化、风俗习惯的不同使得中国人和日本人的思维方式也不同。在做生意的时候，中国人可能不会太顾及客户的想法，自己觉得行就可以了。进购的商品中也往往会有质量不好的，这让我很头疼。

【BTV】当地政府会有一些积极的政策去支持外资企业吗？

【秦书】其实也不需要好的政策，只要能够遵守商贸交易的规则就好了。如果大家都能平等地好好遵守规则就好了。外资企业和中国企业是一样的，所以制定相应的法律和政策，大家都来遵守才是最好的。如果大家都不遵守，不管制定什么好的政策都没有意义。

【BTV】如果您是义乌市的管理者，您将会怎样帮助外资企业，比如资金的投入？

【秦书】这个，我认为不是资金问题。资金可以自己努力得到，我觉得是提高商家的诚信度，这在商品交易中是最重要的，如果大家都被骗也就不会来这里了。大家到这里都十分努力，希望做长期有效的投资，这样才能达到利益的最大化。

【BTV】能谈谈您对义乌这座城市的印象吗？这个地方好吗？

【秦书】这里不错，大家都很努力地工作着。

【BTV】最后一个问题，您对义乌的城市建设有什么看法呢？

【秦书】义乌城建方面还是有不足之处的。我希望政府能够提高义乌这个城市的效率。提高了效率，改善市容，大家都会来这里，不然大家可能会觉得义乌跟不上时代的步伐，没有与时俱进。比如说马路上的车流量，我看义乌经常堵车堵得很厉害，如果有人能够好好调查每个路段在不同时间的车流量，根据这个把道路扩宽或者在其他方面进行改善，我想更能提高效率。大家都是从很远的地方来，有的时候只能在这里待上一周或两三天，所以效率很重要。

【BTV】感谢您对我们活动的支持，在百忙之中抽空接受我们的采访，非常感谢。

【秦书】哪里哪里，你们都辛苦了。

团队成员：侯琳琳，侯朋

桜の夢

作者：侯　朋　指導教師：蔡　蕾

夜は徐々に訪れながら、ネオンが輝いていく。雅やかで暖かい雰囲気に溢れたような喫茶店があったり、内装がそれぞれ違った外国レストランなどもあり、この町の夜景に引き付けられた。この時、町を歩きながら、心に打たれたリズムに従い、五線譜が跳ぶような音符を思い出した。レストランのきれいなガラス窓を通し、肌の色や服の異なる外国人は、店内に集まり、椅子にどっかり腰掛け時間を潰していた。彼らの笑い声に交じった音楽のリズムは窓を通し、空中を流していくような気がするのだ。それから一日中働いてきた義烏人もそこに来てゆっくりと外国料理を楽しみ、美味しいコーヒーを味わうなど、彼らの夜遊びに浸っている。ここはイスラム風の建築、アラブの伝統的な音楽、異言語や異なる肌の色を持っている人で賑わう。どこの言葉か不明瞭な文字で書いてある看板など、この町の国際化を感じさせられた。こここそ真の「西洋風」、「地球村」と言うことを深く体験した。

中華民族の伝統的な美徳を伝承した義烏人は開放、包容を胸に抱き、世界中の方々を迎えていく。世界の小物卸売り場の所在地として、義烏は世界の国際化の発展を確かに推進しつつある。と共に、この町の発展にも大きな変化をもたらした。世界中からの商売人はユニークな文化を持ってきたから、この町の生活が豊富になってきた。そして、皆はずっと頑張って自らの夢を追求している。「中国の経済が世界市場に繋がる高速道路」と呼ばれたこの中国の小町はグローバル化に従い、少しずつ変わってきた。

一日中、日本人を探し回ったが、結局、日本人が一人も見つけられなかった。私達は落胆し、もう諦めようと考えたが、義烏の異国風の町で多くのレストラン、喫茶店、日本料理屋などを辿って、なんとか日本人企業家の古賀さんという男性を捜し当てた。初めて会った時、そのわざと手入れした眉が印象的だ。日本で見掛けの手入れを重視することは礼儀だと古賀さんが言われた。互いに挨拶を済ませてからインタビューのことを助けてくれるかと頼んだ時、断るかもしれないと心配で堪らなかった。思いかけないことは、訪問の旨を説明してから古賀さんは納得した様子を表した。インタビューを含め、私達の心に残された古賀さんのイメージは親切で活気の溢れる日本青年だったことである。取材を深く掘り下げるために、私達は料理のことを話してお互いの緊張感を緩めた。古賀さんは「中国料理の鴨の煮込みが大好きだ」とおっしゃった。しかし、私はザリガニに目が無いと言ったら、古賀さんは首を横に振りながら、「日本人はザリガニを余り食べない」と言われた。中国ではザリガニは、人気の料理として好まれているが日本では全然違った。まるで中国人は日本の納豆がどうしても受け入れられないというようなことだろう。これが中日両国のカルチャーショックだろう。義烏に対するイメージと言ったら、道が汚いし、市政府は町の外観に更に力を入れるべき、市民の素養の育ちも大事だなど、古賀さんは自分の真実の感想を言われた。この町に色々な不足があるのに、親切で友好な義烏人やこの町に対する好きな気持ちに影響を及ぼさない。ところで、古賀さんは大通りを横断しようとしたが、他の中国人は皆、横断歩道を無視してそのまま直接道路を渡っていたが古賀さんは遠回り、ゴーストップなしの横断歩道にじっとして自動車が通り切った時に足早に駆け抜けた。このような簡単な動作から古賀さんの規律正しい面が明らかになった。

また、「中国の夢」という最近盛んな話題と言えば、古賀さんは自分の夢を詳しく教えてくれた。「中国語をぺらぺらしゃべれるのが当面の夢だ」とおっしゃった。義烏の町では中国語をよく話す外国人を見かけた。彼らには異国からこの町に来て、異文化の下で交流し流暢な中国語を身につけるのは共同の夢だと思われる。これは多分一生かかっても忘れられない夢だろう。なぜかと言うと、古賀さんの話によると毎年、日中間で何回も往来しているので、流暢な中国語を使えば、中国の文化がよりよく理解に役立ったはずだと言った。それと同時に、お互いに理解し合うからこそ、うまく付き合っていけるに違いないと思われる。また、率直な古賀さんは目下の中日両国の緊張関係に言及した。両国の関係は経済分野の盛んな往来のように発展し、また、経済面の交流より、国家間、国民間の繋がりは更に重要だと考えられる。一方、人と人との交流がなければ、両国の繋がりが深まるわけがないと言われた。普通の若い商人なのに、日中両国の国民の幸せなどのことも考えて、本当に感心せざるを得なかった。同時にわれわれ中国の若者もお互いの交流と理解を学ぶべきだろう。古賀さんは当面の夢の話だけでなく、将来の夢についても語ってくれた。「お金を沢山儲ける」と率直に回答したが実はお金を沢山儲けるより、自分の「中国の夢」をいっそう重視しているだろう。雑談の時、古賀さんは「家族が何世代も花のビジネスを扱っているので、自分も花に目がないのだ。中国の大都市である上海で花のチェーン店を作るのは真の夢だ」とおっしゃった。それでは、古賀さんの「中国の夢」が桜の満開のように成功することを心から祈っている。

かつて中国の大詩人陸遊の「知識を身に着けるために本を読むだけは足りな

く、実践躬行が大事である」と書いた通り、今回の実践活動を通して自分の能力の不足を深く感じた。授業の時、何回も通訳のことをしっかり勉強したが自分が勉強するべきところがまだ沢山あると気づいた。例えば、社交礼儀、文化の教養、専門知識など多岐にわたる。しかし、自分の能力不足に気づいたと同時に、日本語専攻の無限の就職の未来が嬉しく発見された。嘗て日本語という専攻に迷った私はもっと自信を持ち、日本語をこつこつと勉強しよう。「蒔かぬ種は生えぬ、志があれば事ついに成る」と堅く信じている。

樱花般盛开的中国梦

文:侯　朋　指导老师:蔡　蕾

夜静静地降临,耀眼的霓虹灯、典雅温馨的咖啡馆、各具特色的异域餐厅让你领略这个城市夜的风姿。漫步街道,重金属风格的动感音乐搏动心脏,仿佛你就是那五线谱上跳动的音符。走在街上,透过洁净的玻璃窗可以看到各种肤色穿戴各异的外国客人坐在一起休息聊天,音乐声、欢笑声透过窗户弥漫在空气中。此时,劳累了一天的义乌人也开始来到这里,美美地饱餐一顿外国大餐,再喝上一杯香浓的咖啡,开始了他们的夜间休闲。苏格兰风情建筑、阿拉伯传统音乐、熙熙攘攘不同语言不同肤色的人群、各种认识或不认识文字书写的店名招牌,时刻告诉我这是一个国际化城市。在这里我深深地感到什么才是真正的"洋气",什么叫做"地球村"。

传承中华民族热情好客传统的义乌人,以开放、包容的胸怀喜迎八方来宾。作为"全球最大的小商品批发市场"所在地,义乌着实推动着国际化进程。同时,国际化进程也给这座城市带来了翻天覆地的变化。来自全球各地的外国商人带来了他们独具魅力的声音,展示着风采各异的文化,不懈追求让他们难以自拔的梦想。这个堪称"中国经济对接世界市场最快速的动脉血管"着实体现了全球化浪潮如何改变中国一座小城的发展。

在经过一整天的茫茫人海寻找,毫无收获的我们来到义乌异国风情街。苦心人天不负!我们已经打算放弃的时候,在一家西餐厅遇到了来自日本福冈的古贺先生。初次见到古贺先生,他那刻意修饰过的眉毛让我们印象颇深。据古贺先生讲,在日本,对自己外貌的修饰是一种礼貌。刚开始询问古贺先生能否让我们进行采访的时候,我真担心他会说很忙没时间。出乎意料的是,在道明来意之后,他很客气地让我们坐下,表现出对我们活动的支持。整个采访过程中,古贺先生给我们留下既热情活泼又严谨的现代日本人形象。为了深入采访,活跃气氛,我们闲聊着谈到了饮食,古贺先生说他很喜欢吃中国菜鸭煲。当我说到喜欢吃小龙虾时,古贺直摇头,他说日本人不吃小龙虾。虽说小龙虾在中国被奉为美食,但在日本人们却是对它敬而远之。这也算是中日文化冲击吧,就好像中国人吃不惯日本的纳豆一样。在对义乌的印象上,访谈中我可以听出古贺先生说出了自己的真实感想,如义乌的道路不够干净,他也希望当地的政府能够在市容上多加关注,市民素质也亟待提高。但这些也影响不了他对友好热情的义乌人及这个城市的热爱。古贺先生的高素养我也是目睹过的,如在过马路时我们就直接穿过去,而古贺先生坚持要绕路走人行道，可是由于人行道两端没有红绿灯提示，加上当地车主开车不遵守交通规则，因而他一直站在原地不动，等没车时他才急匆匆穿过。

在谈及“中国梦”这个热议的话题时，古贺先生很详细地告诉了我们他的“中国梦”，目前就是希望自己能够说一口流利的汉语。在这里我可以看到很多外国人在用汉语交流，虽然他们有着不同的文化背景，来自不同的国家，但我相信他们都曾有一个共同的梦，就是很流利地用汉语交流。这对他算是一个很有意义的梦想，因为据他说，他每年多次往返日本与中国之间，一口流利的汉语能帮助他很好地理解中国文化，只有互相理解才能很好地相处。说到这里，坦率的古贺先生主动提及目前紧张的中日关系，他希望两国间交往能像经济关系那样火热，与经济交流相比他认为国家间的民众的交流更为重要，只有人与人之间的交流多了，才能促使两国关系在各方面越来越和谐。对于一个普通的年轻日本商人，能够站在为了两国人民的幸福安宁的高度看待中日关系，这需要怎样的魄力？我不由得想到，国内那些年轻人是否也应该要学会交流与理解呢？另外，在谈及他的长期梦想时，古贺先生很坦然地回答，要挣很多的钱。其实，他希望将来可以在上海开几家连锁花店，与金钱相比，他更在乎自己的“中国梦”。古贺先生家族长期做鲜花生意，一直对鲜花情有独钟。衷心希望他的“中国梦”像樱花一样烂漫盛开。

正如大诗人陆游所言，“纸上得来终觉浅，绝知此事要躬行”。通过此次实践活动，我深深感觉到自己在知识方面的不足。虽然在校期间，多次加强与外教的交流，口语能力也有所提升，但是走出校园，却发现自己要学的知识还有很多，如社交礼仪、文化背景、专业知识素养，等等。在发现自身不足的同时，我也很欣喜地发现，日语专业有着无穷潜力的就业前景。这让曾一度对日语专业迷茫的我更加坚定了踏踏实实地学好本专业的信心！我相信，天道酬勤，有志者事竟成！

佐藤日春

佐藤日春:義烏へのコンプレックス
义乌情结

佐藤日春:義烏で海外の仕入れ係として、今までもう4年経った。最初は会社の先輩から中国のことを聞いてきた。中国に来た後、ますます中国のことが好きになった。とても親切な人で、歌も上手である。

佐藤日春在义乌进行海外采购已经有四年了。最初她是从公司的同事那里听说关于中国的事,来到这里之后,越发喜欢上了中国。她是一个非常热情的女孩儿,而且歌唱得很棒。

義烏へのコンプレックス

佐藤日春

インタビューの記録

【BTV】佐藤さん、こんにちは。

【佐藤】こんにちは。

【BTV】佐藤さんは、今ここで、どんな仕事をしていますか。

【佐藤】そうですね。わたしは今アクセサリーの仕事をしています。つまりね、会社の仕事で義烏に来て、ここのアクセサリーを買って、日本に持って帰ることです。今もう4年です。

【BTV】貴社は日本にございますか。

【佐藤】はい、そうです。日本の渋谷にあります。会社には30人います。みんな仲良くしています。

【BTV】そうですか、それはよかったですね。ところで、貴社は全部日本の方ですか。中国人がいますか。

【佐藤】中国人はいませんが、全部日本人じゃないよ。29人は日本人で、ひとりは韓国人です。

【BTV】いいですね。じゃ、最初はどんなきっかけで義烏に来ましたか。

【佐藤】そうですね。最初は義烏のことまったくわからなかったですが、会社に入った後、会社の先輩から義烏のことを聞きました。なんかとても面白いところだそうで、いずれ機会があれば、行ってみたいなと思っていました。だから、自分で会社の海外の仕入係を申請しました。

【BTV】なるほど、じゃ義烏に来てから、中国と日本はどんな違いがあると思いましたか。

【佐藤】違うところといえば、いろいろあると思いますが。

【BTV】じゃ、佐藤さんがその中で最大の違いはなんだと思いますか。

【佐藤】うんん、やはり最大の違いは人込みかな。あなたの知っているとおり、日本は小さくて、人も少ないですから。あとはゴミの捨て方も違います。日本人はゴミをちゃんと分類してから捨てますが、ここに来てから中国の方はあまり分類しないという感じです。

【BTV】そうですね。中国は大国ですから、人もいっぱいで、だから人込みはとても込んでいます。ゴミの捨て方については、中国は大きすぎて、管理しにくいから、まだいい方法が見つからないです。わたしもゴミの分類に賛成します。

【佐藤】そうですね。

【BTV】じゃ佐藤さん、もう義烏の生活に慣れましたか。

【佐藤】はい、もうすっかり慣れました。義烏の方はとても親切で、いい人ばかりです。

【BTV】それはよかったですね。佐藤さんはここに来てもう4年ですね、じゃ中国語ができますか。

【佐藤】いいえ、普段わたしは日本にいて、2か月に1回、一週間だけ中国にいます。それに中国語はわたしにとって難しすぎる。だから、中国語ほとんどできないです。

【BTV】ああ、そうですか。両国間駆け回って、大変ですね。

【佐藤】義烏のことが好きですから、旅行みたいな感じでとても楽しいです。

【BTV】本当にいい気分ですね。ところで、義烏は全国小商品市場として有名ですが、佐藤さんの視点からまだ改善する必要があるところがありますか。

【佐藤】そうですね、わたしから言えば交通問題かな。人がいっぱいで、わたしたちみたいな外国人から見れば、交通が少し不便です。

【BTV】なるほどね、わかりました。じゃ佐藤さんはここの人について、どう思いますか。

【佐藤】ああ、エネルギッシュで？とてもパワーがあるかんじがしますね。

【BTV】そうですか、どうしてそんなふうに思いますか。

【佐藤】ここの人の生活リズムが速いからかもしれない。

【BTV】ところで、義烏での国際貿易を促すために、地元政府は2011年3月から全面的な貿易改革を実行してきました。ご存知ですか。

【佐藤】いいえ、あまりしらないです。

【BTV】じゃ、簡単に言えば貴社の売り上げは2011年より上がりましたか。

【佐藤】2011年より、上がりました。

【BTV】そうですか。お忙しいところで取材を受けてくださって、誠にありがとうございました。

【佐藤】はい、どういたしまして。

団体：劉李，劉璐，尚夢丹，肖琳

叙事记录

【BTV】佐藤小姐，你好。

【佐藤】你们好。

【BTV】佐藤小姐，请问你现在在这里做什么工作呢？

【佐藤】我现在正在做饰品采购的工作，也就是在义乌低价购入饰品，然后运回日本出售。我工作已经有四年了。

【BTV】请问贵公司位于哪里呢？

【佐藤】我们公司位于日本的涉谷，有 30 名员工，大家都相处得很好。

【BTV】这样真好。话说回来，你们公司里都是日本人吗，有没有中国人呢？

【佐藤】没有，虽然没有中国人，但也不全是日本人，有 29 个日本人和 1 个韩国人。

【BTV】那么请问，当时是怎样的一个契机让你来到义乌的呢？

【佐藤】一开始我对义乌一点也不了解，但进入公司之后，从同事那里听说了很多关于义乌的事，觉得非常有趣，心想如果有机会一定要去那里看看。后来，我自愿申请成为了公司的海外采购员。

【BTV】原来如此，那么来到义乌之后，你是否发现中日之间有不同之处呢？

【佐藤】说到不同之处，我觉得有很多方面。

【BTV】那么佐藤小姐你觉得最大的不同点是什么呢？

【佐藤】嗯，我觉得最大的不同还是拥挤的人群吧，就如你所知，日本是个小国，人口不是很多。还有就是扔垃圾的方式有很大不同。我们日本人会对垃圾进行仔细的分类处理之后再回收，而这里的人们好像不怎么会进行垃圾分类，直接扔的比较多。

【BTV】是啊，的确是这样，中国是一个大国，地大物博人口众多，所以会感觉比较拥挤。至于垃圾处理方面，由于中国地域辽阔，实行起来比较困难，仍未找到有效的好方法。不过就我个人而言，非常赞成垃圾分类处理。

【佐藤】的确如此呢。

【BTV】那么佐藤小姐对义乌这里的生活已经习惯了吗？

【佐藤】是的，已经非常习惯了，义乌的人很热情、很友好。

【BTV】那真是太好了。话说佐藤小姐来到这里已经四年了，那么你会说中文吗？

【佐藤】不会，我平时大多数时间还是待在日本，每两个月来一次义乌，每次大概待一周左右时间。而且中文对我来说很难，所以基本不会说中文的。

【BTV】哦，这样啊。你经常奔走于两国之间也很辛苦啊。

【佐藤】因为我很喜欢义乌，感觉来这里就像旅行一样，所以感到很开心。

【BTV】你的心态可真好。话说回来，义乌作为全中国的小商品市场是非常有名的，从你的角度看，你觉得义乌还有哪些需要改进的地方吗？

【佐藤】就我而言应该是交通问题吧。因为人多，对我们这些外国人而言，交通不是很方便。

【BTV】原来如此，我明白了。佐藤小姐你觉得这里的人给你一种怎样的感觉呢？

【佐藤】啊，应该是那种很有活力，很有力量的感觉。

【BTV】这样啊，那你觉得这是什么原因呢？

【佐藤】可能是这里人的生活节奏比较快吧。

【BTV】话说回来，你知道义乌当地政府从2011年3月开始实行了全面的贸易改革来促进义乌的国际贸易发展吗？

【佐藤】不知道，我不太清楚。

【BTV】那么就简单地来说，贵公司的收益自2011年以后与之前的相比有所提高吗？

【佐藤】是的，相对于2011年之前的有较为明显的提高。

【BTV】非常感谢你在百忙之中接受我们的采访。

【佐藤】太客气了，不用谢。

团体成员：刘李，刘璐，尚梦丹，肖琳

義烏への旅行

作者:劉　李　肖　琳　指導教師:蔡　蕾　蔡　亮

義烏に行く前に、全国の小商品市場としての名はよく聞く。この目で見た後、もう一度確認した。義烏は北京ほど歴史の重み、上海の繁盛には比べものにならないけど、別の意味でとても繁昌している。最初の「羽替え糖」から全国第十個「経済特区」まで、義烏は30年の発展を積んできた。ここに玲琅満目の商品があるし、絶えない外国の友人もいる。

この忙しい都市の中に行き来すると、まるで小商品の海に身を置いたような感じである。いろいろな商品がめまぐるしく、あちこちにさまざまな肌色の外国の友人が歩いている。特に義烏国際商貿城では外国の友人がいっぱいである。彼らは大部分仕事の関係でここに来たが、義烏の風景を見るために観光に来た客も多かった。

こんな忙しい外国の友人の中で、海外の仕入係を担当している日本から来た佐藤日春さんと出会った。会社の海外の仕入係としてもう4年であった。義烏といえば、佐藤さんには言い尽くせない言葉がある。これまでに義烏のことはあまり知らナるたっが、同僚の紹介のもとに、この都市を知り始あ、だんだん好きになった。義烏に来た後、佐藤さんはここに対して特殊な感情が生まれた。

佐藤さんが仕事についての話をした時、興奮して私たちに言った。仕事が大変だが、とても楽しくやっている。毎回の仕事を義烏への旅行だと思って楽しんでいる。地元の人の生活リズムは早いが、人はとても友好的だと佐藤さんが言った。だから、ここが大好きだ。しかし、足りない所もたくさんある。佐藤さんにとっては最大の問題は交通問題であった。こんなに忙しい都市では、交通は非常に重要なことで、これは義烏の改善する必要がある一面である。もう1つ改善する必要があるのは中国のゴミ処理の問題である。日本より、中国人の人数はずっと多い。だから中国でゴミ処理は難しく、今はもう深刻な問題になった。これこそはちょっと困らせると思ったが、いつかゴミ処理の問題がうまく進むことを期待していると佐藤さんが言った。

ずっと前、中国人が外国に行って留学するとか働くとか、いろいろな面倒なことと出合って、一人でやらなければならないって、すごく大変だとよく聞いた。一方、外国人が中国での生活は快適みたいだと思われている。実はそうではなく、外国人にとって、中国で苦しいこともいっぱいあると思われている。今度の活動を通じ、私の考え方がいろいろ変わってきた。

活動終了後、私はそう思った。今回の活動は外国の友人にとっても自分にとっても非常に有意義である。外国の友人はその活動を通し、もっと直観的に義烏への感覚や意見が発表できるし、そして我々にとっても、これも自分を鍛えるいいチャンスである。外国の友人との会話を通じ、いろいろなことを学んできた。そして自分の専門レベルも上がった。新しい角度で自分の考えをあらためて見れば、面白いものが見つかるかもしれない。それはどんな素敵なことだろう。

義烏の発展と進歩は知られている。しかし、トップ市場という位置にまだまだ遠いと思っている。近い将来、義烏市政府は関連政策措置を導入することにより、より多くの外国の友人は義烏に来、義烏のことを知り、義烏は正真正銘の世界の小商品市場になれると願っている。

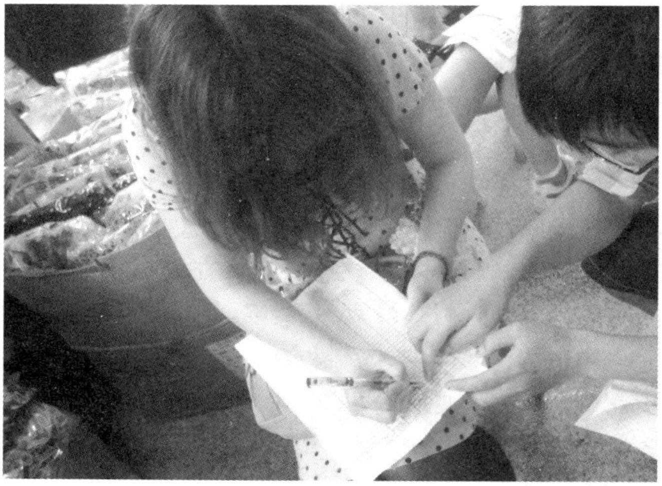

佐藤小姐填写联系方式摄影　刘璐

义乌之旅

文：刘　李　肖　琳　指导老师：蔡　蕾　蔡　亮

来到义乌之前，义乌作为全国小商品城的大名早已如雷贯耳。亲眼看见之后，我更坚定了这一想法。义乌虽没有北京历史的厚重、上海城市的繁华，但是这里却别有另一番底蕴，从最早的“鸡毛换糖”发展到全国第十个“经济特区”，义乌经历了30年的市场变迁。如今这里有琳琅满目的商品和络绎不绝的外国友人。

穿梭于这个忙碌的城市之中，仿佛也置身于小商品的海洋。各种各样的商品令人目不暇接。随处可见的是各种肤色的外国友人，特别是在义乌国际商贸城，他们大多数是来做生意的，不过也不乏来观光旅游的，为的是想一睹义乌风采。

就在这些忙碌的外国友人之中，我们有幸遇见了来自日本的佐藤日春小姐，她负责公司的海外采购已经有四年了。说到义乌，她有说不完的话。虽然之前对义乌的事不太清楚，但是在同事的介绍下，她开始认识并喜欢上了这座城市，来到义乌之后她更是对这里产生了一种特殊的情感。

当谈起她的这份工作时，她兴奋地告诉我们，虽然工作辛苦，但是她做得非常开心。因为她把每次的工作都当作一次到义乌的旅行。她说虽然这里的人生活节奏很快，但是很友好，她很喜欢。但是义乌也有不足的地方，她觉得最大的一点就是交通。在这样忙碌的城市中，交通是非常重要的，这是义乌有待改进的一个方面。另外，由于国情不同，中国与日本在垃圾处理问题上也有很大不同，这让她有点不适应，希望中国的垃圾分类也能顺利进行。

以前，一直听说中国人去其他国家留学或工作，会经历很多困难，很多事情必须独立完成，而外籍人士在中国生活看起来却十分容易。其实并非如此，他们在中国生活也会遇到各种困难。通过这次活动，我的很多想法都有了很大改变。

虽然活动时间很短，但我却觉得这次活动无论是对外国友人还是对我们自己都很有意义。外国友人通过我们的活动，可以更加直观地将他们对义乌的感觉和需求表达出来。而对于我们，这也是一次很好的锻炼机会，通过跟外国友人的交谈，我们学会了很多书中学不到的知识，也提高了自己的口语水平。同时，也学会了用不同的角度和眼光去审视自己的想法，从中发现更多有趣的东西，这是多么棒的事情啊。

义乌的发展与进步是大家有目共睹的，但是只有更好，没有最好，相信在不久的将来，会有更多的外国友人认识义乌、来到义乌，让义乌成为名副其实的“世界小商品市场”。

木田清隆

木田清隆:僕は仕事がたくさんできる

能者多劳

木田清隆:日本 JULIA 会社からの仕入れ係だ。韓国語と英語ができるし、長年に渡り、多国の間で商品を外国から仕入れ、安い商品を国内へ輸入している。とても忙しく、ほとんど休みもない。

木田清隆是来自日本 JULIA 公司的一名采购员,他精通韩语、英语,常年在多国间采购货物,从国外进口便宜的商品运回国内,很忙碌,几乎不休假。

僕は仕事がたくさんできる

木田清隆

インタビューの記録

【BTV】じゃ、今からよろしいでしょうか。
【木田】はい。
【BTV】今一人で中国で生活していますか。
【木田】してないです。日本から仕事に来ました。
【BTV】あ、そうですか、いつ義烏に来ましたか。
【木田】月曜日に来ました、明日帰ります。
【BTV】明日日本に帰りますか。
【木田】はい。
【BTV】義烏が好きですか。
【木田】はい。
【BTV】例えば何ですか。
【木田】僕は仕事がたくさんできるからすきです。
【BTV】そうですか。本田さんにとって義烏で一番ひきつけるのはなんですか。
【木田】ここです。古手市場です。
【BTV】ここの食べ物をどう思いますか?
【木田】おいしいですよ。
【BTV】余暇にどう過ごしていますか。
【木田】余暇がないです。休みもないです。
【BTV】義烏の人との生活に慣れたのですか。
【木田】もう一回。意味が分からないから。
【BTV】ここでの生活のスピートが速いですから、もう慣れたのですか。
【木田】ああ。はい、大丈夫です。
【BTV】ここで投資していますか。
【木田】ただここへ仕事に来ました。
【BTV】じゃここで買った物は日本へ?
【木田】はい、輸出します。
【BTV】ここで買い物の理由は日本のほうが高くて、ここはやすいのですか。

【木田】それもあるし、あと種類がたくさんあるから。

【BTV】じゃ、木田さんにとって、ここに来て何が一番大事なのですか。

【木田】お店が一番大事です。

【BTV】ここでどう貿易していますか。

【木田】貿易は船で貿易します。

【BTV】仕事にかけては何の調査がありますか。

【木田】調査ですか。値段と、後は数、…

【BTV】ここの貿易がうまいですか。

【木田】うまくない。

【BTV】ここの競争は激しいですか。

【木田】ここでの競争は激しくないです。

【BTV】日本は?

【木田】日本は激しいです。

【BTV】ここの文化と日本の文化は何か違いますか。

【木田】えーと、いっぱい違う。

【BTV】例えば?

【木田】例えばタクシーも違うし、トイレも違う、後は人の考えも違う、本当に難しいです。

【BTV】ここで自分で運転しますか。

【木田】しないです。怖いです。

【BTV】方向が反対ですか、日本が左ですね。

【木田】日本が左です。

【BTV】ここの交通は大変ですね。

【木田】大変です。あそこも車いっぱい。

【BTV】義烏でたくさんの外国人がいますが、ここで外国人の友達がいますか。

【木田】います。

【BTV】例えばどこの人ですか。

【木田】インド人です。

【BTV】言葉が通じますか。

【木田】はい。

【BTV】日本語で?

【木田】英語とか韓国語とか

【BTV】お友達の生活が大丈夫ですか。

【木田】たぶんそうと思います。

【BTV】義烏の人をどう思いますか。

【木田】やさしい人です。いいですね。
【BTV】はい、どうもありがとうございました。

团体：鄭立冬，楊俠劍，章李可

叙事记录

【BTV】那么，我们现在可以开始采访了吗？
【木田】可以了。
【BTV】你现在是一个人在中国生活吗？
【木田】不是，我是从日本到中国来出差的。
【BTV】那你是什么时候来义乌的呢？
【木田】星期一到的，明天就要回去。
【BTV】明天回日本？
【木田】是的。
【BTV】你喜欢义乌吗？
【木田】喜欢。
【BTV】举个例子，在哪一方面？
【木田】我在这里有很多事情要做，所以很喜欢。
【BTV】这样啊，对于你而言，义乌最吸引你的地方是哪里？
【木田】是这里的旧货市场。
【BTV】你尝过这里的食物吗，感觉怎么样？
【木田】非常好吃。
【BTV】你的闲暇时间是怎么度过的？
【木田】我并没有空闲时间，不休息。
【BTV】在义乌，你和当地人相处还习惯吗？
【木田】请再说一遍，我有点听不懂你的意思。
【BTV】这里的生活节奏很快，你已经习惯了吗？
【木田】是的，完全没问题。
【BTV】你在这里有投资吗？
【木田】只是来这里工作。
【BTV】那你要把这里买的货物运到日本去吗？
【木田】是的，进口到日本。
【BTV】那么来这里买东西的原因是这里便宜，日本更贵？
【木田】那是其中一个原因，另外一个原因是这里的商品种类很多。
【BTV】对你而言，在这里最重要的是什么？

【木田】最重要的就是这家店。
【BTV】那你是如何进行发货的呢？
【木田】一般都是船运。
【BTV】在工作期间你进行过调查吗？
【木田】会的，在价格还有数量等方面。
【BTV】你在这里交易很顺利吗？
【木田】并不是很顺利。
【BTV】那这里竞争很激烈吗？
【木田】并不激烈。
【BTV】那日本呢？
【木田】在日本很激烈。
【BTV】这里和日本的文化差异大吗？
【木田】很大。
【BTV】打个比方？
【木田】例如出租车、公厕，还有人的思考方式不同，真的好麻烦。
【BTV】你在这里一个人开车吗？
【木田】不开，很可怕。
【BTV】因为方向是相反的吧，日本是靠左行驶。
【木田】日本是靠左的。
【BTV】这里的交通很糟糕啊。
【木田】的确很糟糕，在这里附近一带就有很多车子，经常堵车。
【BTV】在义乌有很多的外国人，你在义乌有外国朋友吗？
【木田】有啊。
【BTV】哪个国家的呢？
【木田】印度。
【BTV】你通晓他国语言吗？
【木田】是的。
【BTV】通晓哪种语言呢？
【木田】英语和韩语。
【BTV】你朋友的生活没有压力的吧？
【木田】我想应该是的。
【BTV】你对义乌人的印象如何？
【木田】很亲切的一群人，这样好了吗？
【BTV】好了，谢谢您的配合。

团体成员：郑立冬，杨侠剑，章李可

三ヶ国語ができる仕入れ係

作者：章李可　鄭立冬　指導教師：蔡　蕾　蔡　亮

長期間、出張する人にとって、いつも家族と一緒にいることができないのは残念なことだと思われているが、木田さんはそうではなく、僕は仕事がたくさんできるからここがすきだと言われた。

歴史の原因かもしれないが、義烏で生活している日本人はあまり多くない。七月六日、私たちは一生懸命さがしたが、義烏商品市場のアクセサリー店の入り口で木田さんと出会った。当日の気温はとても高かったが、市場の中はとても涼しかった。しかし、木田さんの額の汗から見ると、あの時彼の忙しさがわかった。

取材の時、お互いに見知らぬ人だから、木田さんはちょっと堅苦しく見えた。外見から見ると、いつも海外で奔走するかもしれないから、体は弱くなく、逆に高くて元気一杯だ。思っていた日本人と全然違う。あの時、彼は忙しくて、アクセサリーの仕入れをしているが、何分間の時間を割いて、私たちのインタビューを受けてくれた。

インタビューする時、木田さんは義烏で長時間生活するのではなく、ただここへ出張に来たということがわかった。この日本人が多くない町で、彼は日本人同士の友達も多くないが、日本語、英語、韓国語三ヶ国語ができるおかげで、大部分の友達は当地の外国の商人だ。義烏で生活している友達もここの生活に慣れたという。私たちが余暇はあるかと聞いたとき、木田さんはまじめに否定した。全然冗談ではない。確かにとてもいそがしそうだ。義烏の日本商人は多くないから、競争は激しくないが、貨物を本国に輸入した後、競争も激しくなった。

日本で車は左運転だから、木田さんはここで運転しない。なんといっても習慣は変わりにくいからだ。また、義烏の交通にちょっと不満で、交通渋滞は高度発展している町にとって通弊だ。義烏の人がやさしいと、木田さんはそう思った。今義烏で生活している彼はあちこち奔走して各種の貨物の値段を調査することも忘れなく、毎日休みの時間を仕事に使って、どんなに疲れるか想像できない。しかし、木田さんの話によると、これは本当に普通のことだった。私たちは本当に感心させられる。帰国した後、きっともっと疲れるでしょう。仕事のことに夢中になって、休憩すること、全然気にしていないが、さすが戦後厳しい状態から立ち上がった民族だ。

科学技術の発展に伴って、人々の消費水準もだんだん高くなり、商品の販売は価格から質で勝負することにかわってきた。現状から見ると、義烏小商品の輸出が多くの原因で、あまり楽観的ではない。東日本大震災の後、義烏は多くの日本からのオーダーを受けた。ろうそくや懐中電燈、マスク、ラジオなどの緊急物資の輸出量が大幅に増加した。しかし、日本からのオーダーが増えたが、多くの経営者は受けたくないという。日本からのオーダーは利益が高いが、要求も厳しいし、多くの企業の目から見ると、ちょっときつそうだ。関係者の話によると、日本のオーダーは欧米などと違って、製品出荷検査は抜き取り検査ではなくいちいち検査するそうだ。OEM 企業が日本の会社のための製品は最高の出荷率も80％にすぎなく、殘りの部分は不良品として処理するしかない。義烏では毎年日本への輸出量は大きくなく、3％一 5％ぐらいしかないという。それなのに、これをきっかけにして、義烏には製品の品質管理に工夫し、市場を拡大させることができると思っている。

義烏の卸売市場に約 6 万店舗あり、日用小商品販売量は世界中、最大規模だ。近年、多くの「日本製」も義烏市場に入り、中日両国の経済交流が深まるにつれて、両国間の製品同士をお互いに促進している。義烏小商品市場がきっと新しい段階に踏み込むと信じている。

精通三国语言的采购

文:章李可 郑立冬 指导老师:蔡 蕾 蔡 亮

我觉得作为一个长期出差在外的人,无法经常与家人团聚是一件很悲剧的事情,但是木田先生本人并不是这么认为,他说:"我因为能够从事很多工作而感到自豪。"

可能是历史原因,生活在义乌的日本人并不多见,7月6号下午我们好不容易在义乌小商品市场的一家饰品店门口遇到了正在采购货物的木田,虽然当天气温很高,但是在市场里还是很凉爽的,然而从木田额头上的汗可以看出当时木田有多么忙碌。

作为一个日本人,我们采访时他还是显得有点拘束,毕竟我们互不认识,而从外表看由于长年奔波海外的关系,所以他身体并不瘦弱,相反很是高大强壮,与我们印象中的日本人的形象截然不同,当我们采访他时,他正在采买一些小饰品,显得很忙碌,但是他还是抽出了一些时间,接受了我们的采访。

闲聊中我们了解到木田先生并不在义乌常住,只是出差到此,而在义乌这个日本人并不多见的城市,他的朋友也并不多,大部分都是在当地的外国商人,而能交到外国朋友,也多亏了他懂三种语言,日语、韩语和英语,而当我们问他在这里是否有休息时间的时候,他很认真地回答没有,的确很忙。大概是当地的日本商人并不多的原因,所以竞争并不激烈,但当货物运回本国的时候,那竞争就变激烈了。

在日本由于车辆都是靠左行驶,所以木田本人并没有在中国开车,毕竟习惯是很难改掉的,而他对义乌当地的交通并不是很满意,交通堵塞对于一个高速发展的城市是一个通病。他对当地人的印象不错,认为大家都很友好。而生活在义乌的他,仍然不忘四处奔走调查各种货物的价格数据,可以说他把每天可以用来休息的时间都用在了工作上,很难想象这样有多累,但从他的语气可以听出,这对他本人而言是一件稀疏平常的事情,令人佩服不已。也许他回国后可能会更累吧,但从他认为在义乌干很多活而感到自豪这点看来,他热衷于工作,并不在意休息与否,真不愧是从二战困境中崛起的民族。

由于科学技术水平的不断发展,人们的消费水平也越来越高。商品销售已从主要以价格低廉取胜逐渐转向以质取胜。但是,从目前情况来看,义乌小商品出口由于诸多原因,现状不是很乐观。日本大地震后,义乌接到了很多的日本订单,如蜡烛、手电筒、口罩、收音机等应急物资出口量大幅增加,虽然日本订单增多了,但许多商户并不愿意接单,因为日本订单虽然利润高,但要求较为严格,甚至有些苛刻。业内人士透露,日本客商的订单不像欧美等地的订单,产品出厂检测不是抽样检测而是逐一检测，代加工企业为日本客商生产的产品最高的出厂率也就80%多，其余都得当次品处理，虽然义乌每年的对日出口量并不是很大，只有3%左右，但义乌可以借此契机在产品质量上下功夫，用日本订单来检验自己。义乌的批发市场共有约6万家店铺，日用小商品的批发销售量为全球最大规模。近些年也有不少“日本制造”进入义乌市场，随着中日两国间经济交流的不断加深，两国间产品互相比较、互相促进，我相信义乌的小商品市场将会发展到一个新的高度。

采访结束后的合影

杉本哲夫(右二)

杉本哲夫:中国式の奇跡
中国式奇迹

杉本哲夫:日本で日用雑貨の販売をしている。一番早く義烏へ商務活動に来た日本商人の一人である。その分野に何十年間の経験もある。毎年、中国に来る。趣味は清酒、料理、旅行などである。

杉本哲夫在日本从事日用品交易,是最早一批来中国开展义务商贸活动的日本商人,在这个领域已积累了几十年的相关工作经验。杉本哲夫每年都要来中国,他的兴趣是清酒、料理、旅游等。

中国式の奇跡

杉本哲夫

インタビューの記録

【BTV】杉本社長、初めまして、よろしくお願いいたします。

【杉本】皆さん、初めまして、よろしく。

【BTV】今日はインタビューをうけてくださって、本当にありがとうございます。

【杉本】どういたしまして。

【BTV】では、社長は中国にいつきたんですか。

【杉本】今回は一ヶ月前に日本から来ました。たぶん一年に二、三回です。はじめて来たのは十二年前のことです。

【BTV】そうですか。すばらしいですね。貴社は何の会社ですか?

【杉本】売られているのは日用雑貨で、俺がここに来たのもこのためです。日用雑貨の市場規模がおおきいし、商品の種類もいろいろだし、値段も安いし。とても便利なんですね。

【BTV】そうですね。社長は中国語に詳しいですか?

【杉本】日常用語は大丈夫かもしれませんが、ビジネス用語はちょっと......それで、通訳をつれてきました。

【BTV】あ、そうですか。ビジネスの交流は一般通訳に任せて、これを通して、商業活動を進めます。だから、通訳のような職業は対外貿易に従事した貴社にとって、とても大切なのでしょう。

【杉本】まったく賛成です。今、日本語を専攻する中国の大学生も、中国語を専攻した日本の大学生もますます増えています。両国の経済活動に重要な影響をもたらして、だから、私の会社はこれからいいことを、そして、通訳たちも自分の仕事に誠意をつくして、ほんとうにいい人たちですね

【BTV】なるほどね。ところで、社長はもう中国の生活に慣れましたか。

【杉本】それはまだ無理ですね。よく来たんだけど、中国語が下手なので別のところへいかない、商務活動をのぞいて大体ホテルにとまっていて、日本料理店で食事をしています。それが私の生活の全部です。

【BTV】それでは、寂しいのではないでしょうか?

【杉本】そうですね。交流の不便なので、遊ぼうにも遊べない。どうしよう

もない。

【BTV】残念ですね、実は義烏ではいろいろな面白いことがあります。たとえば、当地の料理がおいしいし、そして、名所旧跡もたくさんあります。余裕な時間があれば案内させていただきます。

【杉本】期待いたします。本当に有難うございます。

【BTV】さて、次にもう一つ聞きたいんですけど。今の日中関係に対して何か意見を持っていますか。

【杉本】わたちの思いから言うと、友好関係をいっそう深めて、最も重要なのはお互いに理解を深めて、歴史の問題を正しく認識して、一緒に前に進むということです。

【BTV】はい、どうもありがとうございました。

团体：楊侠剣，鄭立冬，陳林杰

叙事记录

【BTV】杉本社长，初次见面，请多多关照。

【杉本】各位同学，初次见面，你们好。

【BTV】今天，社长先生能接受我们的采访，真的很感谢。

【杉本】不用那么客气。

【BTV】社长先生，您是什么时候来中国的？

【杉本】这次是一个月前来中国的，一年大约两三次。第一次来中国已是 12 年前了。

【BTV】是这样啊，真是了不起。请问您公司是销售什么的呢？

【杉本】销售的是日用品，这也是我来到这里的原因。义乌的日用品市场规模很大，商品的种类很多，价格也很便宜，非常方便。

【BTV】原来是这样的啊，请问您擅长说汉语吗？

【杉本】会说几句基本的日常用语，但商务用语就有点……所以，我带来了翻译。

【BTV】正如您所说的，商务交流一般要靠翻译，通过翻译的交流来进行商业洽谈，所以像翻译这样的职业对于从事对外贸易的贵公司来说是非常重要的吧？

【杉本】你说得很对。现在，无论是日语专业的中国大学生，还是汉语专业的日本大学生都在不断增加，他们对两国的经济活动产生了重大影响，而且，我公司也受益良多，年轻的翻译们对自己的工作也是尽心尽责，真是一群可爱可亲的人。

【BTV】您现在已经习惯中国的生活了吗？

【杉本】日常生活还是有点困难的，虽然经常来，但是我的汉语水平还是不行，去不了更多的地方。平时除了商务活动外，我大部分时间都是待在酒店，以及在日本料理店吃饭，这就是我在中国的全部生活了。

【BTV】那您不会感到寂寞吗?

【杉本】嗯。因为交流不方便，所以即使想去游玩也游玩不了，真是没有办法啊。

【BTV】真遗憾。实际上在义乌有许多有趣的事物。例如，当地的菜肴是很美味，当地的名胜古迹也有很多。如果有空的话，就让我做您的导游吧，带你们去游览。

【杉本】真的很期待呀，非常感谢。

【BTV】接下来，还有一个问题想问您，您对现在的中日关系有什么看法?

【杉本】从我的角度来说，我觉得要进一步加深彼此友好关系，最重要的是要加深相互的理解，正确地面对历史遗留下来的问题，一起向前发展。

【BTV】好的，非常感谢您。

团体成员：杨佚剑，郑立冬，陈林杰

杉本社长在接受采访中

雑貨の海洋、買い物の天国

作者:陳林杰　楊侠剣　指導教師:蔡　蕾

かつての中国は、国力が衰弱し、いつも他国にいじめられ、今の中国は国力が強大し、各国も中国と協力しようとしている。義烏はその良い例の一つである。

義烏市は浙江省の中部に位置し、金華市、金大道盆地の東部で、2012年の住民の平均収入は44454元で、連続長年中国大陸で一位であった。また義烏市は一番目の、中国唯一の県レベルの経済特区で、中国東部の唯一の中国の最大陸港である。

義烏は悠久の歴史と深い文化をもっている都市だ。一人当たりの収入水準も高級車の量も中国大陸で首位、中国で最も豊かな地域の一つである。義烏は、世界最大の小商品集散中心だ。国連、世界銀行などの国際権威機関に確定される世界一大きな市場だ。義烏国際商貿城は国家観光局から認定された中国はじめてのAAAA級ショッピング観光区で、「雑貨の海洋、ショッピングの天国」とは文明の義烏の代名詞だ。義烏は市場に基づいている都市で、浙江省中部地域の中心都市だ。

過去数十年間、中国の経済は急激に不思議な方式で発展してきた。特に、対外貿易の領域において、世界の注目を集める成果を取得した。そして義烏は全体として中国の縮図の存在だ。30年前の義烏はどんな様子なのか、たぶん想像しにくいだろう。その時の義烏は中国の貧しい郡の中の一つで、世界にも知られなかった。耕地面積が町の大部分を占め、家屋は低く、道は狭かった。現代都市の姿がぜんぜん見えなかった。しかし、今の義烏は30年の発展を通じ、困難も一つ一つ克服した後、ようやく世界一の小商品市場になった。高層ビルが林立し、道が広くなった。すっかり現代都市の姿になってきた。それは奇跡だろう。ただこれらは、確かにたいしたことではない。最も重要なのはここに集まってきた世界各地からの商人だ。杉本社長の話からわかるように、それは一つの小さな義烏の発展だけではなく、中国の全体の抬頭だ。中国の発展のために世界が中国の巨大市場に注目し、義烏のような小さい都市の国際化を促進している。かつての「鎖国」から今まで30年の改革開放にかけて、中国はゆっくりと世界に近づいてから世界の潮流に達することができた。特に義烏国際貿易センターで、毎日外国商人が様々な言葉で話している。ここに来てから、まるで中国ではないというような感じがある。これは中国人としての私の誇りだ。

熟睡した獅子が目を覚ました後、そのもたらした変化はどうなっているのか。

改革開放30年以来、中国はドアを開け、積極的に世界と交流するので、中国の変化が世界中に知られるようになった。

今回の取材を通し、私たちは義烏調査の過程の中で、すでに義烏の急速な発展をつくづく感じている。もちろんこのすべては政府の政策と義烏市民の努力から切り離せない。義烏小商品は世界各地で販売されている。その製品は品質も良く、価格も安く、すごく人気があるという。

義烏の市場は決して消えず、奇跡も続いていくと私はずっと信じている。

小商品海洋，购物者天堂

文：陈林杰　杨侠剑　指导老师：蔡　蕾

曾经的中国，国力衰弱，总是被他国欺负；现在的中国，国力强大，各国都想要与中国合作。义乌就是一个很好的例子。

义乌市位于浙江省中部，地属金华市，位于金衢盆地东部，2012 年居民人均收入高达 44454 元，连续多年居国内前列。同时，义乌市是第一个也是中国唯一一个县级市“经济特区”，中国东部唯一也是中国最大的陆港之一。

义乌是一座具有悠久历史和深厚文化底蕴的城市。人均收入水平、豪车密度在中国位居前列，是中国最富裕的地区之一。义乌是全球最大的小商品集散中心。被联合国、世界银行等国际权威机构确定为世界第一大市场。义乌国际商贸城被国家旅游局授予中国首个 AAAA 级购物旅游区，“小商品海洋，购物者天堂”是文明的义乌代名词。义乌是一座建在市场上的城市，亦是浙江中部区域的中心城市。

在过去的几十年中，中国的经济以不可思议的方式迅猛发展，特别是在对外贸易领域上取得了举世瞩目的成就，而义乌就是整个中国的缩影。你很难想象 30 年前的义乌是怎么样的，那时的义乌还只是中国的一个贫穷县城，不为世界所知。它的耕地占了整个县城的大部分面积，房屋低矮，道路狭窄。但是，经过 30 年的发展，在克服一个个的困难以后，义乌终于成了世界第一的小商品市场，高楼大厦鳞次栉比，道路宽广通畅，完全是一副现代都市的模样，这真是一个奇迹。如果仅仅是这些，也没什么了不起，最重要的是这里聚集了来自世界各地的商人。从杉本先生的口述中，我们看到的不仅仅是一个小小义乌的发展，更是整个中国的崛起。中国的高速发展让世界看到了中国这个巨大市场，于是乎也促进了像义乌这样的小城市的国际化。从曾经的“闭关锁国”到至今 30 年来的改革开放，中国从慢慢与世界接轨到如今赶上世界潮流。特别是在义乌国际贸易中心，每天外国商人络绎不绝，听到各种各样的语言，如此国际化的义乌让作为中国人的我深感自豪。

当一只沉睡的狮子从睡梦中醒来之后，它所带来的变化又将会是怎样呢？在改革开放 30 年以来，中国打开国门，积极与世界进行交流，让世界认识中国。

这次采访，我们在到义乌调研的过程中已经深切地感受到了义乌的快速发展。当然这一切，除了离不开政府的政策之外，也离不开义乌市民的努力。义乌小商品销往世界各地，物美价廉，深受人们的喜爱。

我深信义乌的市场是绝对不会消失的，奇迹还将继续。

第七章

Tales of Yiwu

品读义乌

导言

走访义乌之前，我们的团队成员就曾用“头脑风暴”的方式，描述过各自心目中的义乌形象。商品世界、外商云集、充满机遇等队员们热议不已的话题，虽然难以勾勒出一个完整而生动的义乌，但正是这些支离破碎的想象或者众说纷纭的逸事，让一位位热情如火的青年迸发出深入了解这个熟悉而又陌生城市的决心与渴望。义乌，我们心向往之！

对于90后的我们，义乌的过去是个谜团，难以复制的传奇静候我们去倾听；义乌的现在像位行者，洗尽铅华的足迹值得我们去追寻；义乌的将来是篇待续的史诗，再续辉煌我们责无旁贷。三年，可以让青年人与这座城市从最初的陌生走向熟知，像是一场浪漫的牵手；三年，可以让青年人与这座城市演绎出许多的话题与故事，如同一次接力对话。不断发展的城市，年年更新的队员，所有的变与不变，始终伴随着一个声音：我来了，义乌。

义乌初印象

文：楼星烨　指导教师：李　炜　蔡　亮

2011年7月，热浪袭袭，义乌国际商贸城外人流熙攘，步履匆忙，浙江大学宁波理工学院"用声音叙事"团队的成员们穿梭其中，开始了他们探究义乌外籍人士在华成功经商的奥秘之旅。在这之后的2012年和2013年暑期，同样有一批批着装统一、充满朝气的青年学子，或是行走在义乌的大街小巷，或是驻足于街头的咖啡店，或是停留在商品城的店铺，他们用镜头和声音聚焦义乌外籍人士的中国故事，用生动的文字记录义乌的发展历程，在多元文化的交融中解读富有时代意义的义乌精神，在行走的汗水中发现义乌最有可能的未来。

一、选择义乌

2011年5月6日，义乌市作为唯一一个县级市国际贸易综合改革试点全面启动的消息如同一声春雷，响彻大地。国家综合配套改革试验区是我国为顺应经济全球化和区域经济一体化，在科学发展观指导下建立的以制度创新为主要动力、以全方位改革试点为主要特征，对全国社会经济发展带来深远影响的实验区。截至2013年5月，国家已批准确定了上海浦东新区等11个综合改革配套试验区，另外还设立了区别于"配套"的"综合改革试验区"4个，义乌就是其中之一。从中国经济和世界经济发展趋势来看，加快转变中国外贸发展方式，推动中国内外部经济和贸易平衡发展，既符合科学发展的内在要求，也是积极参与国际竞争的现实需要。义乌市是中国对外贸易有独特优势和影响力的地区，以义乌为试点，目的是有针对性地解决中国对外贸易中存在的突出问题，探索建立有利于科学发展和社会和谐的新型贸易制度和管理体制。义乌市国际贸易综合改革试点全面启动对于加快实现发展方式转变和贸易强国目标，具有重要的战略和现实意义，也预示着新的机遇、新的希望和新的挑战。

与此同时，"用声音叙事"团队历经四年发展与成长，积累了丰富的实践经验，吸引了更多的师生参与，也在迫切思考新的方向。立足宁波，又要走出宁波！一时间，寻找新的"阵地"成为团队讨论的重点。"用声音叙事"团队的成员们集思广益，各抒己见，并敏锐地捕捉到：义乌的发展将是浙江，乃至全国经济领域改革的前沿与风向标。用声音发现义乌、记录义乌、诠释义乌迎来了时不我待的机缘。

如果说，试点国际贸易综合改革是选择义乌的历史机缘，那么，探寻义乌的具体实践仍需有强大的价值诉求作为支撑，仍需将丰厚的文化挖掘视为己任。如此方能不虚此行！

自改革开放以来，浙江经济发展迅速，常被视作市场经济的先行者、拓荒人。义乌又是浙江市场的典型，其敢为天下先的开创信念、艰苦卓绝的奋斗历史、与众不同的发展模式、历久弥新的独特文化与魅力，像是一串串璀璨耀眼、引人追逐的瑰丽宝石，给予我们想象她、走向她、拥抱她、难以拒绝她的足够理由。

众所周知，“勤耕好学、刚正勇为、诚信包容”的义乌精神和源于“草根经济”却又超越“草根经济”的义乌模式吸引着政、学、商界的目光。对于专家学者，更多关注于义乌丰富的学术研究价值；对于政、商人士，更多的是义乌经济发展模式的参考价值；而对于青年学子，义乌必将是一本诲人不倦的教科书，一片学生观察认知社会的沃土，一座指引青年人紧跟时代脉搏的灯塔。

有人用“集聚”一个词来概括义乌模式，这里是商品的集聚地，也是全球商人的集聚地。然而，我们会专注于淘宝上的义乌商品，却对义乌商品的渊源一知半解；我们会感慨义乌如今的繁华，却对义乌发展的艰辛历程知之甚少；我们能考察义乌模式，却未能对义乌精神详加解读。让青年学生走进义乌，用行、访、录、叙来观察义乌、感受义乌、记录义乌，或许是最直接、最有效、也最为有趣的方式。

二、义乌初印象

俗话说：好的开始是成功的一半。为保证实践活动顺利、有序推进，实现预期成效，“用声音叙事”团队实践走访初期，团队成员就投入到紧张的筹备工作中。一方面，由外语学院老师带队，两次赴义乌了解情况，期间，我们拜访了义乌市委宣传部等政府部门，寻得支持；同时，走访在义乌工作的校友，借助校友之力解决团队食宿、外籍人士联络等实际困难。另一方面，团队成员针对义乌外籍人士国籍分布广泛等特点开展高密度、大强度的业务培训，精心设计调查问卷，采访提纲几易其稿，不断优化。经过近两个月的准备，成员们成竹在胸，跃跃欲试，一次“用声音叙事”的全新尝试拉开了序幕。

虽说“凡事预则立，不预则废”，但是，万事开头难。义乌支队调查走访初期仍是困难重重。随机走访的外商多因商务繁忙而不能深入；约访外商也会因工作安排而错过时机；受访外商国籍分布广泛，语言交流不畅等问题逐渐凸显出来。是在收效甚微的现实面前选择放弃，还是在疲惫交困的艰难时刻选择坚持，队员们毫不犹豫地选择了后者。回想起当时队员们头顶烈日仍群情激昂的场景，不由得感到兴奋与欣慰。

为破解困局，团队成员发挥团队优势，审时度势，及时研判，从寻访区域、约访时间、沟通技巧、团队分工等多方面着手，修改方案，寻求突破。功夫不负有心人，团队成员在合作中实现共赢，在汗水中经历成长，在成功时分享愉悦。历时近半月，团队成功实现涉及 100 余名外籍人士的走访计划，并对多名外商进行了深度采访。

初次接触义乌，虽历尽艰辛，却也收获了对义乌最初的认识。在我们走访的所有外籍人士中，有87%的男士，占据绝大多数。从年龄分布来看，26～35岁的青年占43%，是主力，36～50岁年龄段占41%，由此可见，来义乌经商的外籍人士以青壮年为主。从调查中我们了解到，在义乌经商超过3年的外商占47%，其中超过6年的有22%，总体来说，有新来的“探路者”，也有“老马识途”的忠实客户，受贸易模式影响，流动性较大。来义乌的外籍人士最关注，也最欣赏的是义乌的投资环境，不过受访外籍人士中有7%左右的人是因为家庭原因才来到义乌，他们对义乌的历史文化、生活环境都给予认可与好评。据了解，在义乌经商的外籍人士中，20%左右已经购置房产，有久长期居住的居打算；另有近60%的义乌外籍人士则选择了租住公寓，他们认为义乌的服务行业比较发达和完善，对于需要四处奔走的经商者非常便捷与经济。

就在“用声音叙事”团队初次走进义乌期间，全英文义乌城市形象宣传片“Yiwu Vignette Series”恰好在CNBC财经电视台亚洲频道和世界频道播出。这部由CNBC摄制组专程赶赴义乌，采访拍摄多位外商在义乌生活经商情况制作而成的宣传片由两部分组成，一部分是义乌精粹，另一部分展现的是城市、市场、产品、展会等四个方面专题，3分15秒的宣传视频再一次让“小商品海洋，购物者天堂”的义乌形象蜚声海外。在众多受访的外籍人士眼中，义乌就是一个“群商荟萃，商品丰富，商业文明，商机无限”的天堂。

接受采访的很多外商说，他们来义乌就是为市场而来，义乌国际商贸城就是他们理想的市场。来自伊朗的外商Kumarkauac说：“义乌实在是一个经商的好地方，现在我们全家都在义乌，并准备在义乌定居，把生意做大做好。非常感谢政府，给我们提供了一个这么好的经商乐土。”他表示，来义乌经商是一件很美好的事，并愿意介绍更多的朋友来义乌。

义乌170余万种小商品让来自全球的外商们目不暇接，流连忘返。伊拉克外商Jimmy感慨道：“义乌的商品应有尽有，只有你想不到的，没有你买不到的。”他风趣地描绘着第一次在博览会上目瞪口呆、惊叹为何会有如此多产品的景象，“这在我的国家，是想也不敢想的。”来自南非的帅小伙Bruise坦诚地表示：“义乌给了我大开眼界的机会，能在义乌经商是我的荣幸。”

“义乌，一个你来了还想再来的地方，不为别的，只为那琳琅满目、出乎意料的奇特小商品。”我们的小队员在初次穿梭于义乌国际商贸城时发出了如此感慨。据了解，义乌国际商贸城一期就有近10000个摊位，如果在每个摊位驻足超过2分钟，逛完整个商城得花半个月时间。在与外籍人士的走访交流中，“用声音叙事”团队的成员们深切地感受到义乌的活力和生机，深深体会到义乌人的勤劳与好客。透过义乌“小商品”，我们更加能感受到融入义乌血脉，“承东接西”、“接轨国际”、“辐射全球”的包容与大气。

在调研义乌期间，队员们用自己的方式感受着义乌的变化和发展，用自己的语言记录下外籍人士眼中的义乌印象，用自己的行动传递出青年人建设城市的热忱。选择义乌，“用声音叙事”的成员们不是为了淘商品，而是要在这片炽热蓬勃的土地上淘知识、淘文化、淘能力。

义乌说“义”

文:沈　洁　马莉莉　张斯惠　指导教师:李　炜　蔡　亮

引言

“义”,繁体作“義”,下从“我”,意指“手持兵戈”,引申为“为信仰、为目标、为旗帜而战”;上从“羊”,《三字经》说“羊初生,知跪乳”,本就寓意“孝义”,又意“祭祀之牲口”,寓意“牺牲”。合二为一,“義”即意为“甘愿为信仰与目标而自我牺牲”,彰显遒劲雄浑之力,意达舍我其谁之大义。千百年来,独特的自然条件和历史人文环境铸造出“义乌”和“义乌人”特有的精神内涵与道德品质,他们“崇孝义、重情义、讲信义、明大义”①。“义”及其背后的那些美丽故事传递和诠释着城市之魂、商贾之道和处事之学。

一、颜乌葬父,城市之魂源于“义”

古人云:“羊有跪乳之恩,乌有反哺之义。”据《本草纲目·禽部》载:“慈乌:此乌初生,母哺六十日,长则反哺六十日。”大意是说,小乌鸦初生时,老乌鸦找寻食物喂养六十日,待到此消彼长,小乌鸦长大了,老乌鸦却不能自己找寻食物的时候,小乌鸦便会找食喂养它的母亲,哺与反哺,时日上基本相同,大致都是六十日。乌鸦反哺的故事经过一代代人的口授心传,已为众人知晓。当今社会,萦绕在人们心头的“反哺情结”仍是维系家庭和谐的精神支柱。

在浙江中部有一处地方,其名来源于人世间“孝鸟乌鸦”的故事,那便是义乌。

西汉经学家、文学家刘向(约公元前77—公元前6)在他所著的《说苑》一书中记载:“颜乌,乌伤人。亲亡,负土为大冢,群鸦数千,衔土相助焉。乌既死,群鸦又衔土葬之。”这是历史上关于颜乌的最早记载。颜乌以其感天动地的孝德备受历代推崇,有关他的神话故事在义乌广为流传。

颜乌,乌伤人。先祖从鲁国(今山东一带)迁居而来。父颜凤。颜乌一家人独居荒原,以耕作为生。生活虽苦,但合家团圆,日子倒也过得舒心。只是,灾难偏找穷苦人,颜乌的母亲因操劳过度、身体极度虚弱而离开了人世,丢下年幼的颜乌与父亲相依为命。颜乌的父亲颜凤,受祖上被称为圣人的颜渊“一箪食、一瓢饮而不变其志”的思想影响,对颜乌言传身教甚笃。他既当爹又当娘,辛辛苦苦地把颜乌

---

① 朱小燕:《义乌人义字当头——听义乌老板讲“吃亏”的故事》,浙江在线新闻网站,2006年5月18日。http://zjnews.zjol.com.cn/05zjnews/system/2006/05/18006625721.shtml.

拉扯大。家境的贫困、生活的磨难，培养了颜乌勤快、孝顺、善良的品格①。

颜乌体贴父亲年老体弱，不让父亲干重活。从田头回到家里，总是抢着做饭炒菜，且每次都等父亲吃好了才拿起筷子。夏天，蚊子肆虐，颜乌总是给父亲打扇驱蚊；冬天，颜乌总是用自己身体温暖被窝后再请父亲安睡。

有一次，颜乌发现有一只小乌鸦因腿伤而落在地上"呱呱"呻吟着。颜乌将它抱回家，精心地治疗、喂养，把小乌鸦的伤治好，养大一点后，便放它飞回蓝天。从此，鸟儿们将他当作好朋友，这只乌鸦常领着一群群乌鸦在他家房前屋后盘旋，久久不肯离去。

天有不测风云，人有日夕祸福。颜凤因一场大病撒手西去。颜乌悲痛万分，哭了三天三夜。颜乌家贫如洗，附近也没有什么人家，安葬父亲只得靠自己。他拼命地挖，工具坏了，用手挖，又整整挖了三天三夜，直至双手血肉模糊。经受着伤心、劳累、饥饿的颜乌，终因体力难支晕倒在地。

颜乌的爱心、孝心深深地感动着乌鸦。那只曾被他救过的乌鸦领着一大群乌鸦"呱呱"飞来，它们衔着泥来帮颜乌筑坟。乌鸦们不顾喙在啄泥时被磨破，在流着殷红鲜血的情况下仍然不遗余力，全力以赴，慢慢地，一座由团团紫红色泥团堆砌而成的坟掩埋了颜父。

筑好坟后，乌鸦渐渐离去。可是不久，乌鸦突然又多了起来，过路行人甚为奇怪，过去看时，才知道颜乌由于过度悲伤和劳累，死在父亲的墓旁。孝子颜乌死后，乌鸦再次衔土掩埋，将颜乌葬在其父坟墓旁。为纪念颜乌，人们在这里建起了祠堂，称为孝子祠；为了纪念那些筑坟受伤的善良乌鸦，人们把这一带称作乌伤。秦始皇平定江南后，这里正式建县"乌伤"，至公元 624 年，改称义乌。

传说中，当年乌鸦啄泥而成的大坑积水成塘；乌鸦衔泥途中休息的地方因掉了不少泥块，也堆成了一座小小的馒头山。据当地老人回忆，传说中的那个水塘应该就是现在义乌市客运中心北面的秦塘；堆成的小土山也因前些年城市扩建被取土造路，成为城中北路的一段，大概位置在义乌登峰机械有限公司附近。

援引国际在线 2014 年 2 月 19 日的《义乌概况》描述，义乌位于浙江省中部，地处金衢盆地东部，东、南、北三面群山环抱，南北长 58.15 公里，东西宽 44.41 公里，面积 1105 平方公里。义乌东邻东阳市，南接永康市、武义县，西连金东区、兰溪市，北接浦江县和绍兴的诸暨市，市区以丘陵为主，兼有中低山、岗地、平原等多种类型，与永康市交界的大寒尖，为全市最高峰，北部大陈江边的瓦摇头为全市最低点。

义乌境内最长的河流义乌江源远流长，孕育着一代代聪明、勤奋的义乌人。"骆丞草檄气堂堂，杀敌宗爷更激昂"，在素有"文化之乡"的义乌，先后出现过三国东吴名将骆统、"初唐四杰"之一骆宾王、宋代抗金名将宗泽、金元四大名医之一朱

① 引自义乌资讯网，http://www.eyiwu.com/person/n9675.htm。

丹溪、南宋著名政治家徐侨、现代教育家陈望道、文艺理论家冯雪峰、历史学家吴晗等历史名人。

根据《宋史·卷三百六七·列传第一百一十九》记载，北宋之末、南宋之初的抗金名臣宗泽，为人刚直豪爽，时常针砭时弊，先后在浙江龙游、山东胶州等地为官，勤政爱民，政绩显著，深受百姓爱戴。公元1127年，宗泽以67岁高龄留任东京，领兵与金兵隔着黄河对峙，招岳飞于麾下，屡次打破金兵入侵，自此宗泽威震天下。建炎元年七月起，宗泽一年上疏24次，力劝宋高宗还京，以图恢复北方失地，均为奸佞所阻，这就是著名的《乞回銮殿疏》。上疏屡被阻后，宗泽忧愤成疾，疽发于背。临终前，他仍不停念诵“出师未捷身先死，长使英雄泪满襟”的诗句，表达自己不能为国尽忠尽义的呼唤与遗憾。

宗泽出生在义乌山村石板塘一个贫寒的家庭，受到“耕读传家”思想影响，自幼就参加劳动，农闲时则读书识字。在他十几岁时，举家迁到交通相对便利、商贸文化也较为发达的廿三里地区。在这里，宗泽耳闻目睹了宋王朝的吏治腐败和外敌侵扰，萌发了救国救民的思想抱负。不到20岁的宗泽毅然辞家外出游学，历时十余年，就学之地多达数十处。他不仅悉心求学，研读“古人典要”，而且学以致用，考察社会，了解民情，孜孜不倦地追求治国之道，逐步看清了整顿吏治是解决政治腐败的关键所在；同时眼看辽国、西夏屡屡入侵，也产生了靖边安境、为国效力的思想，他认真研读兵书，苦练武艺，迅速成长为一个博学广识、文武兼备、富有理想和抱负的青年。可以说，义乌的传统文化、自然环境给了宗泽成为一名将臣、能臣的最初土壤，他一生为义，一生守义，一生赴义都与他自小生活的义乌休戚相关。

有关义乌的尚武重义的史事远不止于此。明朝杰出军事家戚继光就有过如此感慨：“征战半生，天下强横之徒，我大都曾见过，却也从无畏惧。但如义乌人之彪勇横霸，善战无畏，实为我前所未见，让人闻风丧胆，可怕！可怕！”话虽如此，但戚继光看重的正是义乌人无畏无惧、勇猛刚毅的战斗精神，在他的征召下，一支4000义乌人的戚家军组建而成，成为反击倭寇的一把利器。

金元四大名医之一朱丹溪从千里求师到救济世人都以“义”字当先。纵观朱丹溪一生，有苦有泪，尤其是当他立在风雨中，乞求罗知悌收他为徒，教他习医时的情景，那是何等的毅力与勇气，为了一个目的，即使千折百转，不达目的仍誓不罢休。就是到了今天，这种精神仍值得颂扬和学习。朱丹溪用一生为世人树起做人、做事的榜样。

近代著名诗人、文艺理论家冯雪峰，不仅是湖畔诗社的创建人之一，也是少有的参加过二万五千里长征的作家。他担任过中央苏区党校副校长，也曾被国民党囚禁于江西上饶集中营；他与鲁迅、瞿秋白是挚友，也曾被错划为“右派”，蹲过牛棚。但是，他唯一不变的是对文学的喜爱，对工作的追求。历史学家、社会活动家吴晗，虽然没能走出“文革”那场浩劫，但却留下“留取丹心照汗青”、“文章憎命达、魑魅喜人过”的一生写照。还有著名思想家、教育家、中国共产党创始人之一陈望道，他在家乡分水塘的柴屋里首译了《共产党宣言》中译本，为中国革命点燃了圣火，照亮了新民主主义革命的道路。正是义乌先贤身上那种崇文尚武、重义尚礼的高贵品质造就了义乌精神。

义乌精神是义乌人民在长期的社会实践，特别是市场竞争过程中，在正确的价值观念体系的支配下，逐步形成和优化出来的具有鲜明个性特征的群体意识，具有时代性、传承性、独特性。义乌人不仅头脑聪明、善于经营，骨子里更有一种刚烈、耿直、讲义气的性格。现如今，义乌 160 多万人口中多半为外来者，仅外商就有八千多人，来自 100 多个不同的国家和地区，慢慢都已融合成了新义乌人。

义乌是一座没有围墙的城市，是一方涌动着激情的热土。义乌的城市是开放的，义乌的人们是包容的，凡是到过义乌的人，从很小的事件中就可以感受到，无论在农村还是在城市，彼此间交流都是用普通话，这一方面是因为说话者分不清对方是本地还是外地人，而另一方面则是其根子里透着一种自信与尊重。在义乌有个不成文的传统，倘若两个人在生意上遇到纠纷，需要调解或是仲裁，在同责情况下当地政府部门往往会偏向于外来经商者。走在义乌的大街上，你会看到各式各样的基督教堂、清真寺等建筑，在义乌，宗教的多元存在已然渐变为一种文化，一种与众不同的存在。

义乌，虽说城市不大，却也有着自己特别的节日与习俗。

红糖节，就是义乌的一项盛事。根据《义乌县志》的记载，义乌种蔗制糖的历史已经有 400 多年了。据传。义乌燕里村是“甜蜜事业”的发源地，早在清顺治年间，燕里村人就已经掌握种蔗制糖之法，到清乾隆年间，义乌人就将红糖制成姜糖，并开始了换取鸡毛的营生。让义乌红糖真正名声大振的是在 1929 年(民国 18 年)，由义乌黄培记生产的红糖在当届西湖博览会上荣获特等奖。自此，义乌红糖开始畅销全国，远销海外。20 世纪初，糖蔗区以佛堂、义亭为主，30 年代开始逐渐扩大，遍布全县，到 1946 年达到鼎盛，种植面积超过 6 万亩，居全省首位。每年冬至是甘蔗成熟的时候，义乌的村村镇镇都弥漫着浓浓的糖香。为了保护和开发义乌红糖产业，不断弘扬红糖文化，提高义乌红糖的知名度，从 2005 年起，义乌市政府在义亭镇每一年都会举办红糖节，引来无数客商。

元宵节，义乌有一个传统习俗——迎龙灯。迎龙灯源于农村，每家每户将灯笼绑在板凳上，并把板凳连接在一起，形成一条长长的灯龙。对于龙灯，义乌人极其敬重，无论大人小孩，都不允许肆意跨过，龙灯过处，每户人家都要在门前放烟花，意图吉庆。龙灯在村子里绕行的时候，如果遇上了小池塘或转弯处，后面的向后拉，前面的向后退，也总有人一不小心掉进水池，或栽一跟头，顿时引得围观者哈哈大笑。元宵迎龙灯给安静的山村以喜庆、祥和的感觉，着实为元宵夜增添了一分喜气，一份快乐。

义乌历史久远，名人辈出，古迹众多。铸造于后周广顺二年(952 年)的双林铁塔，建于宋嘉定六年(1213)的古月桥，建于清嘉庆十八年(1813)年的黄山八面厅，明清乔亭蟹钳形墓葬群，朱丹溪墓，冯雪峰故居，松瀑山摩崖题刻，善慧傅大士塔等省市级文物保护单位，以及双林寺、德胜岩、瑞峰寺等十多处庵堂、寺庙①，都积淀了厚重的文化，记录着众多鲜活的历史故事。

现在的义乌，正以自己的方式延续着“颜乌葬父”的感动，在激荡的历史长河里，与众不同地走向世界。

二、鸡毛换糖，商贾之道立于“义”

信和义的经营理念已经融入了义乌血脉里！可以说，没有信和义，就没有义乌市场今天的辉煌。

不论是“颜乌葬父”，还是“鸡毛换糖”，无不体现一个“义”字。“颜乌葬父”自不必说，而“鸡毛换糖”这种特别的商业模式能在义乌这片土地上，历经各个历史时期奇迹般地得以延续，并创造出义乌现在的商贸奇迹，得益于义乌市政府开给“敲糖帮”们的一张长期证明：“这是我县传统的支援农业措施之一。”正是这张证明给了“鸡毛换糖”足够的支持与空间，这不能不说是种义举！

义乌农业自然条件极其恶劣：多丘陵，少平原，交通尤为不便，但勤劳勇敢的义乌人却凭借“鸡毛换糖”的精神，在改革开放之后迅速崛起，使义乌成为目前全球最大的小商品集散中心，被联合国、世界银行等国际权威机构确定为世界第一大市场，创造了全国乃至全球的现代经济神话。

“百样生意挑两肩，一副糖担十八变；翻山过岭到处走，混过日子好过年。”过去，义乌最出名的就是鸡毛换糖，几百年来，鸡毛换糖曾经是许多义乌农民重要的谋生手段。80 后的一代还能从依稀的记忆中找到满巷子“经货担子”跑着的影子。现如今，走乡串户、沿街叫卖的鸡毛换糖人用手中的拨浪鼓摇出了亚洲最大的小商品批发市场，这就是发生在浙江义乌的真实的历史现实。

义乌鸡毛换糖的历史渊源可追溯到明末清初，一直延续到 20 世纪 80 追着年代，以义乌的红糖加工业为基础，大约经历了三百多年的历史。据《义乌县志》记载：“早在清乾隆时，本县就有农民于每年冬春农闲季节，肩挑糖担，手摇拨浪鼓，用本地红糖熬制成糖粒或生姜糖粒，去外地串村走巷，上门换取禽兽毛骨、旧衣破鞋、废铜烂铁，博取微利。清咸丰、同治年间，糖担货色增售妇女所需针线脂粉、髻网木梳等小商品。抗日战争前夕，本县操此业人数增至近万，发展成为独特性行业——敲糖帮。”②县志中所提及的敲糖人便就是我们现在口中常说的鸡毛换糖人，三百

---

① 《魅力义乌：认识义乌的历史名胜》，浙江在线 http://jq.zjol.com.cn。

② 傅根洪：“敲糖换鸡毛：义乌的商路历程”，《西湖》2005 年 05 期。

多年来，他们的足迹遍及大半个中国。

义乌向来是以农业经济为主，人口的众多加上土地的贫瘠，使得当时不少农民只能自寻出路，搞起副业。鸡毛换糖属于小本买卖，只要能熬制成糖就可以开张营业，无须多少资本，也不需什么高深技术，所以即便是贫穷破产的人也可从事，只要他舍得花力气，不怕辛苦，因而外出换糖相对来说是一条简便谋生之路。

据了解，最早鸡毛换糖人其实做的是售糖营生，只是用糖换钱，不做其他买卖。因为换糖人卖价便宜，态度又好，讲究信义，每到一地，深受欢迎，生意兴盛，带动了越来越多的义乌人不断加入换糖大军。随着商贩日渐增多，又受限于市场规模，商贩间的竞争异常激烈。不过，这些头脑灵活又精明能干的农家商贩，在经营过程中采取变通机动的经营方式，一方面勤劳耕耘，走向更为广袤、遥远的地区进行经营；另一方面，各商贩也在不断扩大经营范围，不再限于现金交易，同时以糖换物，而且所换物品范围极其广泛，以废铜烂铁、牲畜禽毛为主，后来也兼卖一些日用针头线脑之类的小商品。

鸡毛换糖生意虽说“卑贱”又辛苦，却是义乌农民发家致富的一条重要渠道，代代相传，从者如流，连绵不断。

回顾过去，换糖人命途多舛、历经坎坷。新中国成立以后，直至20世纪80年代中期，义乌都一直有人从事着鸡毛换糖的生意。然而，1949年后农村逐步实行集体化，鸡毛换糖受到了限制，外出换糖人数有所减少。在“大跃进”和“文革”时期，鸡毛换糖处于最低潮，一度被当作资本主义尾巴来批判。尽管经营环境恶劣，为了生计，有些人仍旧“偷偷摸摸”地干着，期间从未中断过。改革开放后，政策日渐放宽，换糖人这才扬眉吐气，堂堂正正地做起生意。义乌在全国率先放宽个体户工商登记，允许农民经商，允许开放城乡市场，放开手脚经商的农民如鱼得水，纷纷加入经商队伍。随之而来的是换糖队伍空前壮大，工商部门还特地发放临时敲糖换鸡毛许可证，各换糖人有了合法经营的身份，鸡毛换糖的规模又重新得到发展与恢复，在20世纪80年代初达到了新的高峰。这期间，部分经营户通过经商初步完成了资本的原始积累，买进机器办起加工厂，形成了“前店后厂”工商一体的家庭经营模式。

鸡毛换糖生意历经数百年历史沧桑，其商业形式与内容在不断发展与更新。早时换糖人外出所带货物一般只是本地所产的红糖，及用红糖加工的各种糖粒糖块，以换取鸡毛；将所交换来的上好的羽毛加工后出售，余下的用来做肥料。随着时间的推移，他们的糖担里逐渐增加了针线、发夹、手帕、头巾之类的货物，改变了单一的鸡毛换糖经营方式，增售日用小商品，并逐渐以此为主业。到20世纪七八十年代，换糖人应时而变、与时俱进，开始转变经营策略。20世纪70年代后期，一些换糖人专做长途贩运生意，逐渐也由此形成了一条小商品采购渠道。同时，部分心灵手巧之人开始自己摸索加工一些小商品，在集市上售与外出换糖人及消费者，逐渐地，一个自发的小商品市场悄然形成，这就是义乌小商品批发市场的雏形。

“这个地方原来很穷，农业自然条件不好，很多农民只好外出经商，摇拨浪鼓卖糖。义乌市政府在当地老百姓生存都困难的情况下，在很多地方都在驱赶‘马路市场’的时候，只能考虑接纳他们，使之能够生存下来。不敢说义乌市领导有先见之明，当时只是出于一种本能：为了扶持农民，为了发展经济。”中共浙江省委党校副校长、浙江行政学院副院长马力宏说道。[①] 正如马院长所言，今天的义乌是拨浪鼓里摇出来的。

义乌人敢为天下先。1984 年，面对纷繁复杂的局势，义乌县委却做出决定对外开放义乌小商品市场：“允许农民进城经商，允许长途贩运，允许城市市场开放，允许多渠道竞争”，[②]由此义乌的小商品市场发展一发不可收拾。这正是政府顺应人民的要求，主导建设、开放市场，激励人民搞市场经济，经济发展大踏步前进的真实写照。三十年后的今天，人们读到这些很可能不以为然，因为这些都是常态，是十分正常的现象，但在当时是令人胆战心惊的尝试，是需要极大魄力与勇气的。

义乌市政府的慷慨接纳使当地老百姓的生存条件改善了，从政府角度讲，税收增加了，城市发展就更有底气。而更为让人惊喜的是，市场一经形成，流通量大了之后，商人们就蜂拥而至。一时间，金华、永康等地方的小商品都集中到了义乌，义乌市场逐渐强大，最终发展成为一个小商品集散中心，在全国乃至全世界都颇具知名度。

贸易市场的形成帮助义乌人摆脱了贫困，但却还没有真正地富裕起来。在当时，义乌的企业如雨后春笋般不断兴起，但一箱工艺品的批发利润仅有一二十元。起初，义乌的商品主要来自广州、宁波和温州等地方，只有极少部分是义乌当地加工制造的。勤奋聪明的义乌商人敏锐地捕捉到：相比批发贸易，当时的制造业有着相当高的利润。义乌人摸着石头过河，通过原始积累的资本办起了自己的企业。

义乌企业创一代主要是农民出身，没有受过高等教育，他们最强调市场，知道什么好卖就生产什么，相较而言，在对企业的规划与管理方面并不擅长。初创的义乌企业深知成本控制的重要，所雇佣的工人多是来自江西、安徽和湖南等地的农民工，生产产品主要是一些手工艺品和一些简易的日用品，成本大大降低，生产方式也极为灵活，眼下生产的袜子不受顾客欢迎，第二天就能换个款式，新款过段时间不好卖，继续更换款式，一直坚持顾客导向，以满足顾客需求为主要经营理念。久而久之，很多企业都形成了属于自己的品牌，这也成就了后来被称为“草根经济”的义乌企业发展模式。

随着时代的变迁，义乌始终能紧跟潮流，在坚持把商贸业作为主导产业的同

---

① 王红茹：《“义乌模式”的“无为”与“有为”》，民网经济论坛 http://finance.people.com.cn。

② 《义乌小商品：引领国际市场的指挥棒》，中国义乌政府门户网站 http://www.yw.gov.cn。

时，与时俱进，开创兴建了五代小商品市场。在实施兴商建县战略的同时，充分发挥商贸资本雄厚、市场信息灵敏、经商人才众多等优势，积极实施以商促工、贸工联动的战略，引导商业资本向工业扩展，大力发展与专业市场关联度紧密的小商品加工业。五代小商品市场的发展，也见证着义乌人民的机智果敢。他们利用天时，把握政策，深谋远虑，不断推进着义乌经济的跨越式大发展。

依稀还记得在20世纪80年代末，90年代初，村里面兴起"义乌打工"热潮，很多年轻小伙子、姑娘们都到义乌寻求发展。"义乌老板对我们非常好，过完年我们一起去。"春节返乡的义乌打工者不仅为义乌的经济发展服务，还把义乌企业诚信经营、信义为先的良好形象宣传到各个乡村角落。

义乌小商品市场最早起源于20世纪60年代末的廿三里。1974年春节前后，县城稠城镇县前街湖清门也兴起了小商品市场。在那个特殊年代，上级明令禁止、取缔"马路市场"，而半合法的"敲糖换鸡毛"又需要市场，彼此间存在着巨大的矛盾冲突，"两个提篮叫卖"、"批零兼营"的季节性市场悄然孕育。1982年3月26日上午，就稠城市场整顿问题，县政府再次召开由一名副职主持的县长办公会，这就是义乌小商品市场开放前夕著名的"第二次县长办公会议"。1982年9月，义乌县政府正式开放稠城镇小百货市场，当时投资9000元，为铺设水泥板的露天市场，摊位700个，当年小商品市场成交额为392万元。1983年湖清门市场摊位数增加1050个，成交额达1444万元；到1984年，这个市场的成交额达2321万元，商品主要销往义乌周边县市。与此同时，党的十二大胜利召开，湖清门市场发展迎来新的春天。时年，在县工商局的直接领导和有关部门的配合下，湖清门小百货市场进行大规模整顿，"秩序井然，面貌一新"，义乌第一代马路市场被正式认可，其后发展的速度超出了任何人的意料。

在当代中国经济奇迹中，曾经一而再、再而三地发生过"凹地效应"。当时的义乌小商品市场也是这样的一块凹地。义乌太祖殿畈的第二代棚架集贸市场开张后，近两千个摊位迅速摆开，每天前来交易的超过万人，其中六成以上为外地人，申请进场者络绎不绝。随着第二代小商品市场的兴起，经商农民纷纷迁往义乌。1984年，义乌县委县政府提出"兴商建县"的方针，放宽企业审批政策，简化登记手续。义乌全县掀起经商办厂热潮，年底个体户突破1万户，小商品市场成交额2321万元。据统计，1986年，义乌市场的成交额突破1亿元，辐射范围从周边县市延伸到省内外。① "凹地效应"的形成，使市场的发展完全超出了人们的预计。刚开业不久的义乌第二代棚架集贸市场马上又显得太小了，市场再度扩建，已势在必行。

中国小商品城第三代棚架市场于1985年11月动工兴建，场址选在环城路以东、前大路与标准件厂之间地块，总投资440万元，1986年竣工开业，设有固定摊

---

① 《改革开放三十年篇：重温义乌》，中国义乌政府门户网站 http://www.yw.gov.cn/。

位4096个，占地4.4万平方米，市场内建有综合商业服务及工商、税务、邮电、金融等管理服务大楼。其后经过多次扩建，至1990年底，中国小商品城第三代建设已形成占地面积5.7万平方米，设有固定摊位8503个，临时摊位1500多个的全国最大的小商品专业批发市场。1991年小商品市场成交额达10.33亿元，首次突破10亿大关。这时，小商品市场的地位和作用开始被越来越多的人所认识，很多义乌人自觉不自觉地融入整个市场。

第四代大型室内柜台式市场于1991年开始动工兴建，1992年投入使用，共有摊位7100个。3月在国家工商局首次公布的全国十大市场名单中，义乌小商品市场名列榜首。8月，义乌小商品市场更名为"浙江省义乌市中国小商品城"。1993年义乌小商品市场走上了股份制的发展路子，创立中国小商品城股份有限公司。1994年6月4日，中国小商品城第四代市场二期工程通过交工验收，至此小商品城建筑面积扩大到22.8万平方米，摊位数增至23000个。1995年中国小商品城成交额达到152亿元。①

进入21世纪，义乌小商品市场走上了国际化的发展道路，为顺应国际化发展需求规划建设了第五代的专业市场——中国义乌国际商贸城。国际商贸城的建设秉承"科学的规划、一流的设计、现代化的建筑"理念，致力引领传统集散型市场向现代化国际市场飞跃。义乌国际商贸城作为义乌建设国际性商贸城市的标志性建筑，共设有五区，分三个阶段建设。2011年5月5日，国际商贸城五区市场投入使用，自此，历时10余年建成的第五代义乌专业市场全部开业。这个主要由国际商贸城、篁园市场、宾王市场三个主体构成的宏大市场，营业面积超过400万平方米，商位7万个，从业人员和日客流量均超过20万人，已然成为我国，乃至全球最大的小商品集散中心。到过义乌国际商贸城的人都会感叹这里的商户林立，商品众多。

从第一代市场到第五代市场，义乌先后五易其址、十次扩建，实现了从最初的"马路市场"、"棚架市场"向大型现代化室内交易商场的跨越，市场发展步步为营、稳扎稳打，先占领国内市场，再进军国际市场，不断捕捉商机，赢得发展机遇。

改革开放以来，义乌坚持和深化"兴商建市"发展战略，以培育、发展、提升市场为核心，大力推进工业化、国际化和城乡一体化，走出了一条富有自身特色的区域发展道路。近年来，义乌全面落实科学发展观，致力于"创业富民、创新强市"，着力打造"三中心两高地"，即国际小商品贸易中心、国际小商品创造中心、国际小商品会展中心、区域物流高地和区域金融高地，努力把义乌建设成为国际商贸名城。②义乌市抓住市场发育先机，发展以小商品流通为主的商贸业，不断积累资本、扩大

① 陆立军："中国小商品城的崛起与农村市场经济发展的义乌模式"，《经济社会体制比较》，1999年01期。

② 楼春秋，方向阳："义乌全面建设国际商贸名城"，《金华日报》，2008年7月23日。

规模,促进商业资本向制造业和城市基础设施建设等领域扩张,推动了工业化、城市化、国际化进程,开辟了一条商贸主导、联动发展、创业富民、创新强市的特色发展之路。坚持从实际出发,充分利用市场先发优势,以创业创新为动力,以小商品流通为载体,推进市场化,带动工业化,催生城市化,演进为国际化,创造了“无中生有、有中生奇、无奇不有”的义乌奇观,①迅速涌现出一大批有规模、有品牌的龙头企业。

纵观义乌的经济发展,其鲜明特点是:由“鸡毛换糖”开始,利用市场先发优势和集聚功能,发展以小商品流通为主的商贸业,不断积累资本,扩大经营规模,促使商业资本向制造业和城市基础设施建设等领域扩张,实现市场与产业、城市的联动发展,推进区域经济工业化、城市化、国际化的进程。在近年的高速发展中,他们一靠党的改革开放政策,二靠人民群众的首创精神,三靠信义经营的口口相传,逐步奠定了自己小商品市场的龙头地位。

三、吃亏是福,生命之光荣于义②

义乌,世界最大的小商品批发市场,每日交易量汇聚成“义乌指数”,被称作全球小商品贸易的“风向标”和“晴雨表”。市场是义乌经济的最大特色和优势,自1982年在全国率先创办小商品市场以来,经过五易其址、九次扩建,义乌已形成以中国小商品城为核心,通信市场、家电市场、旧货市场、汽车城、义乌装饰城、物资市场、义乌农贸城、家具市场、二手车交易市场、木材市场、出版物中心等11个专业市场与20多条专业街相支撑,运输、产权、劳动力等要素市场相配套的市场体系。

拥有两千多年历史的义乌,从一个名不见经传的农业小县城发展到如今享誉国际的商贸名城,这“涅槃”般的发展,不可不谓是中国的一个经济奇迹。义乌的成功是中国改革开放的成功,是义乌人民的成功。从义乌走出来的企业家们一直秉承着“勤耕好学、刚正勇为、诚信包容”的义乌精神,让自己的实际行动成为义乌的响亮名片。

在义乌有这么一些人,他们从小离家,体会过了生活的艰辛,尝遍了人间冷暖,带着执着的梦想走上了创业的历程。从一家家的家庭小作坊到如今的高楼大厦,一位位曾经单打独斗的人们如今已经成了成百上千名职员的领头人。义乌承载了太多人的理想与坚持,他们用各自的经历书写着义乌的商业神话,他们的人生就像是一部传奇电影,每个人都是其中的主角,他们用亲身经历向我们诉说,坚持梦想,懂得吃亏才是成功的捷径。如果说义乌向世人缔造了一个商业典范,那么就不得

---

① 王彩芳:“义乌市场创造活力探究”,《浙江师范大学学报(社会科学版)》,2011年06期。

② 以周晓光、胡腾的《女人就是要发光》为素材来源编写。

不提这其中的奠基人们，他们没有光环，既普通又非凡。在这众多义乌商人里，周晓光女士就是一位坚持“做生意首要是做人”，懂得“吃亏是福”的典型缩影。

周晓光，一个来自贫困山区、贫困家庭的农家女，16 岁就在全国各地走街串巷卖小商品的“小货女”，一头利索的短发，精干却不尖锐；一脸和蔼的笑容，温暖且不失柔和，是千万义乌人中的一个平凡却又不平凡的女子。

“我的经商之路是从外出做小生意开始的。”那时的周晓光刚满 17 岁，第一次一个人独自远行，目的地是上海。那时上海城隍庙的小商品交易市场正是萌芽阶段，还不太成熟的她，便想去那里碰碰运气。妈妈担心初次离家的晓光，便让她借住在一个上海的亲戚家。本不想麻烦亲戚的她却因为囊中羞涩，最后还是无奈地住进了亲戚家。

周晓光每天起早贪黑，因为不想给亲戚添麻烦，明明没有吃饭却也含糊地答应他们说她吃过了。每天与城管“斗智斗勇”，带着简易的地摊东躲西藏，一个月下来，她虽是省了住宿费，可是却没赚到什么钱，经济的拮据让她已无法立足，终究她还是选择了回家。

彼时的她还不知道，这一段坎坷经历在她的漫长创业路上有着难以估量的价值。也正是上海城隍庙这个让周晓光留下不甘和执着的地方，17 年后她带着新光——这个义乌第一家把分店开到上海的饰品企业，重新回来了。周晓光说她最喜欢的是一个关于蝴蝶破茧的故事：一个小女孩看到一只蝴蝶正要破茧而出，茧壳上只裂开了一个小口，蝴蝶挣扎着想从小口中出来。小姑娘看蝴蝶十分可怜便想帮它，于是拿了一把剪刀帮它剪开了身上的茧，小女孩满心欢喜地站在一边想要看蝴蝶翩翩飞舞的那一刻，可是这一刻始终没有出现，这只蝴蝶永远也飞不起来了。这个好心的姑娘并不知道，蝴蝶从茧中破壳而出是它必经的过程，只有通过挤压、挣扎，它身体中的血才可能流到它的翅膀上，这样才能展翅高飞。就像这只蝴蝶一样，没有经历过过程的艰险怎能拥有自由的翅膀。周晓光在她的这段启蒙路上学到最多的是勇气，勇气助她破茧重生。一只蝴蝶让她看到了她需要前进的方向，和像她一样的千千万万的义乌人，凭借着吃苦的勇气，克服自身缺陷的勇气，面对陌生事物敢于尝试的勇气一直走到了现在。“如果生命中没有障碍，我们就会很脆弱，我们将不能飞翔，要完成化蝶为蛹的过程我们首先得具备奋斗的勇气。”

都说母亲是一个成功企业家的导师，周晓光的创业导师正是她的母亲，一位言传身教的母亲。周晓光的妈妈因为家里的负担重，光是靠种地这点微薄的收入已经无法支撑一个家庭。由于生活所迫，晓光的妈妈先是在家附近的山上开垦出零星的土地种番薯，做成番薯丝拿到城里换面粉，之后又在家中养上家禽补贴家用，遇到不能做农活的下雨天她便帮着别人补尼龙袜子，别看只是小钱，这一天靠补袜子赚的一元多就可以够全家一个月的盐巴钱。正是这一点一滴的积累，他们家里的生活状况渐渐好了起来。1968 年政策有些宽松，晓光的妈妈立刻办了执照，成了岭北地区第一个拿到合法证件的经营户，临近春节她便挑着红糖出去，用“鸡毛换糖”的钱给孩子们做学费。

只有经历过穷苦的人才能知道甘甜的不易，迫于生活压力，晓光妈妈想尽各种方法自食其力。她不把自己禁锢在那一亩三分田的狭窄“土地”上，凭借变通和发现商机的慧眼找到了自己的生财之道。也正是这样，年幼的晓光才能耳濡目染，在创业这条道路上有了第一位启蒙老师，晓光最初生意的技巧就是妈妈教的。“我小时候穿鞋的日子不多，但是总是赤脚也不是办法，我便从爸爸那里学来了编草鞋的手艺。”草鞋不经穿，而且鞋底的稻草也磨脚，晓光便想着改良草鞋，她通过把鞋底的稻草稍稍扎松让鞋底变得柔软从而让自己的草鞋也有了“小小的市场”。从那时起周晓光便学会了改良与变通，这在创业的路上是不可缺少的重要一步。

2008 年，金融危机席卷全球，中国的制造业受到了重大影响，流行饰品业受到了巨大的打击，零售业首当其冲。义乌是全球最大的日用小商品专业市场，全国有 20 多万家中小企业直接向市场供货，市场外向率高达 60%以上，可见国外市场对于义乌这个以小商品为主打的市场的影响之大。当周晓光在美国考察饰品市场时，她便发现市场里登门购物的客流量直线下降，与新光有着十几年合作历史的海外经销商纷纷抱怨市场的不景气，销售量不断下降。她回国后，发现义乌小商品市场的新光门店受到的冲击巨大，到了 2008 年 10 月义乌小商品博览会时，新光的北美市场订单竟然是零。此时的周晓光是平静的，这并不是因为她对经济危机无动于衷，而是她已经找到了规避危机的办法——开辟新兴国家的海外市场。周晓光走的道路是一条变通之路，在金融危机的大背景下她懂得另辟蹊径，这“变通”的思路与义乌这些年内扩外拓的推进市场发展的战略也是密不可分的。为了拓展国际市场，义乌成功举办了义博会迪拜展，参展的企业代表和工作人员赴实地考察，通过洽谈与当地企业合作实现了巨大成交额。

早在 2005 年，周晓光在对欧洲市场的多次考察中就已经看见了危机的苗头，欧洲市场的饰品公司很多都是从一些做鞋帽的外行公司转行而来，因为利润大，很多企业都转行做了饰品业，他们一味地压低价格、恶性竞争，这种同质化的竞争导致了市场赢利空间的不断缩小甚至消失。新光在这“价格战”中遭遇的损失是不言而喻的，但她并未选择放弃，她坚信暂时的吃亏定能迎来新的辉煌。与此同时，新光一度想要开拓法国巴黎等这些发达国家的市场，但是巴黎的一些政策和员工间的文化差异，使得新光的拓展之路举步维艰，而且欧洲的一些发达国家中也不乏百年老品牌，这对于还处于“萌芽”阶段的新光来说是一个巨大的挑战，发达国家的门槛较高，投入与回报不成正比，这些残酷的现实迫使着新光走上一条新路，一条变通之路。

一次海外进修让陷入困局的"义乌商人"周晓光重新找到了公司发展的路径，发达国家的门槛高为什么不转变思路把目光投到拥有巨大潜力的新兴市场呢？正当其他同行们在欧洲市场一筹莫展之时，新光早已经势如破竹地开辟起了新兴国家的市场。周晓光带着公司的相关人员跑到俄罗斯、中东、南欧等地实地考察，全面了解了那里的地理环境、消费特点、生活水平、市场形态、文化风俗、气候特征等，在前期了解充分之后开始有步骤地选择不同的国外城市开设新光经营公司的直营门市店。当一些同行因为迪拜的市场难以开发时，周晓光却是迎难而上，她从别人忽略的市场中寻到了市场的潜力。她亲自考察市场，挑选开发团队的成员，运用产品研发和管理上的强有力的支持体系与个体户进行竞争。

分公司刚刚起步时，新员工对于迪拜是完全陌生的。语言不通、道路不熟、无地落脚……这些困难都成了新光开辟迪拜市场的拦路虎。最初，新门店的客户经理因为语言不通与当地客人沟通困难，他便用国际长途，请国内同事与客人即时沟通。困难从来都不是失败的借口，他每天记录下与客户的谈话内容，强化自己的语言能力，路线不熟他就每天来回走，直到自己成为一个迪拜通。像周晓光这样"草根"一代浙商有个共同特点，那就是"苦难也是一种财富"。

周晓光早在1999年出访欧洲时就想通过与国际知名的大公司合作来提升自身的品牌，然而接洽工作毫无进展，渴望赴奥地利总部考察也未被允许，只是被安排在香港的分公司走访，受到礼节性的接待。经过商谈，虽有合作意愿，但公司却被认为实力不足，婉拒了周晓光的请求。周晓光意识到，只有真正拥有实力，才能得到别人的尊重。一方面，周晓光不断提升自身品牌实力，在2000年的香港展会上，新光饰品大放异彩；另一方面，随着中国加入世界贸易组织，成功申奥等天时机遇，凭借着坚韧与执着，周晓光和许多的义乌商人们冲破障碍，不断加强跨国合作，成功进军国际市场。

"二木成林，三木成森"，在周晓光的眼中，情谊永远高过竞争。

饰品行业门槛低，不需要很多资金投入就可以办起一个小型的加工厂，所以随着饰品行业越来越好，越来越多的商人看中了其中的商机。就是在这个时候，新光公司虽然有了很好的收益，却也遭受了前所未有的人才流失危机。新光创业初期，业务量日益增大，新光公司不断招兵买马，但随着进入饰品行业的人越来越多，新光公司辛苦培养的人才不断外流，很多刚刚培训好的员工或是熟练的操作工，没多久就被其他的饰品企业高薪挖走。起初周晓光还没有察觉，直到她发现自己公司里的经理带着同部门的人在外自立门户，甚至偷偷地带走了公司的工具时她才意识到问题的严峻。

看着自己辛辛苦苦培养出来的人才居然就这样成为竞争对手，周晓光起初非常伤心，看着谎称生病实为跳槽的员工，她深深地觉得自己的善心被利用。一段时间里，她内心焦急，一筹莫展。

事实上，这个坚强的义乌女人并没有被残酷的现实所击倒，她从自己的人才流失看到了饰品市场的蓬勃发展，看到了自家企业很大的发展空间。她想象着：如果整个义乌只有她一家饰品企业，那也许很多国外的商家也就不来义乌了。她明白，外商们正是看重义乌整个行业欣欣向荣的景象，看重义乌极大的发展潜力与竞争力空间。

周晓光释然了！她不但没有为此懊恼，反而加快了培训员工的步伐。她希望通过自己的努力提升义乌整个行业的员工素质，哪怕可能是杯水车薪，她仍乐此不疲。

现在看来，新光这些年的努力并不是徒劳的，它为义乌饰品行业输送了大量的人才，对义乌整个饰品行业的发展有着不可估量价值。周晓光的大气、大义和甘愿吃亏，为自己赢得了他人的钦佩与赞赏，以她的气度为义乌的商业做出了重要贡献。

天下没有不散的宴席，但是情谊天长地久。人才只有不断流动，新鲜血液才能进入，行业的竞争力才能不断提升，正是义乌人如此宽广的胸怀，才为他们自己赢得了广阔空间。可以说，义乌人的成功不是偶然，靠的是义乌商人的包容、诚意与气度。新光公司的副董事长洪周文曾这样评价过周晓光："你是企业家，不是生意人。"没错，极强的社会责任感正是她的人格魅力所在，也是她的立业之本。

周晓光仅仅只是一名在义乌创业的普通人，她是义乌人的放大，也是义乌人的缩影。不经历风雨怎么见彩虹，像她一样的许许多多义乌人用他们的亲身经历诠释大道、大义。记得义乌小天使玩具公司董事长吴云江说过："只要讲诚信，就有做不完的生意。"①据吴总回忆，1997 年与俄罗斯商人的一次 3 万元的赔本生意，让他获得信任，反而促成自己成为俄罗斯最大的充气玩具供货商。

义乌商人如点点繁星，遍布全球，他们的成功正源于对市场的执着，对成功的渴望，更源于他们对企业的理解，对社会的责任，对义乌精神的勇敢践行与不懈追求！

结语

品味绵绵香浓的丹溪红曲，回味从古到今的传奇故事，少有人不醉倒在义乌悠远而迷人的历史，不迷恋于义乌所勾勒出的未来开放景象。有幸的是，"用声音叙事"的团队成员能走进义乌，在这本社会之书中从容行走、快乐叙事。义乌有"义"，义乌讲"义"，义乌行"义"，义乌正在以"义"无反顾的开拓与包容，让每一位与她亲密接触过的人深深折服！

---

① 朱小燕：《义乌人义字当头——听义乌老板讲"吃亏"的故事》，浙江在线新闻网站，2006 年 5 月18 日。http://zjnews.zjol.com.cn/05zjnews/system/2006/05/18006625721.shtml.

参考文献

[1]傅根洪.敲糖换鸡毛:义乌的商路历程[J].《西湖》2005年05期.

[2]改革开放三十年篇:重温义乌[OL].中国义乌政府门户网站 http://www.yw.gov.cn.

[3]季金甫,刘志毅,朱京义,吕华.义乌对外宣传报道精选(2011)[Z].浙江义乌:中共义乌市委宣传部,2011年.

[4]楼春秋,方向阳.义乌全面建设国际商贸名城[N].《金华日报》,2008年7月23日.

[5]陆立军.中国小商品城的崛起与农村市场经济发展的义乌模式[J].《经济社会体制比较》,1999年01期.

[6]魅力义乌:认识义乌的历史名胜[OL].浙江在线 http://jq.zjol.com.cn.

[7]王彩芳.义乌市场创造活力探究[J].《浙江师范大学学报(社会科学版)》,2011年06期.

[8]王红茹."义乌模式"的"无为"与"有为"[OL].民网经济论坛 http://finance.people.com.cn.

[9]朱小燕.义乌人义字当头——听义乌老板讲"吃亏"的故事[OL].浙江在线新闻网站,2006年5月18日.http://zjnew.zjol.com.cn/05zjnews/system/2006/05/18/006625721.shtml.

[10]义乌小商品:引领国际市场的指挥棒[OL].中国义乌政府门户网站 http://www.yw.gov.cn.

[11]中国社会科学院《义乌发展之文化探源》课题组.义乌发展之文化探源[M].北京:社会科学文献出版社,2007年.

[12]周晓光,胡腾.女人就是要发光[M].北京:中信出版社,2009年.

后记

用心讲故事的人

郑　媛

无论如何也不曾想到，一次普通的暑期社会实践竟然在冥冥之中为我的大学生活画下如此浓重的一笔，我不确定这一经历可以在多大程度上改变我的人生，但是我和我的伙伴们都坚信，在那个骄阳似火的夏天，我们在用心讲述与自己青春有关的故事。

2013 年 7 月，在指导教师的带领下，我和"用声音叙事"全体团队成员一起奔赴素有"国际小商品市场"之称的浙江义乌，在这里，我们继续沿着先前队员的足迹探索义乌外籍人士的中国故事（注：2011—2012 年团队两次调研义乌）。于是，在义乌的大街小巷可以看到一群奔波的身影，他们或者在向路人问询地址，或者踌躇在街头寻找访问对象，或者激烈地与队友讨论方案，抑或是成竹在胸地与外商侃侃而谈；于是在这里，他们深切地体会到可以让书本知识鲜活起来的叫实践，可以分担压力的叫队友，可以点拨迷思的叫老师，可以见证传奇的叫时间，可以沟通心灵的叫文化，可以改变世界的叫义乌，可以点燃激情的叫中国。一批批学生和一批批老师正在用心做着一件贴近生活、走进社会的事情，城市就是他们习得知识的课堂，声音就是他们传播文化的媒介；于是，就有了"用声音叙事"的一系列实践成果；于是，我们从宁波来到义乌，再访义乌，三访义乌，我们羞涩也骄傲地欢呼：义乌，我来了！

我知道即使时光流逝，我也会被不断地拉回到这段难忘的记忆。2014 年 1 月 15 号，我代表浙江大学宁波理工学院前往北京参加由共青团中央、《人民日报》指导，人民网主办的"全国大学生社会实践评选活动颁奖典礼"，活动旨在落实习近平总书记在 2013 年五四青年节期间的讲话，鼓励广大高校学子勇担使命，深入基层体察国情、民情，凝聚青春正能量。本届评选历时三个多月，4000 多支团队激烈角逐，200 万网友参与了点评和投票活动。我们的"用声音叙事"团队获得了全国大学生暑期社会实践优秀团队三等奖的荣誉称号。在人民网举办的访谈交流会上，我与来自全国各地高校的优秀团队代表进行了交流，并且展示了我们团队历年来的实践成果。代表们都对我们师生协作、固化社会实践成果的模式非常赞赏，团中央领导也对我们的活动给予了高度评价。被认可总是一件令人愉悦的事情，当心情平复的时候，我也在不断思考，是什么让这支队伍一路走来，又是什么可以让我们一直坚定地走下去。

在暑期调研活动结束后不久，我又去了一趟义乌，身份是外商随行翻译。我陪那位外商逛遍了义乌大大小小的商店，看着他不厌其烦地讨价还价和轻车熟路地下着订单，我的思绪不免又回到了当初的调研主题——外商与义乌经济发展的关系。为什么一座内陆小城走出了一条国际化发展的道路？答案在“鸡毛换糖”的风俗里可以找到，在国际小商品市场琳琅满目的店面里可以找到，在星罗棋布的家庭式工厂里可以找到，在如潮而至的外商心里可以找到。机遇就是在别人想到的时候你做到了，这里有中国经济发展的整体环境，有义乌商业文化的坚实根基，更有这座城市创新和开放的胸襟，正因如此，来自世界各地的外籍商人，不远万里来到义乌，有些人甚至因此爱上了中国文化，长期定居于此。这些都让我们的实践活动变得更加有意义。“中国梦”就是城市的梦、市民的梦，就是一个与其他国家和文化“共享的梦”，城市只有用心才能讲述好一个发展的故事，青年只有用心才能讲述好与青春有关的故事。

用心听故事可以赢得朋友，用心讲故事可以赢得世界，城市如此，人也如此。

（本文作者为2013年“用声音叙事”暑期社会实践调研团队队长）

图书在版编目（CIP）数据

用声音叙事：义乌，我来了：汉英对照/蔡亮主编．—杭州：浙江大学出版社，2014.9

ISBN 978-7-308-13694-5

Ⅰ.①用… Ⅱ.①蔡… Ⅲ.①义乌市—概况—汉、英 Ⅳ.①K925.54

中国版本图书馆 CIP 数据核字(2014)第 186775 号

用声音叙事：义乌，我来了

主 编 蔡 亮

责任编辑 张 琛
责任校对 张远方
封面设计 续设计
出版发行 浙江大学出版社
(杭州市天目山路 148 号 邮政编码 310007)
(网址：http://www.zjupress.com)
排 版 杭州金旭广告有限公司
印 刷 杭州杭新印务有限公司
开 本 710mm×1000mm 1/16
印 张 25
字 数 580 千
版 印 次 2014 年 9 月第 1 版 2014 年 9 月第 1 次印刷
书 号 ISBN 978-7-308-13694-5
定 价 59.00 元

浙江大学出版社发行部联系方式 (0571)88925591；http://zjdxcbs.tmall.com